AF479017

trail

Project realized for dOCUMENTA (13) — 9 June until 16 September 2012
Edited by Natascha Sadr Haghighian, Pola Sieverding, Jasper Kettner
Designed by Ça ira!

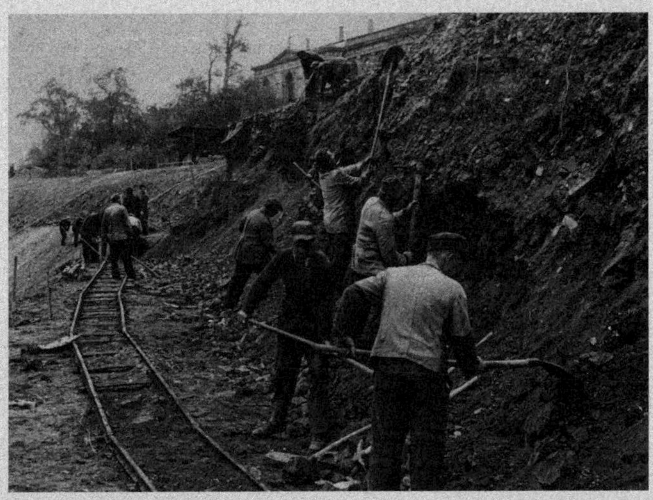

This book is about how we learned to listen to rubble: rubble that used to be a kitchen tile, a doorframe, a brick wall. We found that the rubble carries secrets, secrets that everybody knows about—public secrets. We found a lot of stories in the rubble—stories about becoming animal, about continuities in what we call history, and about ruptures, ruptures that flip and stretch history and turn continuities into unsteady loops. We found history repeating itself under different names.
The book will show how, in the process of listening to the rubble, we lost words and found others. Words that speak the language of things rather than people. And it will include images of the traces that people and things left on a slope that was made of rubble.

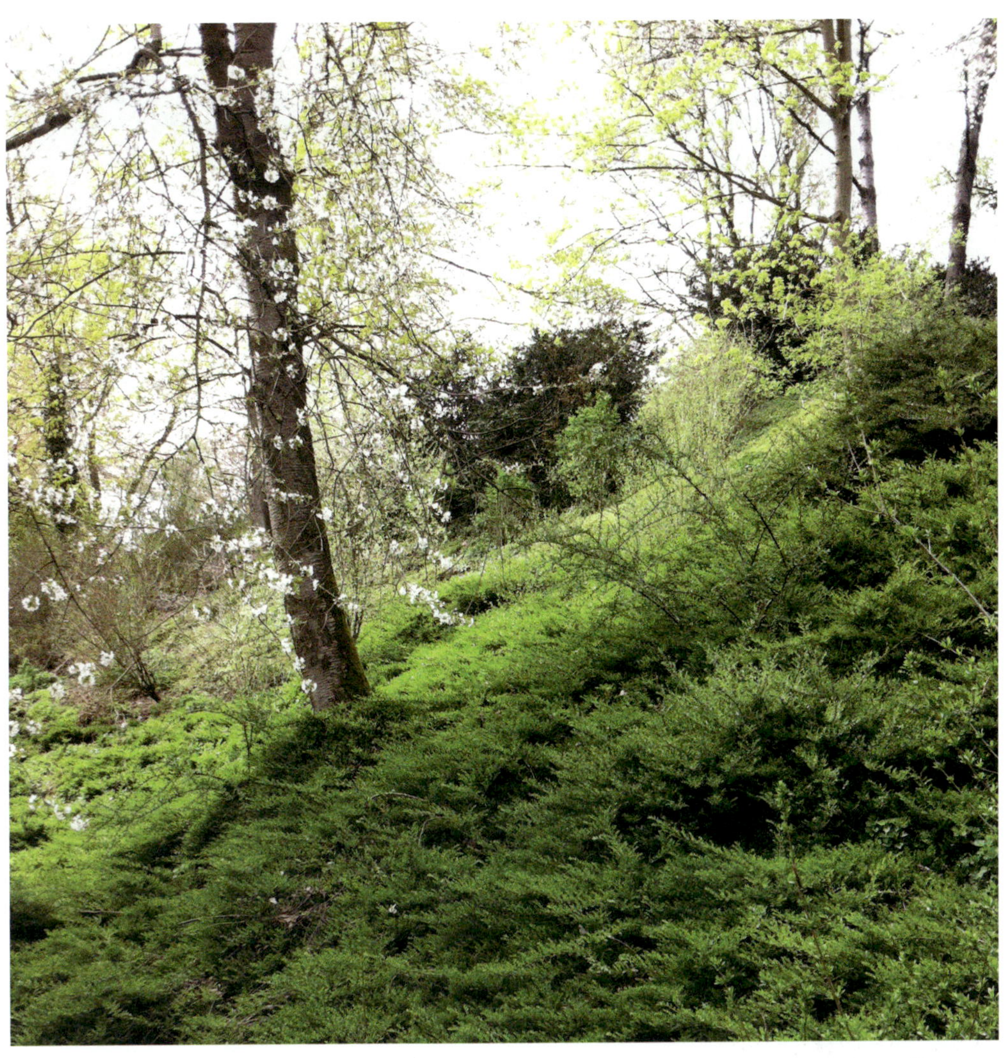

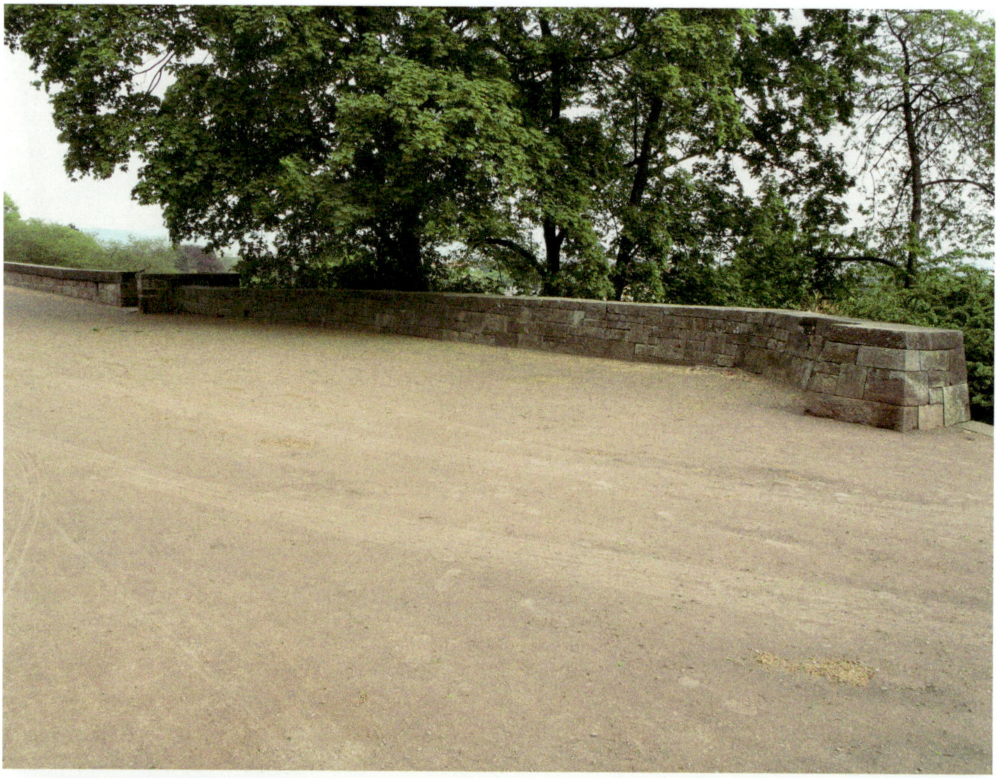

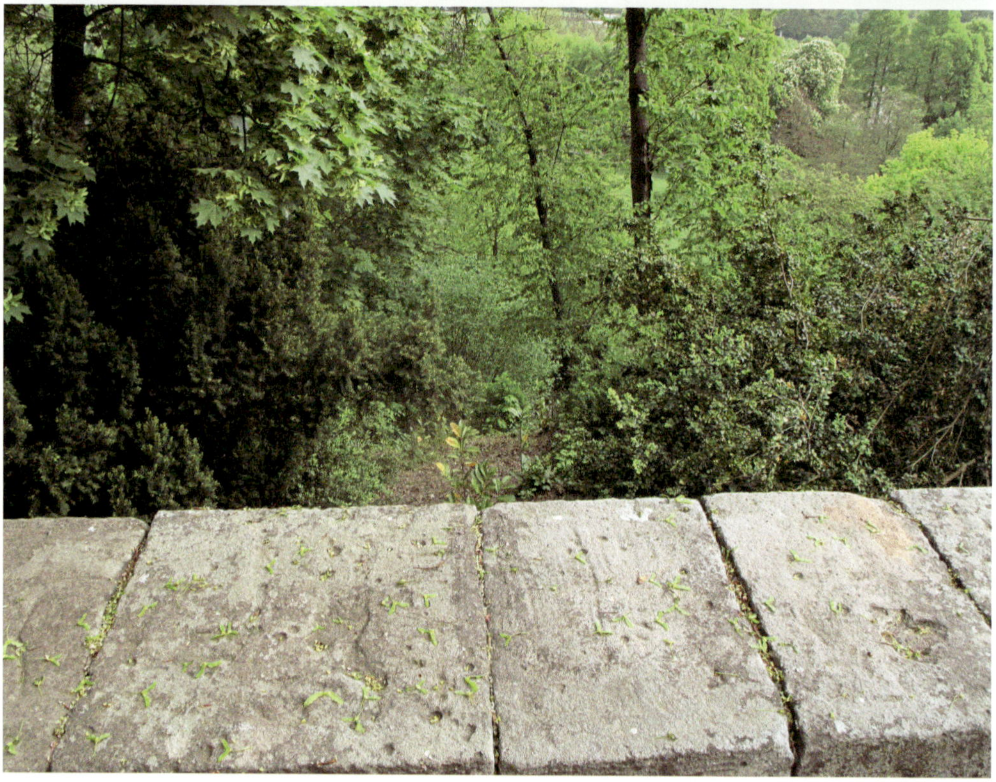

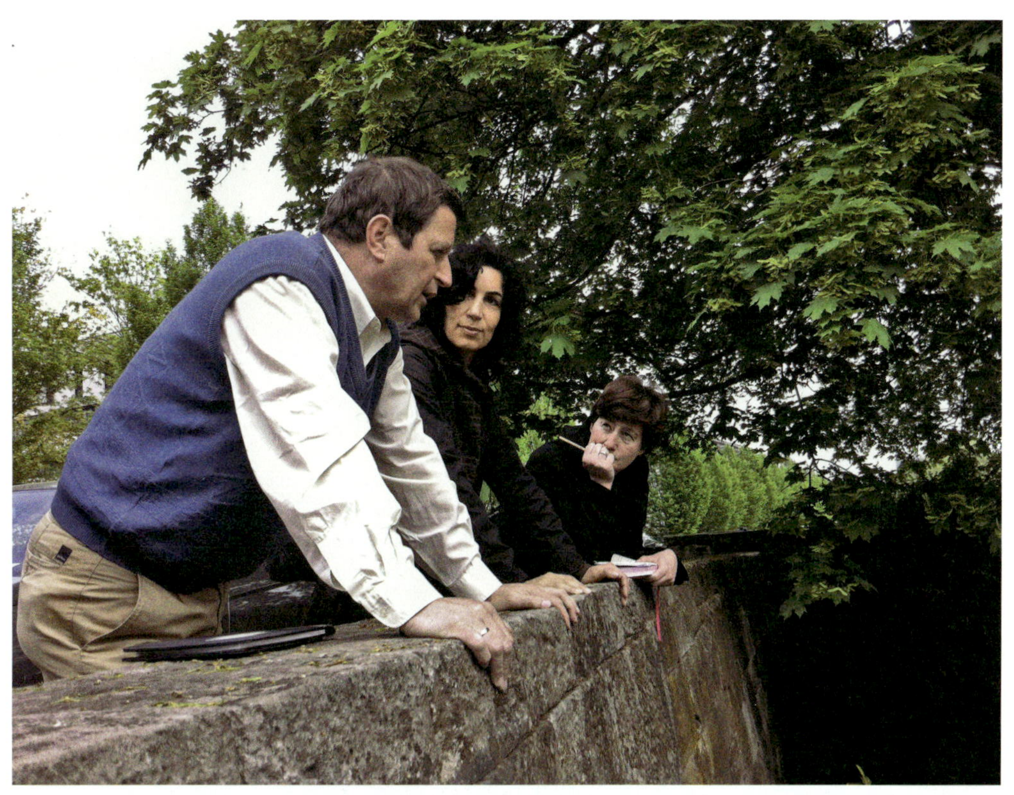

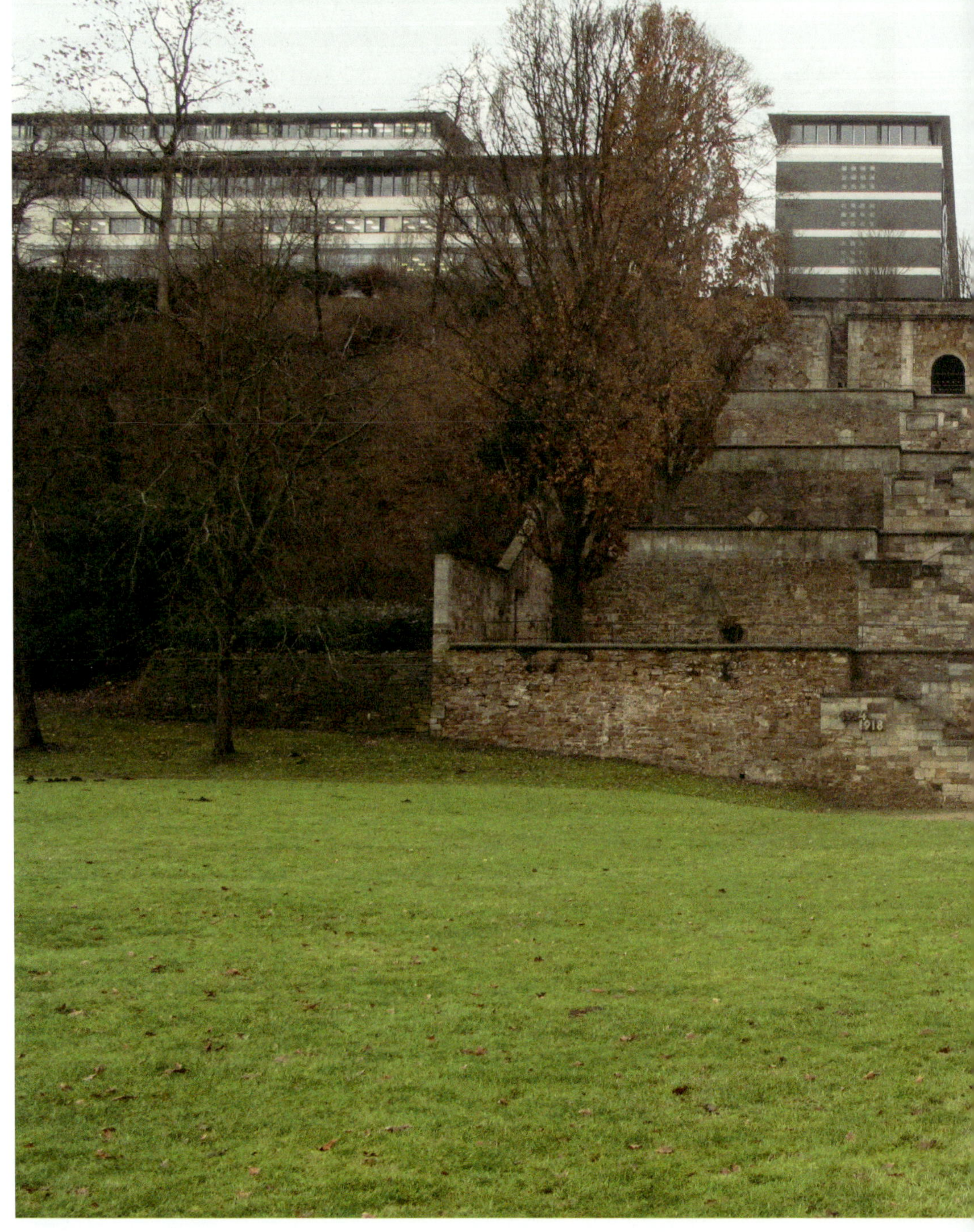

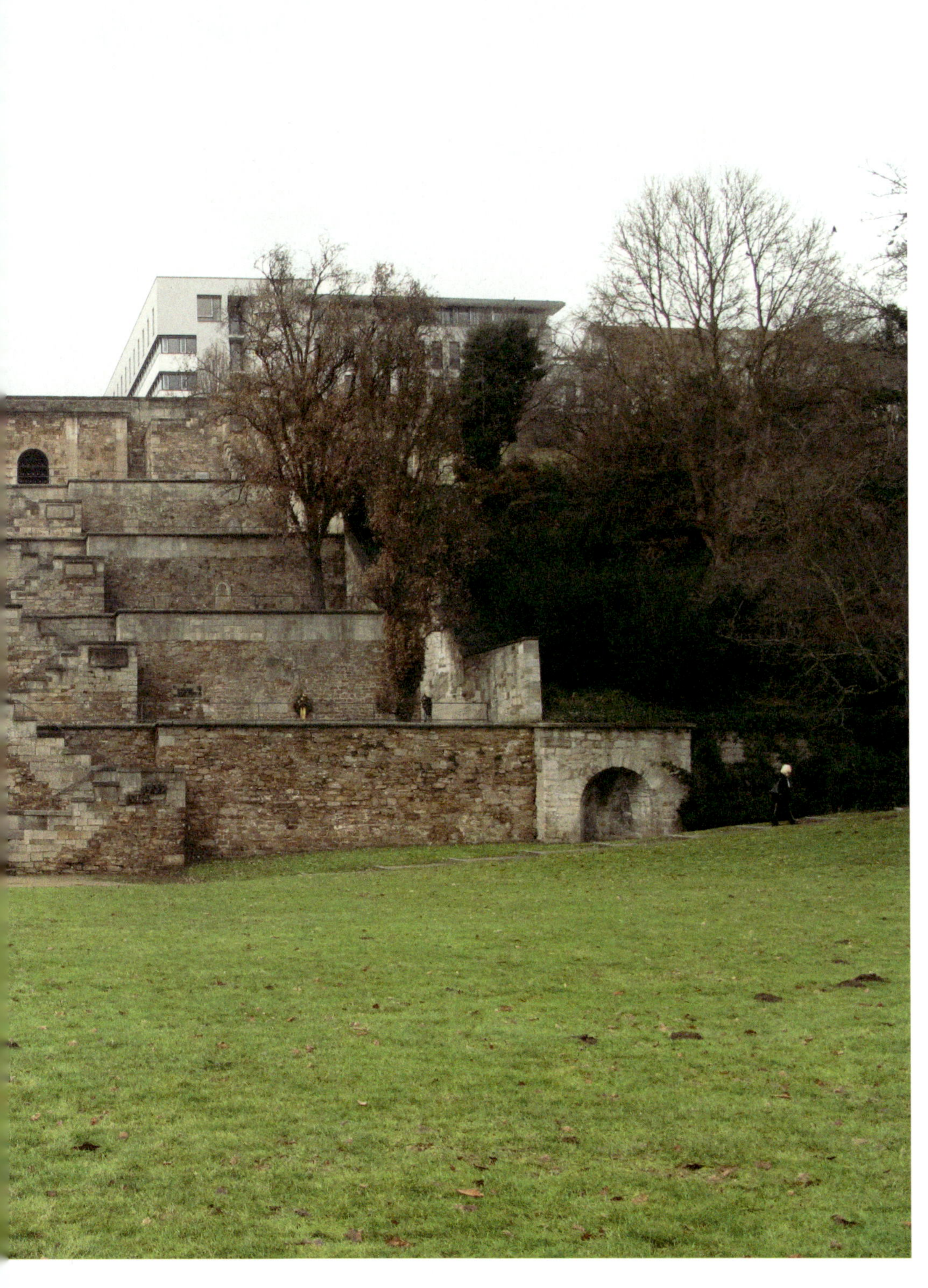

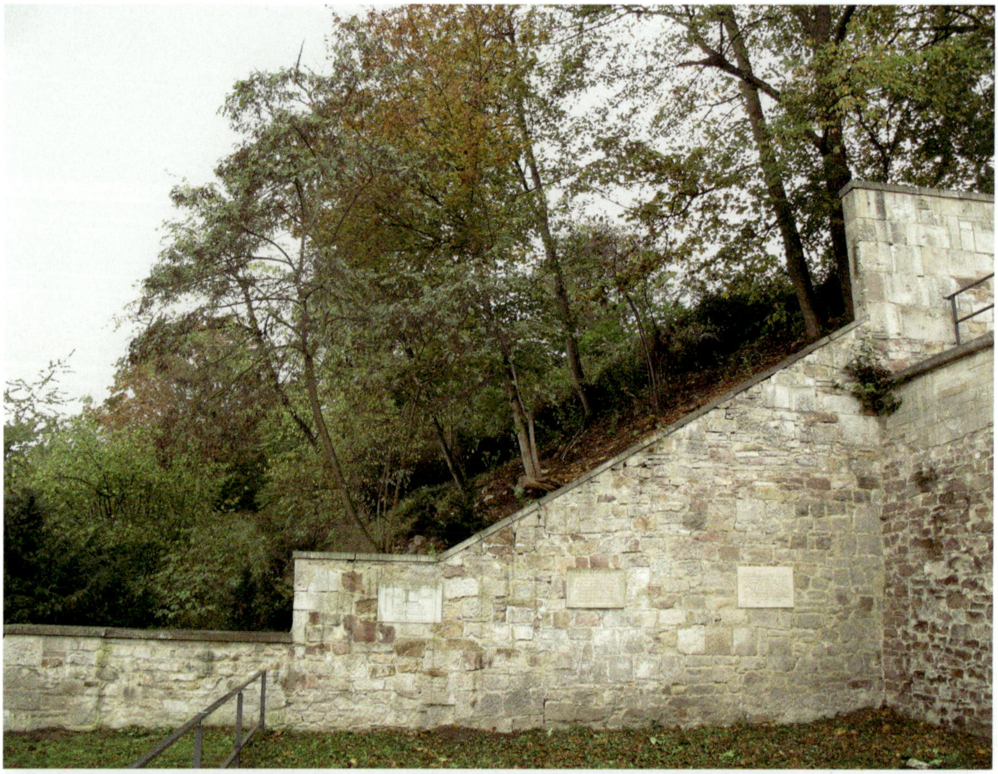

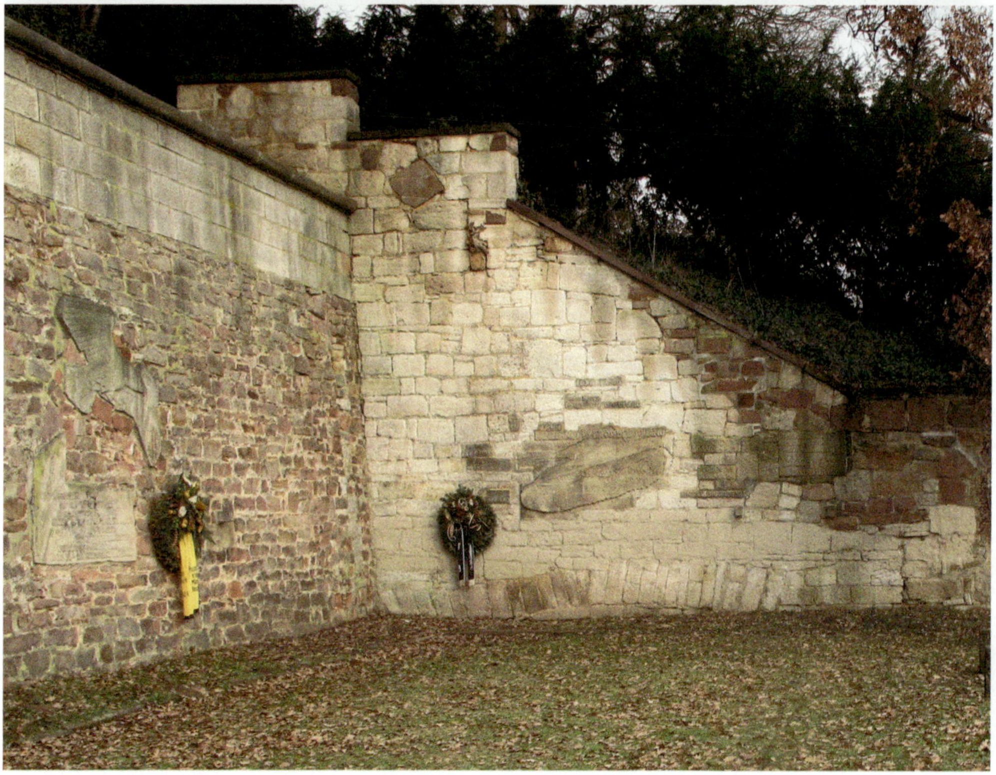

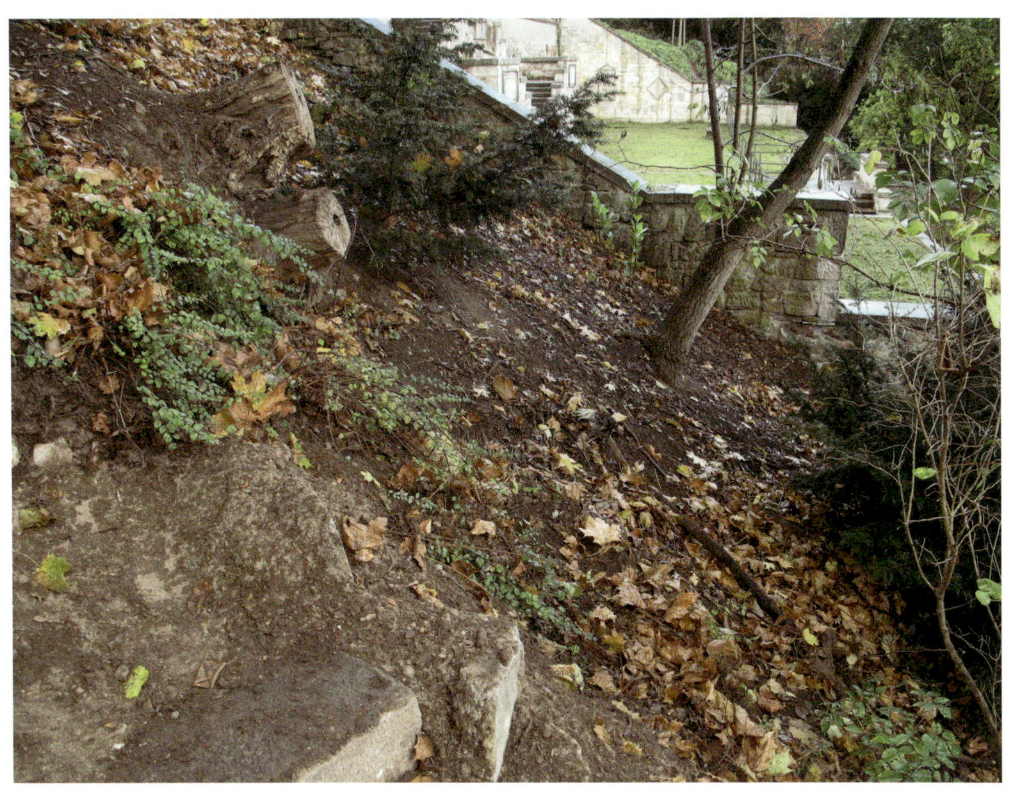

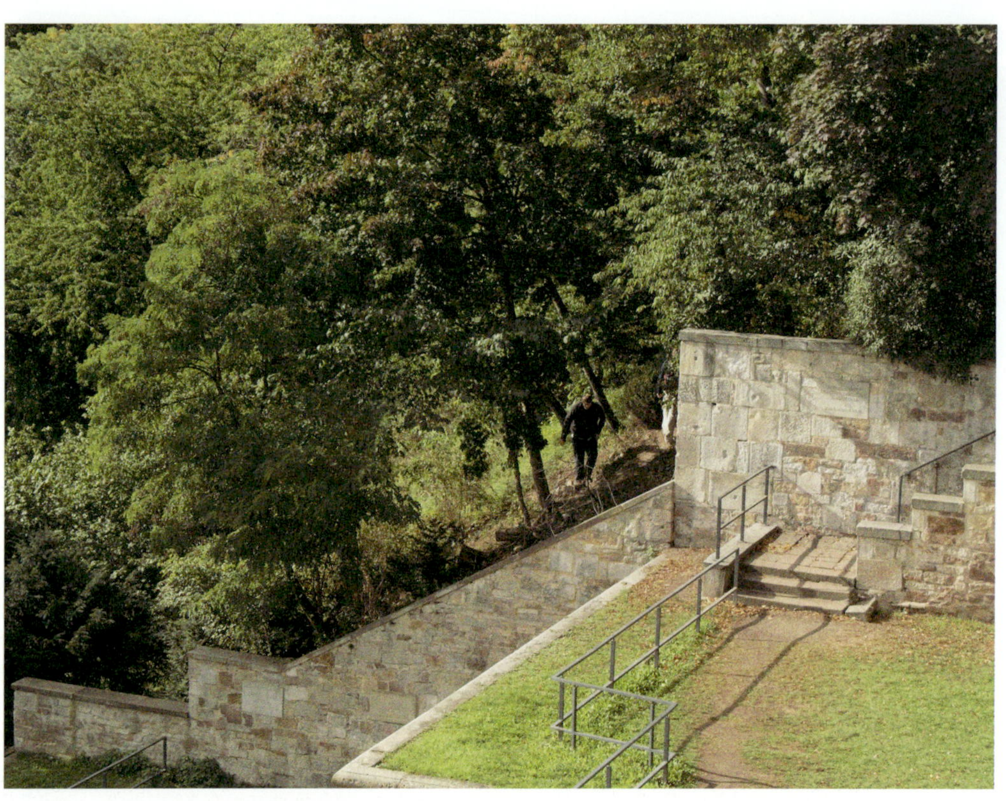

14

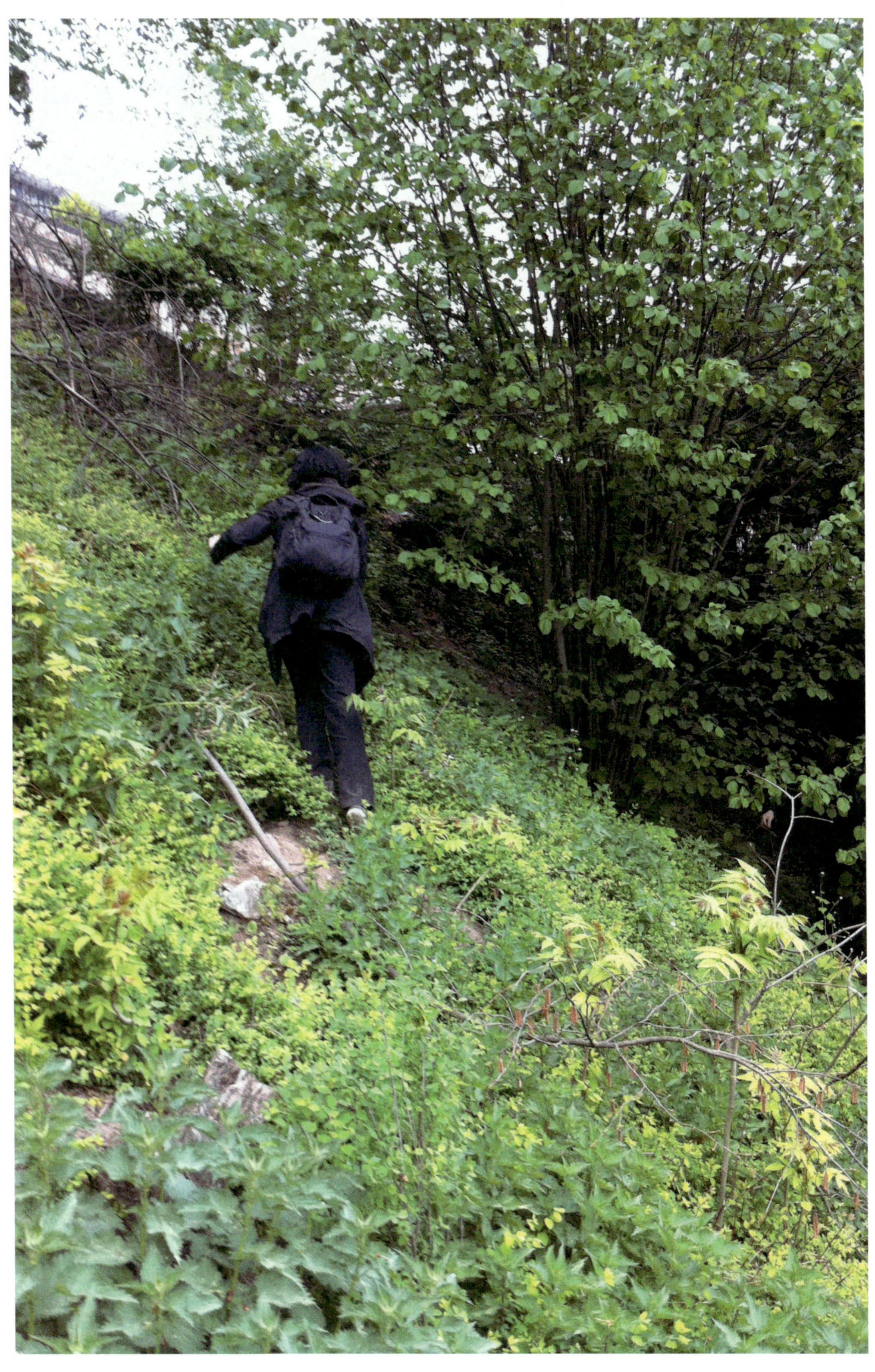

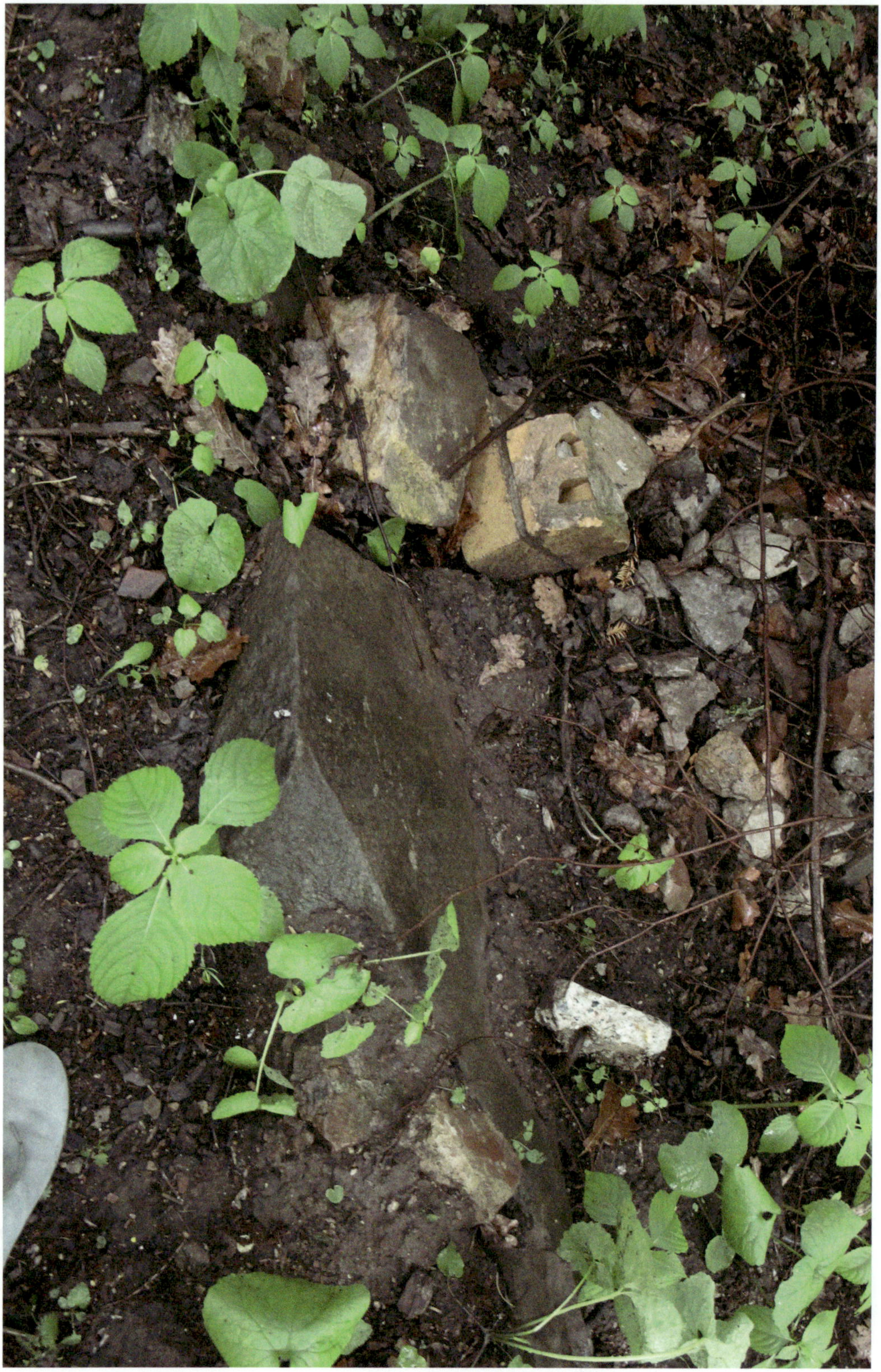

In January 2011, at the first viewing of the various areas proscribed for
dOCUMENTA(13), I notice the Ehrenmal for the first time. Jasper explains
to me that it's a memorial for the fallen soldiers of the First and Second
World Wars. We walk up to it and I'm quite surprised at the unbroken, heroic
gesture and language. The whole place is full of wreaths from the various
divisions of the army, support groups, and generals. The wreaths have
obviously been recently placed beneath the mural relief. On one relief can
be read "Es ward gespannt ein einig Band um alles Deutsche Land [A single
band will be wrapped around the whole of German land]; 1939 JR GD; 1942
PZ GREN DIVGD; 1944 Tank Division of Greater Germany." It also shows a
tank, which I will learn a lot more about later, but at the moment that I'm
taking a picture of it I still don't know any of this. On another relief an eagle
is circling, peering down, its claws already outstretched to grasp its prey.
After climbing the cascade-like steps, we stand there at Schöne Aussicht and
look down onto the Auepark. Jasper tells me that when Via Lewandowsky
proposed an intervention to the memorial in 1992, he ran into trouble with the
so-called 'tradition societies,' veterans' groups with often dubious affinities to
Germany's military past. On the way back home to Berlin, I think about this
and decide that there's no point in intervening in the memorial, because its
singular narrative of history and militarism would always inevitably impose
itself over everything. The best thing would be to ignore it. Still, it occurs
to me that the memorial's staircase is the shortest way to get from Schöne
Aussicht back down to the Auepark. That's a problem. NATASCHA

Since I was born afterwards, I don't have any personal connection to the
World Wars, and I didn't lose any close relatives in them. So war monuments
don't cause me to reflect on the idea of perpetrator-victim/victim-perpetrator,
they just give me a sense of revulsion at the militarism on display there.
The epigraph "Germany must live, even if we must die" on a Hamburg war
memorial is only bearable in the slightly altered version by the Hamburg
band Slime, "Germany must die, so that we may live." Both continue to exist,
the memorial and the song, and you can choose which path you want to take.
Not so with Kassel's Ehrenmal war memorial. This is all about commemoration,
and all manner of critique seems to be taboo. Did those whose deaths are
commemorated here, for instance the tank division of Greater Germany,
actually behave 'honorably,' as the German name of the memorial implies?
Even the plaque commemorating the war deserters, which was only added
later under protest, utterly complies with the look and style of the pre-existing
relief of Kassel's Ehrenmal—and thus also with the logic of war, eternally
reproduced there, which was in fact exactly what the deserters had defied.
JASPER

For dOCUMENTA (13) various venues at Schöne Aussicht are to be used as
well as, significantly, the Auepark that lies below. After talking with Jasper,
I decide to set up a hiking trail right next to and parallel to the memorial.
The trail could serve as an alternative path for visitors to the exhibition.
By means of the trail they come directly into the park, without having to
use the memorial's stairway or the vastly longer park paths that snake their
way down. In order to 'activate' the trail, and in diametric opposition to
the singular military voice of the memorial, a multiplicity of voices lending
their presence will be heard over loudspeakers along the path, giving it their
presence. NATASCHA

Designing a hiking trail is an oxymoron. Such trails tend to result from
a swarm of users. Unrelated to any organizing or guiding principle, their
course emerges from whatever is optimally needed in each specific place.
Inasmuch as the Kassel trail is an ascent or a descent, it may be arranged via
its serpentine quality in a way that resembles a 'natural' trail as it develops.
The symbiosis of genuine and projected trail can already be observed, even
before the opening of dOCUMENTA (13). If the built-in curves are too small,
this gives rise to parallel paths; if whole areas slide down, there are detours.
Or, in the following case of a boy from Kassel, when the purpose of the trail
is transformed: he incessantly runs up and down the slope trying to identify
all the sources of sound, therefore producing direct connections between all
the loudspeakers hidden throughout the slope. The constructed path finds
itself continuously overwritten. JASPER

Jasper sends me a picture. The caption reads "Renaturalization Work at the Kassel Debris Heap: Construction Work for the German Horticultural Show at the Auehang." It shows men using shovels to distribute debris from lorries onto a slope. At the top of the slope you can make out the Neue Galerie. This is the slope where we want to set up the trail. When we start to dig, we find bricks, kitchen tiles, and other pieces of rubble under a thin layer of dirt. The findings open up a number of questions, technical as well as historical. Can a stable path be built at all on rubble? Where does this rubble come from? Why was Kassel almost completely destroyed during the Second World War? What kinds of plants grow on rubble? NATASCHA

Renaturalization, or the contradiction of the concept of 'nature' . . . It occurs to me that quite often efforts are undertaken to frame nature as a site or a condition of 'origin' exactly when it seems necessary to blanket those historical procedures, also known as 'culture,' which require concealment. The slope, made of rubble, becomes a part of the park's formation. The rubble is hidden underneath 10,000 roses and a planted grove of myriad flora. Out of sight, out of mind. A blossoming new beginning, for a new history, with a new past. POLA

The concern that Kassel's residents will continue to use the trail even after documenta is great; that the temporary use of the Auepark will transform into a permanent, unwanted use. Even the plants placed at the entrances to the trail turn out to be superfluous. As throughout the rest of the city, documenta's presence on the slope between Schöne Aussicht and the Auepark quickly falls into oblivion. Kassel, each and every time, after 100 exceptional days, finds itself going back to business-as-usual in a matter of a few days. Alternative routes seem to no longer be necessary. The trail is just another part of the history that nature covers up on the slope. JASPER

Simultaneous to the planning of documenta, the city of Kassel, as part of an unemployment opportunity expansion programm, decides to assign long-term unemployed individuals the task of renovating the former gardens of the Henschel villa, known as the Weinberg, for public use. This is meant to provide a daytime connection from the upper city to the lower city, providing a greener, more dynamic alternative to the other, pre-existing route that runs along a four-lane road. Even here German laws and regulations apply to the necessary work for securing the way, as they do for the removal of the rubble from the Henschel villa and its garden structures. We are more than happy to take the rubble off their hands. JASPER

We climb through the piles of rubble on the Weinberg and search for pieces that could work well as steps. In the meanwhile, I've come to know quite a bit about the Henschel company, so it feels odd to be standing in the rubble of their villas. Henschel's incessant weapons production, which had defined the image of the city during the Second World War and was made possible by thousands of forced laborers, was the main reason for the Allies' bombardment of Kassel. The city was razed to the ground. Much of what's here on the Weinberg has already been arranged according to the size and type of rock, in order to use them later for securing the way. We find bricks, natural stones, and concrete, partly with steel elements. There are pieces of masonry that seem like parts of a puzzle, as if they are waiting around to be placed into an incomplete wall. We wonder what the upper entrance to the trail might look like. It shouldn't look too commodious, so as to immediately signal the route's degree of difficulty. A ladder is in discussion, and for a period of time an opening in the wall alongside Schöne Aussicht, as well. NATASCHA

Actually everything has been clarified. We have found the site, conceived the essential elements of the project, the concrete realization may begin—it is then that doubt, and its emissaries, arrive. Visitors might fall down the slope and suffer the most severe bone fractures. The drama conveyed by some of these sketched-out scenarios can hardly be outdone. Through signage displaying legally-verified disclaimers, as well as verbal warnings from the security personnel, visitors are notified of the risks, as well as the alternative, less dangerous possibility of entering and climbing the trail from its entrance in the Auepark below. By these measures, the project is saved in the end. Fortunately, there is not so much as a sprained ankle in the 100 days of the project; indeed, the trail is empowered by the hordes of visitors, all of whom need no warning. JASPER

By the time I join the project, the physical trail has already been laid out, 'off the beaten path' of the Ehrenmal's staircase. The work on the trail has uncovered potentialities that, alongside the physical experience on site, allow for other modes of conceiving to take place. Together, we start to talk about and research the site, to observe the individual fragments, images, stories, dates, and fictions. Long before I visit the site for the first time, I already have an idea of it. When I finally arrive, I see much of what would remain hidden from the unknowing gaze; at the same time, I am surprised that everything is completely different from what I had thought. This relation of tension turns up again in the various aggregate conditions of the trail: in its physical as well as virtual form, as a form of narrative, as well as in its form as a book. POLA

Archives are what you make of them. They can be reservoirs that set histories free, and they can superimpose histories, in which one layer hides the other. Like how the slope, made from the rubble of the Second World War, is a reservoir.

I imagine it as a turn of the spade that sets histories into motion. The work necessary to lay down the trail reveals the rubble, which in turn seems to be the loose ends of a whole variety of stories. To find these stories, we go to the city archive and the archive of the Henschel company, the largest weapons manufacturer in the city of Kassel during the Second World War. At first, both archives are completely overwhelming. Huge amounts of photos, folders containing newspaper clippings, stories handed down, notes, signatures, references, names, dates, and reports by eyewitnesses in dusty files. These must account for that smell which permeates the archive: dry as dust, a dampness that bites, perhaps caused by the millions of tiny spores, well into corroding the paper that conserves all these histories. At the Henschel archive, also aspiring to be a museum of the history of the company and its eponymous family, we see everyday objects the workers made out of unused munitions after the war. What was cooked in the pots that used to be bombs? POLA

In March 2012, Ute Waldhausen and I drive to Kassel to record voices for the multilingual, onomatopoeic sound installation for the trail. Initially, our plan is to gather the entirety of languages one can hear in Kassel. Herr Boßdorf, director of the Auepark—with whom we are negotiating the trail setup—gives me a list he had put together with his wife of all the languages spoken in Kassel. Finally, we decide against the idea of completeness and instead, start to develop the range of languages based on our own contacts and encounters in the city. In the end, we record six hundred onomatopoeic animal sounds by ten different domestic animals, spoken by sixty-four inhabitants of Kassel, in thirty languages.

The recordings take place, amongst other locations, at the studio of the youth center Schlachthof. Ayse Güleç, director of the education department at Schlachthof, had made this suggestion, as there are German classes on the upper floors of the building where we might find participants. Ayse is well connected in Kassel, and not only does she put the infrastructure for the sound recordings at our disposal, she also greatly helps us with making contact with the people who would later lend their voices to the trail.

I go into the individual classrooms and attempt to introduce the trail. Using hand and foot gestures, as well as a scrawled chalk drawing of the site and the animals, I explain what the project is all about. I also make an attempt at the various onomatopoeic animal sounds to clarify my intention. Everyone laughs. From each class a delegation forms and goes down to the studio on the lower floor of the building. Almost everyone comes from a different linguistic background and there is a lot of amazement and amusement from everyone about the differences between 'wau,' 'woof,' and 'wang,' or 'kikeriki,' 'kookorikookoo,' and 'ghoghogho,' or 'quack,' 'wak wak,' and 'kegul.' There is much laughter on this day, ending with twenty people having provided their voices for the trail. The next day we go to yet another language school, as well as to the Nigerian Cultural Center, and to a housing facility for young migrants; in the end, we have a great deal of very moving, sad, funny, and affectionate encounters in thirty different languages, including regional distinctions between Libyan, Palestinian, and Iraqi Arabic, or Turkish, Kurdish, and Azeri. It's beautiful to see many of the participants four months later, at a picnic held on the trail. NATASCHA

The days in the archive are moments lacking objective distance. One digs
ever deeper in the layers, always finding new strands to follow. "Tiger" was
the name of a tank built by Henschel during the Second World War. Why it
was called this is anyone's guess; we don't find an explanation. The animals
encountered along the way, as we move along the histories of the site, play a
recurring role, revealing the layers and folds through which history is composed.
The Karlsaue was once a zoo; the elephant whose middle jaw bone Johann
Wolfgang von Goethe demonstrated fell and died in the Karlsaue; and animal
sounds are meant to accompany the physical trail Natascha is laying down.
In order to receive an overview of and a relation to the site—this place
that we are observing close-up—we make use of the surveying capacities of
Google Earth. From lofty heights we zoom right in on Kassel, on the Karlsaue,
on the barracks that were occupied by forced laborers during the war, and
then later by migrant workers, and finally, on the grounds of the weapons
manufacturing company Henschel. Today, there stands a Leopard 2 tank in
the courtyard of Henschel, now named Rheinmetall Defense. You can zoom
in on it within a few meters, thanks to Google. Here, once again, we stumble
upon animals: military vehicles, following the tradition of various German
military systems, were provided with animal names. And we immerse ourselves
into the many loops of history: Kassel is yet again one of the largest weapons
producing sites in Germany. POLA

Ground

A slope made of rubble. Landfill.
Bricks, tiles, clay, handles, stones,
glass, and metal you can sell,
debris from the Henschel Villa.
Debris underneath the soil.

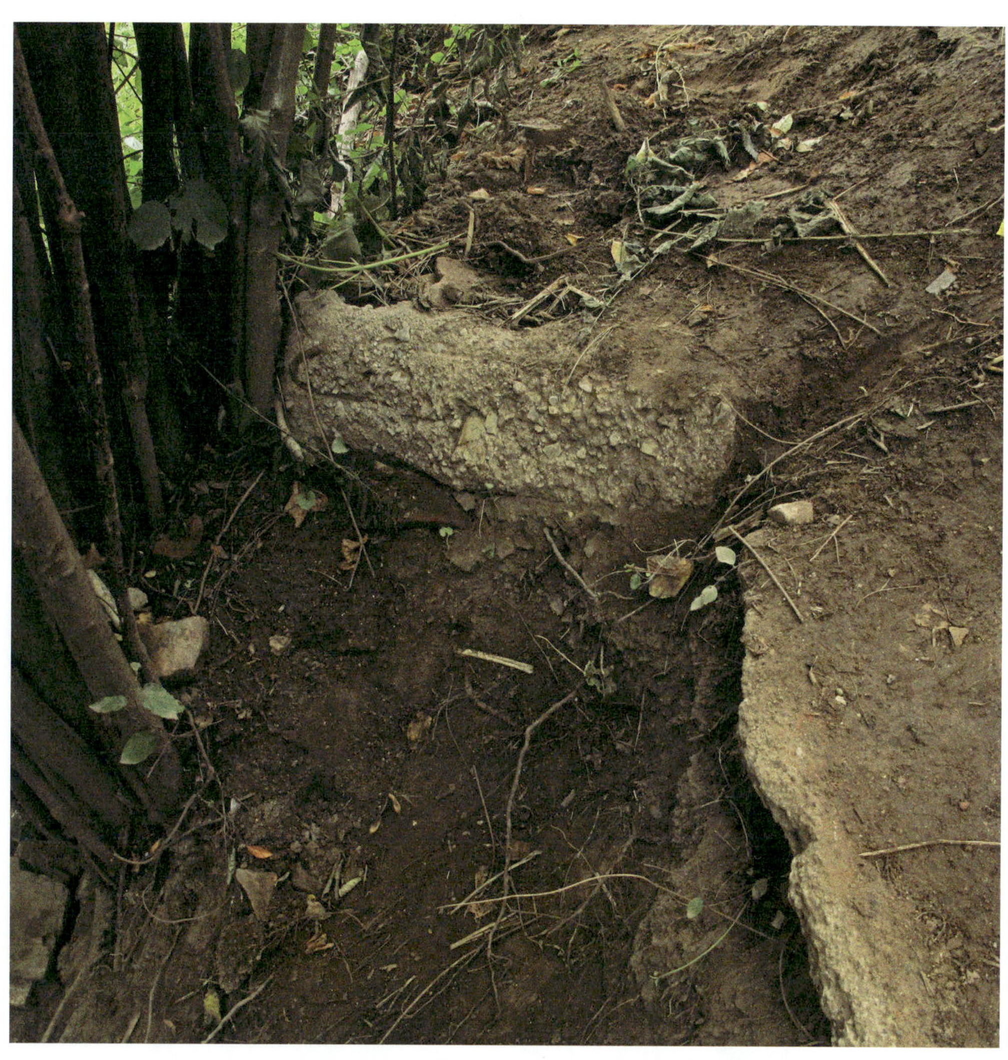

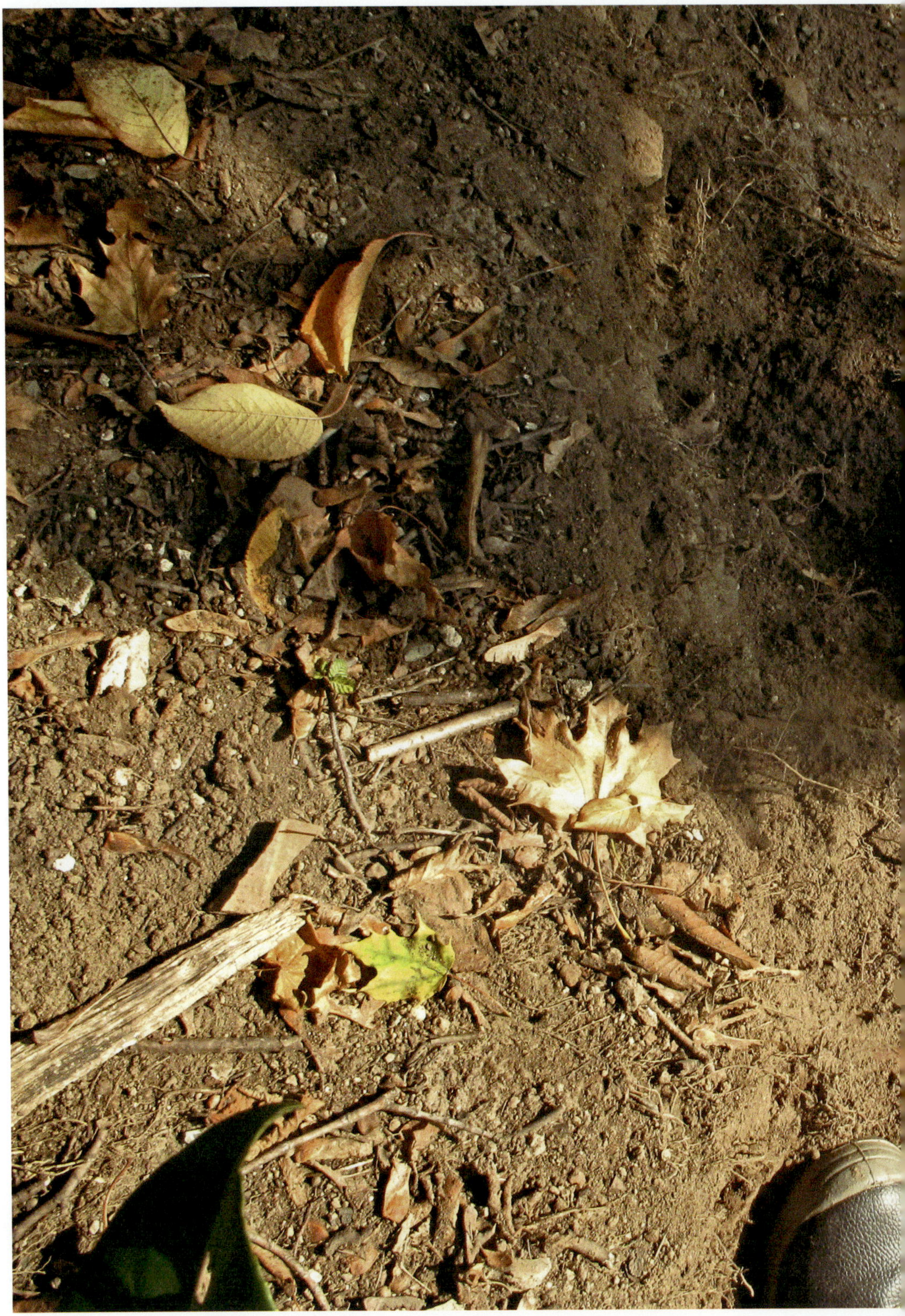

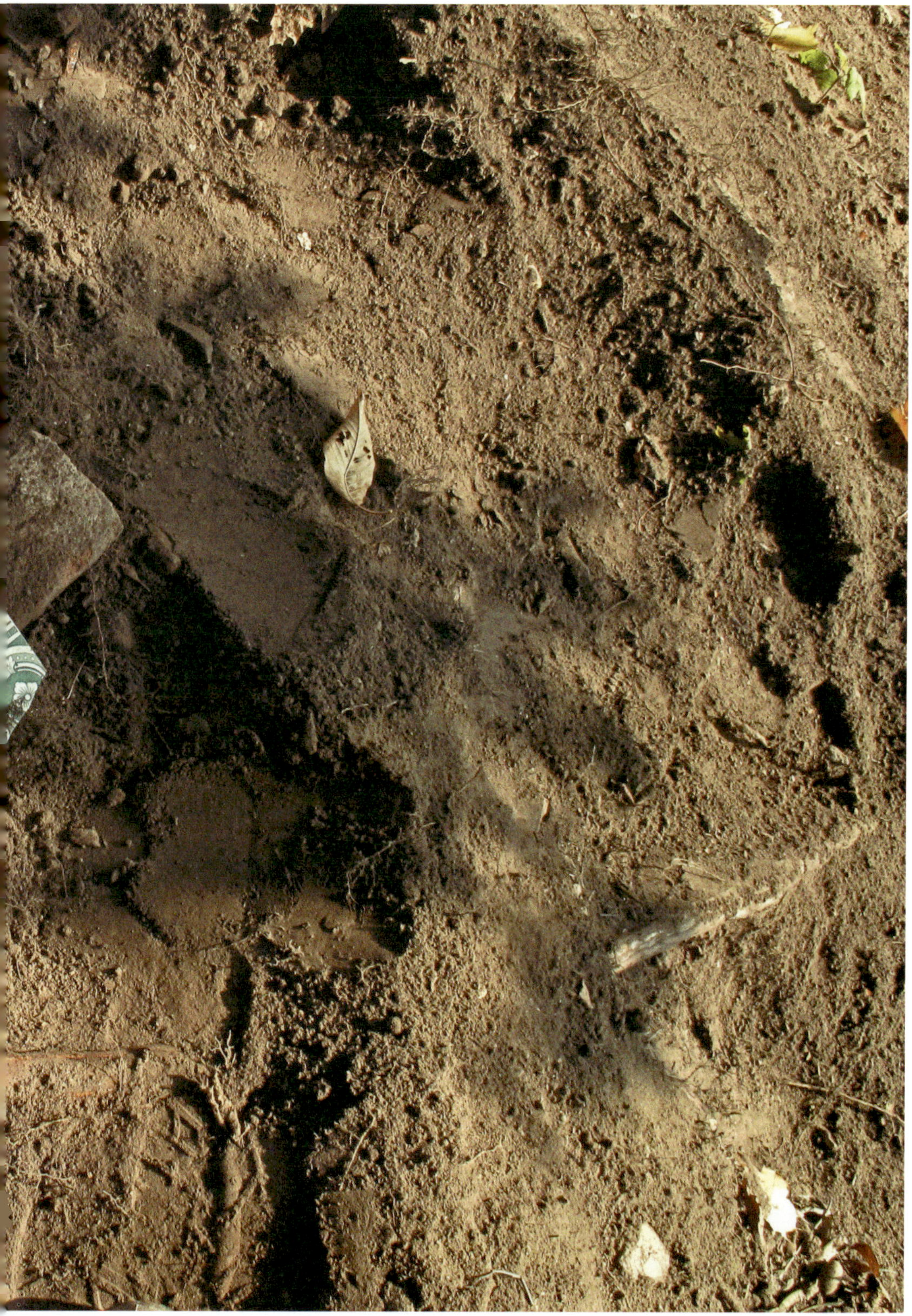

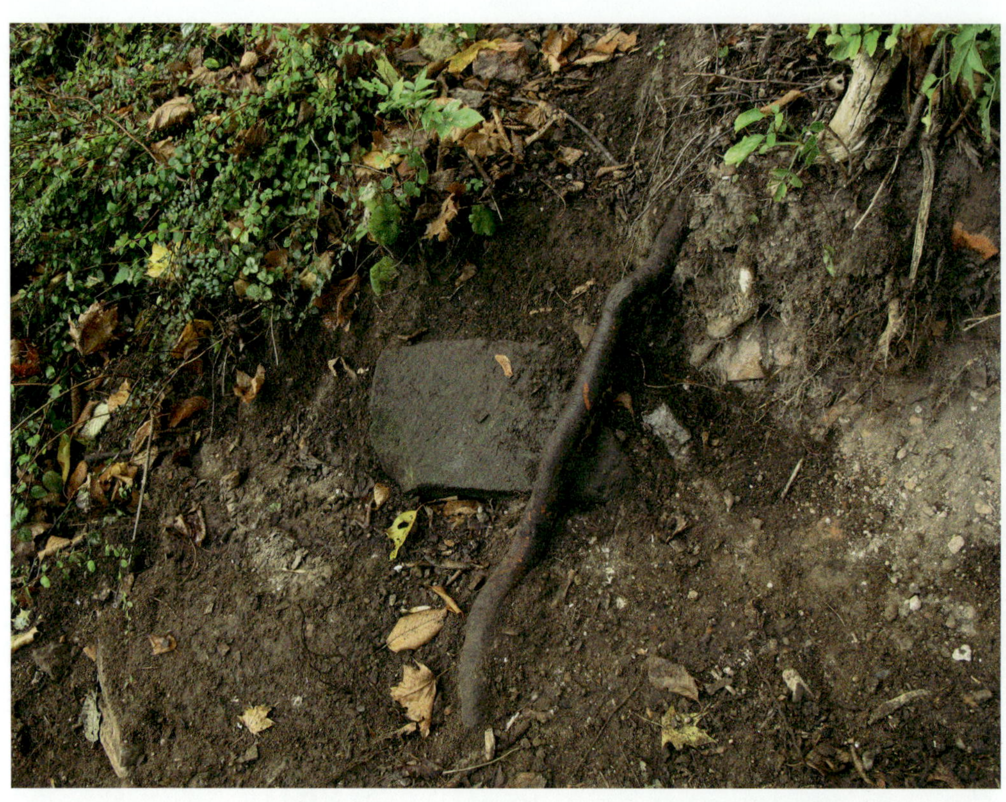

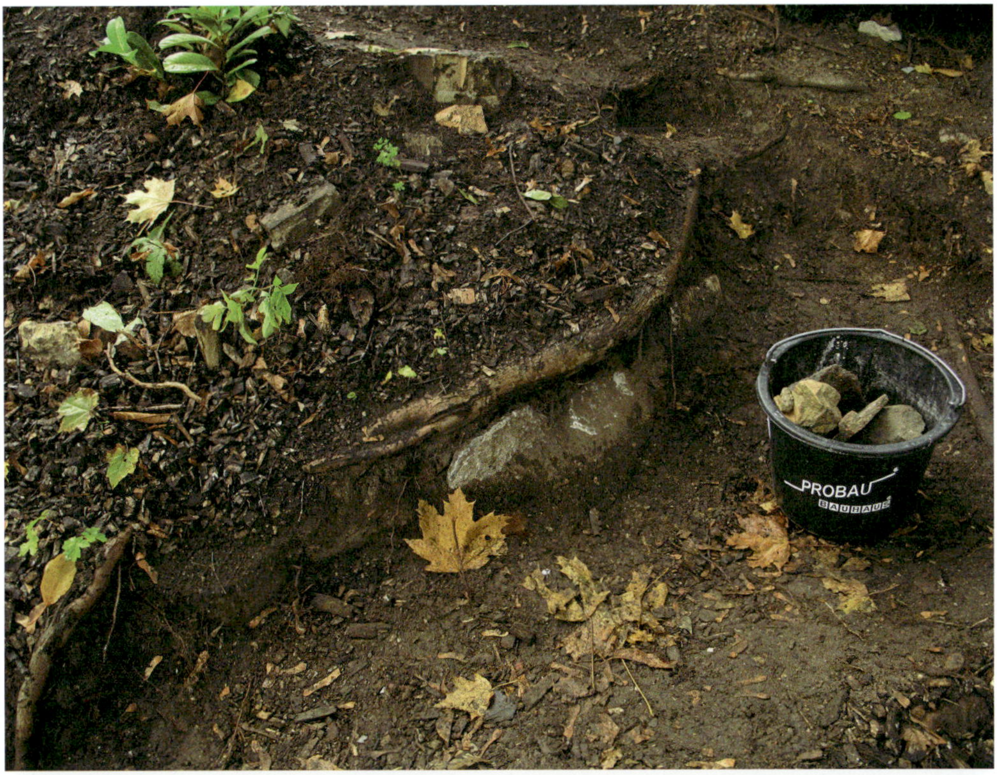

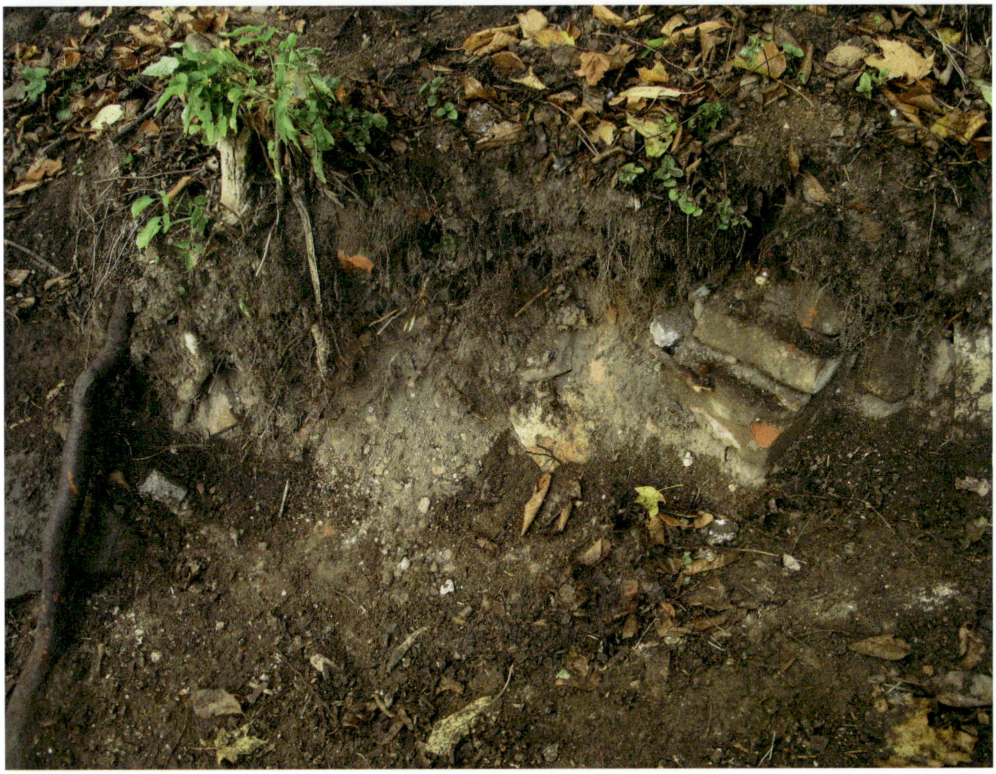

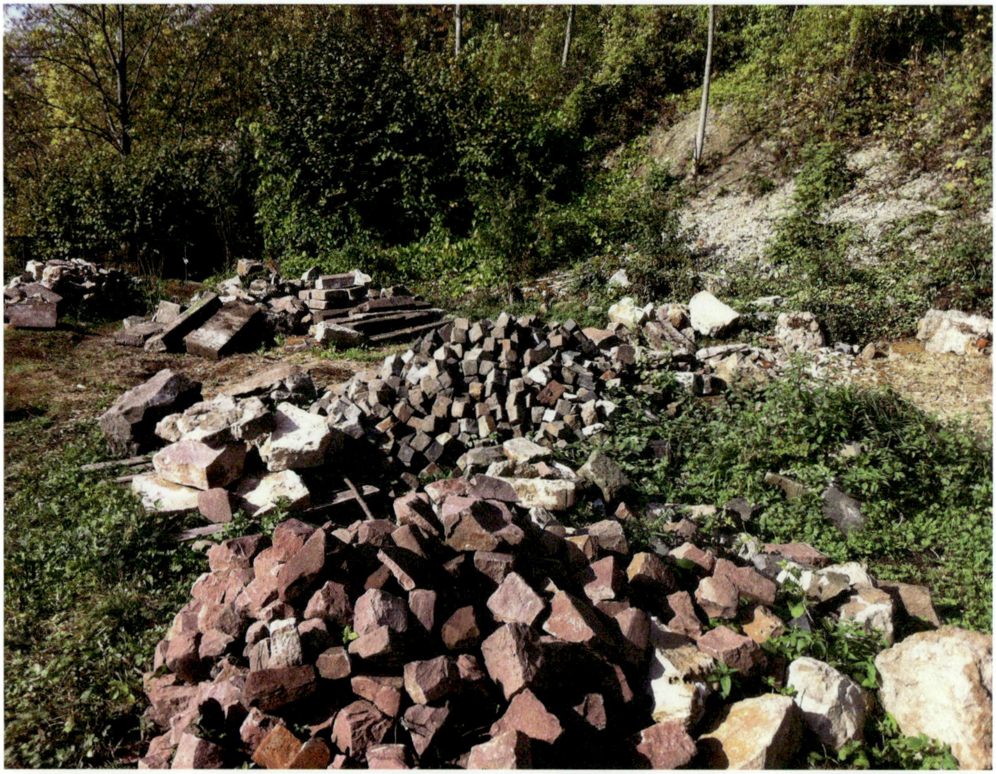

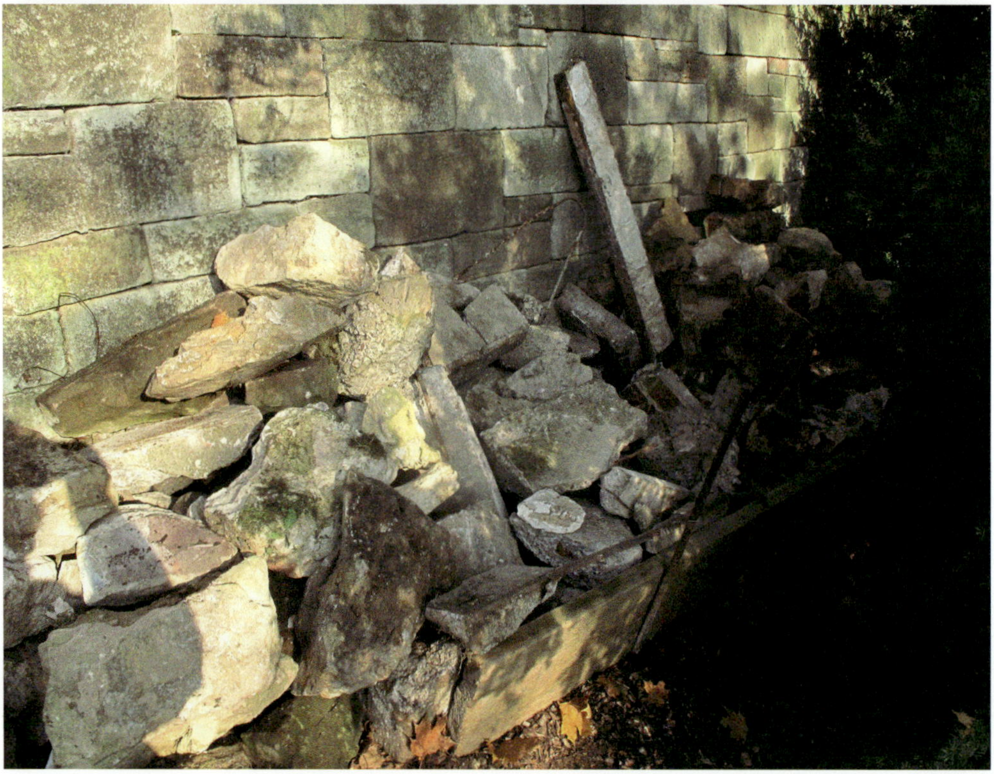

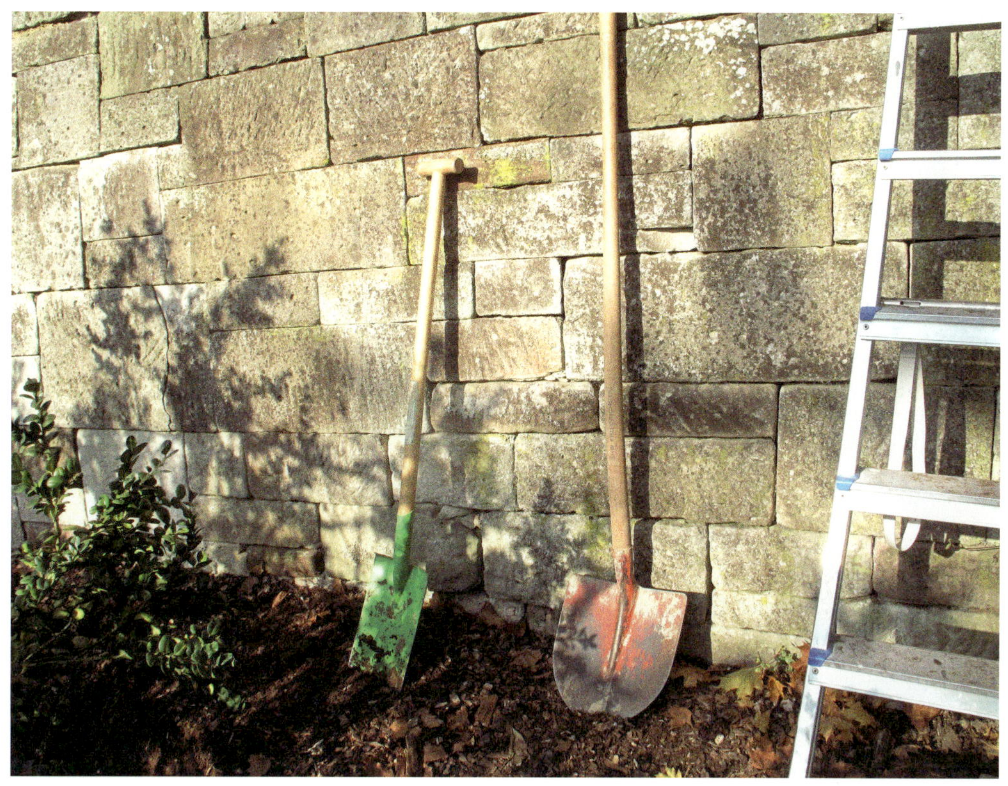

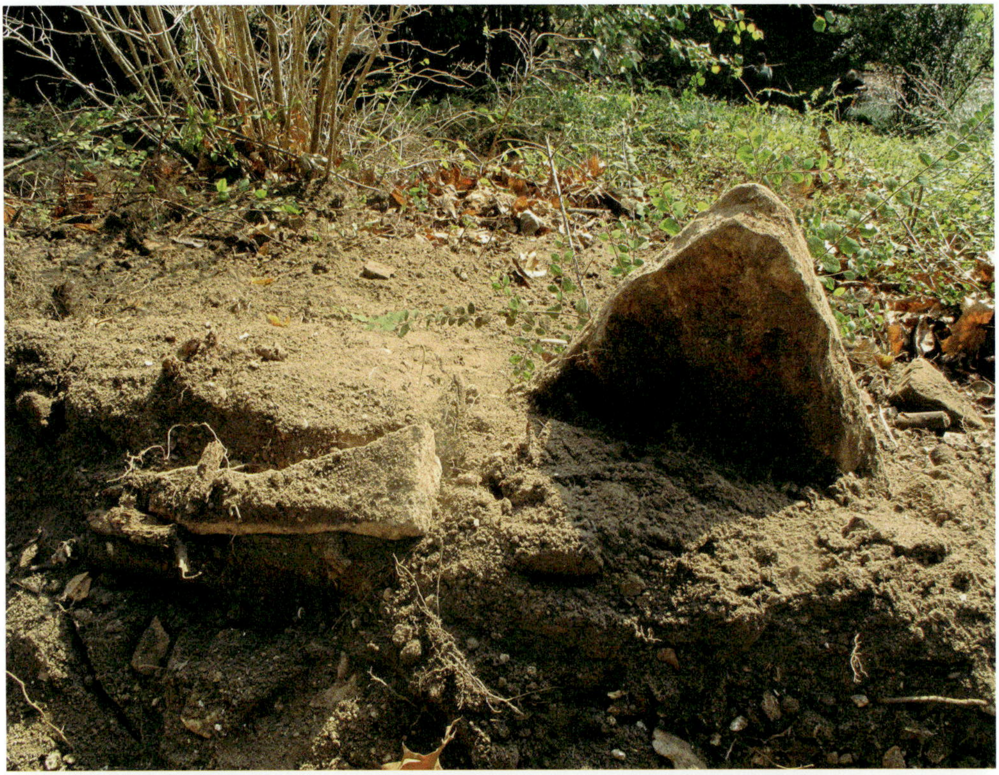

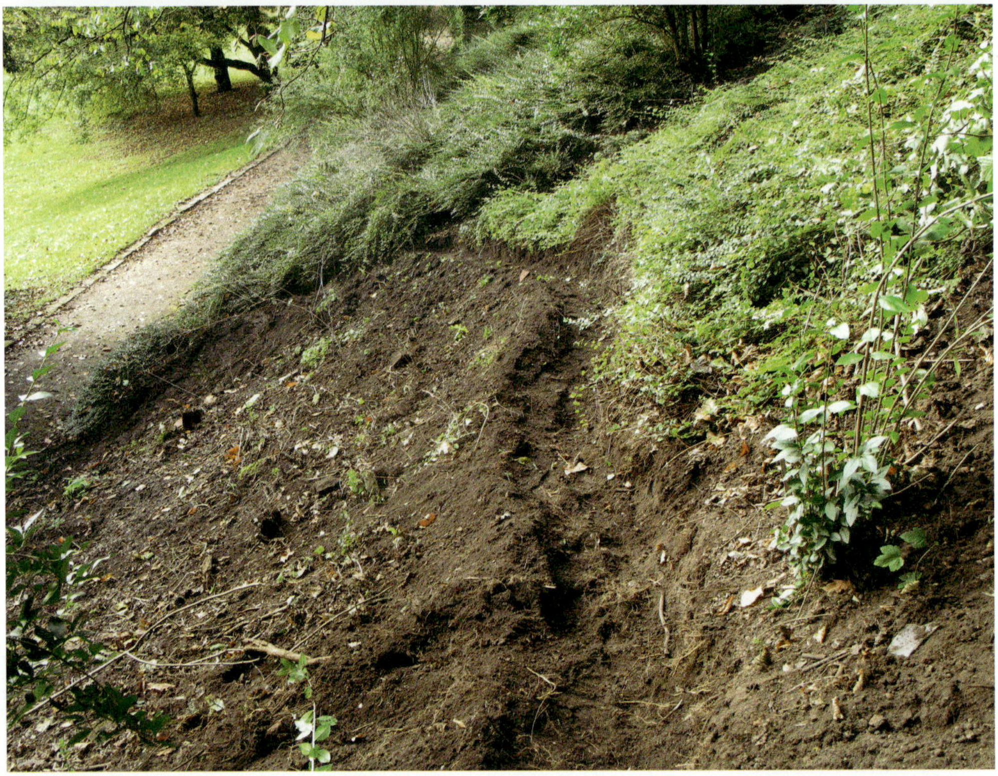

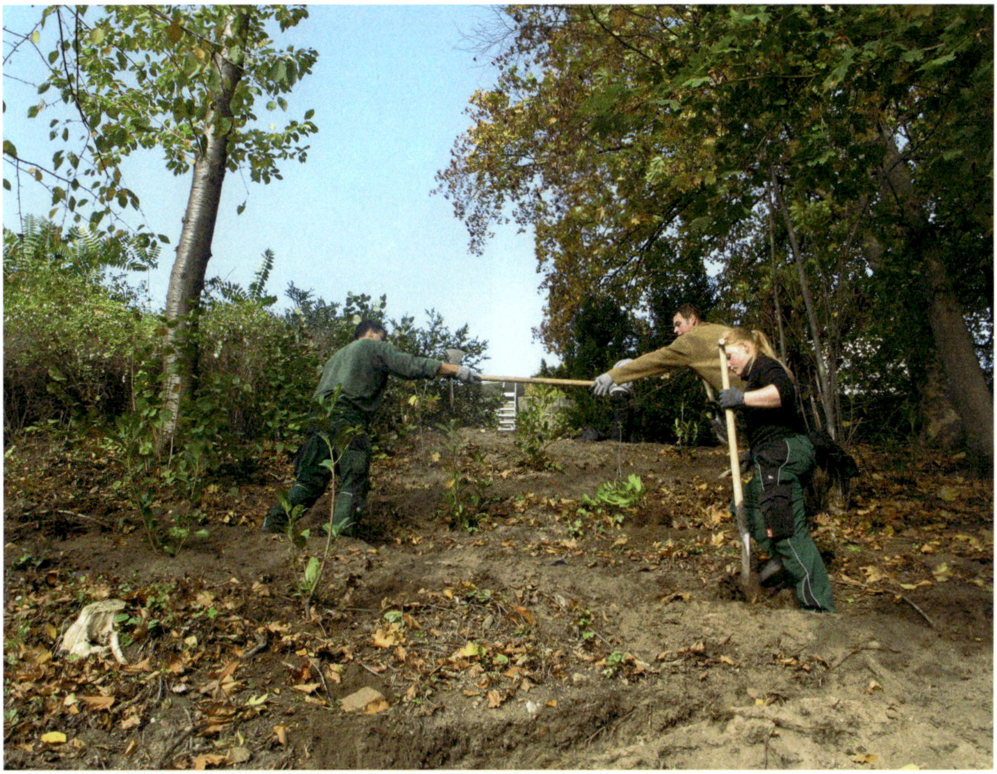

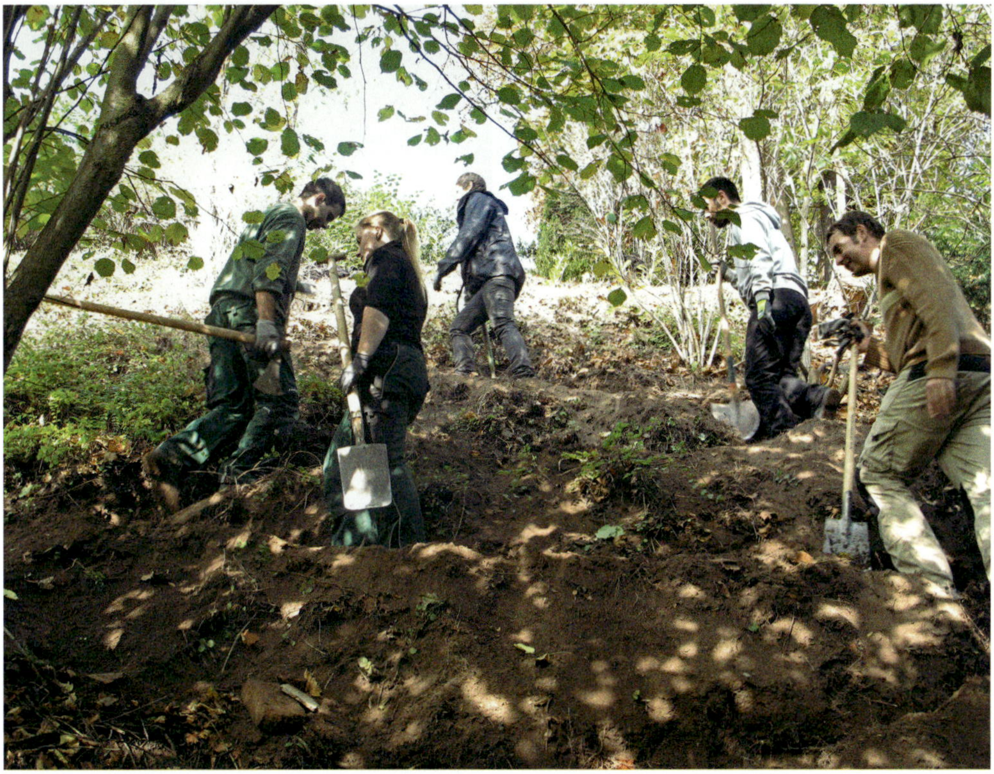

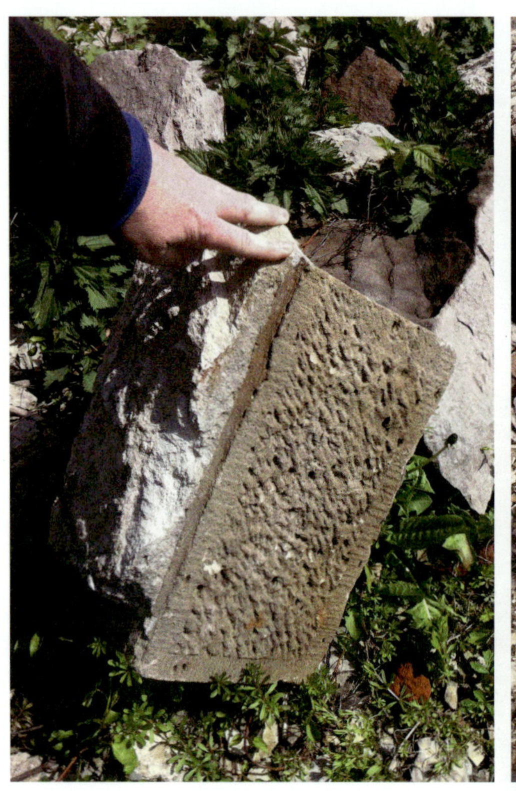

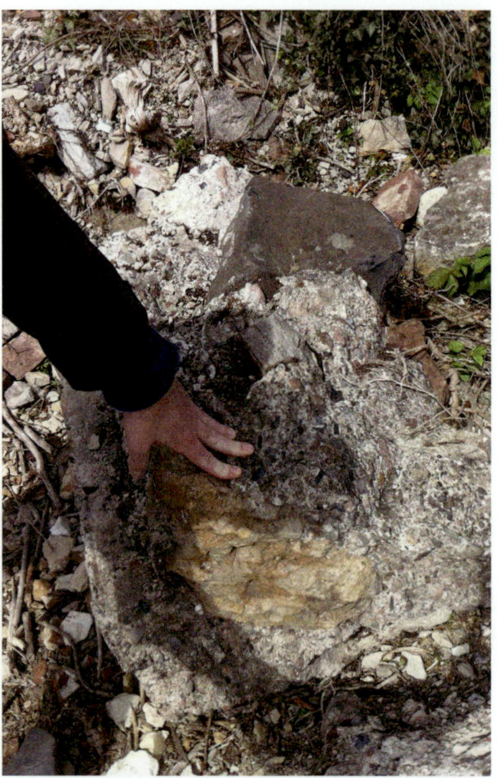

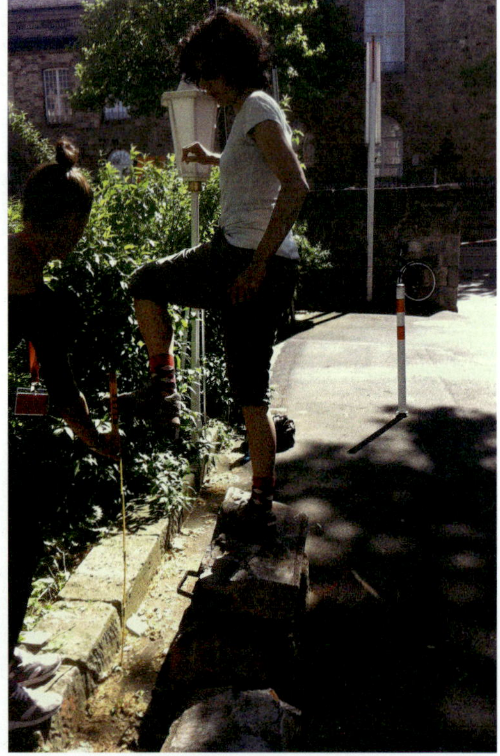

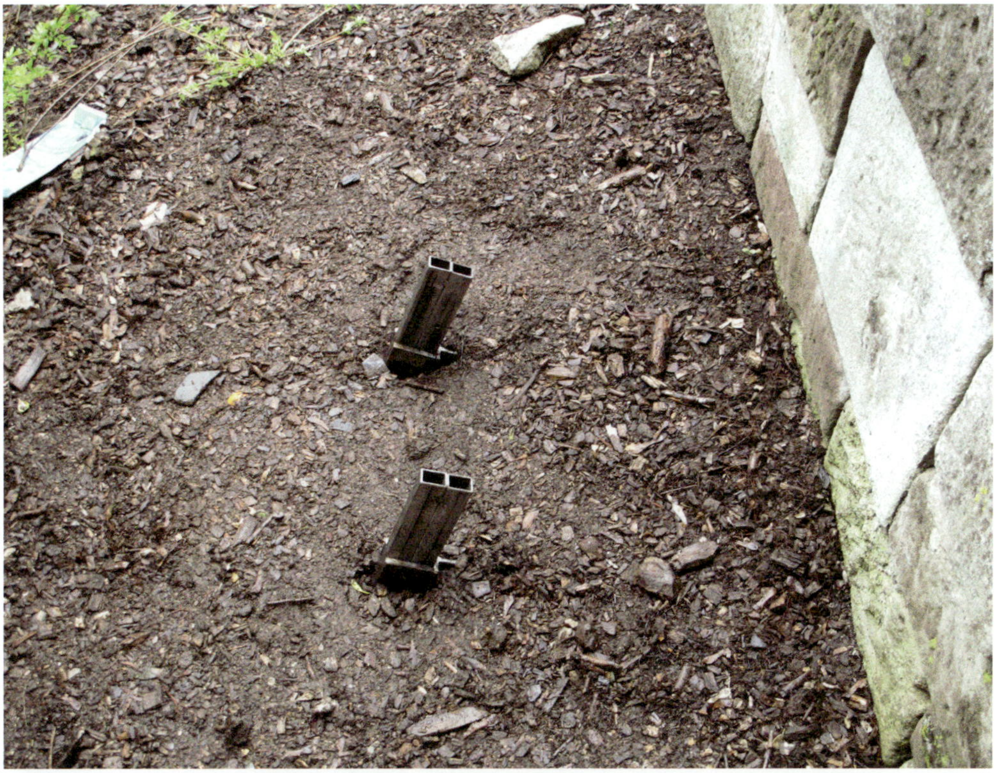

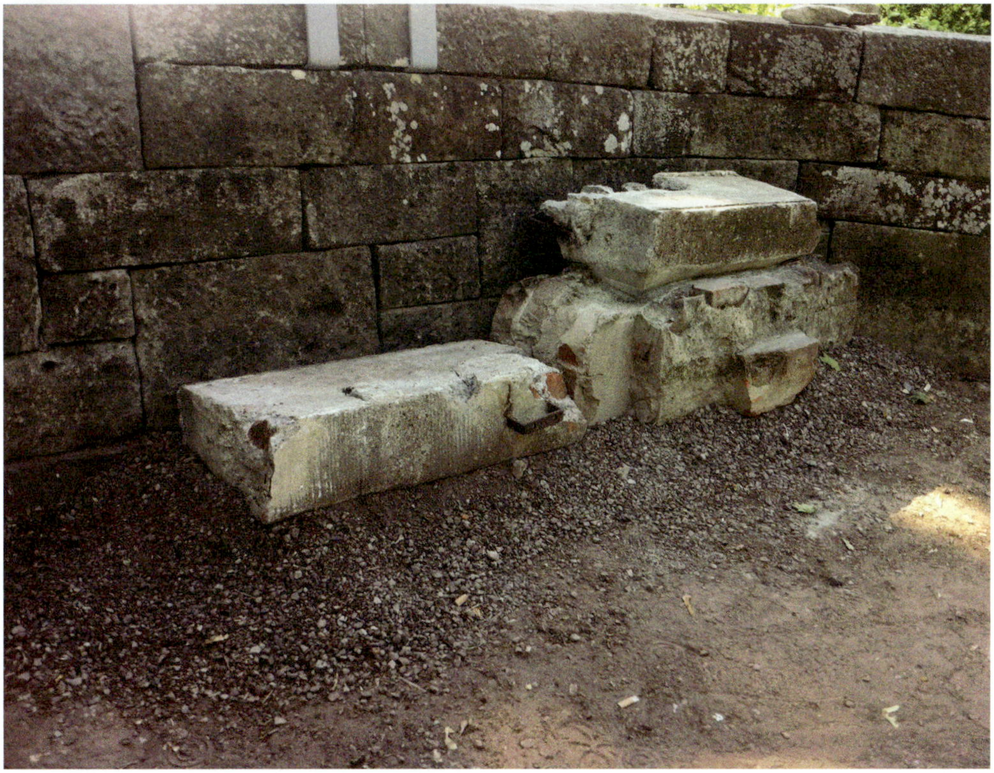

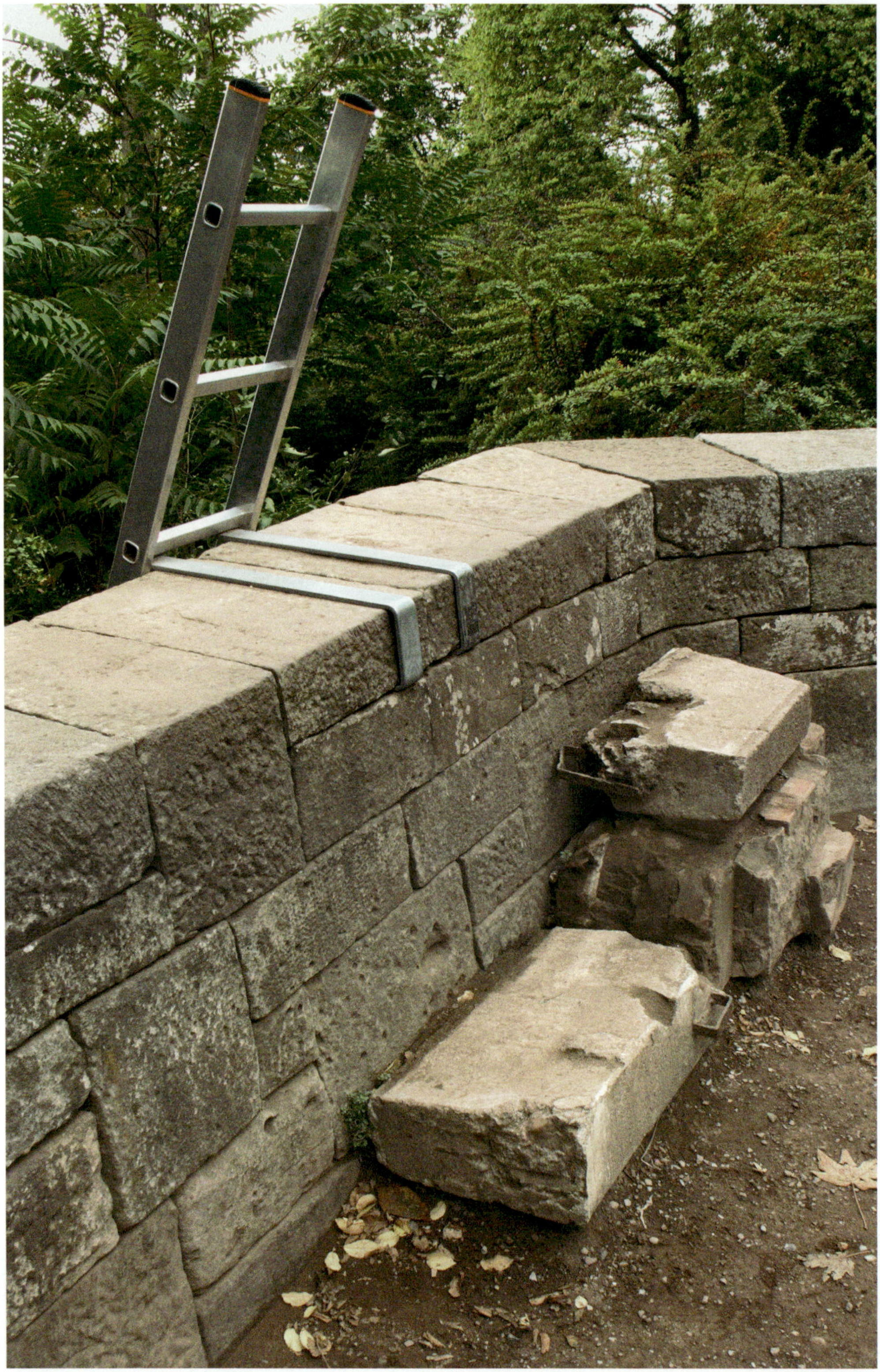

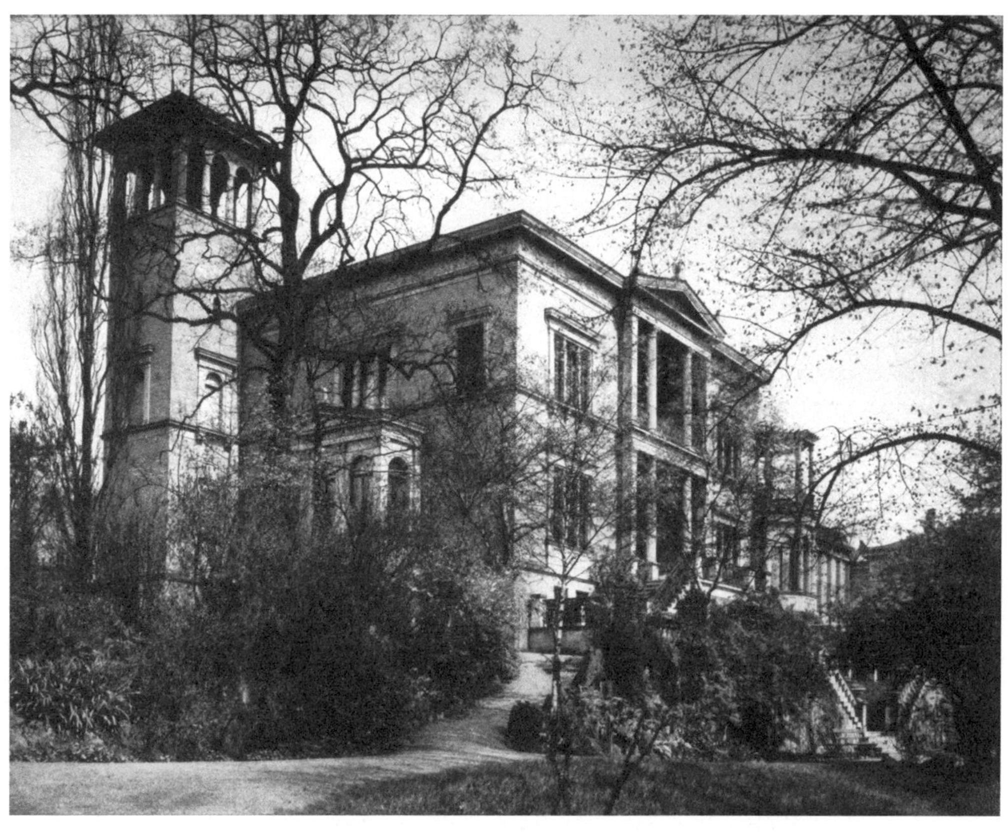

«VILLA HENSCHEL»

Built between 1868-1870 and destroyed in 1945 in a bomb raid.

[SOURCE: HENSCHEL-MUSEUM, KASSEL. REPRODUCTION: POLA SIEVERDING]

Volker Lange advises us during the process of laying the trail on the Auehang. He says we'll need additional material to keep the trail from collapsing beneath us. He would be able to dump some material in front of the slope for our use, rubble that he anyway needs to get rid of, debris from the Villa Henschel on the Weinberg, a neighboring section of the park.

NATASCHA SADR HAGHIGHIAN ‣ Mr. Lange, last autumn, when we began laying the trail on the Auehang, we needed extra rubble to brace the hillside, because otherwise the trail would have perhaps slid down the hill. At that time, you made extra debris available to us. Can you briefly say where it came from and how it became available all of a sudden.

VOLKER LANGE ‹ Well, the debris came from the Weinberg here. The Weinberg is a historical place in Kassel, a heritage-protected garden and park site whose history is full of changes. The Weinberg itself was mentioned as a town for the first time in the fifteenth century, as the village of Weingarten. It is after then that people began making first attempts at wine cultivation, and then the story gets more and more fascinating. The land was owned for the first time, the owners being princes. In the seventeenth century the first terracing was carried out here on the southern slope, after which the princes sold the land, and Bürgergärten [public park] were established. Then—and actually this is what still characterizes the Weinberg to this day—the whole plot was bought up by the Henschel family.

‣ When was that?

‹ Around 1900/1902. Around 1905 there were still two beer gardens at the top of the Weinberg. They were quite popular with Kassel residents. But they were closed when the Henschel family bought the entire plot.
An essential characteristic of the Weinberg plot are these big subconstruction arches that reach over to Frankfurter Strasse. They're huge concrete constructions, among the first concrete constructions of this type that were made here in Kassel, built in 1905. They had become necessary to enable terracing

of the area in the upper part of the Henschel Garden, and to create space
for Haus Henschel, or the Henschel House: the ancestral seat of the family.
Then around 1905/06 the house was built.

‣ There's a Haus Henschel and a Villa Henschel, right? The Haus Henschel
was torn down, and the Villa Henschel was destroyed in the war.

‹ Exactly. The Villa Henschel was completely destroyed in 1945 in a bomb
raid. Today you can only discern leftovers from some stairs that led into the
garden, which also had a really ostentatious fountain. The Haus Henschel
was actually torn down by the Henschel family themselves, allegedly because
the taxes back then were so high.

‣ What happened with the remains of the Villa Henschel after the war?

‹ In the '50s the grounds were made accessible to the public as part of the
1955 BUGA (Bundesgartenschau German Horniculture Show). However, this
applied first and foremost to the upper area of the so-called Henschel Garten.
The lower area, the actual Weinberg slope, actually fell into a deep sleep
like Snow White, since developing it was extremely difficult. There was no
interest in the Bürgergärten anymore either. It became dormant, disused,
the grounds became overgrown. Wild growth climbed, ivy flourished into trees,
and the greenhouse, also one of the first reinforced concrete buildings in
Kassel, became more and more delapidated.

‣ Was it still owned by the Henschel family then? Who became responsible
for the Weinberg?

‹ The city bought the grounds in the '50s. From then on, both the lower Weinberg slope and the Henschel Garden up above were owned by the city of Kassel.

‣ And now you supplied us with debris from that site, debris of the Villa
Henschel. . . . Is the deep sleep over now? Or how did you happen to be clear-
ing out this debris?

‹ So the deep sleep ended in 2005 when the city's Environment and Garden
Agency began to clear out the Weinberg plot. At that time people realized that
it's a very significant, heritage-protected garden layout, and we wanted to safe-
guard these quite distinctive retaining walls, the systems of stairways and old
arches, and the pergolas, the turrets. And so we started exposing the terraces,

mostly in the southern area. At that time we just had to clear aside the
rubble, the trash, the refuse, which was from several centuries. That was made
possible by an initiative that involved unemployed people, who did a lot of
manual labor on these hardly accessible terraces and moved all this material.
A lot of very old, authentic building material was uncovered along the way,
stuff we reused to build stairs and walls. But of course there was also rubble
that accumulated, stuff we couldn't find any use for whatsoever.

‣ You reused debris for parts of the reconstruction?

‹ Exactly. We reused the debris, using sandstone stair blocks, adding
sandstone to walls, reproducing sandstone wall cappings . . . pretty much
everything that could be used in one way or another was used. And in a way,
this is a tradition particular to this location, because you find materials here
from totally different eras. And it simply has to do with the fact that building materials were really quite expensive in the old days, highly valued. And
because of the difficult topography, people repeatedly used what they found.
That's what makes this spot so fascinating: a mixture of different eras can be
found in the material.

‣ I had a conversation with one of the workers who helped heap up the moun-
tain of rubble on the Auehang back then in 1951, and he told me how they
actually earned extra money by finding and removing all the valuable materials
and selling them directly to scrap dealers who were waiting right there on
site. Now here, the debris has been in repose, unlike other sites in the city. Is it
possible to describe what kinds of material or what sort of debris it was?

‹ There was quite a lot of metal, steel . . . basically evidence of the Henschel
family. Steel was a popular construction material back then. We found a lot
of flower bed edgings made out of band steel, band iron. Some of those we
found at their original locations. We put new steel edgings in these places too.
But there was also a lot of plumbing, steel pipes, water pipes; there were
trellises for the climbing plants on the retaining walls; there were bannister
pieces . . . many of the authentic bannisters are still found at the site. Also,
we've decided that we don't want to make it, let's say, 'glitzy,' to restore it all,
but that much of it should stay just as rusty as it looks now, to stay right in
the same spot it's in now so that this place doesn't lose its authenticity.

‣ Could you give a short description of which kinds of debris have made
their way to our trail on the Auehang. What sort of material was it?

‹ Lots and lots of bricks. But also cobblestones, sandstone, basalt paving stones. Some of it was lime-marl debris. The Weinberg is actually a limestone hill, and limestone can be seen cropping out in some places. And then some of it was, let's say, 'natural stone' that was brought here as landscaping stone by the Henschel family. Those stones have big holes and dents.

› And the material, the debris was just lying around in the open? I saw some furrows in the ground, almost like graves, that were full of debris.

‹ Well, because of all the totally different construction activities here, material has gotten churned up and thrown into disarray, above all by the construction of Hochstrasse in the '80s. Back then masses of debris were dumped down the slope, so to speak. And that debris just intermingled with paths, with fences, or with old walls made of natural stone. For that reason, the materials have completely different origins. We've tried again and again to salvage it all. Everything that could be utilized was sorted so that we could reuse as much material as possible here on site.
And the material that we brought to the trail on the Auehang originates primarily from the upper area of the Weinberg. In other words, it's quite probable that a lot of the material was part of the original Villa Henschel that was destroyed in the war.

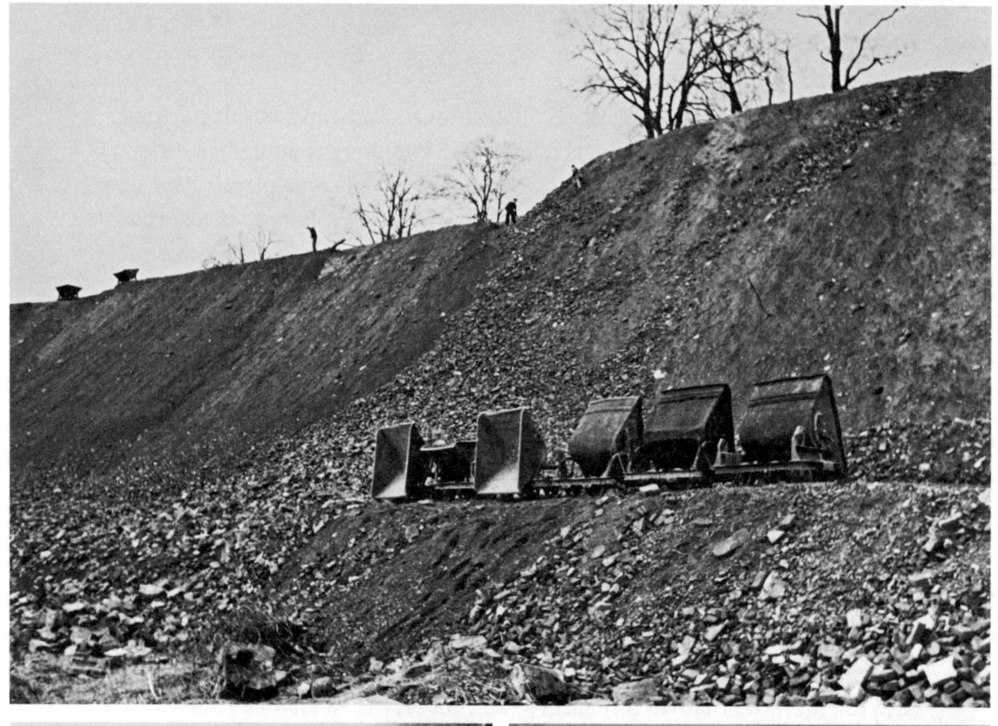

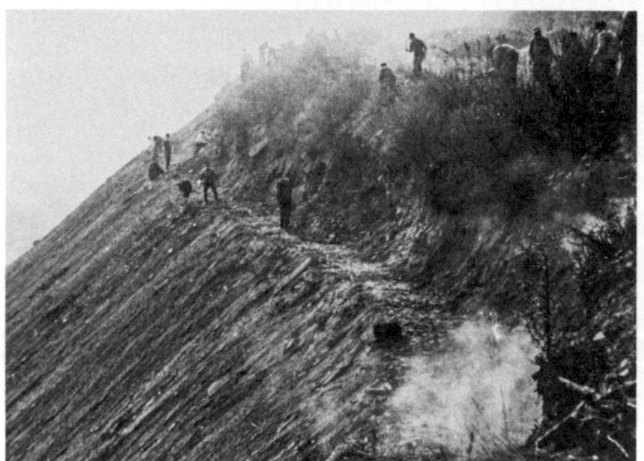

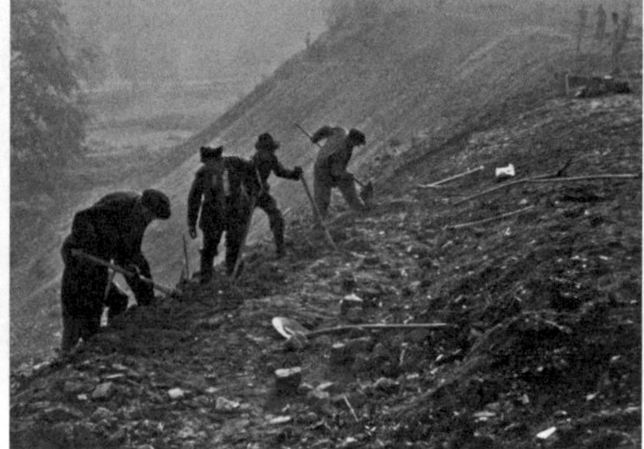

DUMPING RUBBLE OVER THE AUEHANG

Dumping of debris from Kassel's city center onto the Auehang in 1953 in preparation for the 1955 Bundesgartenschau (German Horticultural Show)

[SOURCE: STADTARCHIV (CITY ARCHIVE) KASSEL. REPRODUCTION: POLA SIEVERDING

P. 54 TOP: E4 No. 206, P. 7 - PHOTOGRAPHER: UNKNOWN / BOTTOM: E4 No. 47, P. 12 - PHOTOGRAPHER: UNKNOWN

P. 55 TOP: E4 No. 47, P. 12 - PHOTOGRAPHER: UNKNOWN / CENTER LEFT: E4 No. 47, P. 11 - PHOTOGRAPHER: UNKNOWN

CENTER RIGHT: E4 No. 47, P. 5 - PHOTOGRAPHER: UNKNOWN / BOTTOM: E4 No. 47, P. 5 - PHOTOGRAPHER: UNKNOWN

P. 56 TOP: E4 No. 206, P. 19 - PHOTOGRAPHER: UNKNOWN / BOTTOM: E4 No. 206, P. 11 - PHOTOGRAPHER: UNKNOWN

P. 57 E4 No. 217, P. 31 - PHOTOGRAPHER: UNKNOWN

P. 58 E4 No. 206, P. 6 - PHOTOGRAPHER: UNKNOWN / P. 59 E4 No. 6, P. 42 - PHOTOGRAPHER: UNKNOWN]

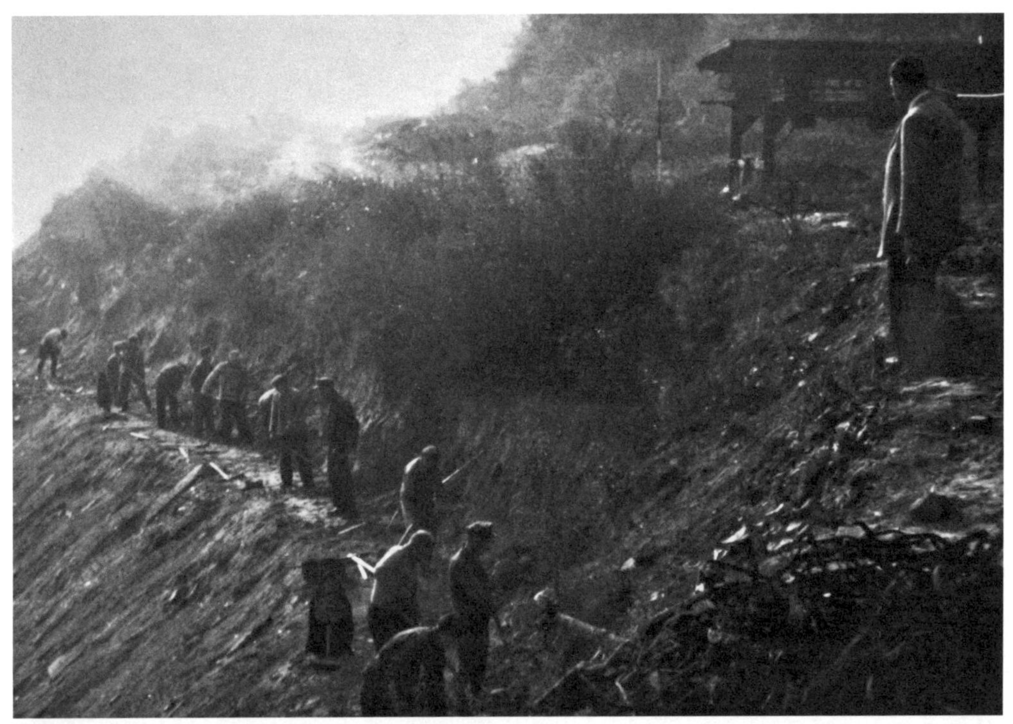

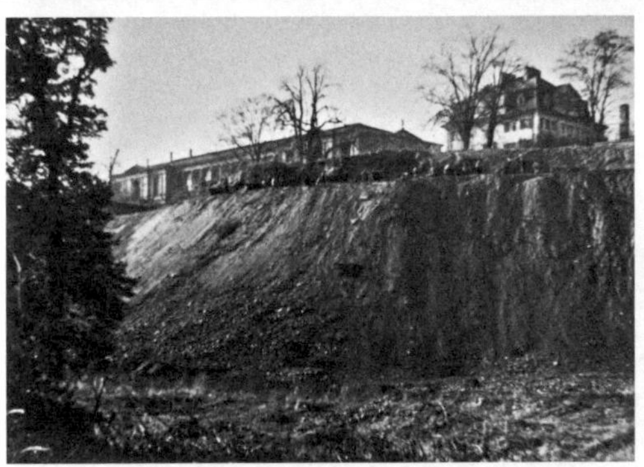

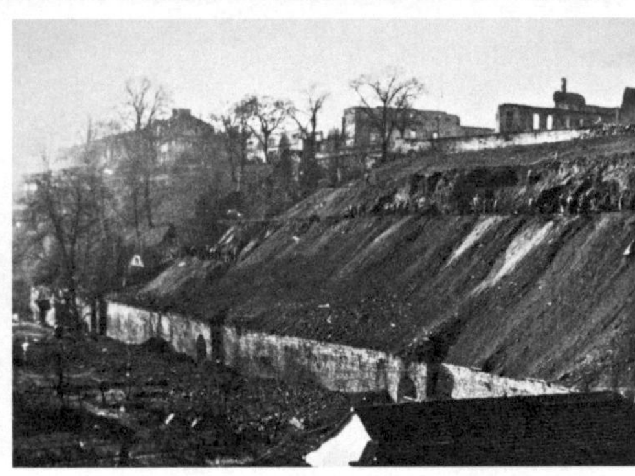

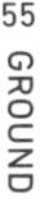

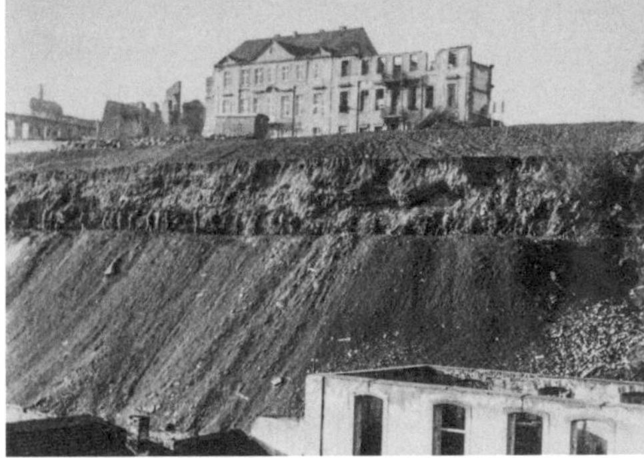

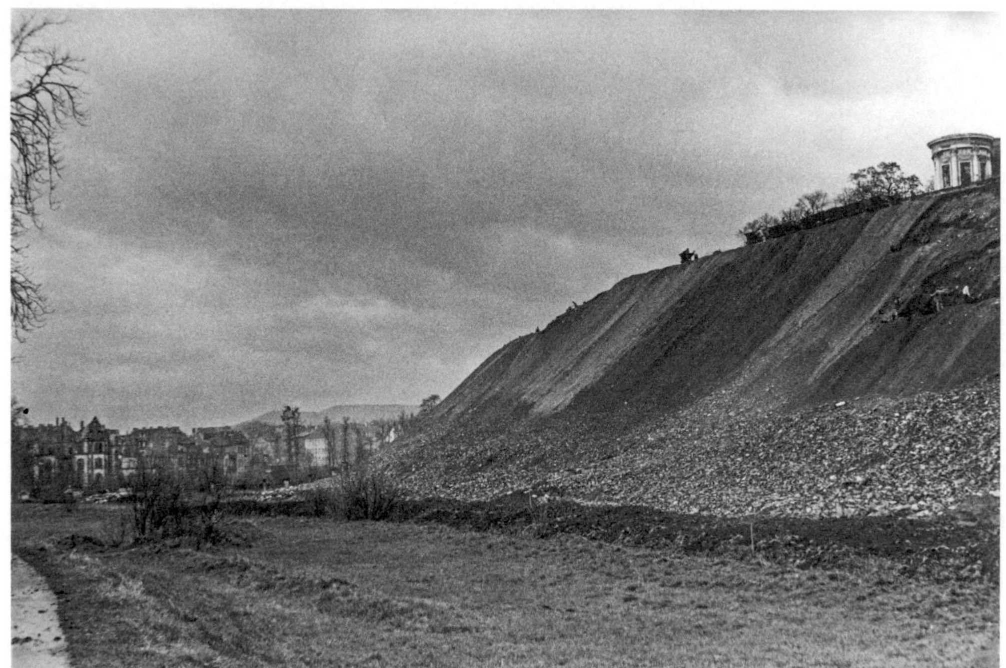

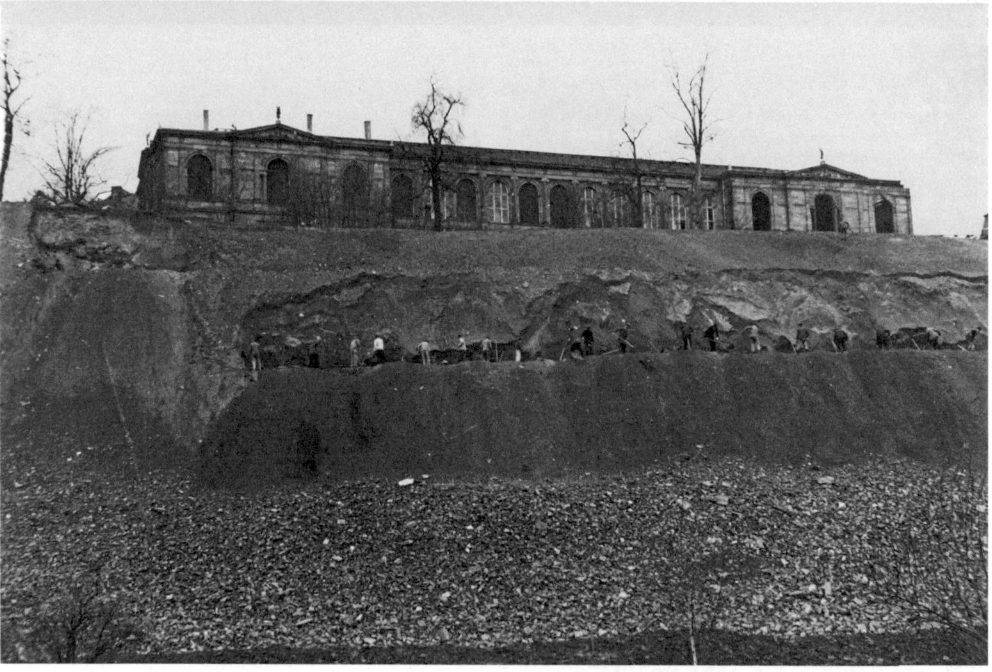

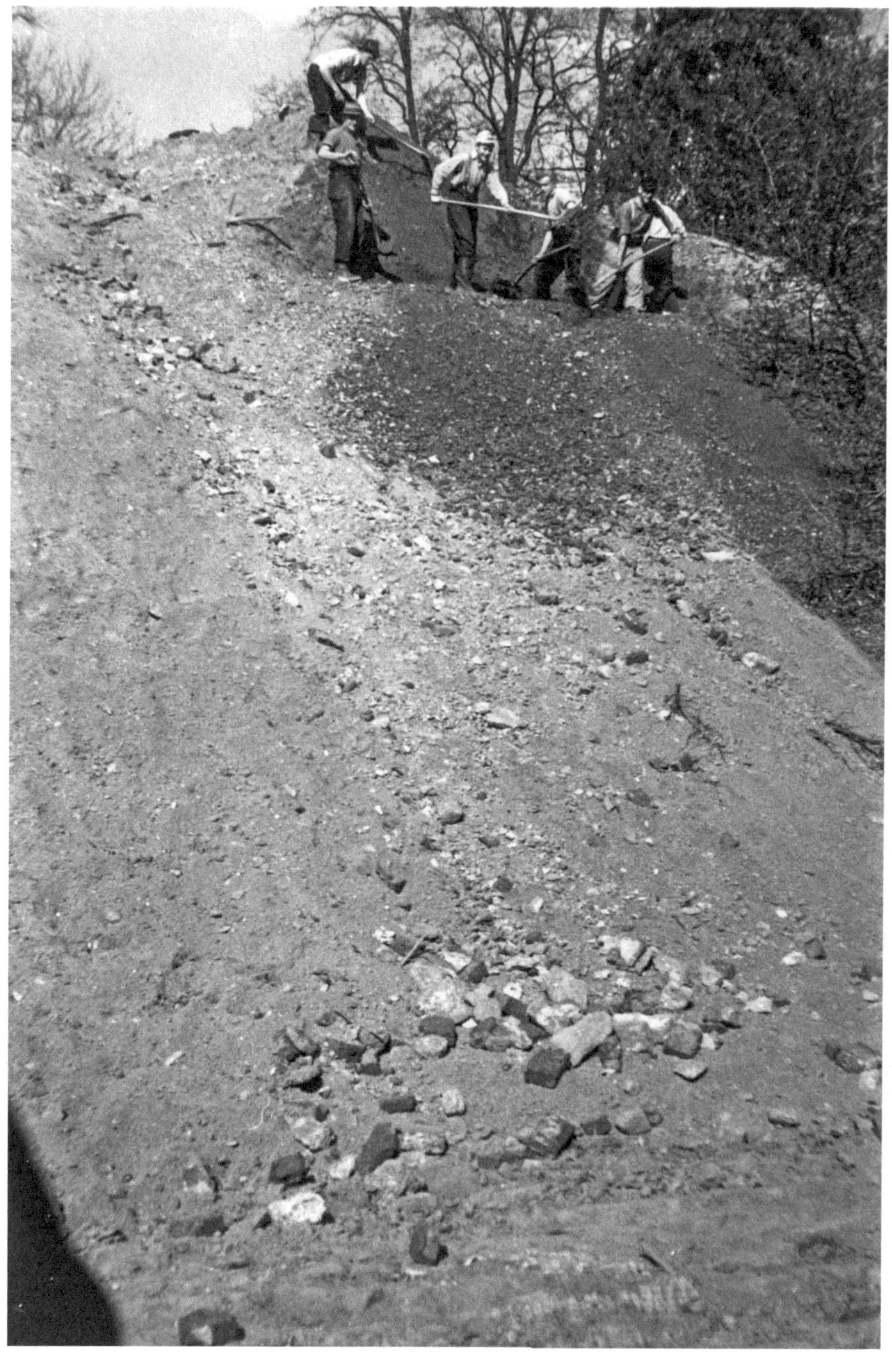

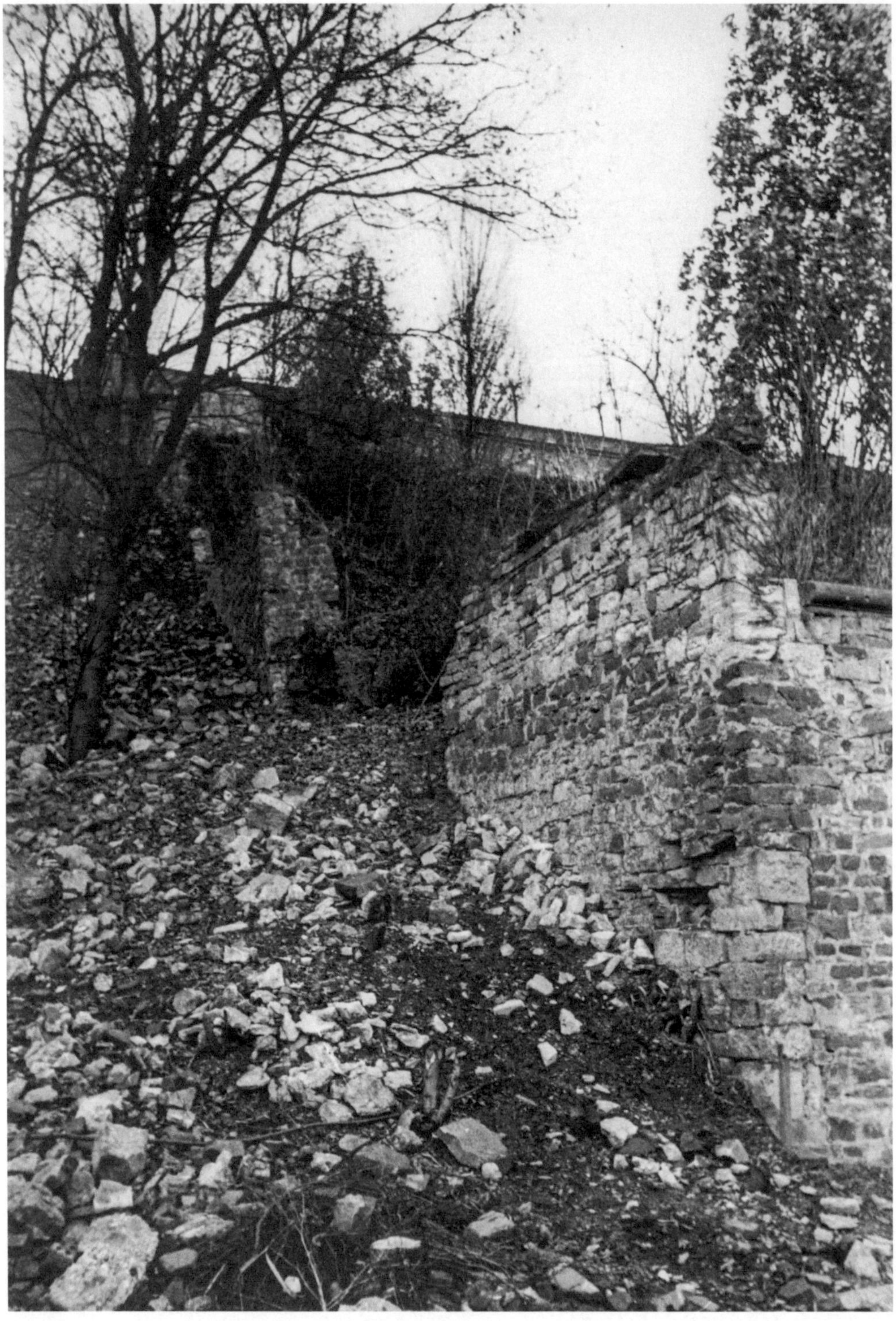

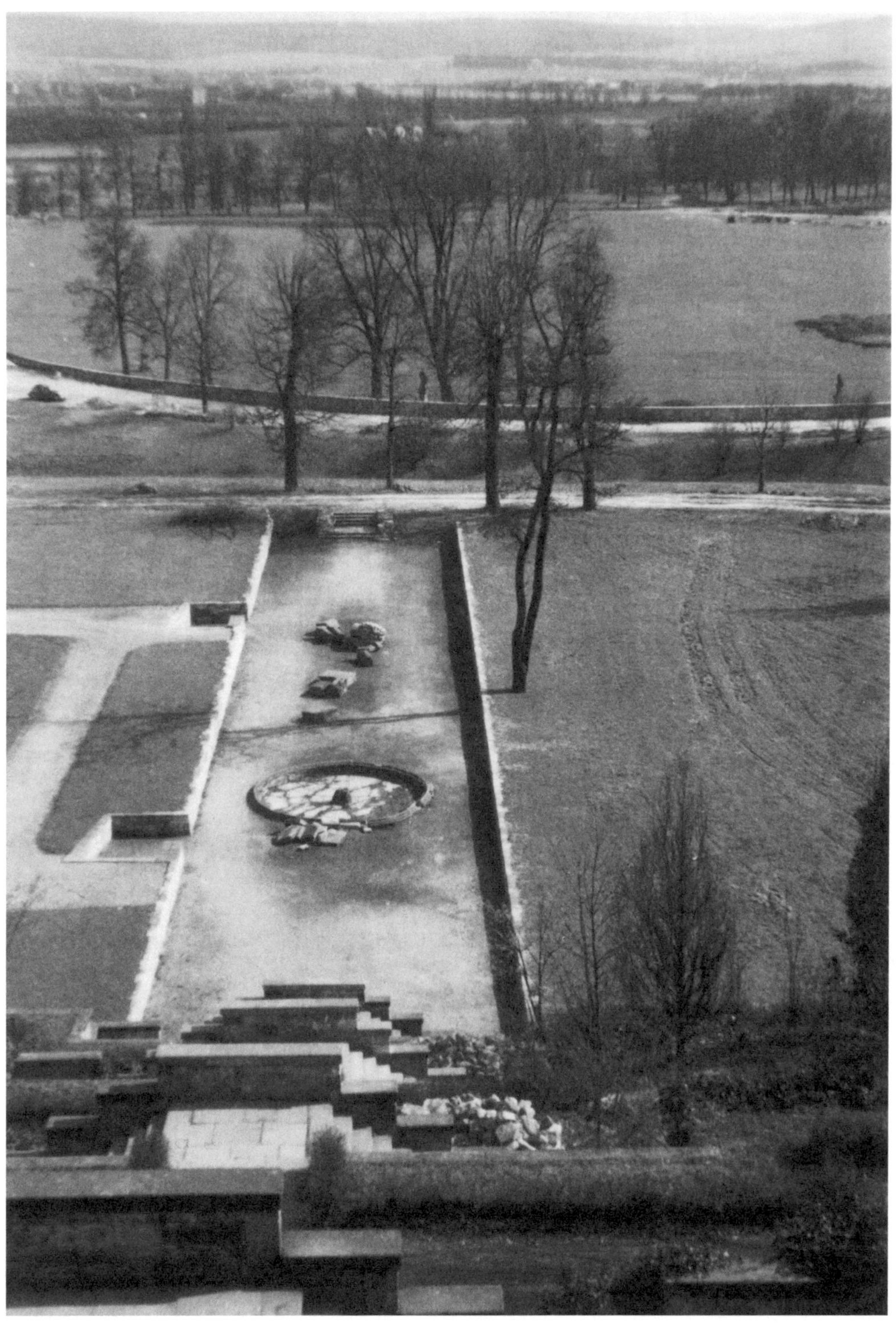

View over the Ehrenmal from Schöne Aussicht onto the Karlsaue, Kassel, ca. 1950

[SOURCE: STADTARCHIV (CITY ARCHIVE) KASSEL / E4 No. 6, P. 42 - PHOTOGRAPHER: UNKNOWN. REPRODUCTION: POLA SIEVERDING]

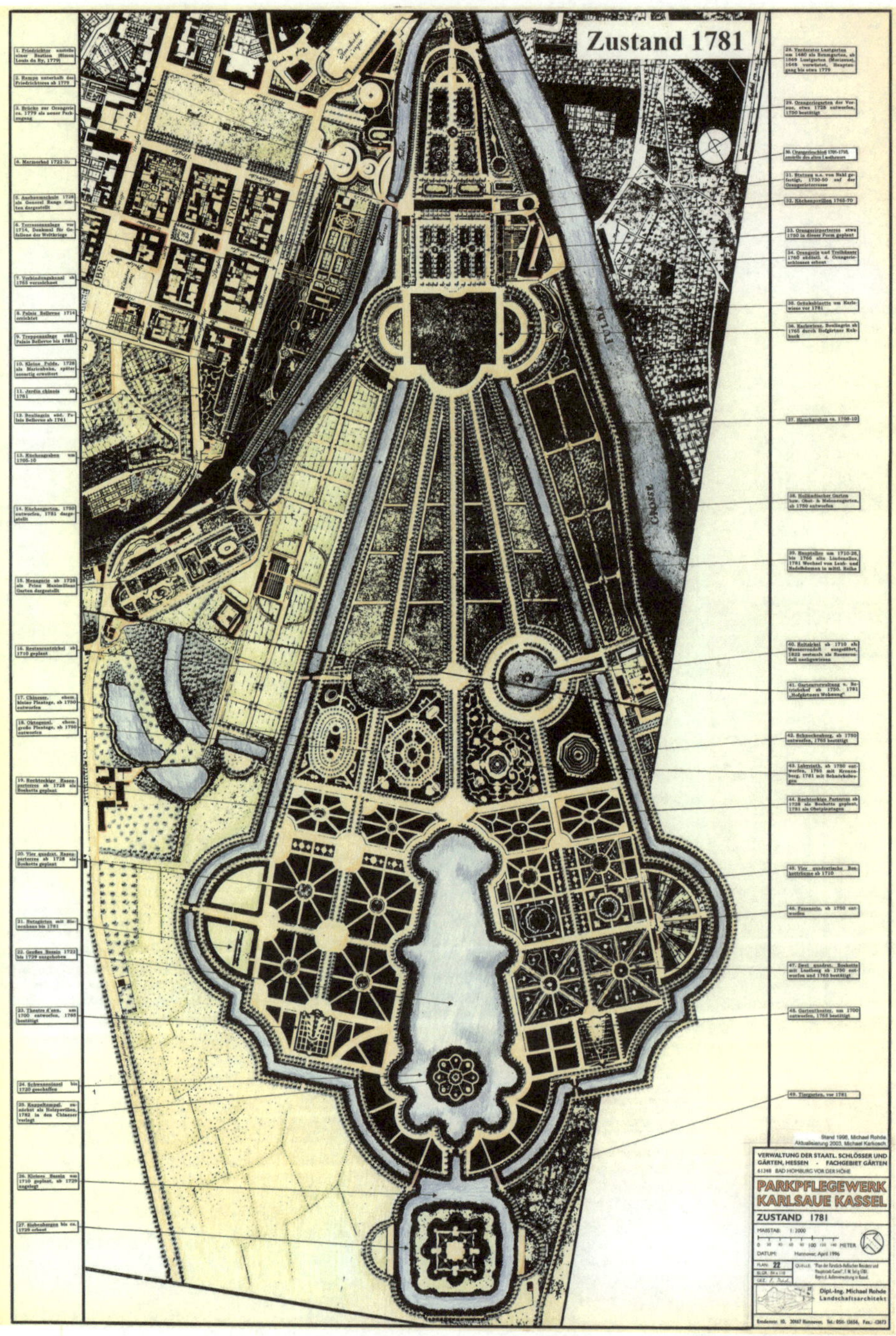

1781 map of the Karlsaue, Kassel

[SOURCE: STAATSPARK KARLSAUE KASSEL, PARKPFLEGEWERK]

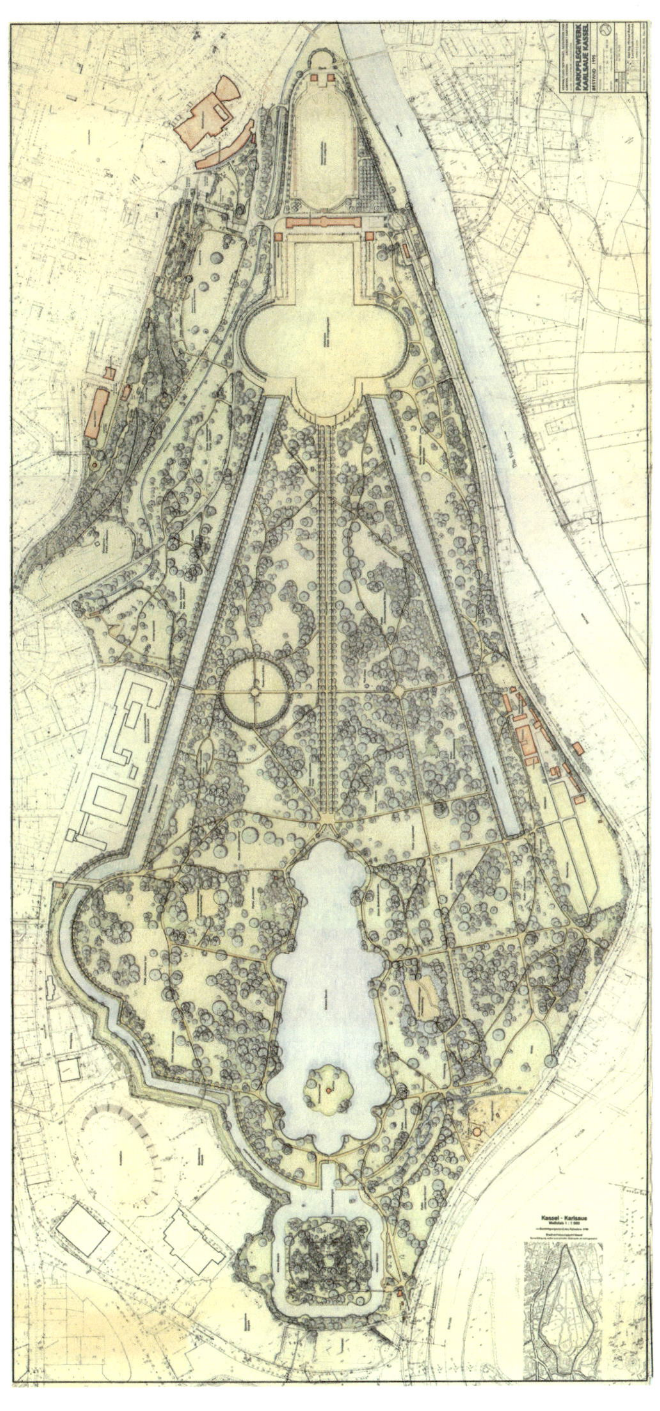

1995 map of the Karlsaue, Kassel

[SOURCE: STAATSPARK KARLSAUE KASSEL, PARKPFLEGEWERK]

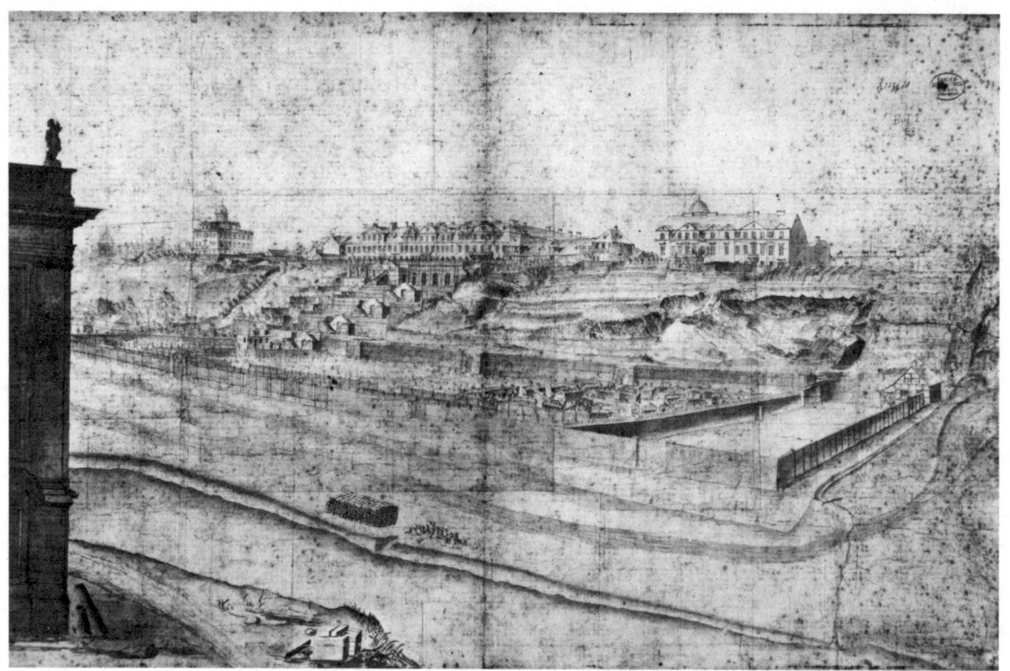

TERRACED GARDEN ON AUEHANG, MASTER BUILDER PAUL DU RY, KASSEL, CA. 1711

The terraced garden on the Auehang, also known as the Prinzessgarten, was built by the master builder Paul du Ry as part of the Palais Prinz Georg on Schöne Aussicht (formerly Bellevue). Orange, lemon, and fig trees grew on the terraces, and wine was cultivated for some time. After World War I, the garden was transformed into a war memorial for fallen soldiers, know as an Ehrenmal.

[SOURCE: STADTARCHIV (CITY ARCHIVE) KASSEL / E4 No. 6, P. 1 - ILLUSTRATOR: UNKNOWN. REPRODUCTION: POLA SIEVERDING]

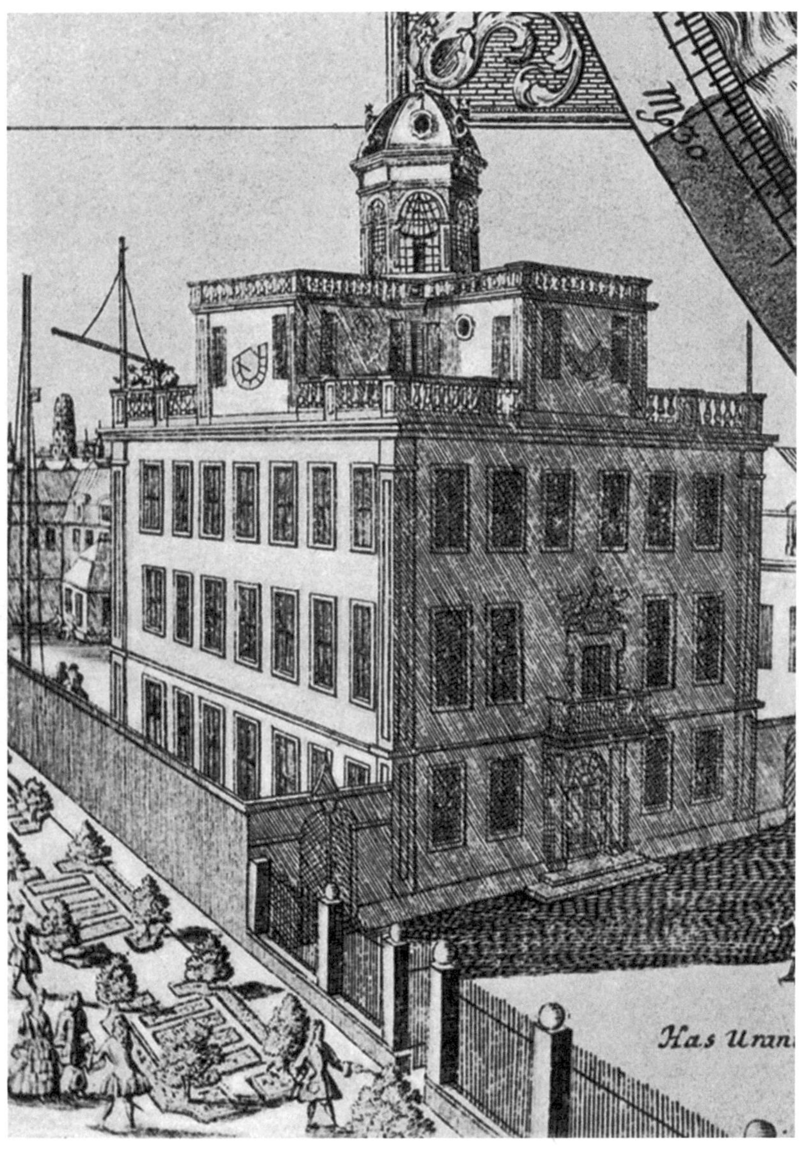

PALAIS BELLEVUE, 1742

The palais Bellevue was built by the Huguenot master builder Paul du Ry. It is located on Schöne Aussicht (formerly called Bellevue) above the Karlsaue. According to the wishes of Landgrave Karl, the Palais was equipped with a state-of-the-art observatory. During the eighteenth century, between the Thirty Years' War and the Seven Years' War, the connection between Baroque landscape architecture, ballistics, and military perspective was written into the city planning of Kassel. This culture of sight lines, panoramas, and alignment, or, in short, this culture of the view is transported from the battlefield into the gardens of France and, with Paul du Ry, to Kassel. This is nicely illustrated in the picture of General Tilly looking out over the city of Hann Münden (page 71). Today the Palais Bellevue houses the Grimm Museum.

[SOURCE: UNIVERSITÄTS- UND LANDESBIBLIOTHEK DARMSTADT. ILLUSTRATION: JOHANN GABRIEL DOPPELMAYR, 1742. PUBLIC DOMAIN]

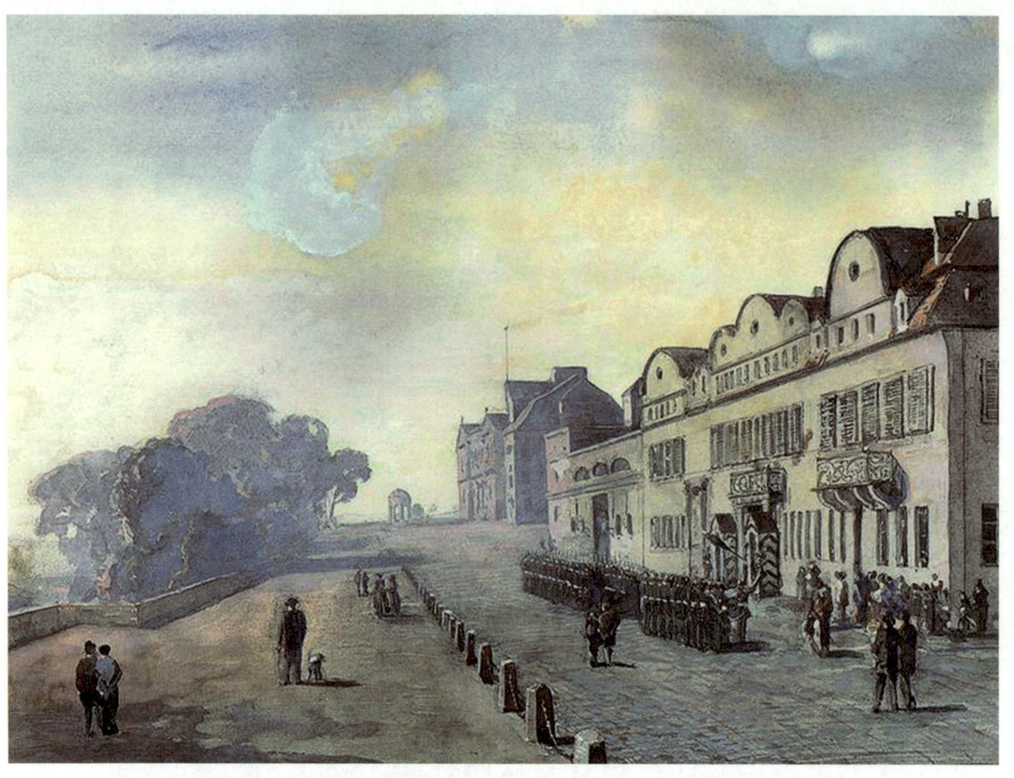

"GENERALKOMMANDO BELLEVUE KASSEL," GOUACHE BY LOUIS KOLITZ (1845–1914)

The picture shows Schöne Aussicht. A soldier corps marches by; flaneurs are strolling. Curious onlookers are bustling up against the house wall of the Palais Prinz Georg to get a glimpse. From 1777 onward, the Palais, built by Paul du Ry, housed the Académie de Peinture et de Sculpture de Cassel, Kassel's first art academy. On the left, behind the trees, is where the Ehrenmal is located today, and right behind that, our trail.

[ILLUSTRATION: LOUIS KOLITZ. SOURCE: PUBLIC DOMAIN]

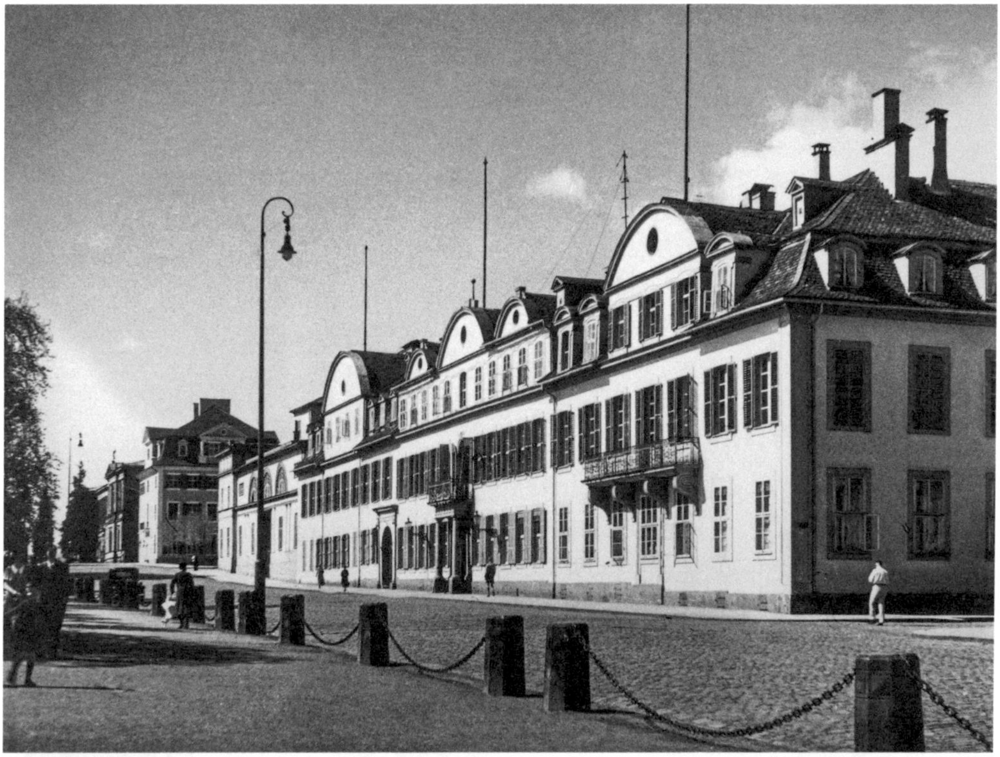

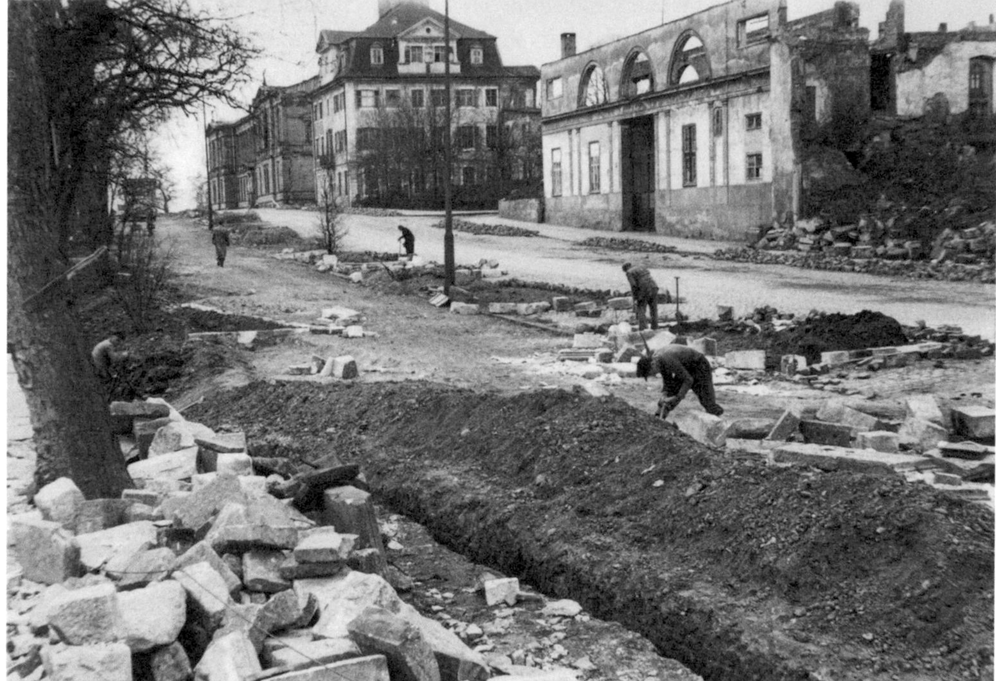

Street views of Schöne Aussicht in Kassel Oberneustadt before and after the bombardments in World War II

Dear Allen,

I hope this message finds you well.

I am writing to you with a few questions concerning your wonderful book *Unnatural Horizons* in connection with my dOCUMENTA (13) project.

I built a 'trail,' i.e. an informal path, on a slope in the city of Kassel between the elevated street level of Schöne Aussicht (Bellevue) and the Baroque gardens of the Karlsaue in the valley below. The trail functions as a shortcut between the upper and lower levels, but also as an alternative to the monumental Ehrenmal, a war memorial in honor of the German soldiers of World War I and II located on the same slope. This memorial used to be a Baroque terrace garden associated with Palais Prinz Georg and became a war memorial only after World War I. The memorial also connects Schöne Aussicht with the park through a symmetrical staircase. When building the trail, we found that the slope is mainly built of rubble and debris from World War II. Working on the trail uncovered the rubble and made visible and tangible what is buried underneath the thin layer of soil.

The role of the military in Kassel struck me as continuously influential, manifesting itself on many levels.

The rubble itself indicates a militaristic loop: Kassel was heavily bombarded during World War II and almost completely wiped off the map because it was home to one of Germany's biggest weapons manufacturers, named Henschel & Son. After World War II tons and tons of debris were shoved down the slope around the already existing Ehrenmal in order to clean up the city. Nevertheless Kassel is once again today one of the main locations for arms production in Germany.

But also the Ehrenmal in its original form was shaped by military knowledge. It was constructed as a terrace garden in connection with Palais Prinz Georg by the Huguenot captain of the engineers, Paul du Ry, a master builder of fortresses, cascades and water constructions. Above the terrace garden on Schöne Aussicht, Paul du Ry also built the observatory Palais Bellevue, which

is now the Grimm Museum. The Karlsaue, a Baroque garden of simultaneously
plays a central role in the city's layout, as well as been a venue for documenta
and other cultural events to this day. The references are manifold. To mention
a few more: Schöne Aussicht with Palais Prinz Georg (1703–1711) and Palais
Bellevue (1714) and the Huguenot quarter behind it (1687) were built on
the former city fortifications of Kassel after the Thirty Years' War; Schöne
Aussicht—as the name already suggests—provides a panoramic view, and the
Palais Bellevue was even equipped with a state-of-the-art observatory.

As you can imagine I immediately felt the need to reread the chapter *"Demate-
rialization and Iconoclasm"* in *Unnatural Horizons*. In this chapter, you explain
how the formalized and geometric application of techniques of visibility in
Baroque gardens connects to military engineering and planning, prefigured by
issues of ballistics and military perspective ('perspective cavalière'). (UH, 50)
How does this military perspective come into play here in the gardens of
Kassel? I would love to know your reading of the layout of the Karlsaue and
Paul du Ry's terrace garden in reference to the arguments you set forth in
Unnatural Horizons.

I would also be curious to know how you perceive specific modes of visuality
that are established in this scenario and their possible purpose or reason.
The Cartesian symmetries of the terrace garden connect to the Baroque
layout of Karlsaue with its alleys establishing visual axes, vanishing points,
and viewpoints that synthesize the mobility of a projectile, embodied by the
visitor traversing the park.

Was it simply the latest fashion that Paul du Ry had brought from Paris
when he sought refuge in Kassel's Princedom? Or did Landgrave Karl knowingly
introduce a culture of geometrization and surveying techniques to the fortified
Kassel of war times? Was Karl and, for that matter Paul conscious that
gardens were and are instruments of knowledge and power?

I came across an image from the Thirty Years' War. Apparently it shows
General Tilly on the so called Tilly Schanze (Tilly entrenchment) looking into
the distance, down onto a city under siege (Hann Münden, 1626) near Kassel.
His gaze parallels the cannon's direction of fire. Do you see the gardens in
Kassel—built between the two great wars of that time, the Thirty Years' War
and the Seven Years' War—as responding to this gaze of conquest and power,
symbolically or otherwise?

How do you read the garden's central role in Kassel's cultural, recreational,
but also representative life? Does it hold an importance that seems to be
ongoing, from its beginnings in the eighteenth century, during the first
BUGA and documenta in 1955, until today, just like the continuous thread of
war-related issues?

I figured that if these visual concepts exist, our trail actually evades them, as it is impossible to attain an overview of it. It does not allow for a grand view or a survey, other than glimpses of the adjacent Ehrenmal and details of the rubble and plants.
I would be most delighted if you could respond or give feedback, even if only briefly.

Warmest regards,
Natascha

Dear Natascha,

I fear that you will be disappointed by this letter, but I am sure that you will understand. I read your proposal with great interest, as it is exactly the sort of project that I would be interested in writing about. The problem is that what I have seen does not even constitute 'paper gardens,' but rather immaterial computer images. As you know, all of my work on landscape—notably *Mirrors of Infinity* and *Unnatural Horizons*, and to some extent *The Wind and the Source*—is based on the lived experience of gardens and landscape, perhaps representing the most useful remnant of my studies in phenomenological aesthetics. If I were able to come to Germany and walk the sites with you, engage in discourse on the motivations for and structures of the project, contemplate and meditate on site, etc., etc., it would have been a pleasure. But, alas, this isn't possible. In some cases, when I know a site intimately, either through frequent visits or by having already written about it—such as Vaux-le-Vicomte, Versailles, Mont Ventoux, and certain Zen gardens of Kyoto such as Ryōan-ji and Daisen-in—I can write without a visit. But this is not the case in the present instance. To write from image would be to betray my epistemology, and to fall into the trap that I have so often criticized in other landscape historians, i.e., reducing the garden to an image, the stroll to a perspective, the synaesthetic to the visual. I am truly sorry to miss this chance to collaborate, and hope that the future holds a more concrete crossing of paths. I wish you the best of luck with this project.

Most Sincerely, Allen

Dear Allen,

Thank you for your considerate response. I fully understand your concerns.
It only confirms the genuine thoughts that speak through your book.
Actually it's very much in accordance with how I discovered all these questions
that were sitting in the folds of the Auehang in Kassel, by spending time
there, by looking and contemplating, with friends and alone.
So I guess your response could be read as an invitation to visitors to do the
same, to walk the sites, and try to engage with them.
The reason why I wrote to you, above all, is that I wanted to make a space
for this project's attachment to your book, which helped me decipher some
of the code inscribed in the landscape. In fact, maybe I also wanted some
sort of confirmation from you that I'm not completely on the wrong track,
misreading all the signs.
This view, the way of looking at this landscape that I tried to lay out in my
questions to you, would have not been possible without your research.
I wanted to share this with visitors. The Auepark will be the focus of attention
this summer as it is one of the main venues of dOCUMENTA (13). I think
Unnatural Horizons is a valuable companion for this site and its visitors.

With best wishes,
Natascha

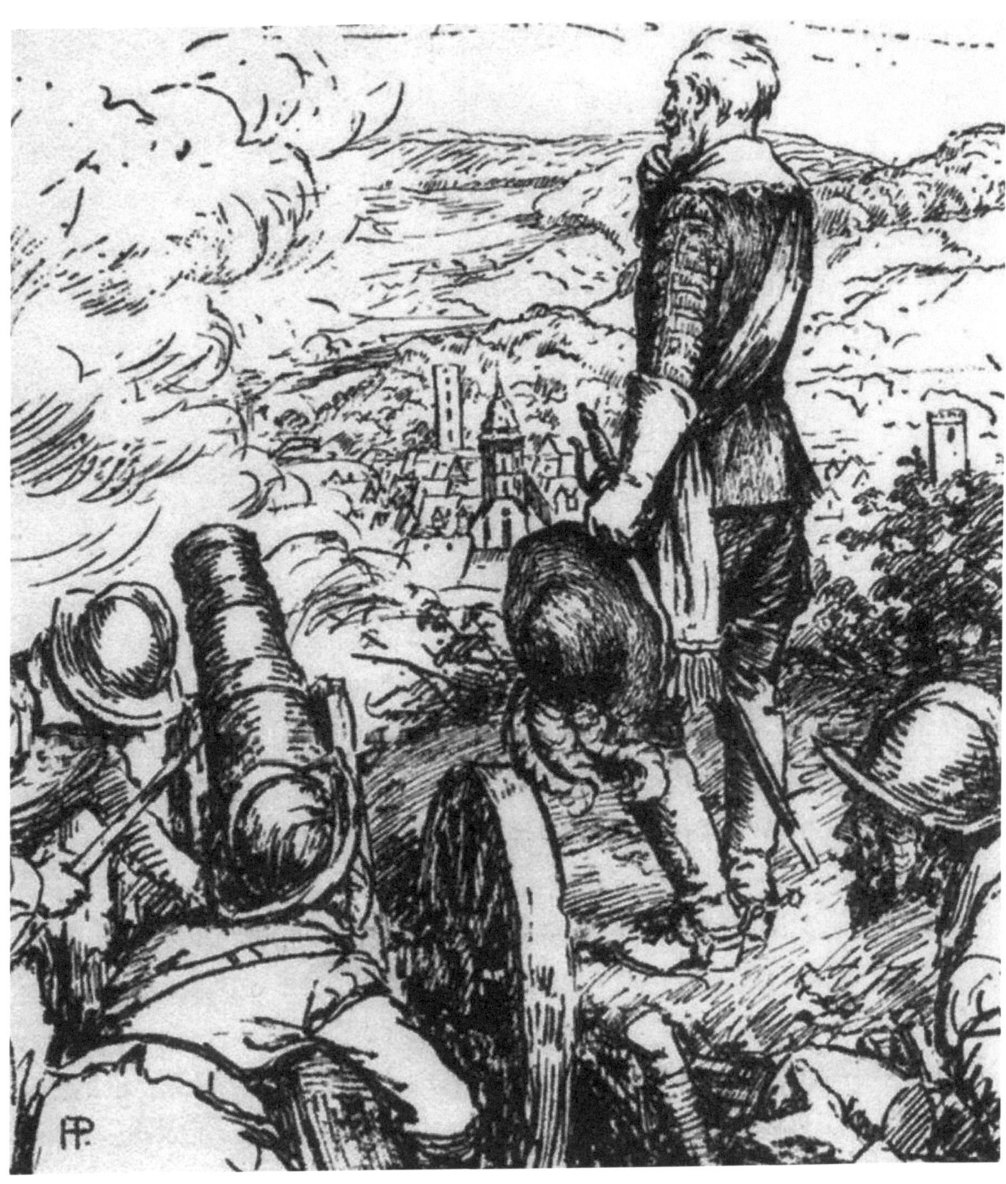

GENERAL TILLY ON THE SO-CALLED TILLY SCHANZE

The picture shows a scene from the Thirty Years' War. In 1626 General Tilly captures the city of Hann Münden after laying siege to it. In this image, he is standing atop a sconce looking out over the city he is about to capture. His gaze runs parallel to the trajectory of the cannon, which is being loaded.

Plants

Lemon trees, orange trees,
and a Princess Garden that is turned
into a war memorial; pioneer woody species,
plants that grow on rubble,
debris flowers, and 12,000 roses
for the German Horticultural Show.

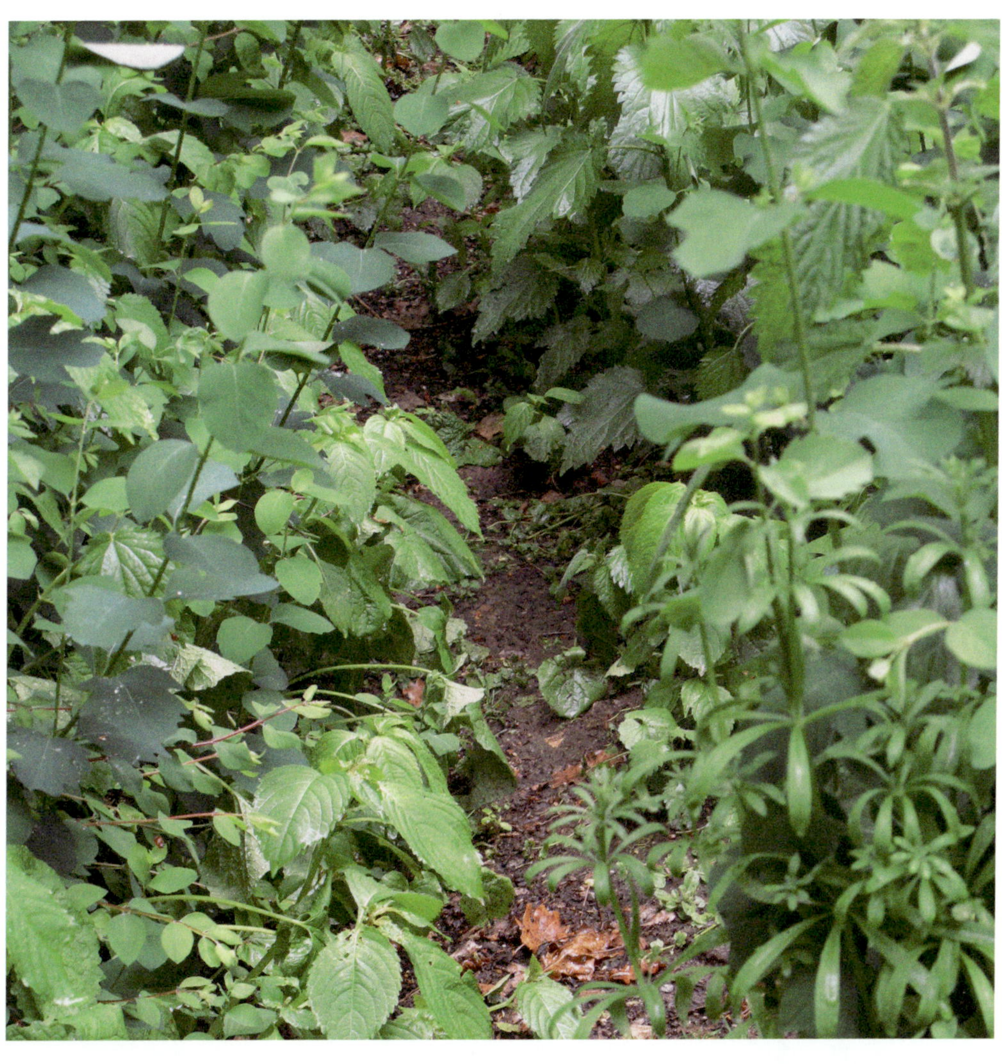

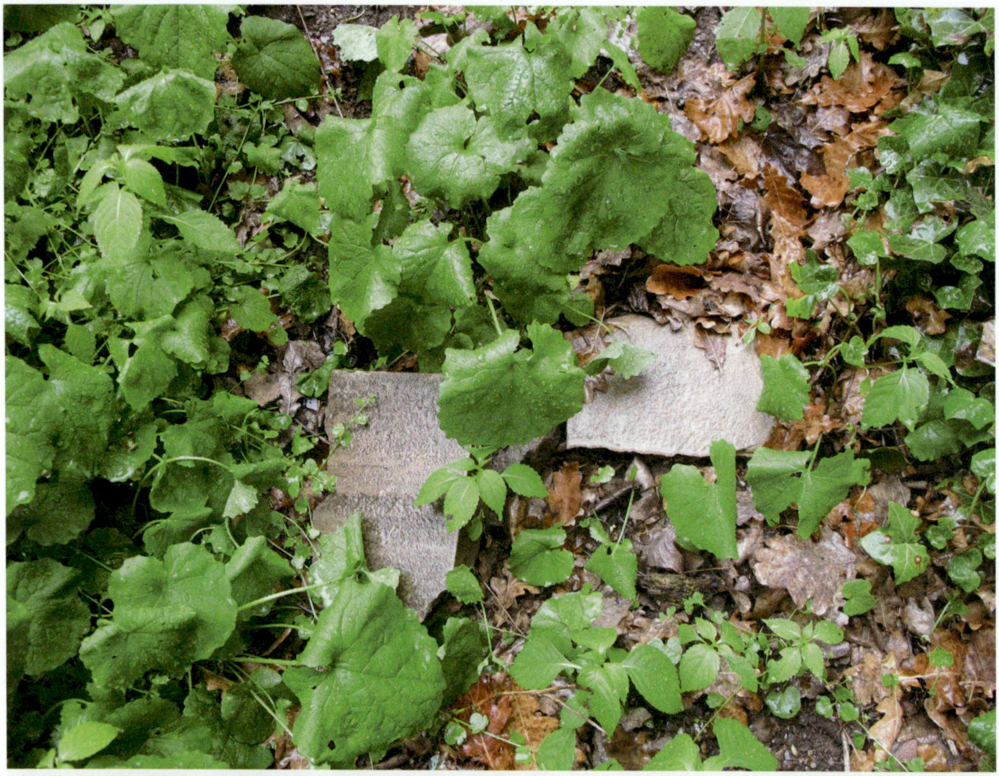

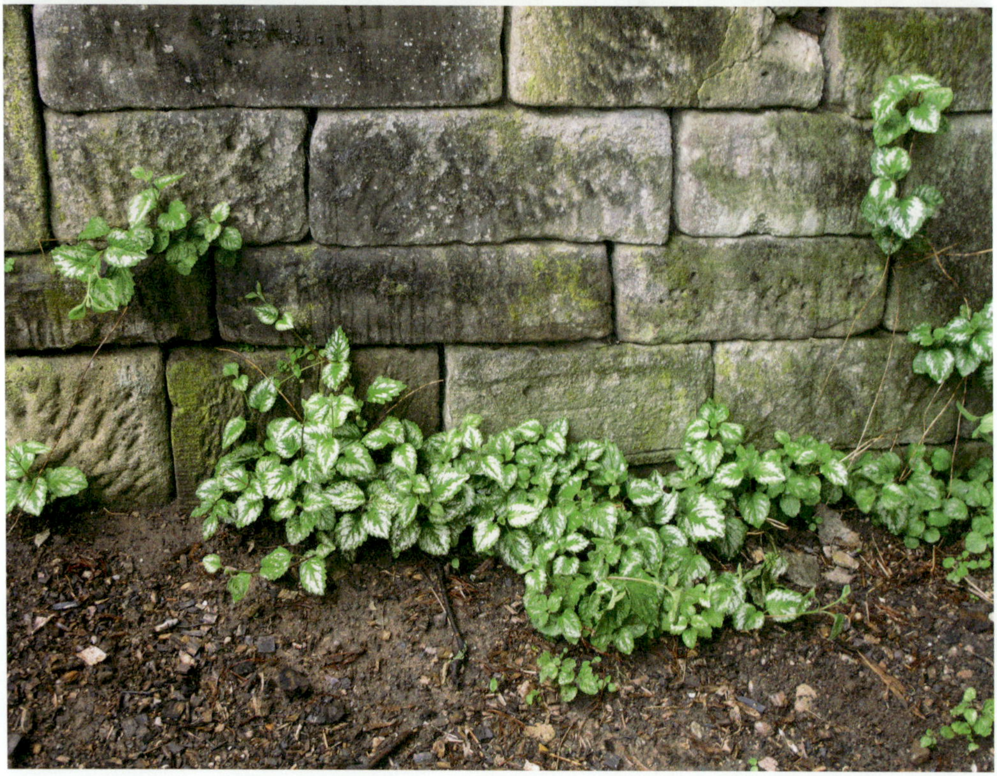

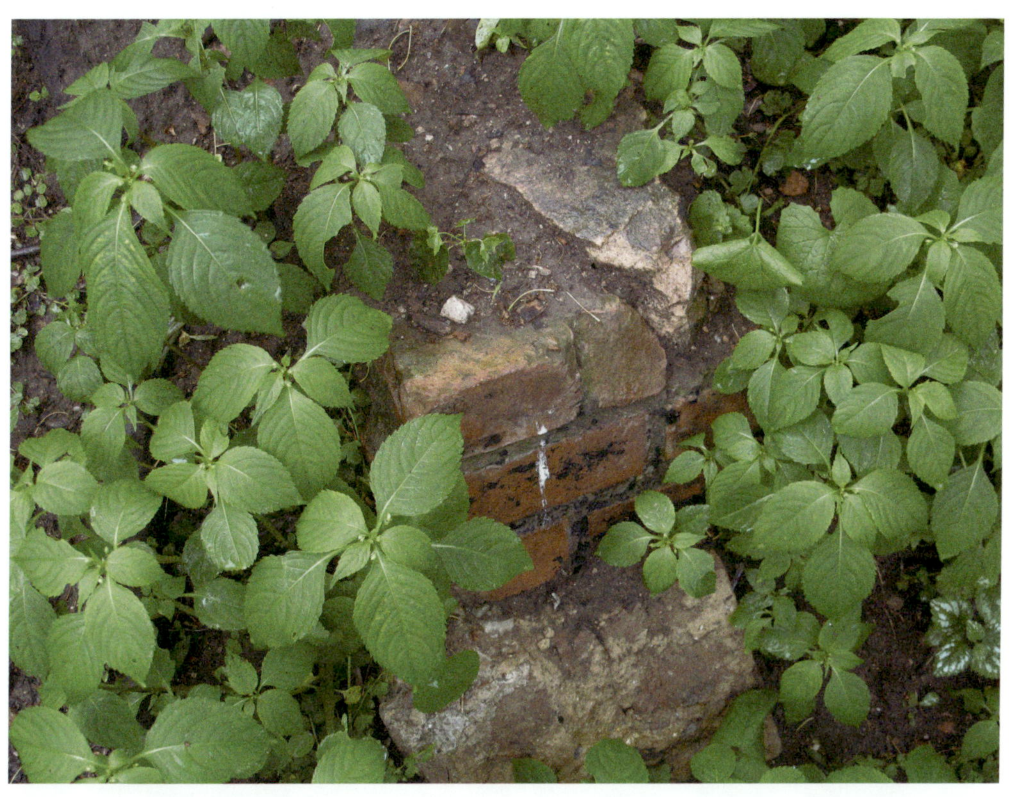

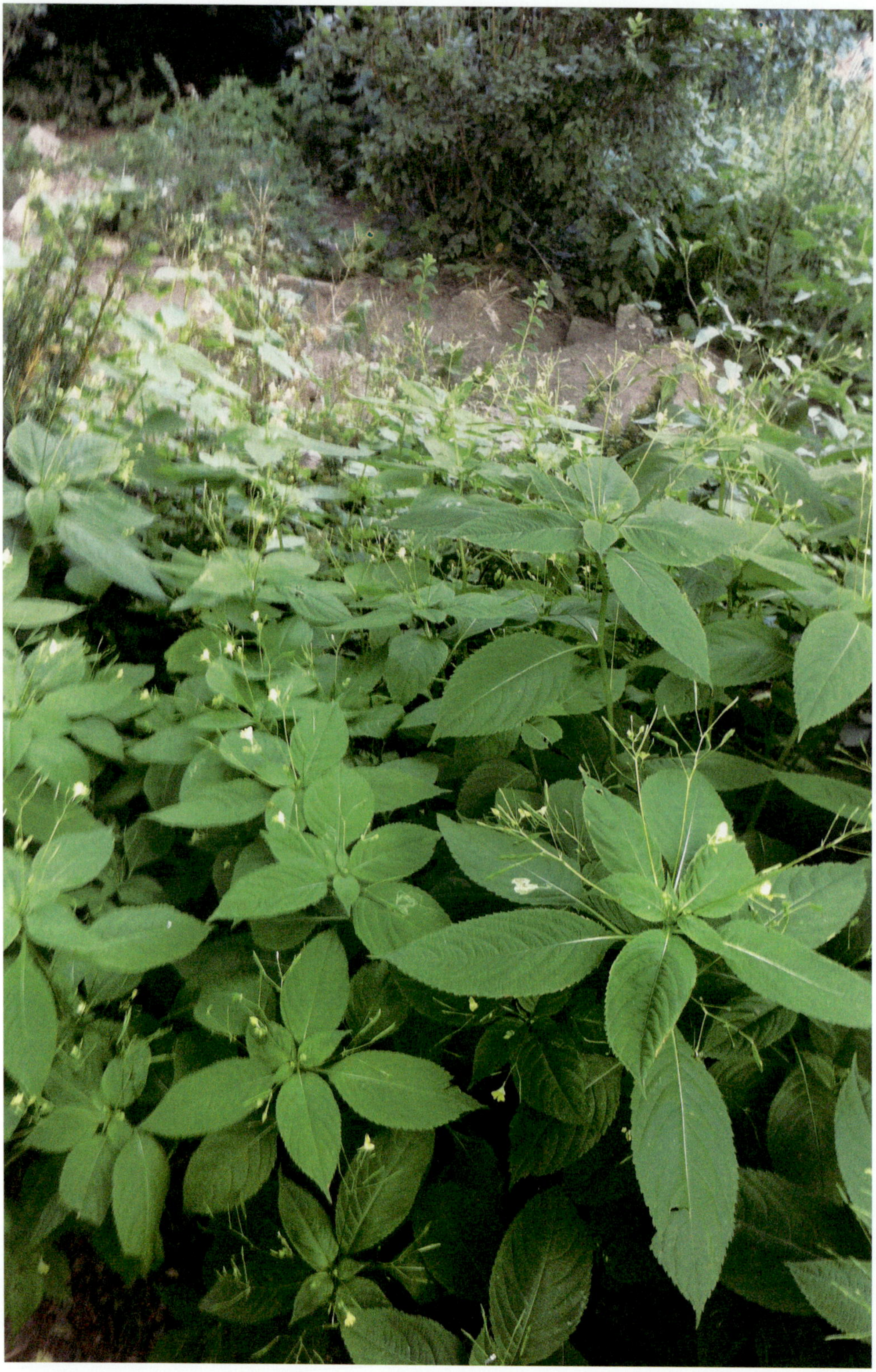

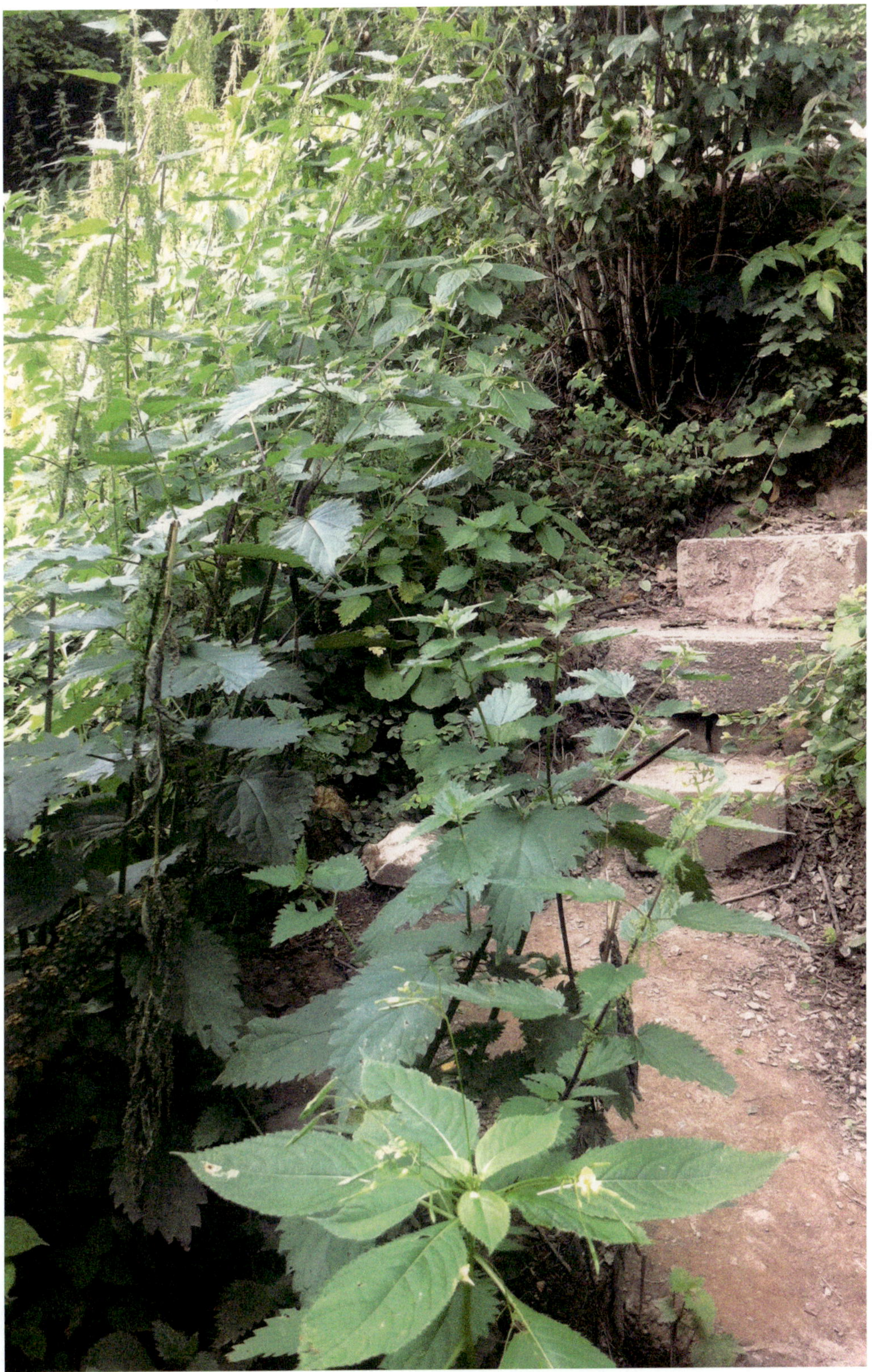

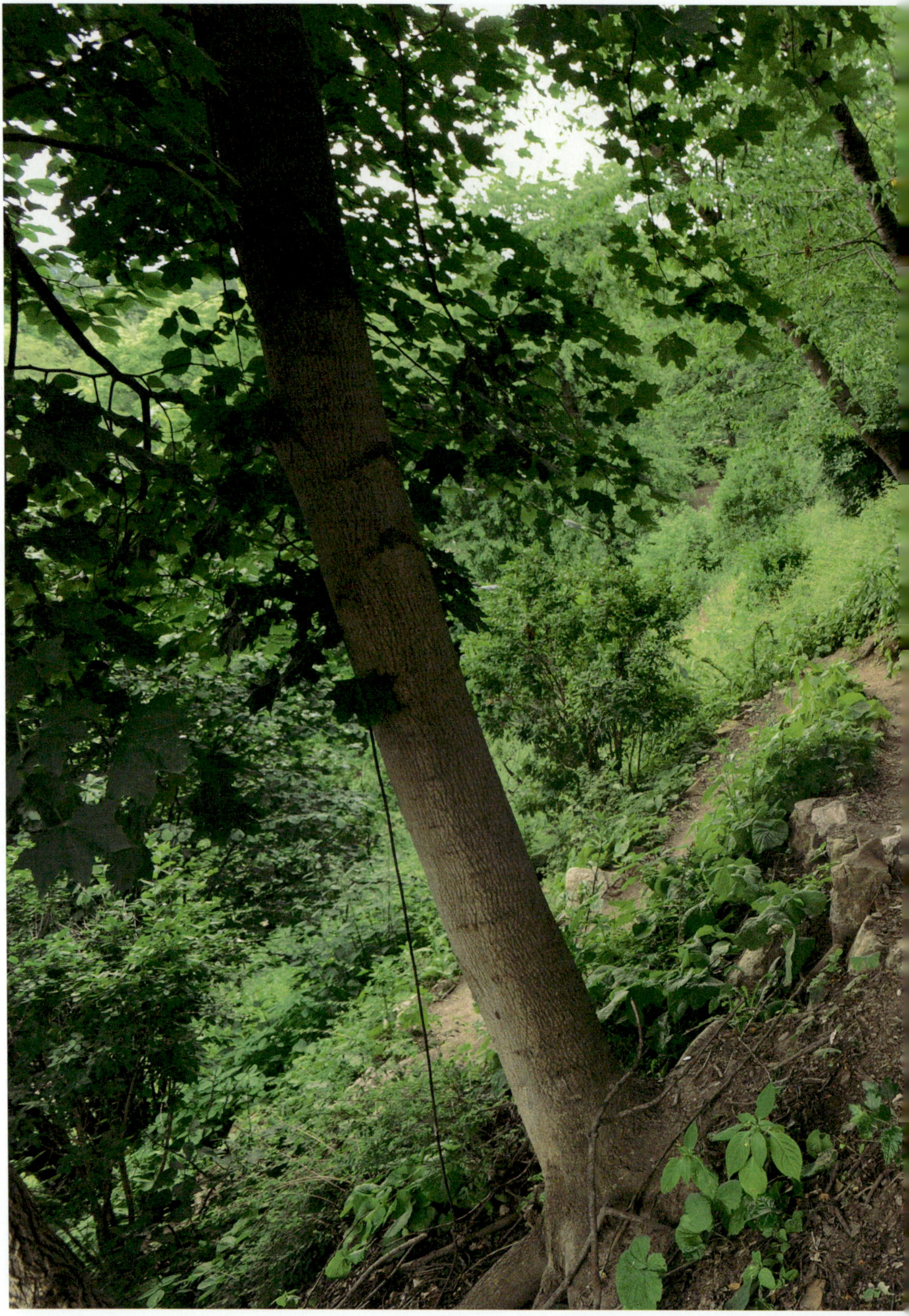

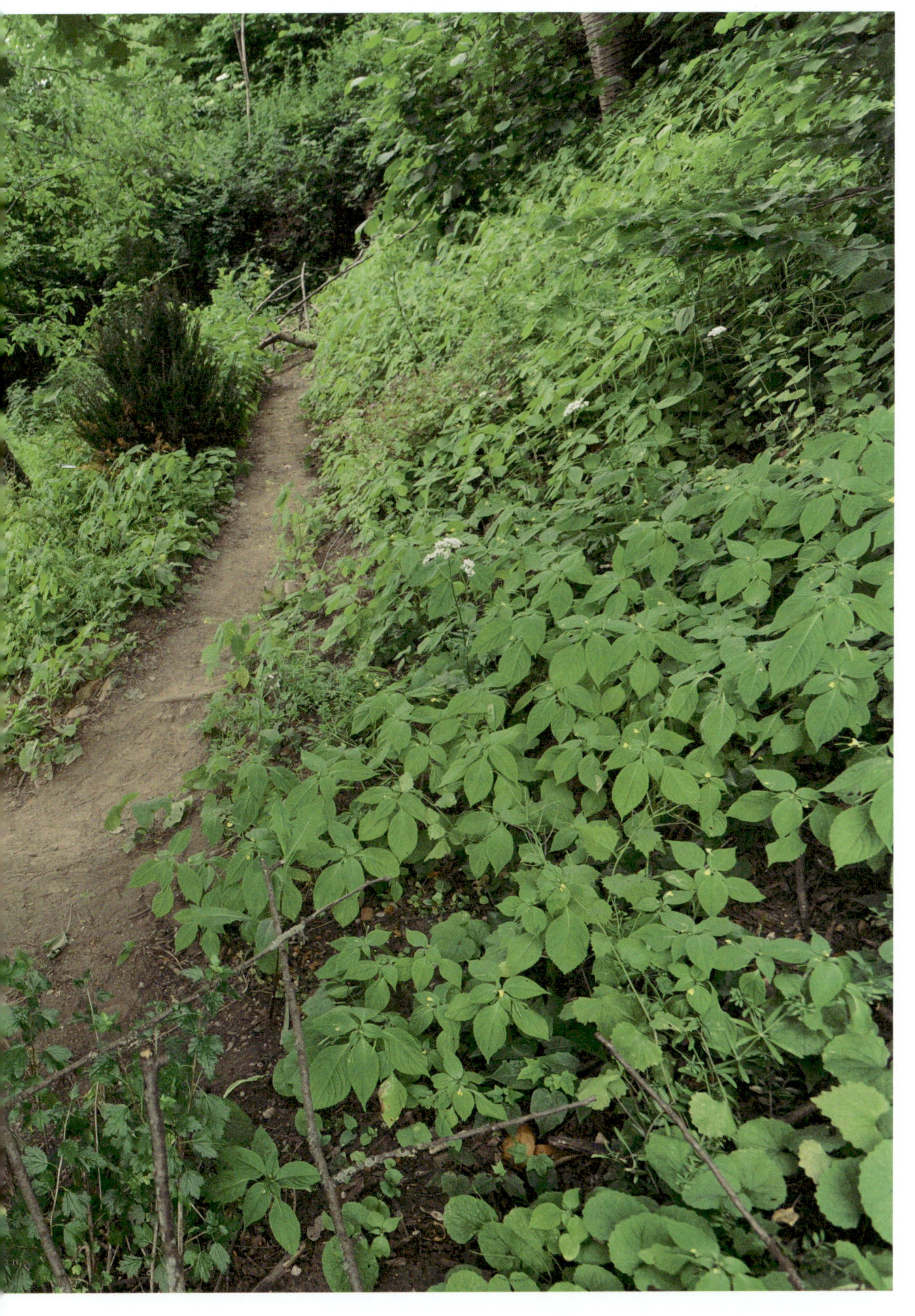

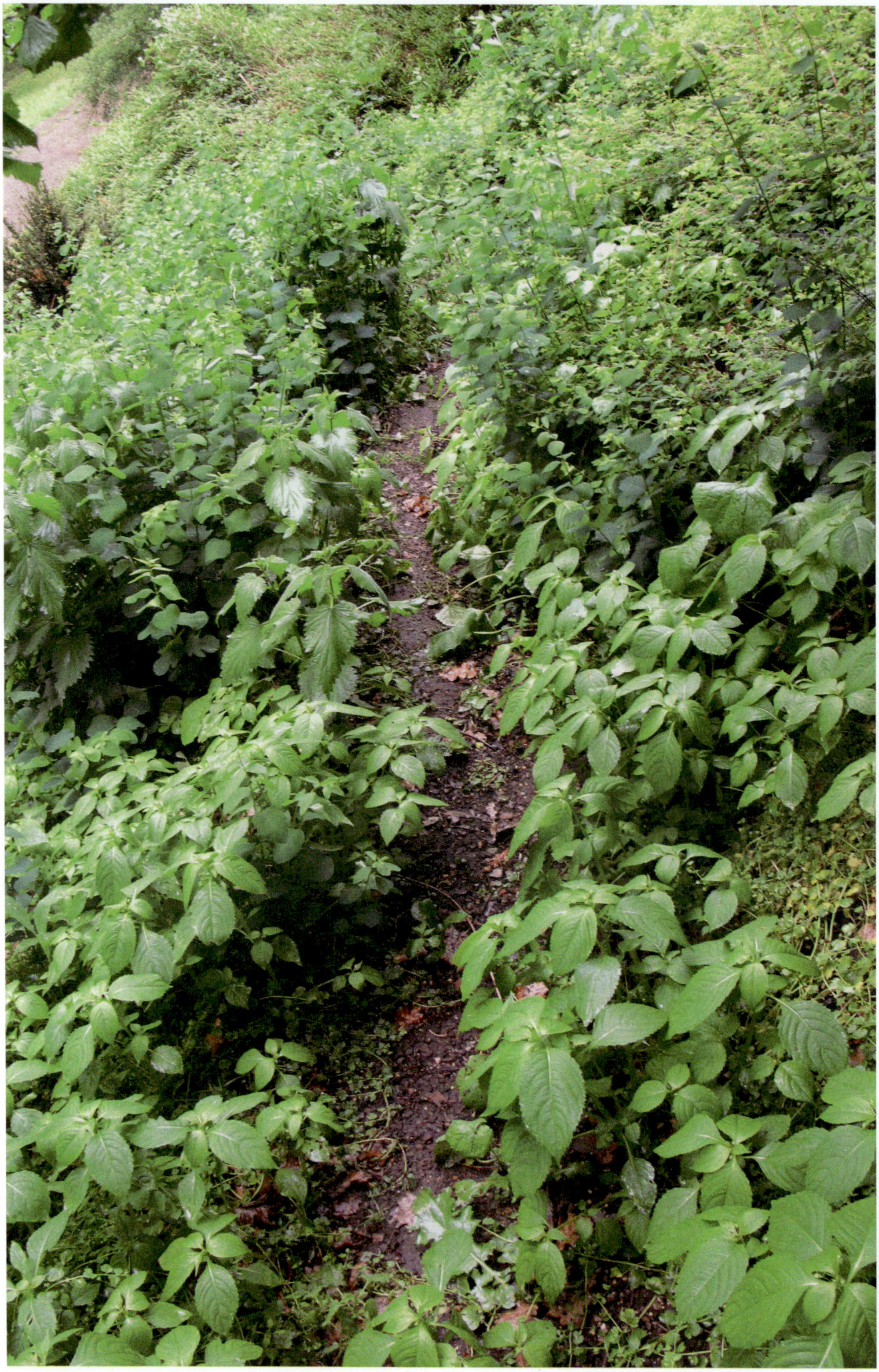

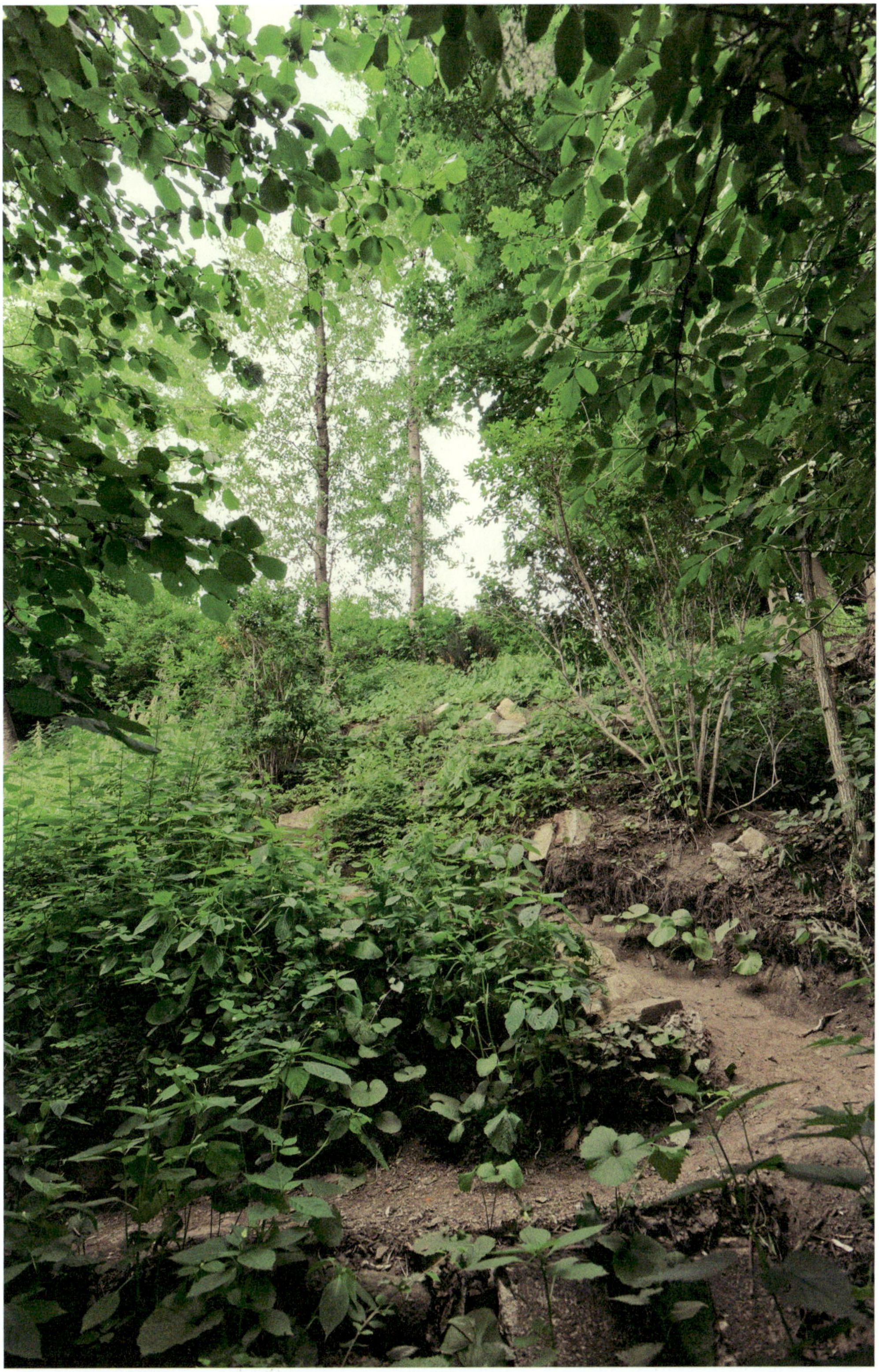

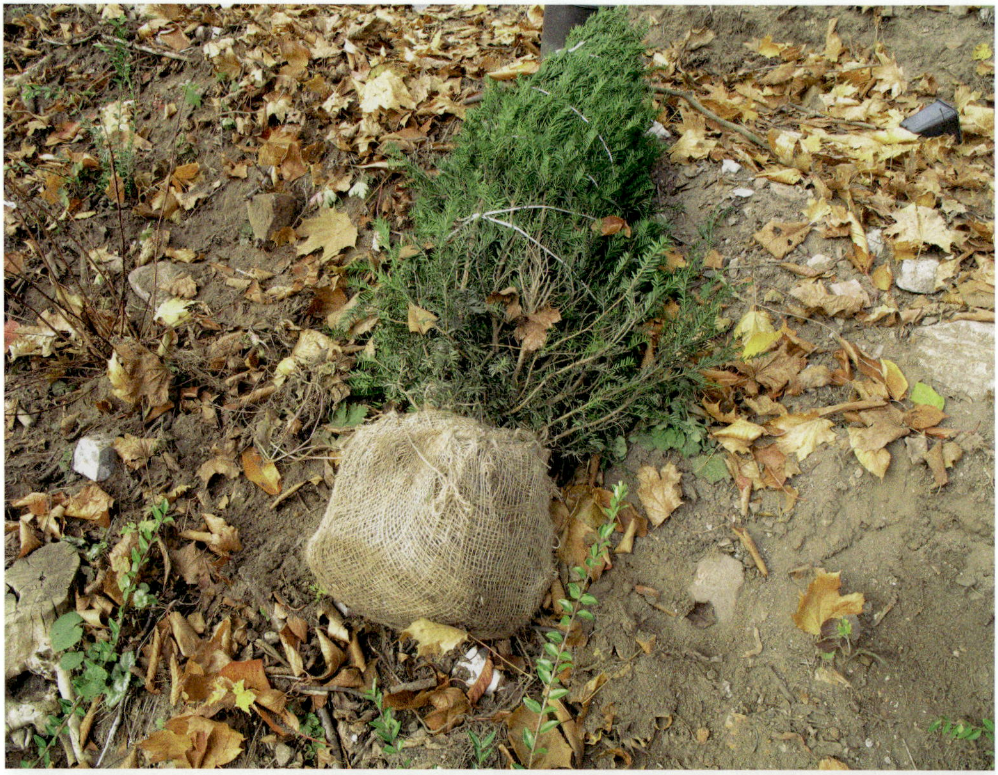

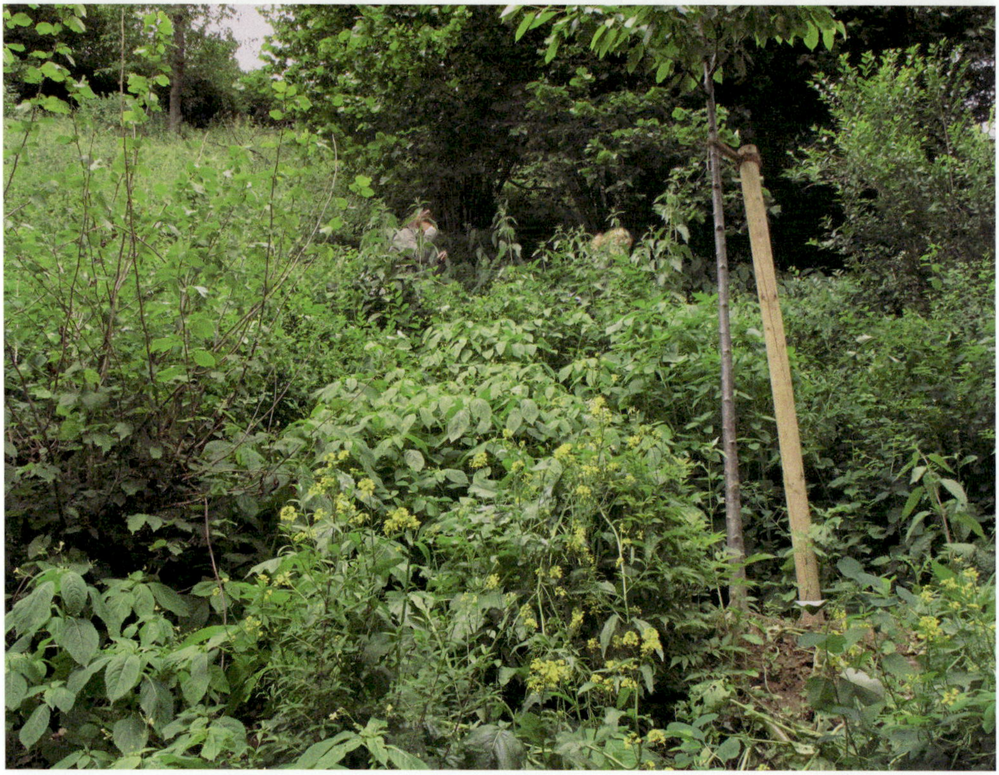

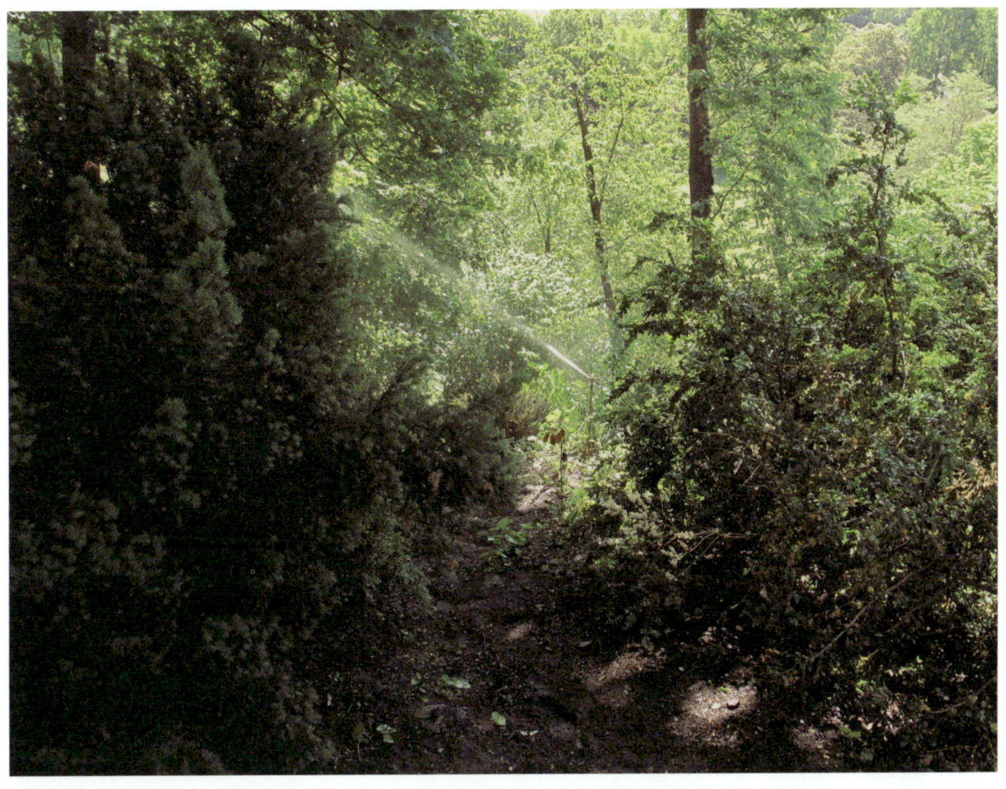

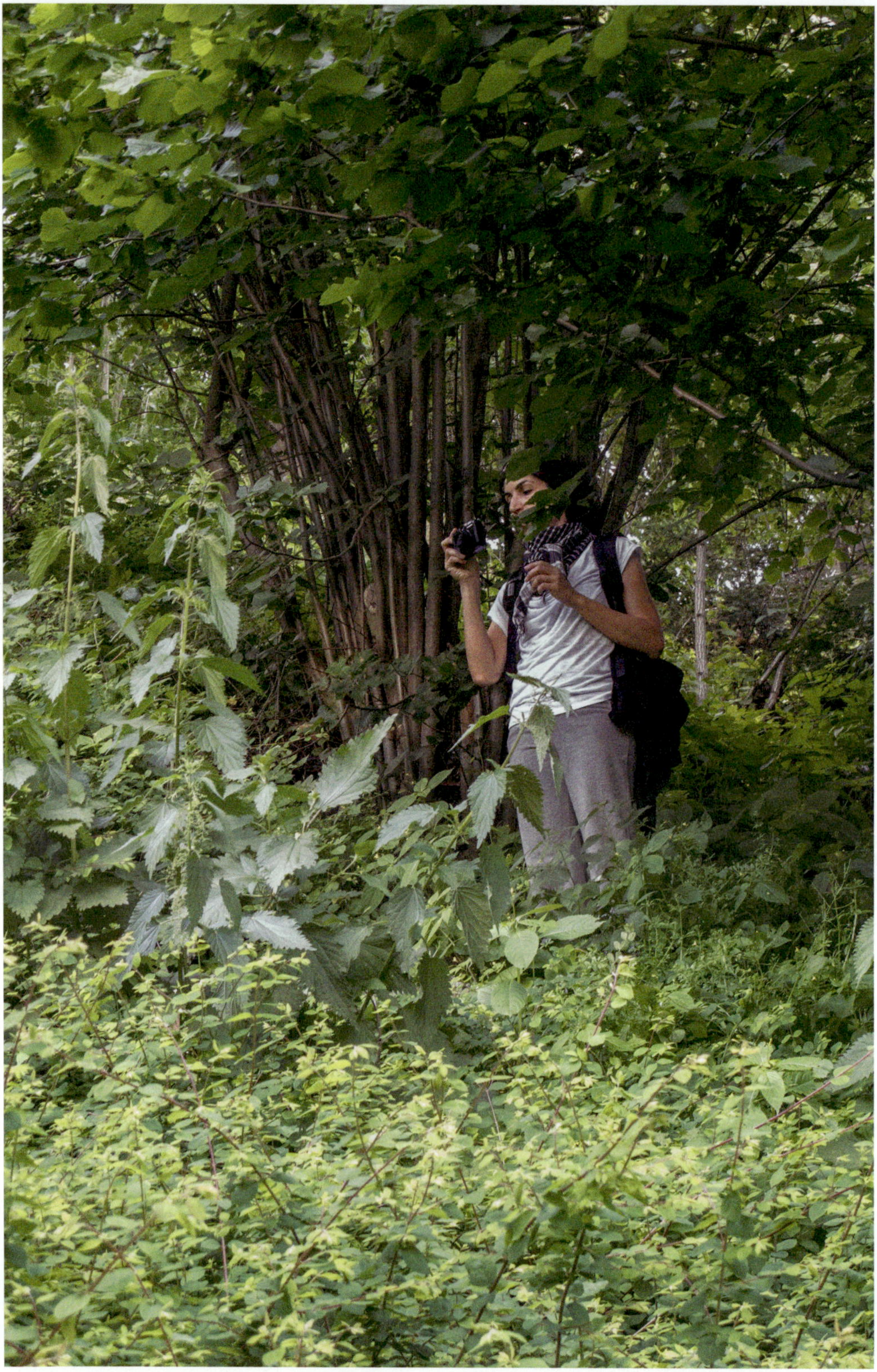

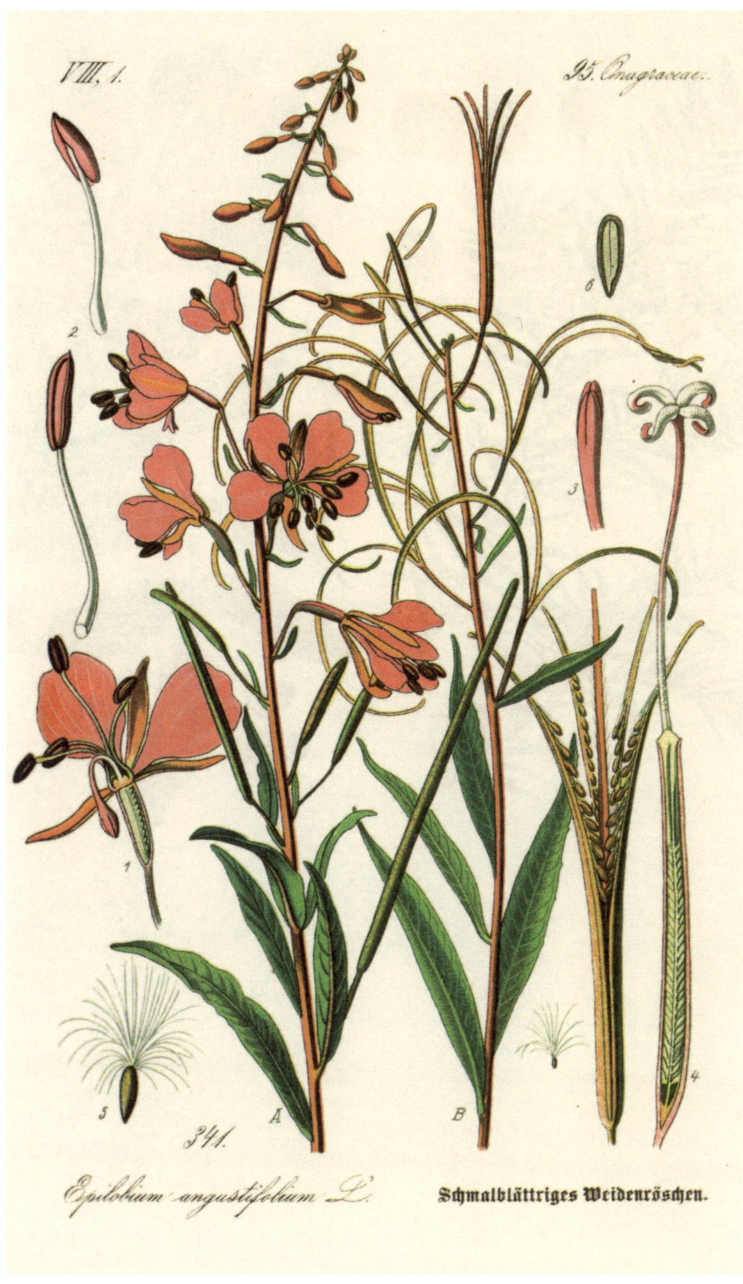

ROSEBAY WILLOWHERB OR FIREWEED

This is a special type of pioneer species from recent history. It grows in urban areas where air raids and ground combat have created expanses of rubble and debris. The term «Trümmerblumen» [debris flowers], which was coined as a reference to unusual plants or those previously unknown to urban spaces, is used quite often when referring to the rosebay willowherb.

[ILLUSTRATION: PROF. DR. OTTO WILHELM THOMÉ: «FLORA VON DEUTSCHLAND, ÖSTERREICH UND DER SCHWEIZ», 1885, GERA, GERMANY. SOURCE: BIOLIB.DE, KURT STUEBER, GFDL]

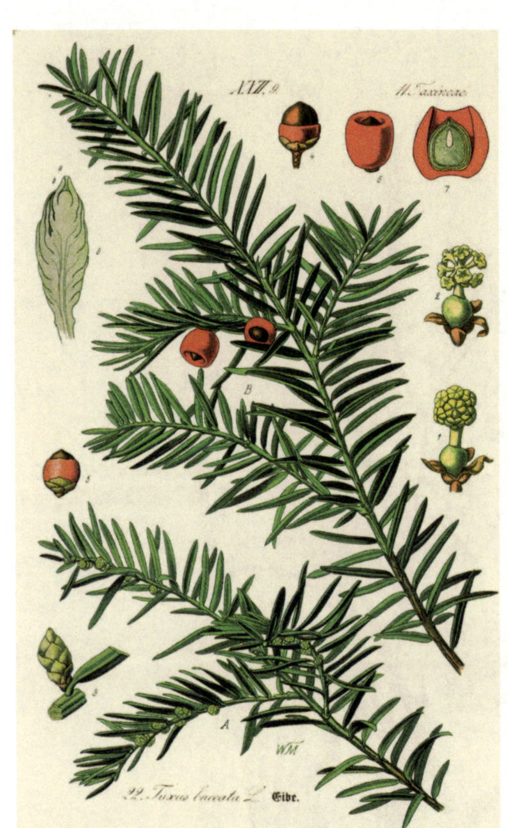

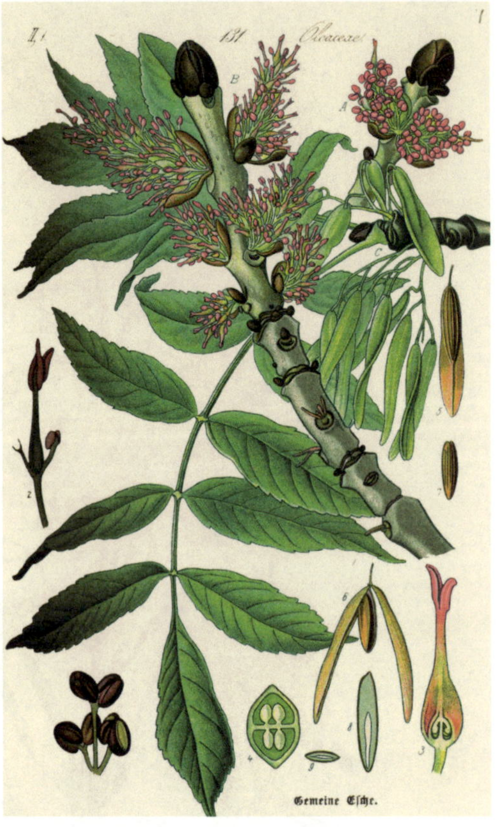

PIONEER SPECIES

(LEFT: TAXUS BACCATA OR YEW PIONEER SPECIES, RIGHT: FRAXINUS EXCELSIOR OR ASH PIONEER SPECIES)

Pioneer species are highly adaptive and robust. They adapt well to locations with no previous growth.

[ILLUSTRATION: PROF. DR. OTTO WILHELM THOMÉ: «FLORA VON DEUTSCHLAND, ÖSTERREICH UND DER SCHWEIZ», 1885, GERA, GERMANY. SOURCE: BIOLIB.DE, KURT STUEBER, GFDL]

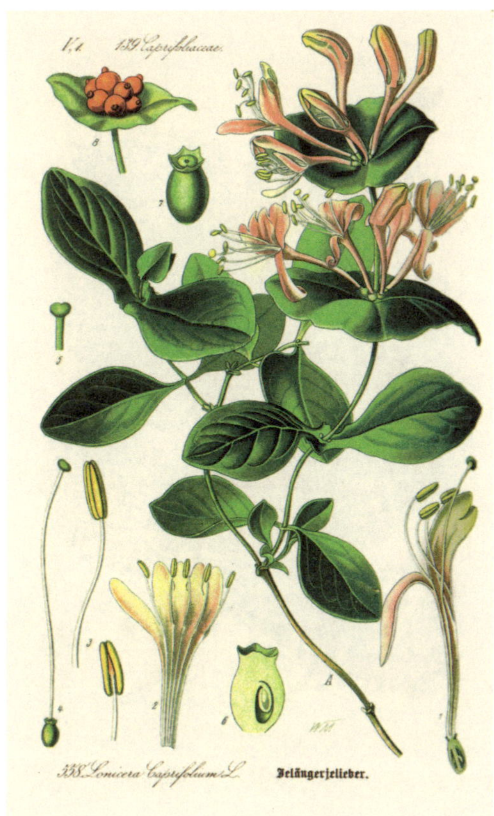

LONICERA CAPRIFOLIUM
OR PERFOLIATE HONEYSUCKLE PIONEER SPECIES

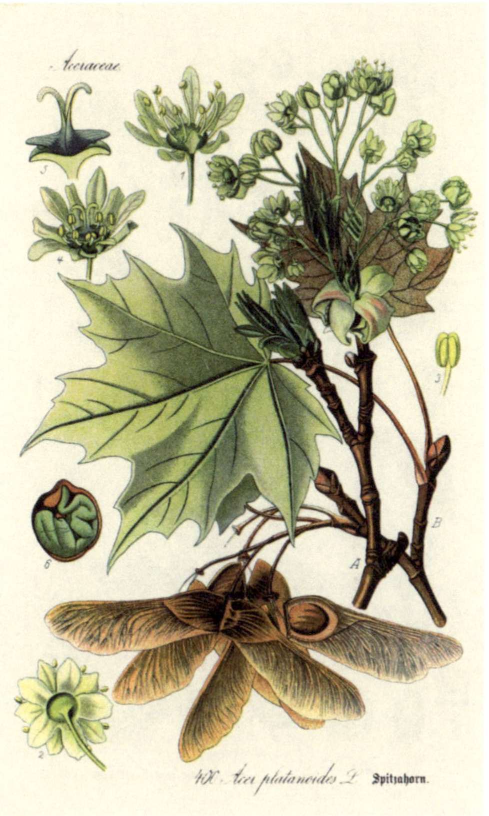

ACER PLATANOIDES
OR NORWAY MAPLE PIONEER SPECIES

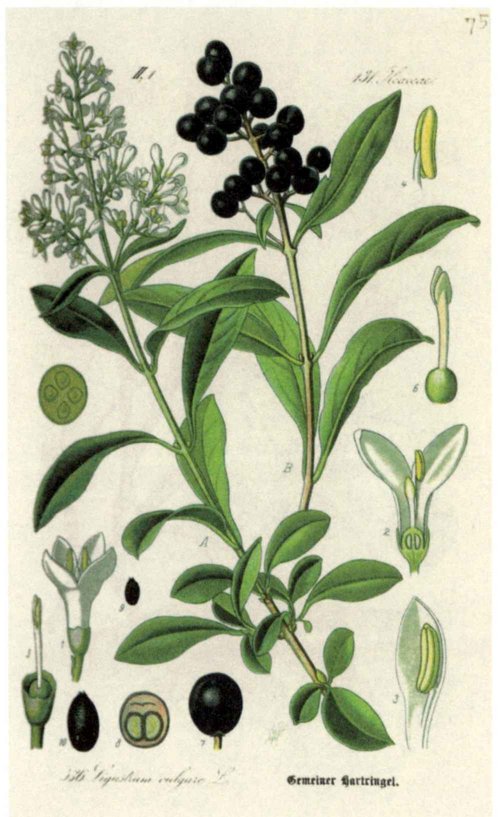

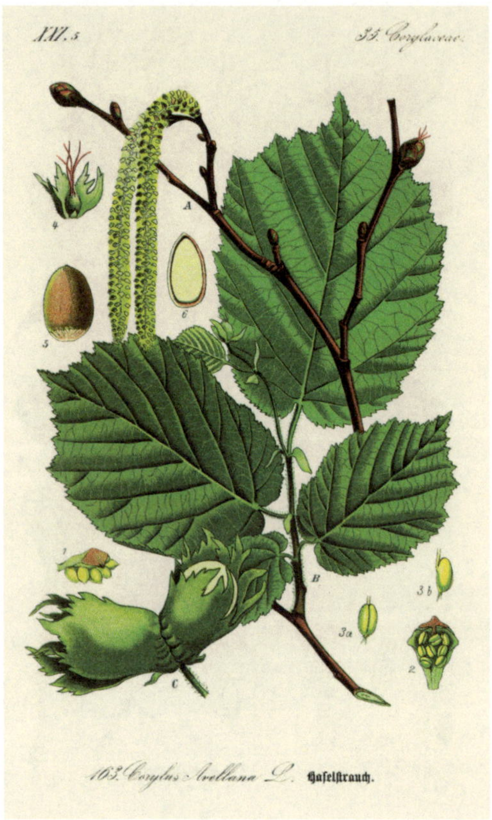

LIGUSTRUM VULGARE

OR WILD PRIVET PIONEER SPECIES

CORYLUS AVELLANA

OR HAZEL PIONEER SPECIES

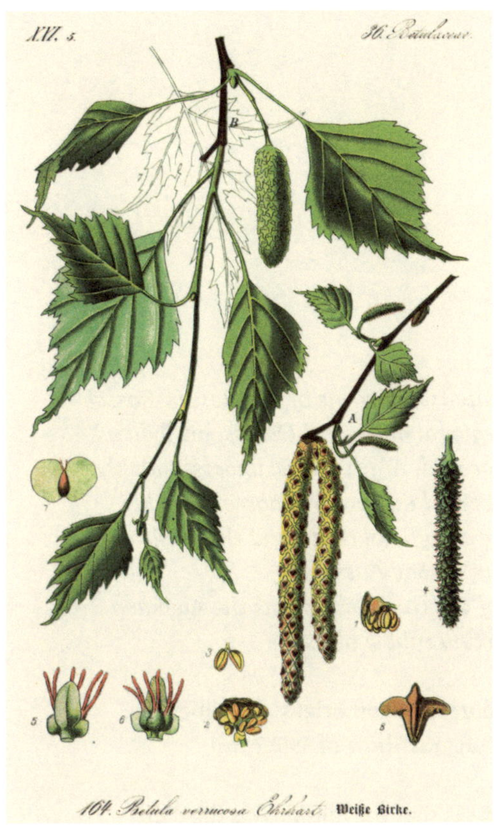

BETULA PENDULA

OR SILVER BIRCH PIONEER SPECIES

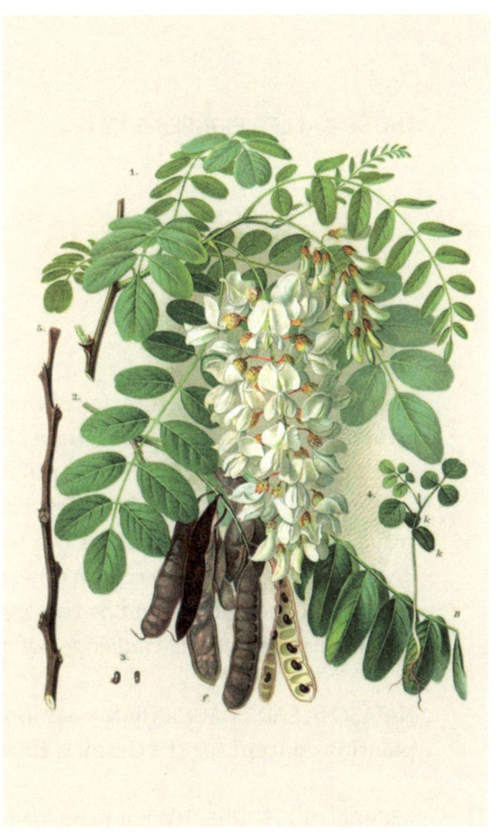

ROBINIA PSEUDOACACIA

OR BLACK LOCUST PIONEER SPECIES

Michael Boßdorf is the director of the state-run gardens of the Hessen-Kassel Museumslandschaft, an association of regional museums. His responsibilities include the Auehang, where our trail is located. At first he is, understandably, rather unenthusiastic about a dirt trail being laid here. We agree that the trail shall not be authorized as if it were an official route and that visitors are to enter at their own risk. We meet at Schöne Aussicht.
It's raining and hailing, and he tells me of the transformations the Auehang has undergone and the challenges of making rubble blossom.

NATASCHA SADR HAGHIGHIAN ‣ Mr. Boßdorf, can you briefly describe the planting concept for the German Horticultural Show of 1955?

MICHAEL BOSSDORF ‹ What happened first is that the hillside was filled in with around two million cubic meters of debris after the war. Then, when it was certain that the 1955 German Horticultural Show would take place here, this bluff, filled with debris, underwent preliminary preparations, meaning it was pulled further out toward the park; or in other words, the hillside's form was changed, becoming flatter. This was done primarily with debris from the old part of the city, from Kassel's city center, with a certain percentage of clay, brick, and sand. How to plant vegetation on it was, indeed, a big problem. The next thing to think about was how to lend the slope firmness so as to avoid a landslide, because this debris, especially in the lower areas, had a thickness of several meters.

‣ Can you explain which problem arose while planting?

‹ The problem was that the debris, due to its thickness, definitely has an immense drainage effect. That means precipitation drains right through the underground layers. The plants, no matter if they're woody plants—trees or bushes, or also the so-called herbaceous layer, perennial shrubs—they wouldn't be able to access any water. That's a big problem, as is the stability of the slope itself. Therefore the first considerations focused on how we could lend it stability, and what kinds of woody plants can even endure this stress.

The answer was to plant the so-called pioneer woody species. Then we also filled the lower areas of the slope a little bit with topsoil, and the amounts we needed weren't available at all: in the end we really had no more than thirty or forty centimeters. Then this was sown with clover, with alfalfa and with legumes so the slope would green and maintain a certain stability, and so its capacity to hold water would improve and stabilize too.

And these pioneer woody species, as they're called, were primarily birch, black locust, ash, maple, and shrubs like privet and yew. That's what was planted here. In the Rosenhang area, a total of 140,000 woody plants were planted. Of course, at first they were all quite small plants. Then they grew to a certain size by the time the Horticultural Show came in 1955, but they were still relatively small. Then over the course of several years, decades afterwards, some plants were removed, which was urgently needed to let the individual plants experience good development, or so their so-called habitus could develop, so the structure of the slope could materialize. That means that over the course of decades plants were removed time and again. It was nevertheless a big problem to always keep the slope stable, and so in recent decades the slope has undergone stabilization measures repeatedly. Tree trunks have been embedded in the slope and stabilized to prevent landslides. Then we kind of had a big problem with rabbits that were undermining the slope, or eroding it.

▸ The whole slope was conceived as a terraced garden while the Karlsaue was in planning. Is that right?

◂ That's right. And that's a reference to the Baroque era under Landgrave Karl. The area which is the Ehrenmal today was the so-called Prinzessgarten, a terraced garden that has, for the most part, kept its original form to this day. And in this terraced garden, in this Prinz-Georg-Garten, there were also lemon, orange, and fig trees. Attempts were made at growing wine there, because the location has great exposure to sunlight. None of this exists in that form today because it would be much too elaborate and expensive. And other than that, the so-called Rosenhang, which stretches from the little temple, the so-called Frühstückstempel, to the Ehrenmal with its large dimensions, was a relatively steep slope before the BUGA [German Horticultural Show] of 1955, and it was also laid out as a terraced garden.

▸ Apart from the roses and exotic plants, did the new concept for the distribution of plants throughout the park incorporate these original aspects? Was it more about showing exotic plants? Is it possible to say something about how the planting in general was?

‹ The Rosengarten was integrated into the overall concept of the 1955 Horticultural Show. That was done by Professor Hermann Mattern, the landscape
architect who was in charge of carrying out the design here. He oversaw
the construction and realization. The Rosenhang in its entirety in this area
of the park was integrated into the 1955 BUGA. And even modelled too. The
park area all the way down to the Little Fulda was correspondingly modelled,
and the realization of the modelling of the terrain was quite successful.
The pedestrian traffic pattern was then adapted and developed, for which
we used a lot of sandstone: partly in the bordering of the paths, and in
the retaining wall in the so-called frontal Rosenhang area, which today is
between the Ehrenmal and the documenta-Halle. Many shrubs were planted
there, lots of roses too. A total of 12,000 roses were planted for the BUGA
'55. There aren't anywhere near that many today, an effect of the bad soil
conditions that I told you about earlier: water and nutrient storage isn't
happening. Roses need significantly richer soil, nutrient-rich soil, and that's
unfortunately not the case here on the Rosenhang. But during the BUGA '55
and a few years after that, too, this place was resplendent in exquisite roses
and shrubbery. And today we're making efforts to conserve this area right
between the Ehrenmal and documenta-Halle in its original form with lots
and lots of shrubbery—there was a lot of blossoming shrubbery in the mix—
and with roses, even with the historical roses that we had here in 1955.
And that's our goal at the moment. We're also making efforts to conserve the
population of woody plants in its 1955 state, and expand it too in the area
of the so-called rear Rosenhang, between Ehrenmal and temple. But we also
wish to to conserve, or regain, the view of the park and of the open landscape
by creating forest aisles and open vistas for the visitors up here on Schöne
Aussicht Bellevue, because that's one of the old magnificent streets of
Kassel from Baroque times. People enjoyed strolling along Schöne Aussicht,
getting a wonderful view over the park to the Orangerie and out onto the
open landscape.

› Could you briefly describe what kinds of vegetation grow on this slope now?

‹ At the moment, there's a high percentage of box and yew. And then there
are cherry trees, oaks, and linden trees. As far as shrubs go, we have privets
and also some cherry laurel. Then wild gooseberries ("Ribes"as well as
"Lonicera"), there are honeysuckle, and in some areas also barberry. Some
hazelnuts, too. There's also the occasional oak tree up here on the slope.

› Which of these are the pioneer species that you mentioned earlier?

‹ Most of them can be counted as pioneer species, but not the box, nor the cherry laurel. But the Lonicera can—they were planted back then, too, as were the hazelnuts. Cherry trees can't really be called pioneer plants, but all the others can.

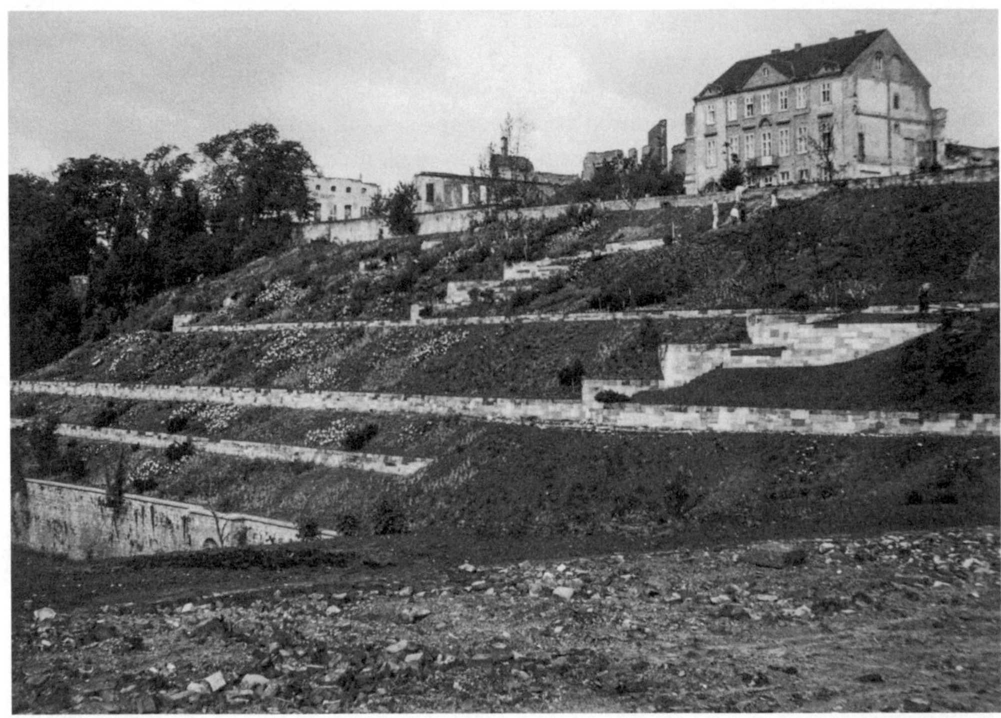

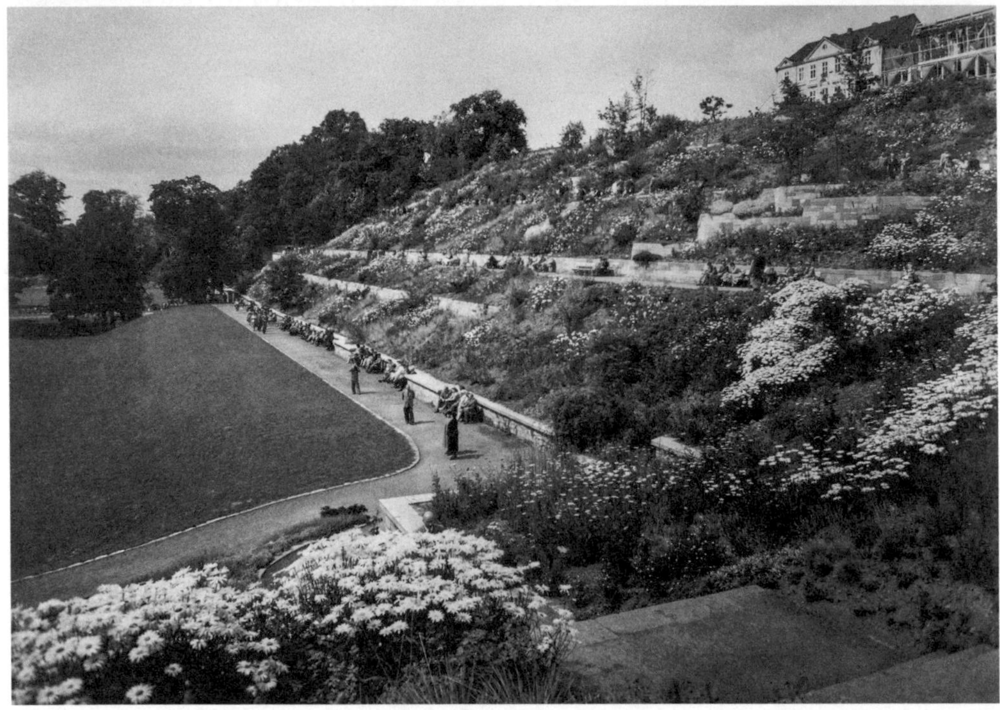

BUGA, TERRACE CONSTRUCTION
Preparatory work for the 1955 German Horticultural Show (BUGA) at the Auehang in Kassel
[SOURCE: STADTARCHIV (CITY ARCHIVE) KASSEL. REPRODUCTION: POLA SIEVERDING

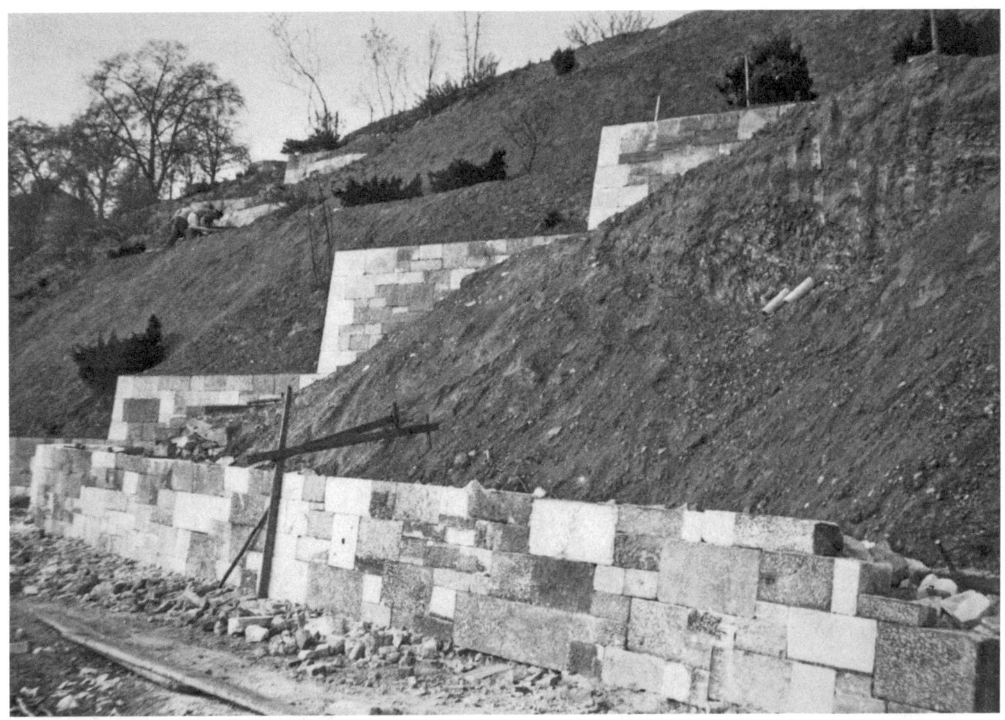

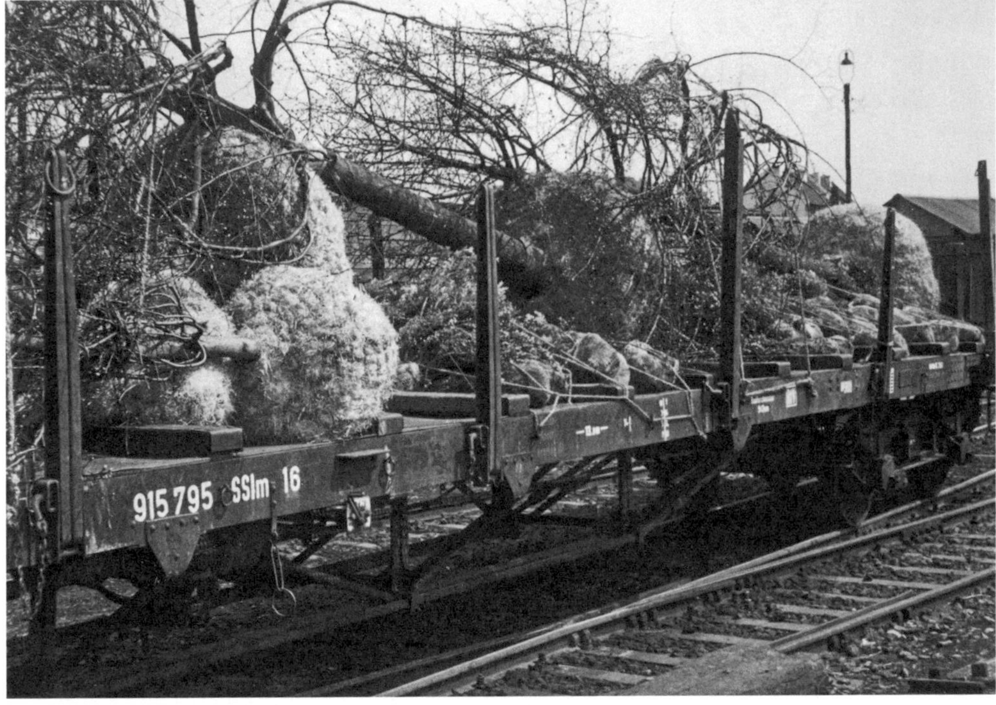

915 795 SSlm 16

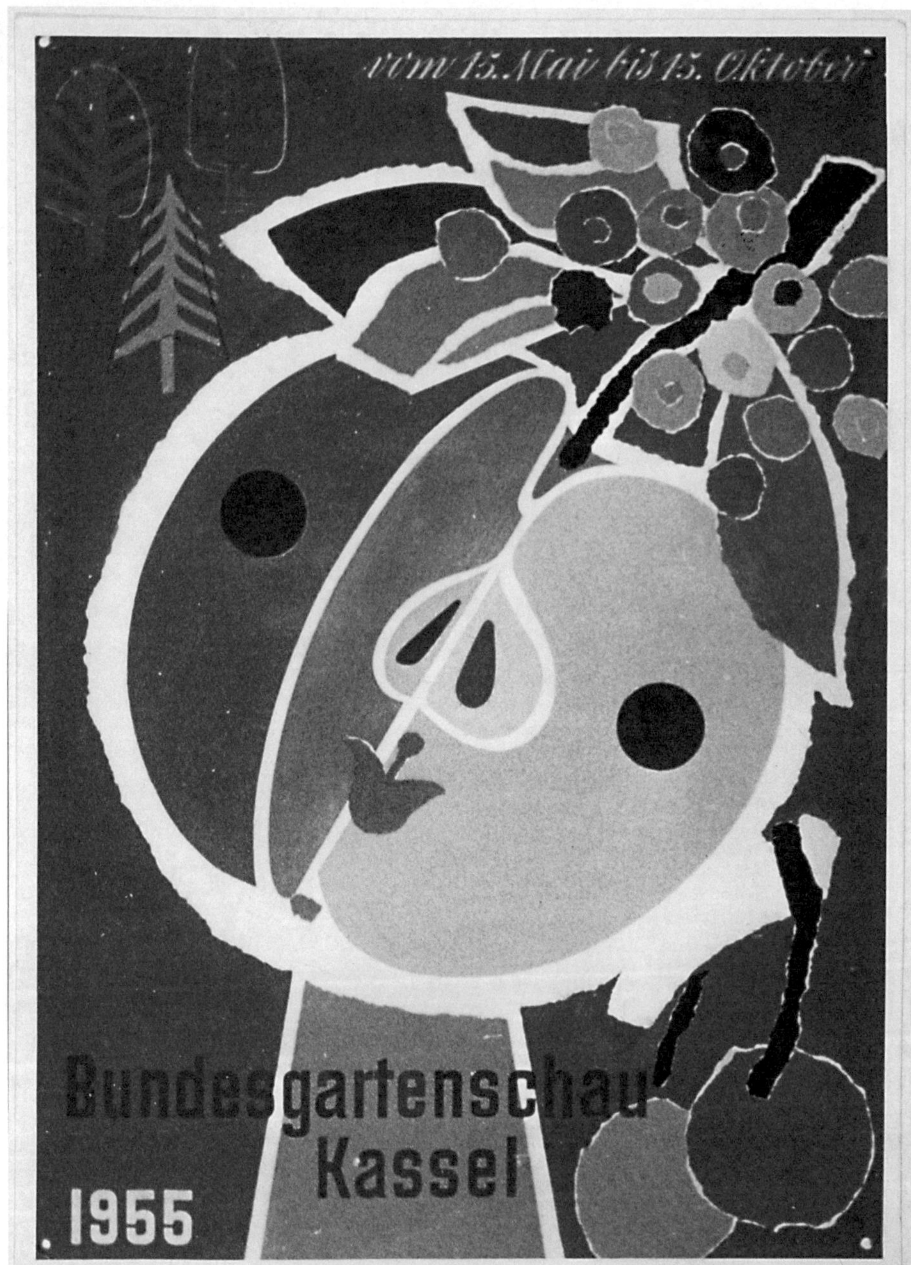
vom 15. Mai bis 15. Oktober
Bundesgartenschau
Kassel
1955

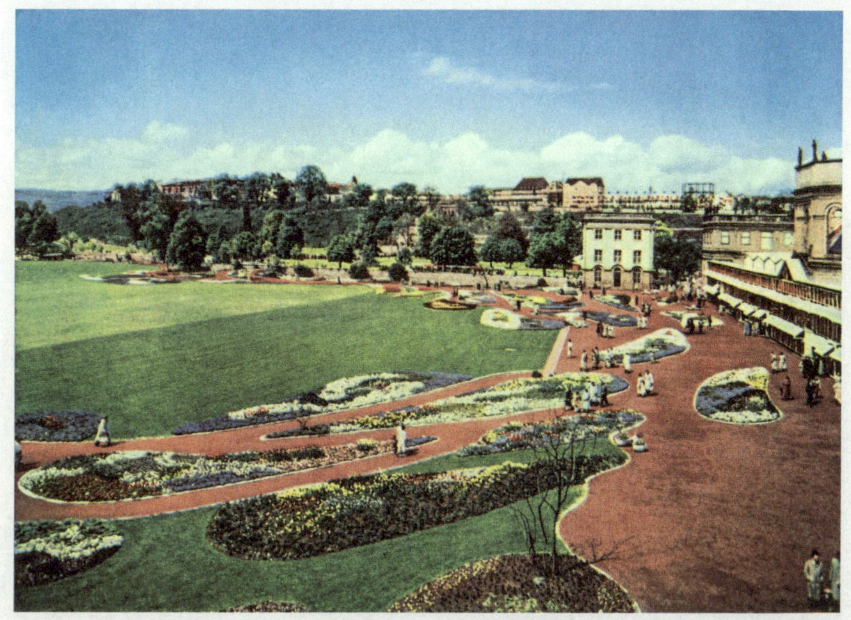

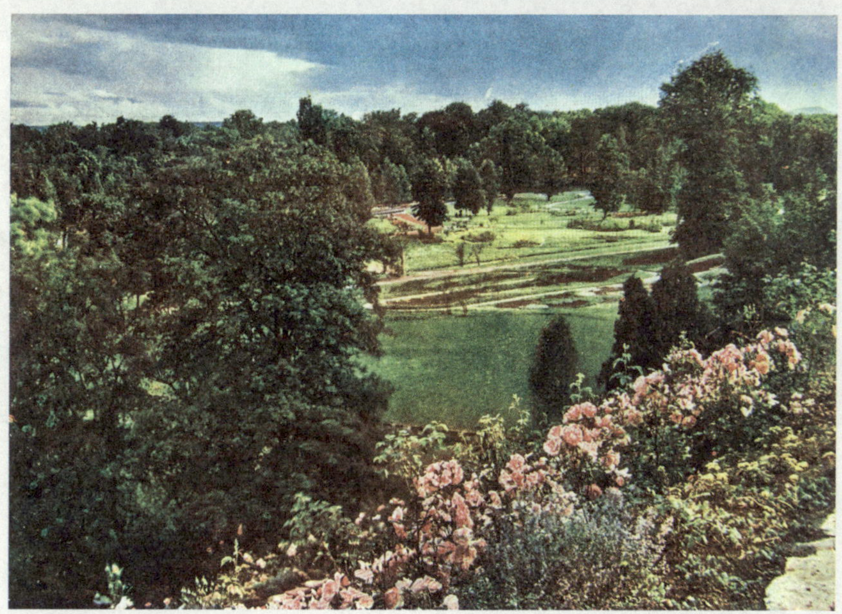

THE ROSENHANG, GERMAN HORTICULTURAL SHOW (BUGA), KARLSAUE, KASSEL, 1955

The colorized photographs show the recently-planted rubble-slope in the Karlsaue at the time of the German Horticultural Show's opening in 1955. According to Mr. Boßdorf, no fewer than 12,000 roses were planted on the slope alone.

[SOURCE: STADTARCHIV (CITY ARCHIVE) KASSEL. REPRODUCTION: POLA SIEVERDING
P. 100   E4 No. 51, P. 1 - PHOTOGRAPHER: KURT FRANZ
P. 101   TOP: E4 No. 207, P. 18 - PHOTOGRAPHER: UNKNOWN, BOTTOM: E4 No. 207, P. 23 - PHOTOGRAPHER: UNKNOWN
P. 102   E4 No. 207, P. 19 - PHOTOGRAPHER: UNKNOWN]

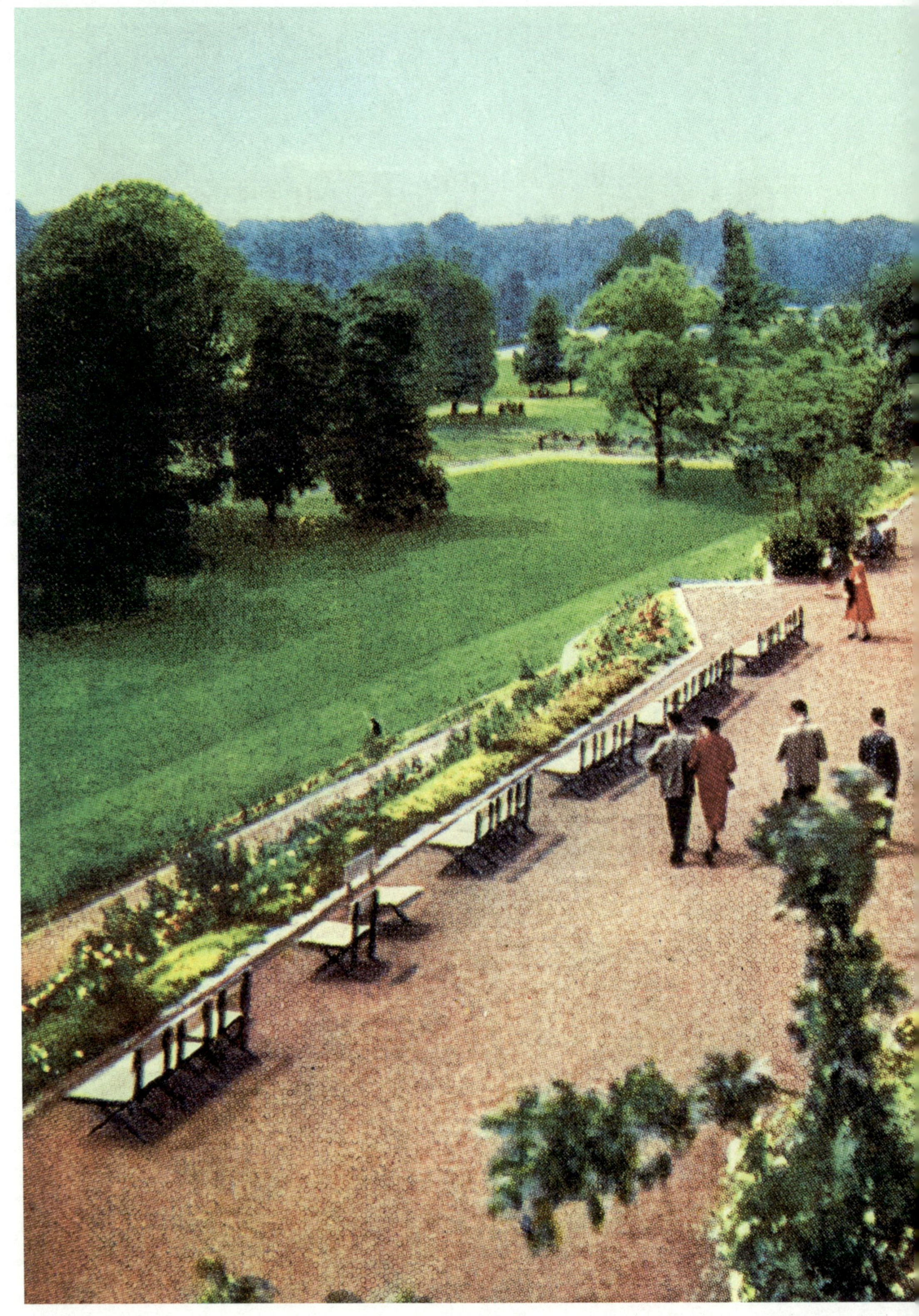

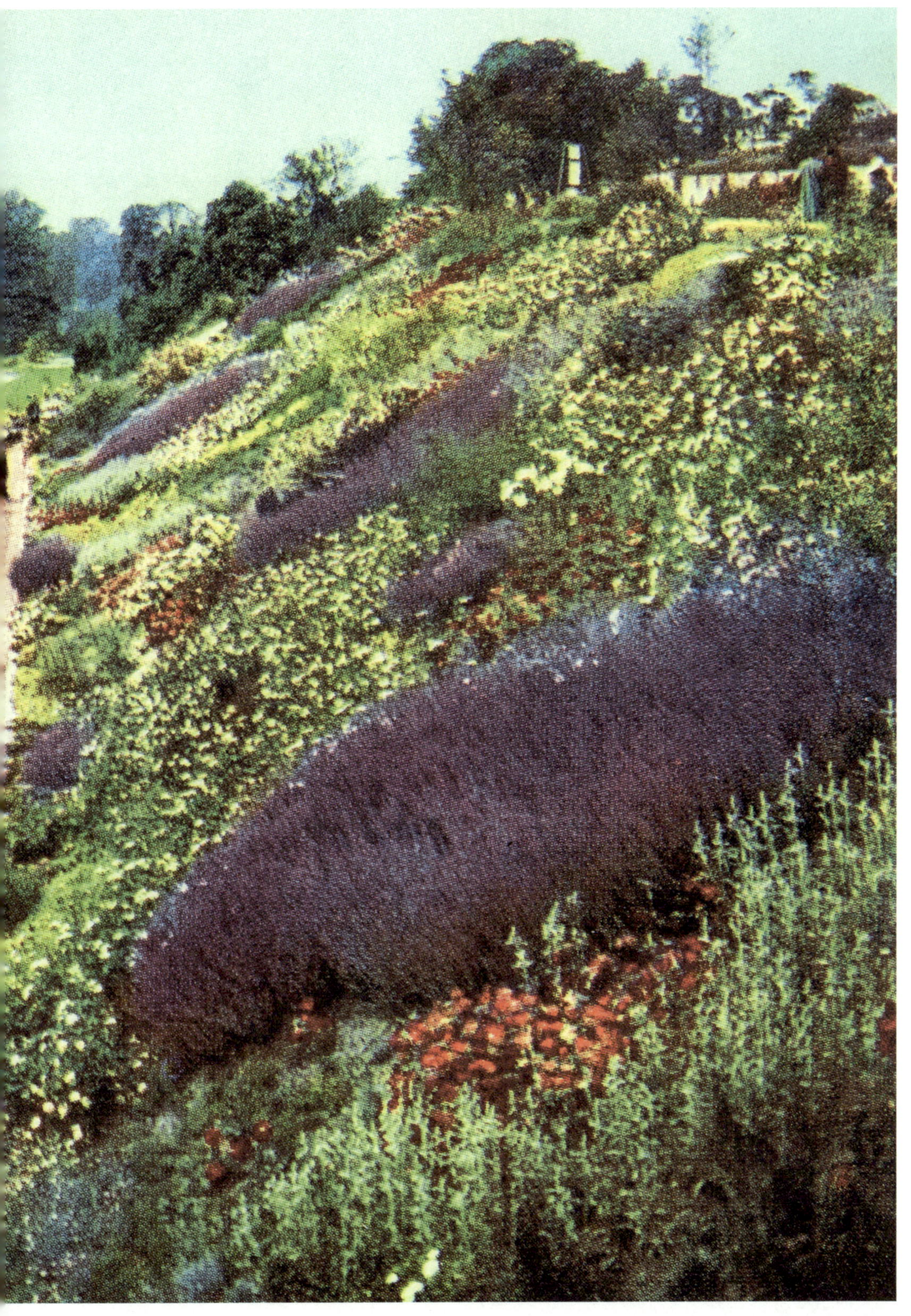

Animals

Dogs, cats, sheep, cows, goats,
frogs, donkeys, ducks, chickens,
tigers, pumas, foxes, martens,
leopards, dingos, elephants,
and lions.

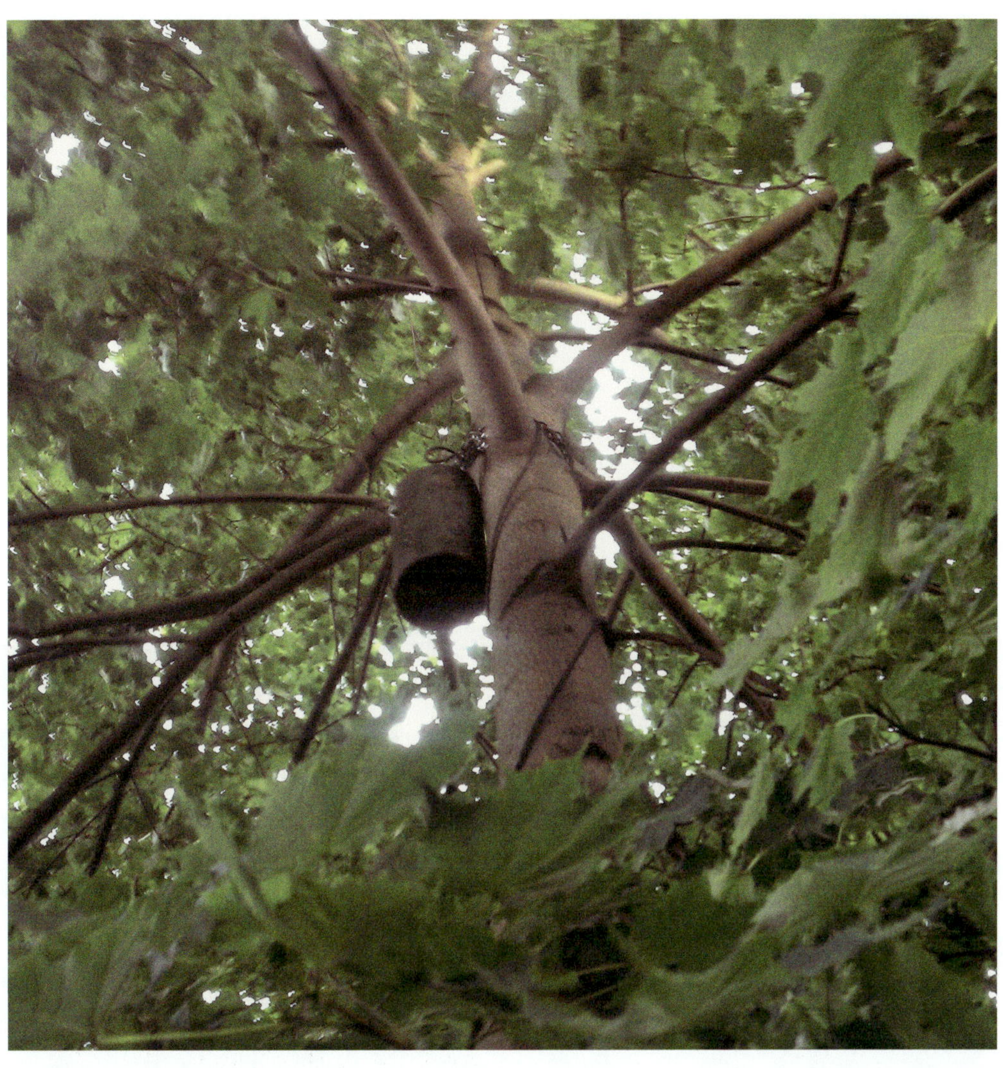

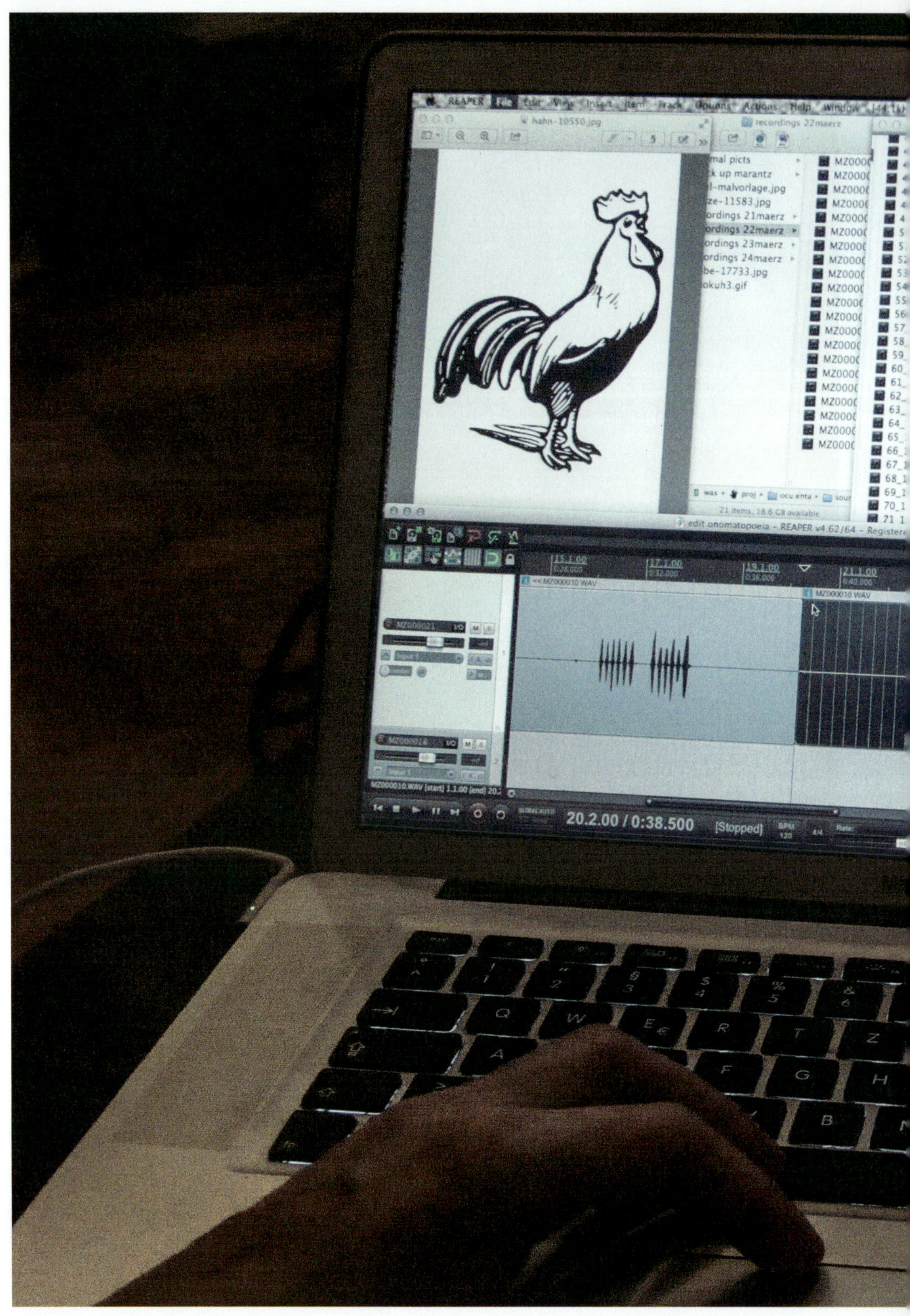

REAPER File Edit View Insert Item Track Options Actions Help Window
hahn-10550.jpg
recordings 22maerz
mal picts
k up marantz
l-malvorlage.jpg
ze-11583.jpg
ordings 21maerz
ordings 22maerz
ordings 23maerz
ordings 24maerz
be-17733.jpg
okuh3.gif
MZ0000
21 items, 18.6 GB available
edit onomatopoeia - REAPER v4.62/64 - Registere
MZ000021
MZ000018
MZ000010.WAV
20.2.00 / 0:38.500
[Stopped]

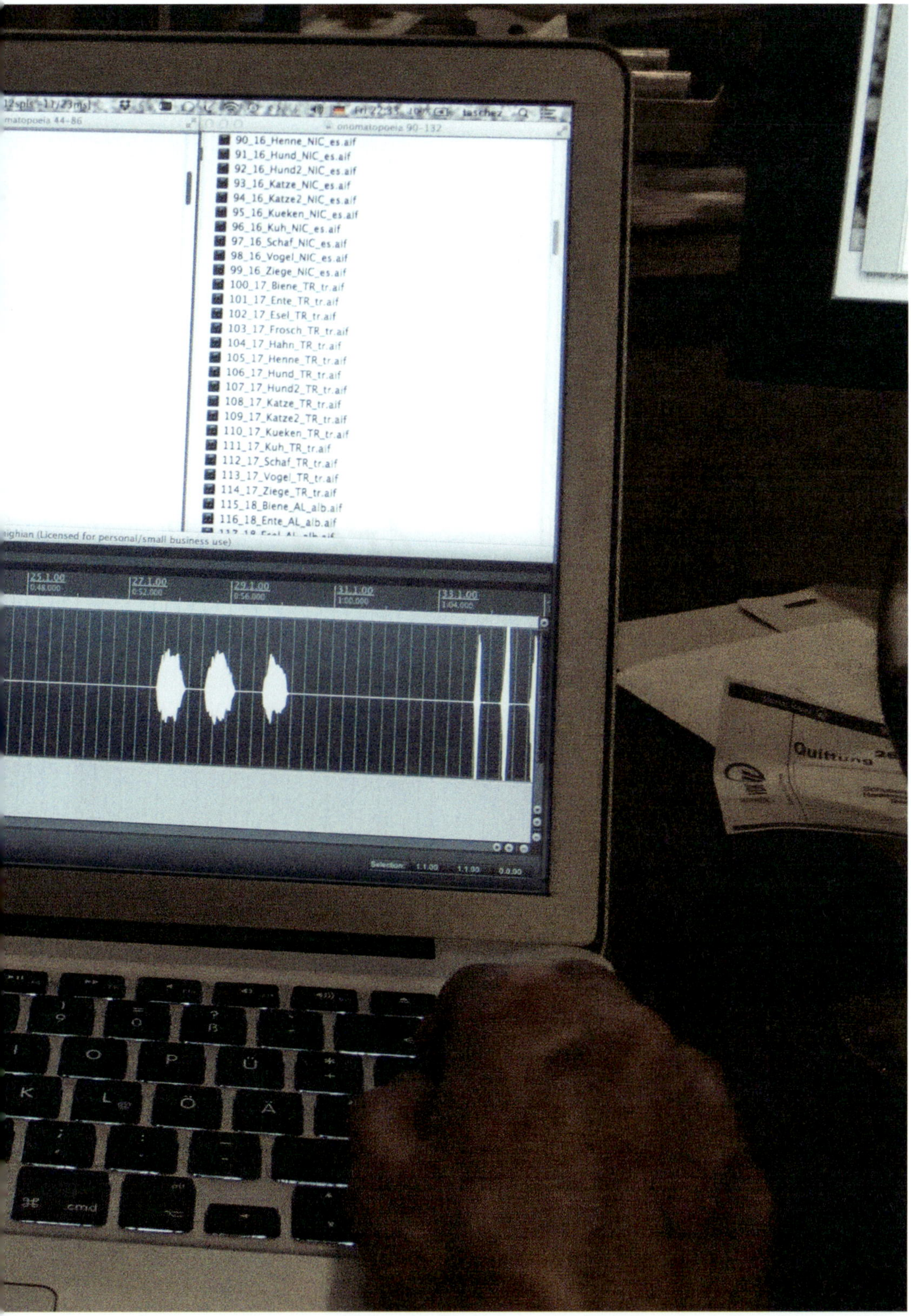

onomatopoeia 90-132
90_16_Henne_NIC_es.aif
91_16_Hund_NIC_es.aif
92_16_Hund2_NIC_es.aif
93_16_Katze_NIC_es.aif
94_16_Katze2_NIC_es.aif
95_16_Kueken_NIC_es.aif
96_16_Kuh_NIC_es.aif
97_16_Schaf_NIC_es.aif
98_16_Vogel_NIC_es.aif
99_16_Ziege_NIC_es.aif
100_17_Biene_TR_tr.aif
101_17_Ente_TR_tr.aif
102_17_Esel_TR_tr.aif
103_17_Frosch_TR_tr.aif
104_17_Hahn_TR_tr.aif
105_17_Henne_TR_tr.aif
106_17_Hund_TR_tr.aif
107_17_Hund2_TR_tr.aif
108_17_Katze_TR_tr.aif
109_17_Katze2_TR_tr.aif
110_17_Kueken_TR_tr.aif
111_17_Kuh_TR_tr.aif
112_17_Schaf_TR_tr.aif
113_17_Vogel_TR_tr.aif
114_17_Ziege_TR_tr.aif
115_18_Biene_AL_alb.aif
116_18_Ente_AL_alb.aif

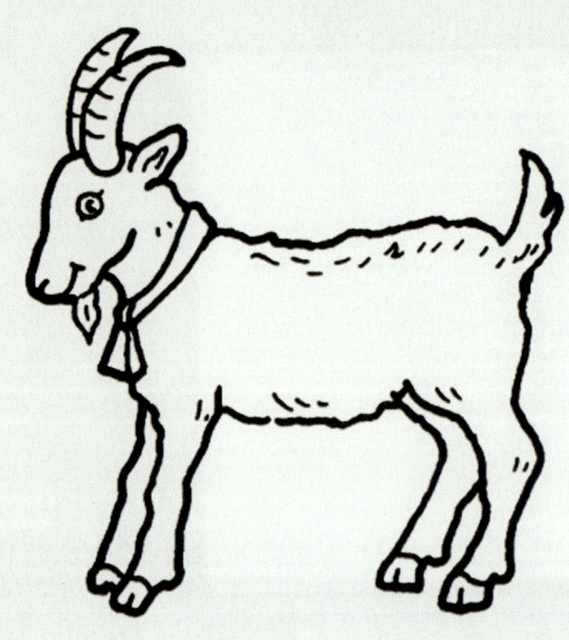

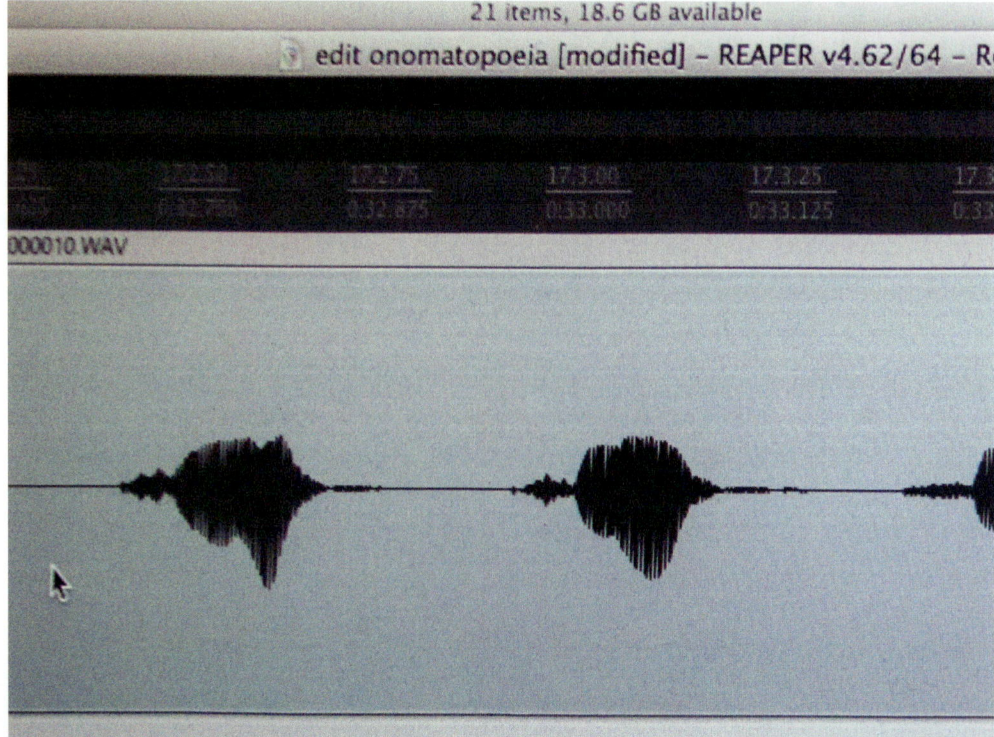

21 items, 18.6 GB available
edit onomatopoeia [modified] – REAPER v4.62/64 – R
000010.WAV

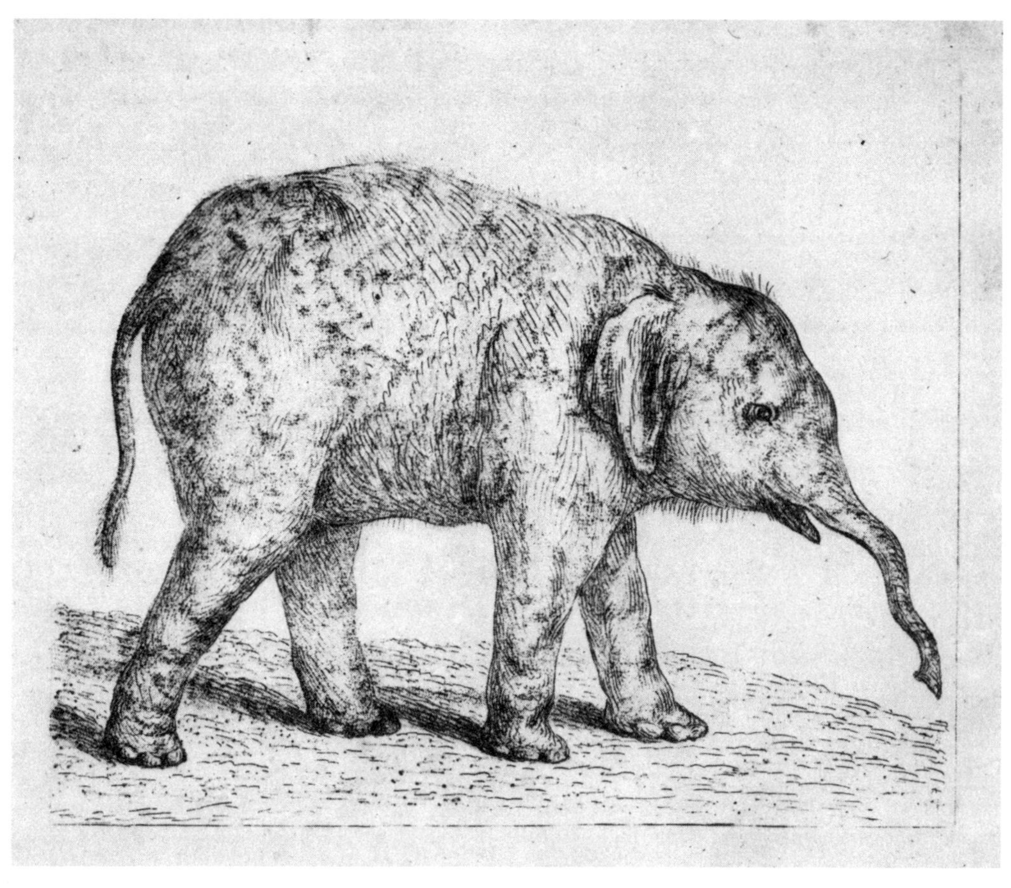

ETCHING OF THE LIVING ELEPHANT BY JOHANN H. TISCHBEIN

In 1773 this Indian elephant was brought at the age of three to Kassel from India or Sri Lanka. At the age of nine he fell down the Auehang and died. It became well-known after its death, and Goethe received its skull as a present from the anatomist Thomas Sommerring, which explains its other moniker, the Goethe Elephant. The taxidermied elephant traveled through Kassel on a truck in 1938, and its photo was featured in every newspaper in town. Its then burned in an air raid, and today its skeleton is displayed in the Ottoneum.

[ILLUSTRATION: JOHANN-HEINRICH TISCHBEIN JUNIOR, CA. 1774. REPRODUCTION: OTTONEUM KASSEL]

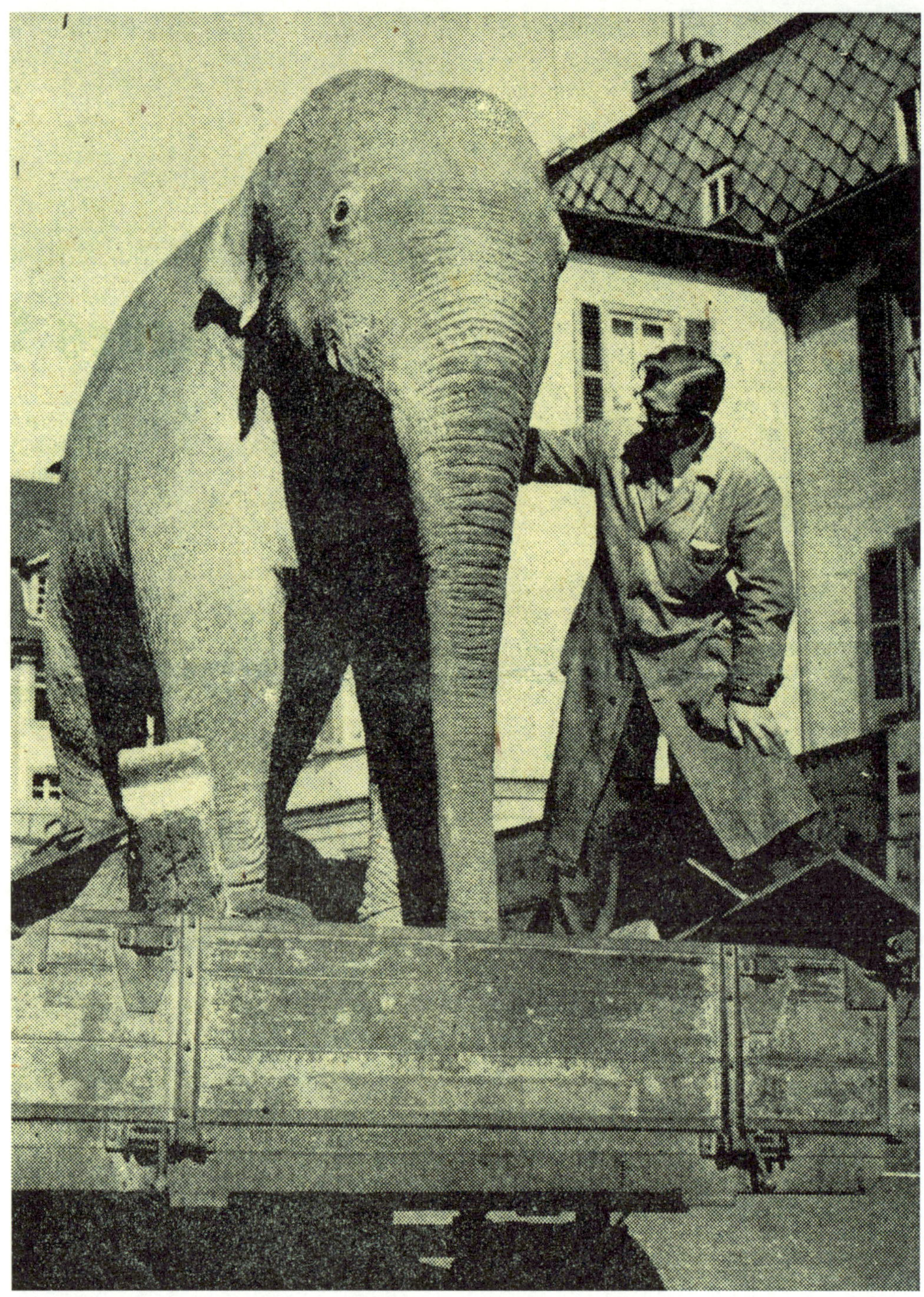

GOETHE ELEPHANT
The taxidermied elephant travels through Kassel on a truck in 1938, and its photo is featured in every newspaper in town.
[REPRODUCTION: OTTONEUM KASSEL]

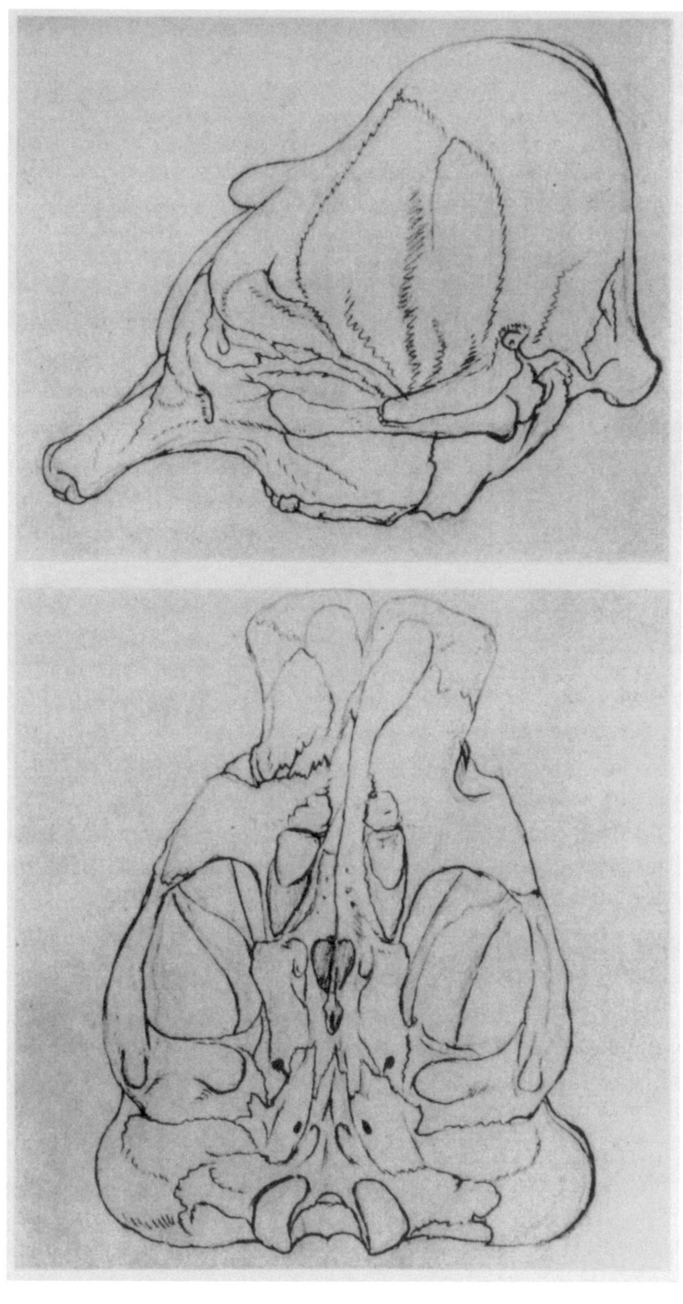

DRAWINGS BY JOHANN C. W. WAITZ FOR J. W. GOETHE, WEIMAR 1784.

[SOURCE: GOETHE- UND SCHILLER-ARCHIV, WEIMAR/"SAMUEL THOMAS SOEMMERRING IN KASSEL (1779-1784)" MANFRED WENZEL (EDITOR).
REPRODUCTION: POLA SIEVERDING]

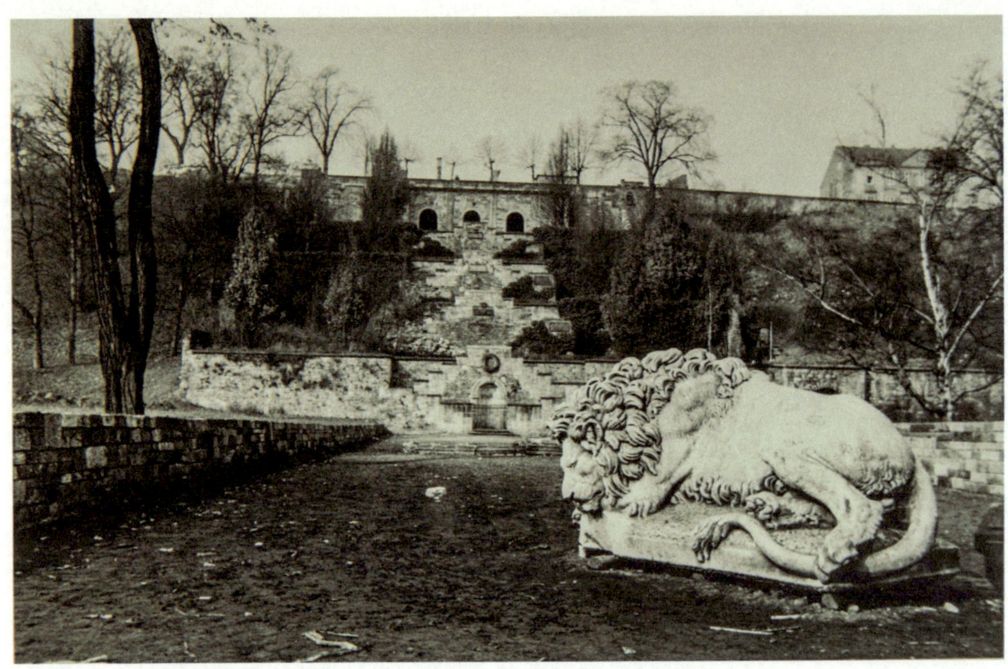

THE HESSENLÖWE [THE HESSIAN LION]
The so-called Hessenlöwe (or, Kurhessischer Löwe) in front of the Ehrenmal in the Karlsaue, Kassel.
These pictures were probably taken sometime between the end of the war in 1945 and the German
Horticultural Show in 1955.

[SOURCE: SOURCE: STADTARCHIV (CITY ARCHIVE) KASSEL / E4 No. 217, P. 41 - PHOTOGRAPHER: UNKNOWN. REPRODUCTION: POLA SIEVERDING]

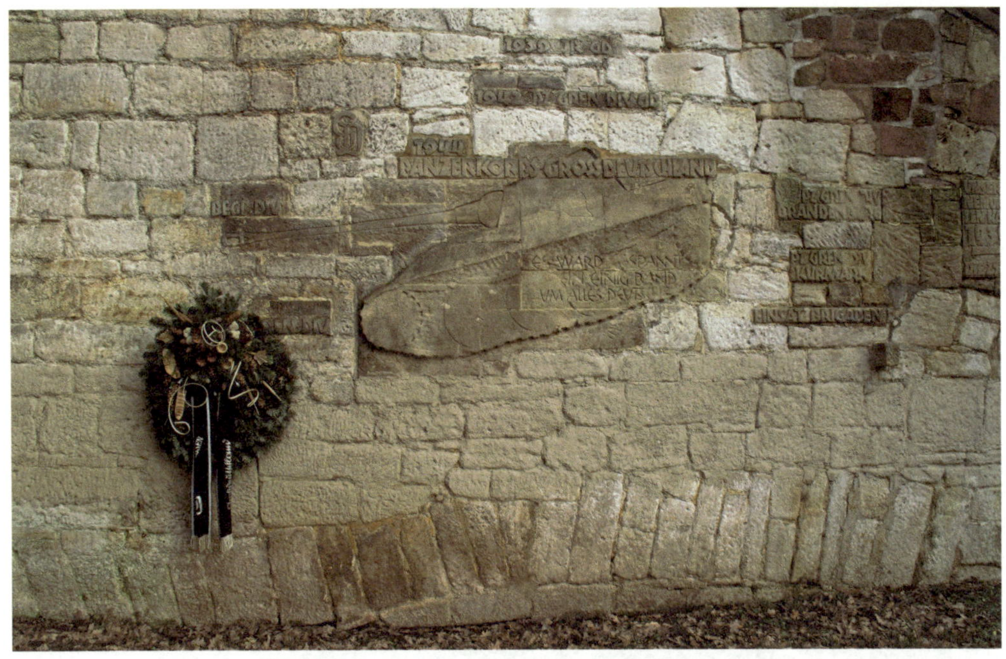

TIGER TANK ON THE EHRENMAL IN KASSEL, 2011

On the memorial to the Panzercorps Grossdeutschland on the lower terrace of the Ehrenmal, I discover the Tiger tank again. It's aimed slightly downward and looks like it is suspended from the relief script. After having to view so many tanks in the course of our research, I recognize it straight away as a Tiger. It looks the same as the photograph of the Panzer VI Tiger I as it is being loaded onto a rail car in the Henchel plant, hovering from two cranes several meters above the ground. It is faithful to the original in every detail, except that its cannon is pointing in the other direction. An attentive reader of a local newspaper indicates later that it might be a Panzerkampfwagen V Panther by Henschel, instead.

[PHOTO: NATASCHA SADR HAGHIGHIAN]

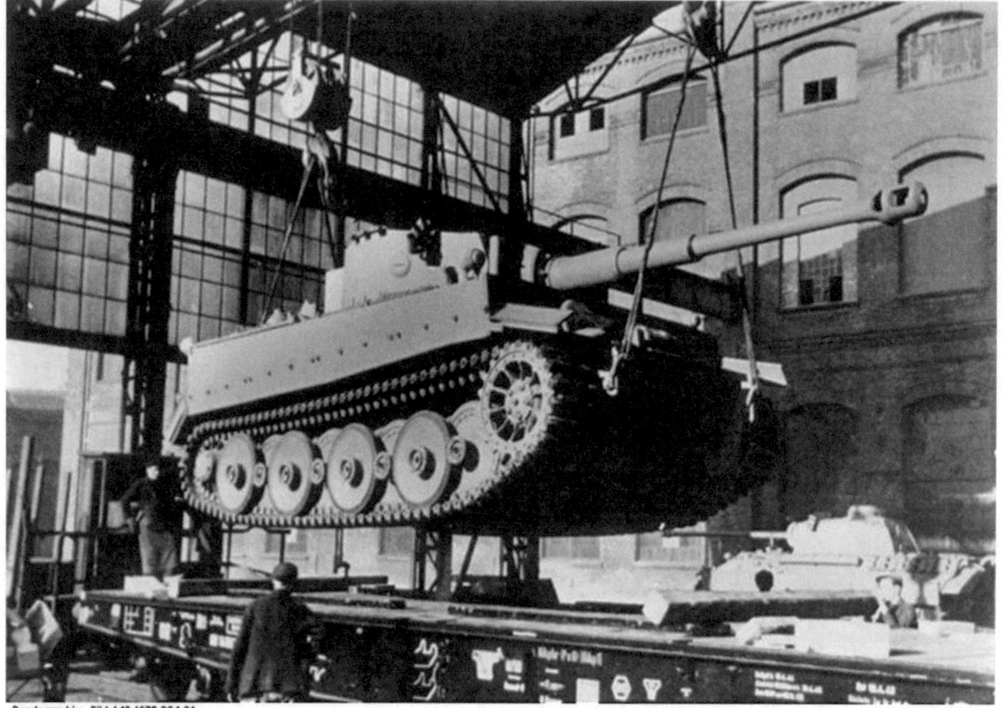

PANZER VI «TIGER I» BEING LOADED ONTO A RAILROAD CAR IN THE KASSEL HENSCHEL PLANT

[SOURCE: DEUTSCHES BUNDESARCHIV (GERMAN FEDERAL ARCHIVE), BILD 146-1972-064-61. CREATIVE COMMONS-LICENCE GERMANY.]

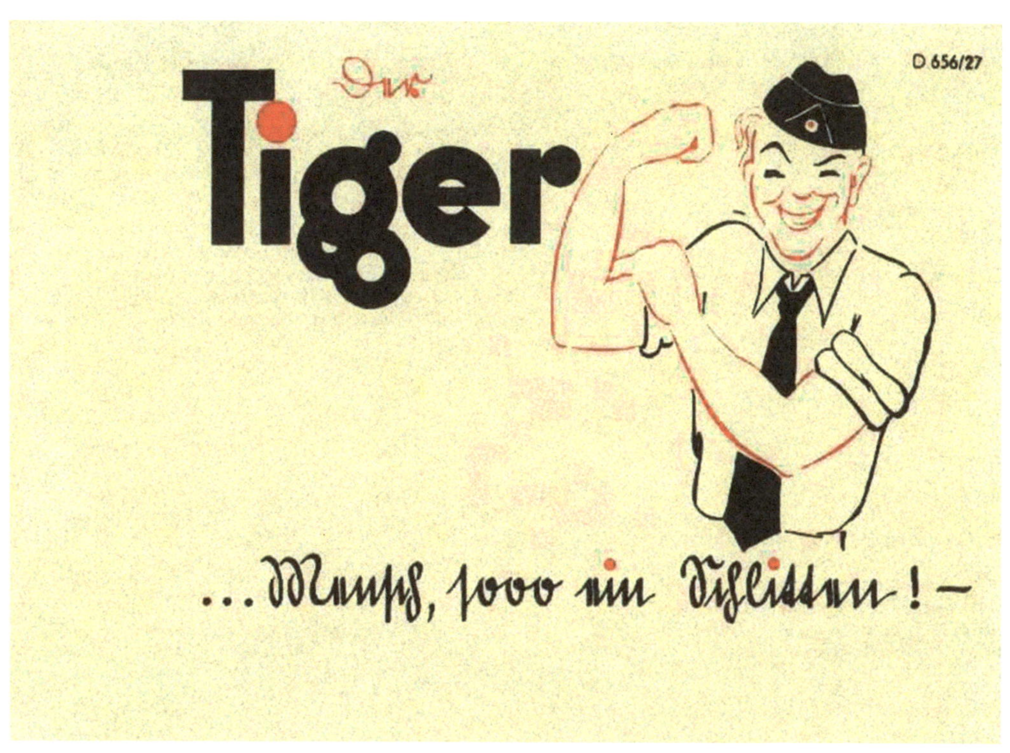

THE TIGERFIBEL

The "Tigerfibel" manual was published in 1943 by the Inspector General of Panzertruppen (tank forces) in order to instruct commanding officers and platoon leaders in the deployment of the Tiger VI heavy tank.

[SOURCE: PUBLIC DOMAIN]

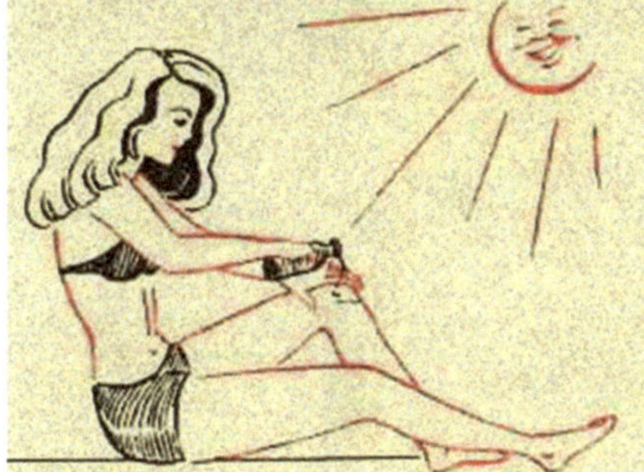

Öl ist ein Schmiermittel

Schon wenn Du Deine Hände miteinander r∈
werden sie heiß. Du brauchst sie gar nicht schnell
mit viel Kraft bewegen. Tust Du aber ordentlich H∈
dazwischen, dann bleiben sie kühl.

Deine Maschine macht 3000 Umdrehungen in
Minute und 700 PS sitzen dahinter. Sie würde bren∈
heiß werden, alles Bewegliche würde sich festfre∈
Du kämst keinen Kilometer weit, wenn nicht Öl
Hitze aufnähme und hinwegspülte. Zu wenig Ö
gefährlich

l ein Brennstoff

n es aus den Leitungen leckt, durch
en ausgeworfen wird, aus schad-
n Dichtungen tropft und sich mit
vermischt, brennt es lichterloh
steckt Spritlachen und den üb-
n Wannensatz an.

el Öl ist gefährlich.

Darum:

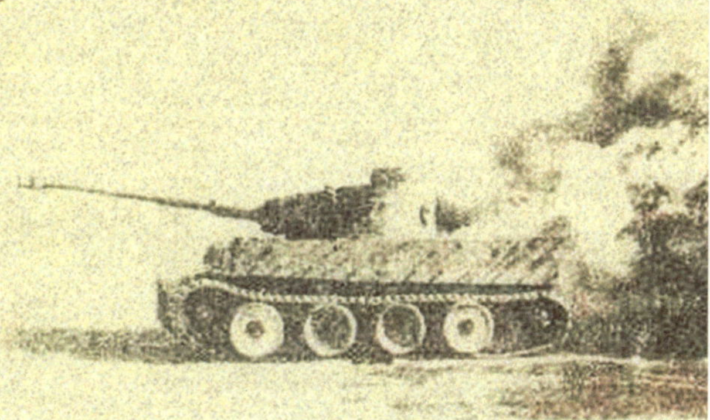

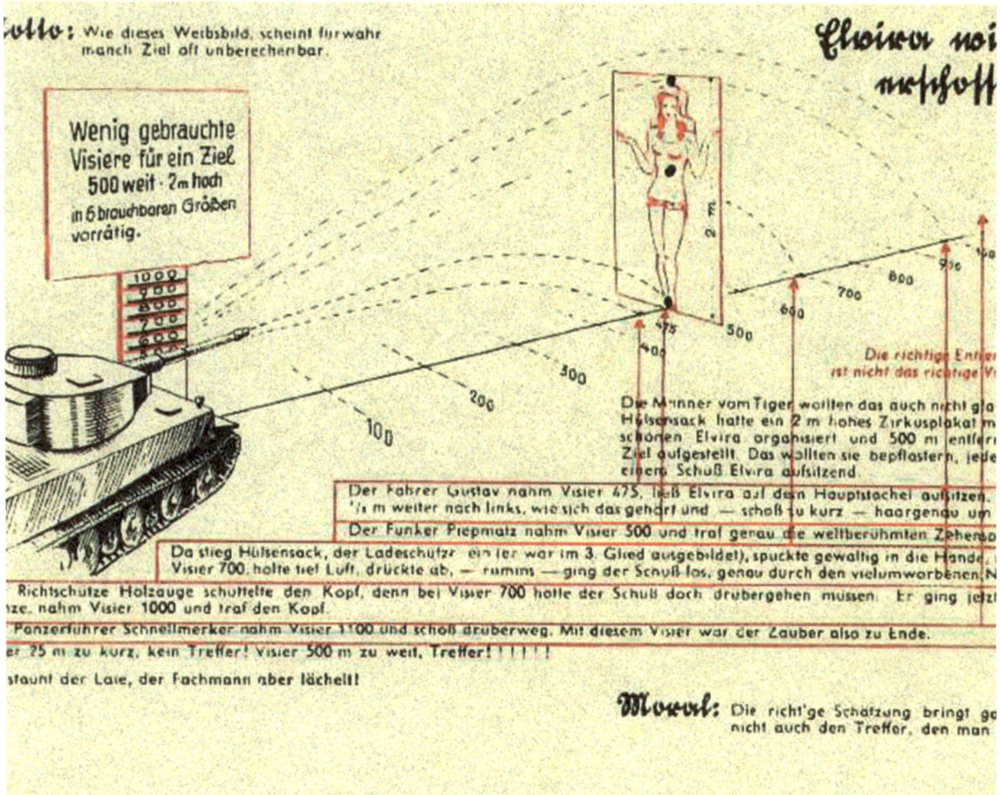

Motto: Wie dieses Weibsbild, scheint fürwahr manch Ziel oft unberechenbar.

Wenig gebrauchte
Visiere für ein Ziel
500 weit · 2m hoch
in 6 brauchbaren Größen
vorrätig.

1000
900
800
700
600

100
200
300
400
475
500
600
700
800
900

2 m

Die richtige Entfer[nung]
ist nicht das richtige Vi[sier]

Die Männer vom Tiger wollten das auch nicht gla[uben]. Hülsensack hatte ein 2 m hohes Zirkusplakat m[it] schönen Elvira organisiert und 500 m entfer[nt als] Ziel aufgestellt. Das wollten sie bepflastern, jede[r] einen Schuß Elvira aufsitzend.

Der Fahrer Gustav nahm Visier 475, ließ Elvira auf den Hauptstachel aufsitzen, ¼ m weiter nach links, wie sich das gehört und — schoß zu kurz — haargenau um

Der Funker Piepmatz nahm Visier 500 und traf genau die weltberühmten Zehen

Da stieg Hülsensack, der Ladeschütze ein (er war im 3. Glied ausgebildet), spuckte gewaltig in die Hände, Visier 700, holte tief Luft, drückte ab, — rumms — ging der Schuß los, genau durch den vielumworbenen N

Richtschütze Holzauge schüttelte den Kopf, denn bei Visier 700 hätte der Schuß doch drübergehen müssen. Er ging jetzt
ze, nahm Visier 1000 und traf den Kopf.

Panzerführer Schnellmerker nahm Visier 1100 und schoß drüberweg. Mit diesem Visier war der Zauber also zu Ende.

er 25 m zu kurz, kein Treffer! Visier 500 m zu weit, Treffer! ! ! ! ! !

staunt der Laie, der Fachmann aber lächelt!

Moral: Die richt'ge Schätzung bringt ga[r] nicht auch den Treffer, den man

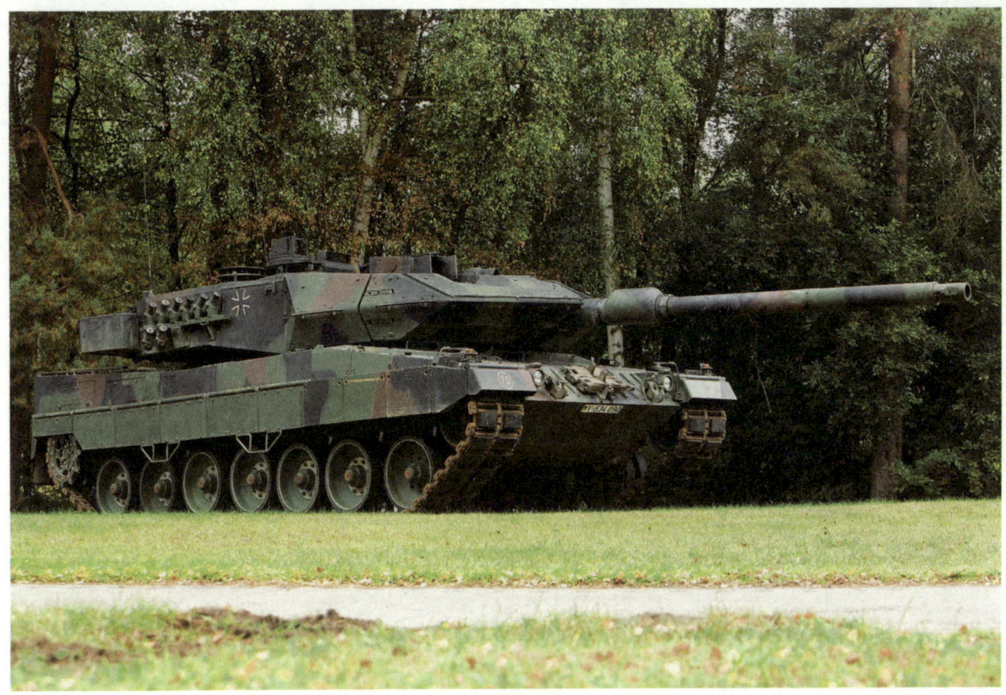

LEOPARD

WEAPON SYSTEMS WITH ANIMAL NAMES

Ever since the manufacture of the Tiger tank, which Henschel developed in 1937 and produced in Kassel from 1942 until the end of World War II, weapon systems made in Germany have been adorned with the names of animals: Leopard, Marten, Weasel, Puma, Cheetah, Lynx, Beaver, Buffalo, Badger, Dingo. The images show track vehicles and wheeled vehicles that are manufactured in Kassel (and other German cities) in the plants of Rheinmetall Defense and Krauss-Maffei Wegmann, which is where the infantry fighting vehicle Puma and the Leopard 2 is currently manufactured.

[SOURCE: BUNDESWEHR MEDIENDATENBANK]

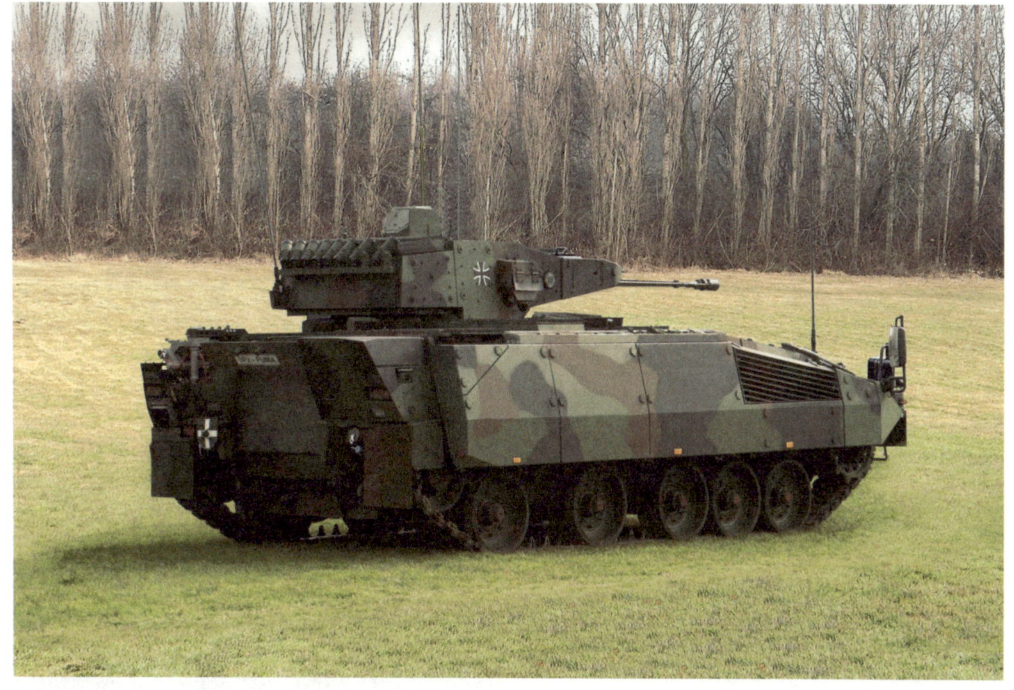

PUMA

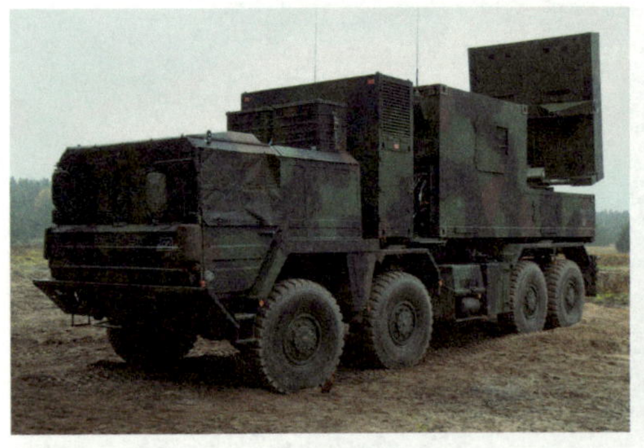

COBRA

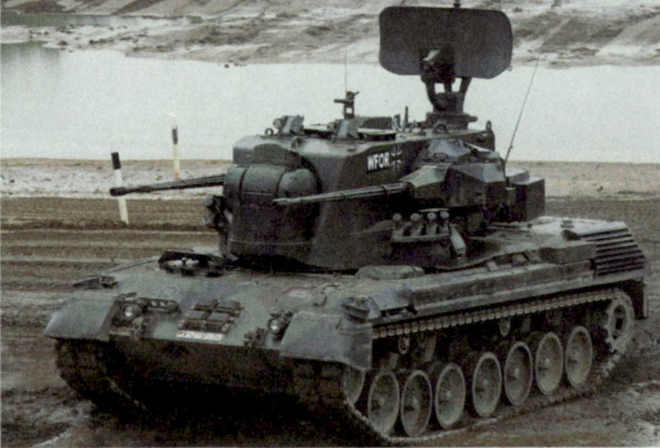
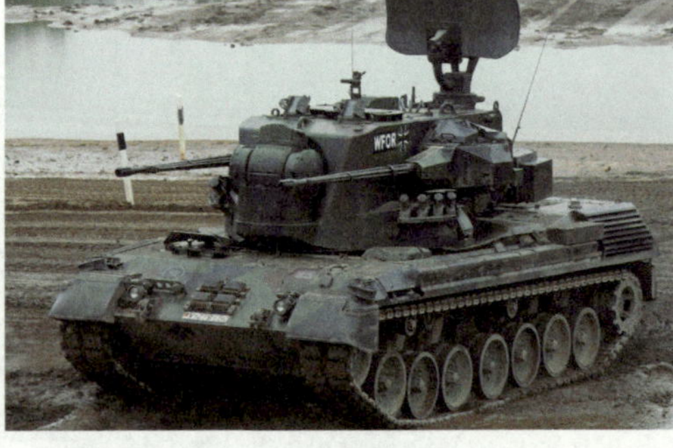

CHEETAH

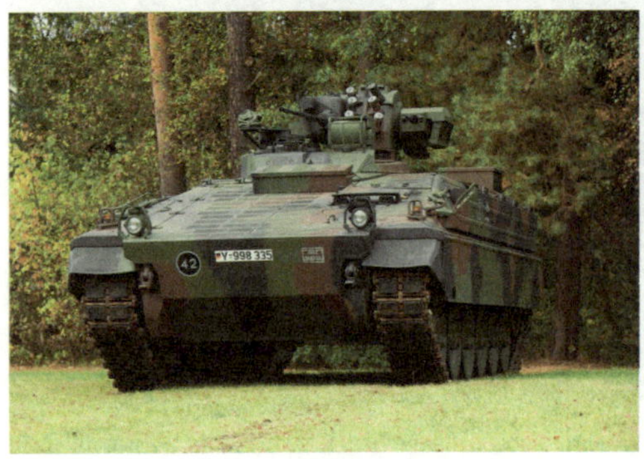

MARTEN

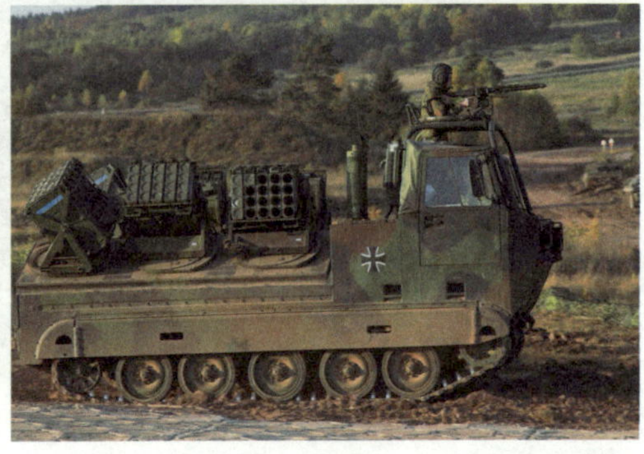

SCORPIO

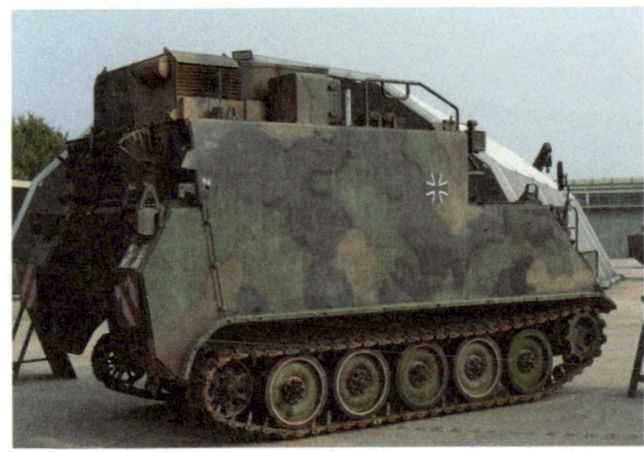

EAGLE

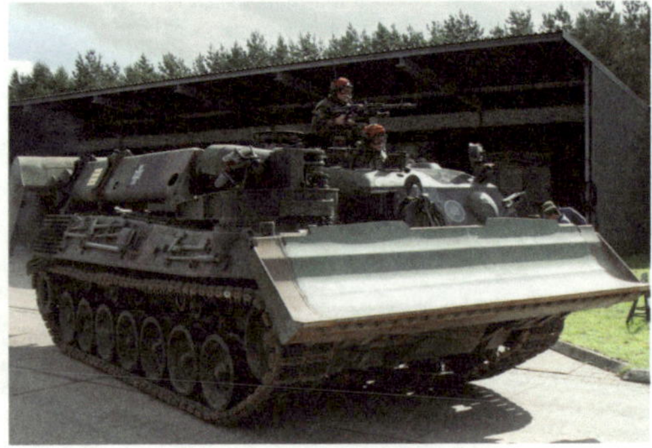

BADGER

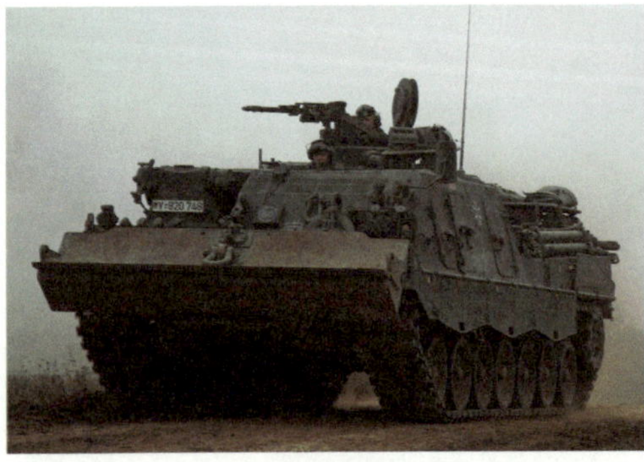

BUFFALO

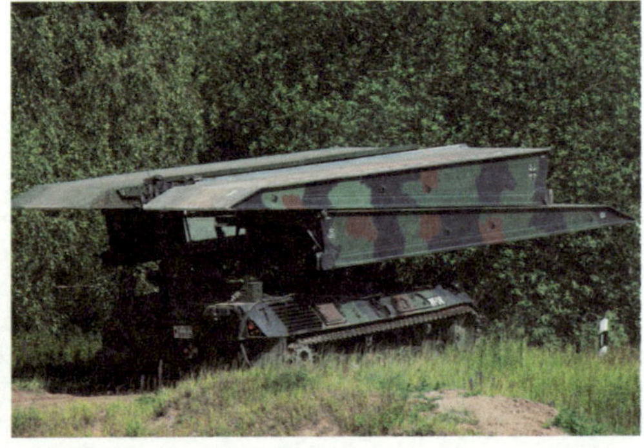

BEAVER

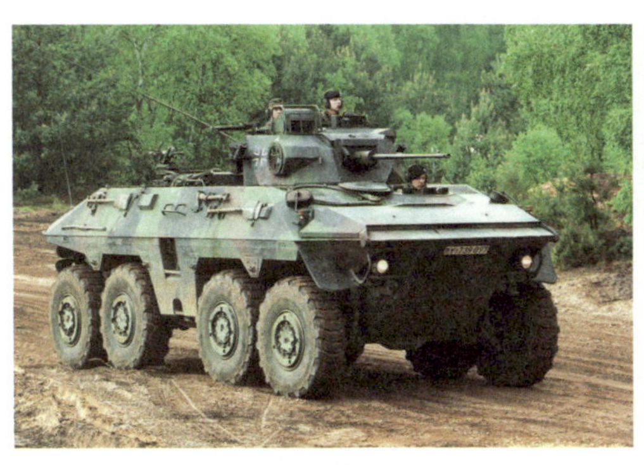

LYNX

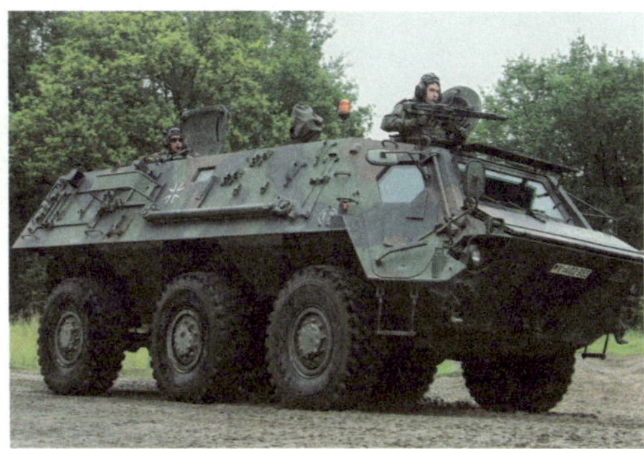

FOX

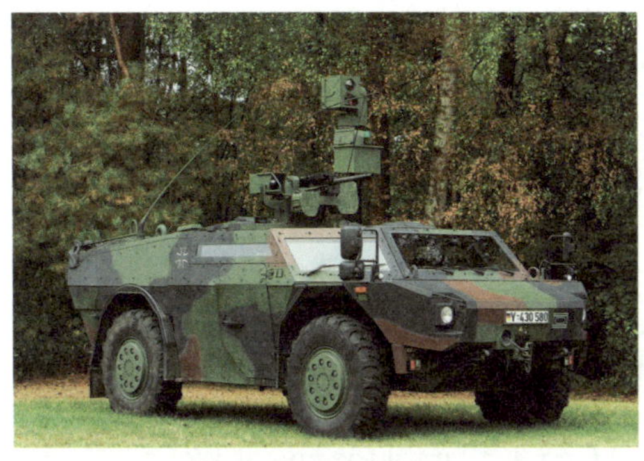

FENNEC

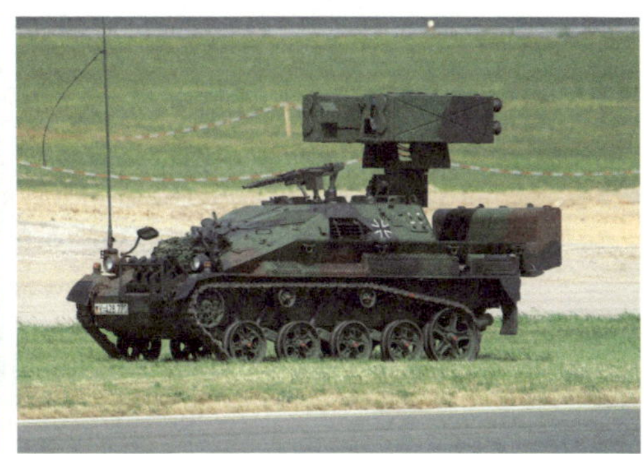

OCELOT

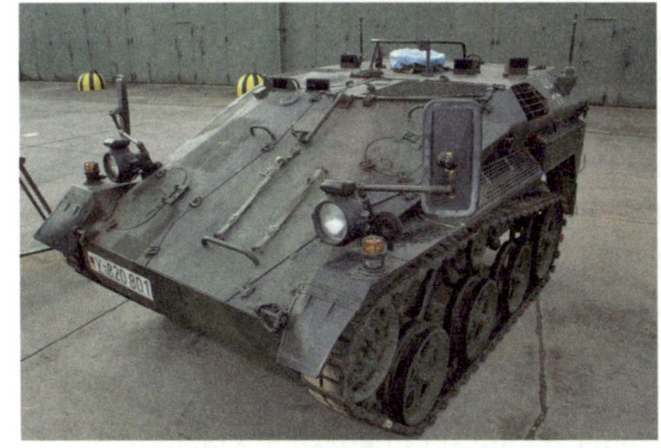

WEASEL

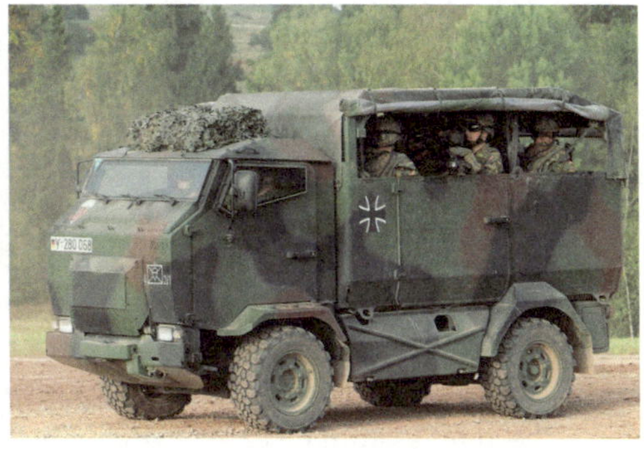

MONGOOSE

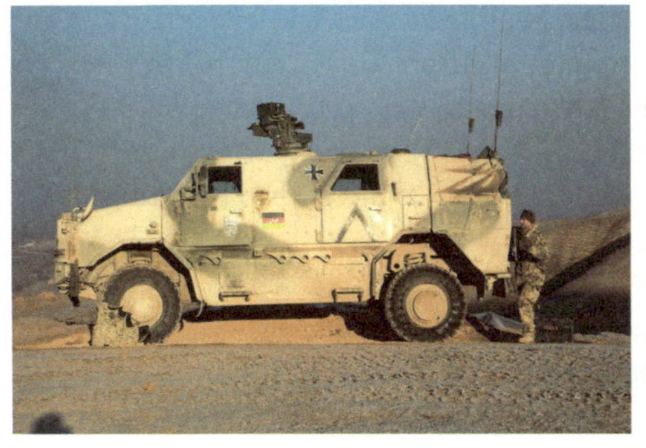

DINGO

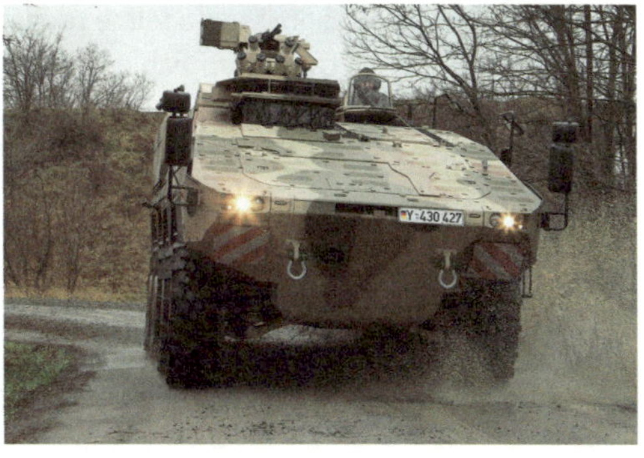

BOXER

Dear Anselm,

Something in relation to the trail has surfaced, and I'm writing to ask if you
could offer a bit of feedback about it.
Kassel's role in arms manufacture was brought to our attention by rubble
originating from the Henschel Villa. There is a noteworthy point particular
to this manufacturing locale, one which has endured until today: its naming
practice. Ever since the manufacture of the "Tiger" tank, which Henschel
developed in 1937 and produced in Kassel from 1942 until the end of World
War II, weapon systems made in Germany have been adorned with the
names of animals: Leopard, Marten, Weasel, Puma, Cheetah, Lynx, Beaver,
Buffalo, Badger, Dingo.

We couldn't find any reasons for this tradition anywhere. Even participants
in the relevant weapons forums could only puzzle over the question, freely
associating about which motivations lie behind this practice.
Benjamin speaks of the magic of language, of the mimetic act through which
objects are endowed with their force or power by the names that designate
them. What sort of mimesis occurs within a track vehicle's process of
'becoming-animal'? Does a highly technologized military believe in magic?
In what form? Are the characteristics of the animal thought to extend to the
vehicle? The litheness of a feline predator, the hunting instinct, the fearlessness,
the quality of the untameable. Or is it a matter of associations conjured in
the mind of the opponent (after all, the German military has resumed its
participation in acts of war)? In other words, is it a question of psychological
warfare strategies? And what actually happens to the soldiers who are sitting
inside of the Tiger?

What other mechanisms of 'becoming-animal' could be pertinent here?
Who or what is being animated? It appears that this mechanism stands in

a peculiar relationship with the 'humanization' of animals, or even devices, but also with the 'de-humanization' of 'becoming-animal,' of beings who don't have the right to exist or whose assigned place is outside of civilized society.

In Kabul, three Dingo 2 patrols drove past us. These are reconnaissance vehicles made by KMW out of Kassel, and German soldiers were sitting inside of them. The dingo is a dog that was once domesticated and that subsequently re-entered the wild milennia ago. To communicate, the dingo uses mostly howling and high-pitched whining sounds, and less often, barking.

I'm also pondering which language is spoken by a dingo from KMW. And when it rolls over Afghanistan, does the tank speak through the dingo or the dingo through the armored vehicle?

How do all of these animals fit into the image of a Bundeswehr that cooly and unemotionally justifies its missions by means of a humanitarian rationale or under the logic of economic interests held by Germany, Europe, or its allies? I find the seemingly well-controlled canalization of the rationalized and the 'animalized' in a system built on Clausewitz's grammar of war, not to mention the images that emerge from that canalization, bewildering. I wonder if this is intended, because one of the effects of German tanks driving through Kabul is the exportation and projection of an image to the outside world. And what about the significant amount of German exports weaponry throughout the whole world—what exactly is exported when a Puma or a Leopard goes to Saudi Arabia?
That's it for the time being. I would be very pleased to receive any feedback, even in reference to particular fragments.

Dear Natascha,

Famously segregated from the human, the animal is indeed already the product
of an exportation. Its position, proportionate to its status as object, lies
outside of social contracts and circles of socialization, yet it still partakes in
these via specific rights related to faculties of bodily sensation—large-scale
livestock farming regularly prohibits 'torture,' but the definition of torture
is obviously subject to a perverse economic rationalization because it only
indicates the pain which is 'too much,' the excess in relation to the 'necessity,'
the 'rational.'
Insofar as these dynamics make the animal into a carrier of social meaning
with a quota of subjectivity rather than into a 'pure' object, the animal—ever
since the establishment of this segregation—epitomizes the emotional, the
affect, the instinct, and so on, all of which are to be understood as prior
to cognition insofar as the animal is pronounced devoid of pronunciation,
bereft of language.

The animal names of German tanks, etc., remind me, in an inversion of sorts,
of the famous caricaturist J.J. Grandville, who developed the caricatural
animal metaphor like no other. What's more, other theories hypothesize
that the animal metaphor—on cave walls, for instance—is the origin of
language. But shouldn't we revise this history? How can it be that the image
of the animal is so terrifically meaningful? Aren't we actually witnessing
the revelation of aspects of society here, displayed and layed out via the
detour of the animal? It appears to be about something 'language' cannot
express, even though this something is as plain to see as what a Grandville
drawing manifests: the plane of society's affective-mediating constitution
upon which it 'naturalizes,' normalizes and internalizes its power relations
and hierarchies; or the plane that one could perhaps call 'the implicit,' or in
Michael Taussig's words, the 'public secret,' or even the 'nature' of society,
if only the term 'nature' weren't used with such a banefulness aimed at the
non-human, who, starting with Hobbes, have been thrown in with society's
'worst,' those whom society calls into being as its antithesis and dustbin.

Of course, one could also turn the formula inside out and say it's the animal
who we have to thank for 'language'—an ambivalent formula which would
probably bring us further. For then we would also be indebted to the animal
for 'the human,' who gets produced in a perpetual interior and exterior separation from the animal ever since this demarcation 'pronounced' the animal
devoid of 'pronunciation.' This is a language that is cut off and a human

who is cut off, and the cut itself constitutes the locus of power. But of course this export recurs precisely in the 'nature' of society, which is henceforth to be called the emotional-mediating-affective constitution of society, and in capitalism, the economy—the only place where modernity has still allowed itself to speak in earnest of 'animal spirits.'

What percentage of the infamous prowess of German exports does the weapons industry account for? I don't have the numbers on hand, but I remember having recently read a statistic that set it at a shockingly high level. But an odd quietness has set in regarding the Germany's arms exports, probably also because industry and politics alike have learned to mask the greater part of those exports in a wide variety of ways, like only exporting the necessary technology and not the finished product. This too is without a doubt a sort of quasi-animalistic operation—camouflage, or sailing under the cloak of an image, below the threshold of identification. And the nation's export data follows its own logic. It is tidily rationalized, and thus unites with other affects. Affects of economic trajectories, of geopolitical tectonics, of dislodged patriotism ("we're proud of our economy"), all of which are affects that have nothing to do with what is really being exported here, or which economic "circulation" the exportation really occurs within.

The great export regimes under the European civilizations of recent centuries are, however, stuck in a crisis that's hard to ignore. Essentially, this 'export regime' consists in a mechanism that projects discriminations and exclusions from the internal space of European culture onto an outside. Madness, which becomes an object of medicalization in psychiatry, is an example of this. The export regime draws imaginary borders that separate an outside from an inside, a negative from a positive (or vice versa), whereupon the separation is masked and naturalized (objectified, as in a syndrome), thereby bestowing the status of dustbin for Europe's garbage upon the Other (system-inherent violence), who is subsequently appropriated as the figure of the outside or the different in order to facilitate real exploitation, identity construction, and self-mythologization. Another example of a such a multifunctional figure of exclusion, real subjugation, and imaginary appropriation can be found in the figure of the barbarian or primitive. For a certain period of time, the concept of 'nature' functioned precisely so: a projected outside, product of a border whose production is masked. The export regime that is invested in nature is plunged into crisis when that which is exported returns; when, for instance, hippies seek out 'wild' nature and find only garbage; when in *The Beach* Leonardo DiCaprio looks for the outside of nature on an island and finds war as the state of nature; or when CO^2 issuing forth from the paradigmatic export architecture, embodied by the smokestack, returns as the greenhouse effect.

Therefore, with regard to the German tanks, we must ask in what form and at what point in time the export returns. That it returns is beyond question, and maybe this form of animal magic, this return of that which is excluded from consciousness as non-consciousness is, in fact, the contemporary form of magic. And the export is already exercising magic now in this very moment. Here, as we ruminate on how we obtain our immediate 'identity' from the sum of our exports and from their successful masking.

Dear Anselm,

It's interesting how you say that the exported animal/machine complex's return, occurring in one way or another, is beyond question. This confirms the continuities and circulations I'm constantly observing in the investigations for the trail.
This return is also contained in the rubble of the Auehang. The weapons industry in Kassel supplies Hitler's war machines, the allied bombers transform the city into a pile of rubble, the piles of rubble are cleared away in order to transform Kassel into a leading location for arms manufacture, and roses are planted on the rubble. An exercise in imagination seems to suggest itself: imagine the debris of the future covering everything. Here, too, we have a strange masking or camouflage effect: the rubble disappears under flowers. But actually these events ought not to return or repeat themselves either, especially not in the form of the becoming-animal of a whole nation. It is explained thus: the magic of the legendary Tiger tank is infused into the Leopard or the Puma in one form and one form alone: favorable job statistics and gross domestic product. The question is, will the animals comply... ?

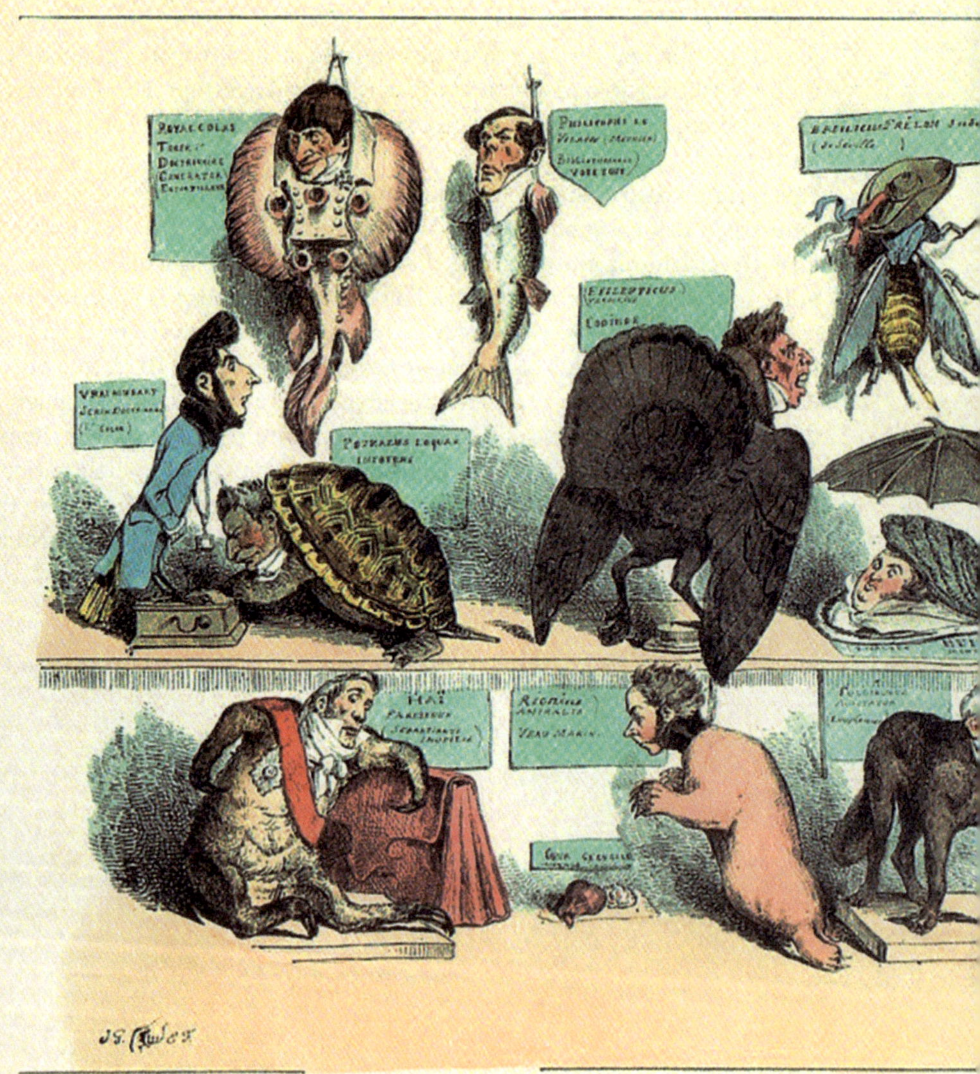

«CABINET D'HISTOIRE NATURELLE» (CABINET OF NATURAL HISTORY), 1833

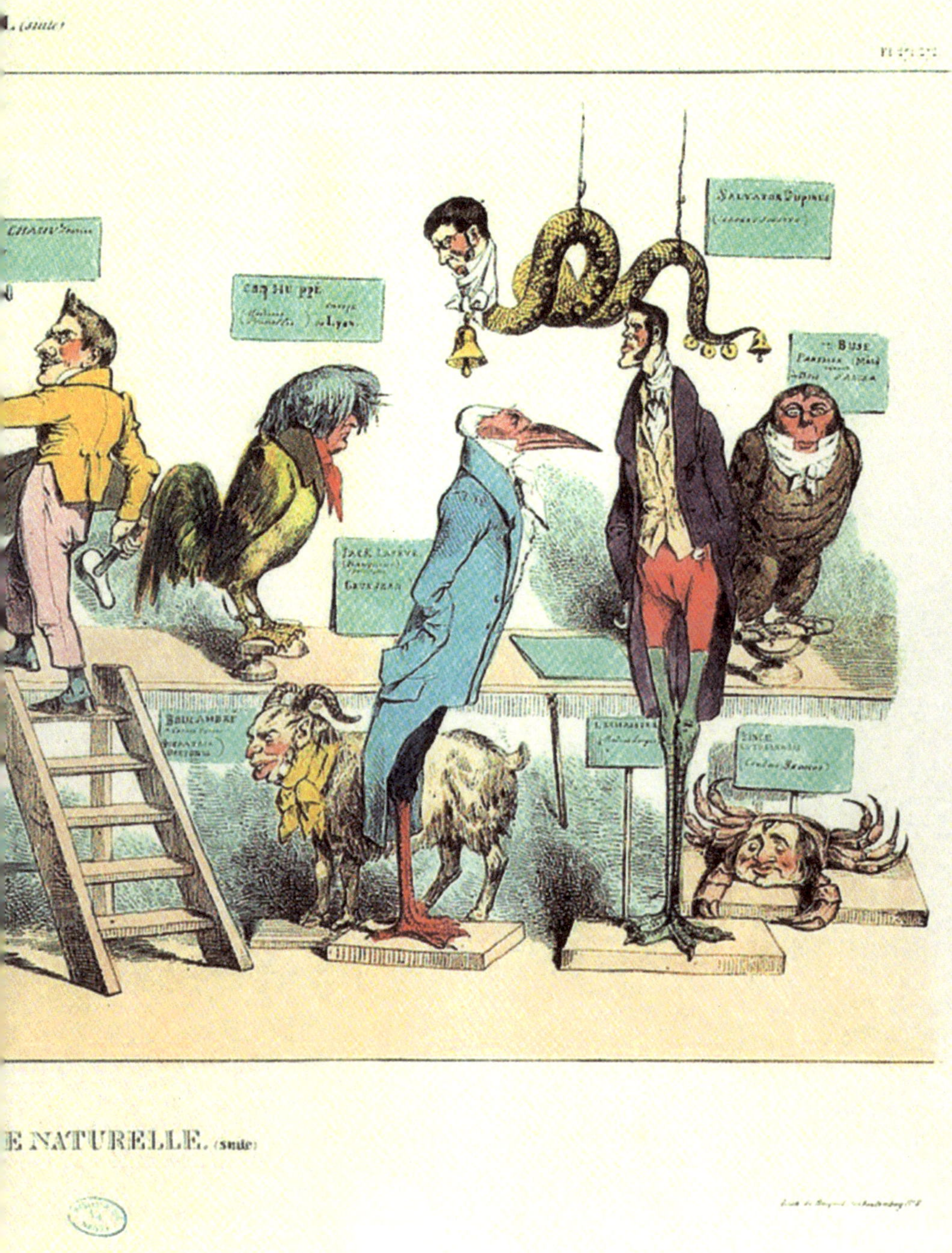

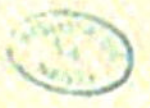

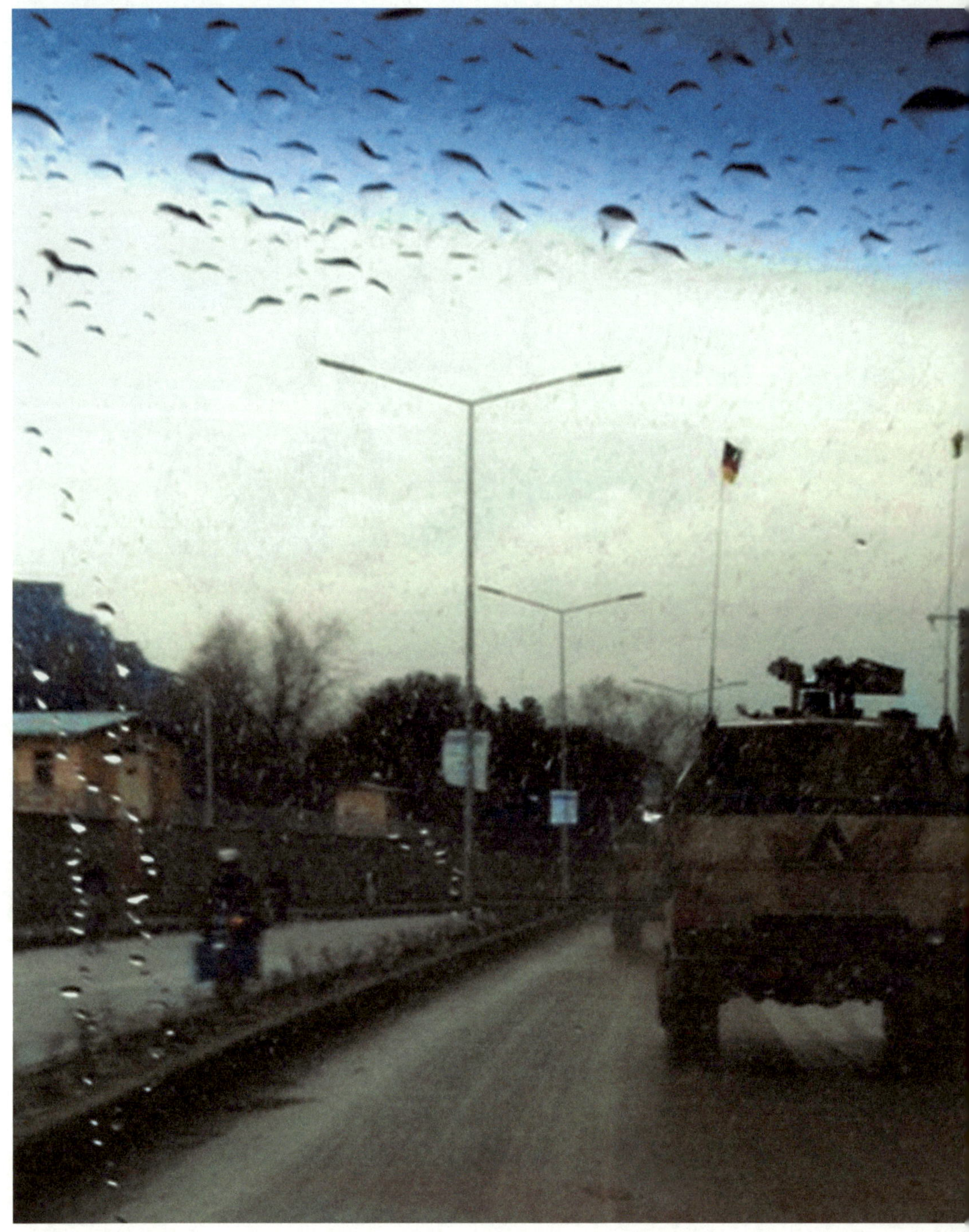

DINGO IN KABUL

Three Dingo 2 patrol vehicles drive by us on Asmayi Street in Kabul. The Dingo is a reconnaissance vehicle, produced by Krauss-Maffei Wegmann (KMW) in Kassel. German Bundeswehr soldiers were sitting inside the Dingos.

[PHOTO: NATASCHA SADR HAGHIGHIAN]

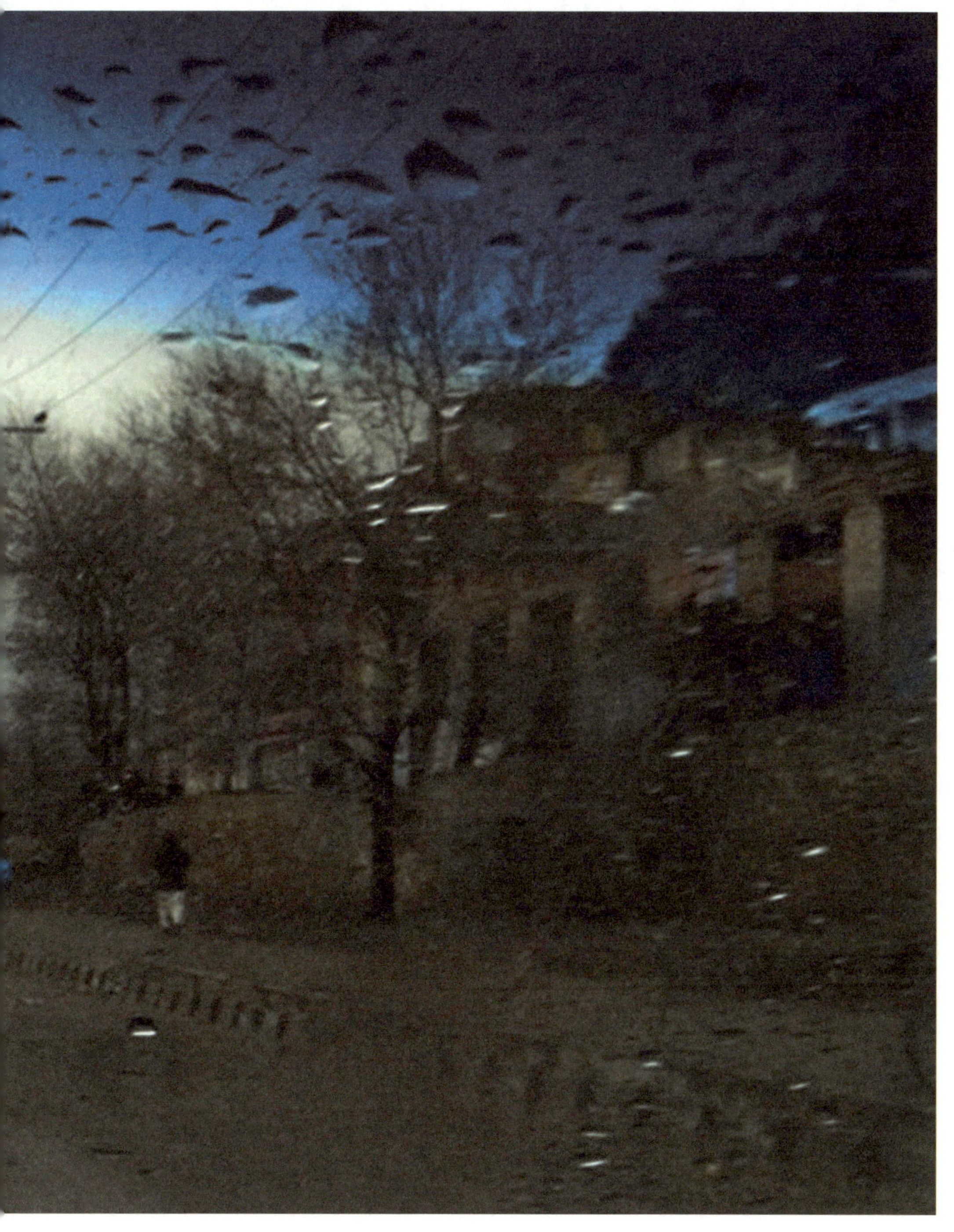

People

People who we met coincidentally,
people who know things
or are good at explaining things,
people who live or at some point lived in Kassel,
people who build cannons and bells.

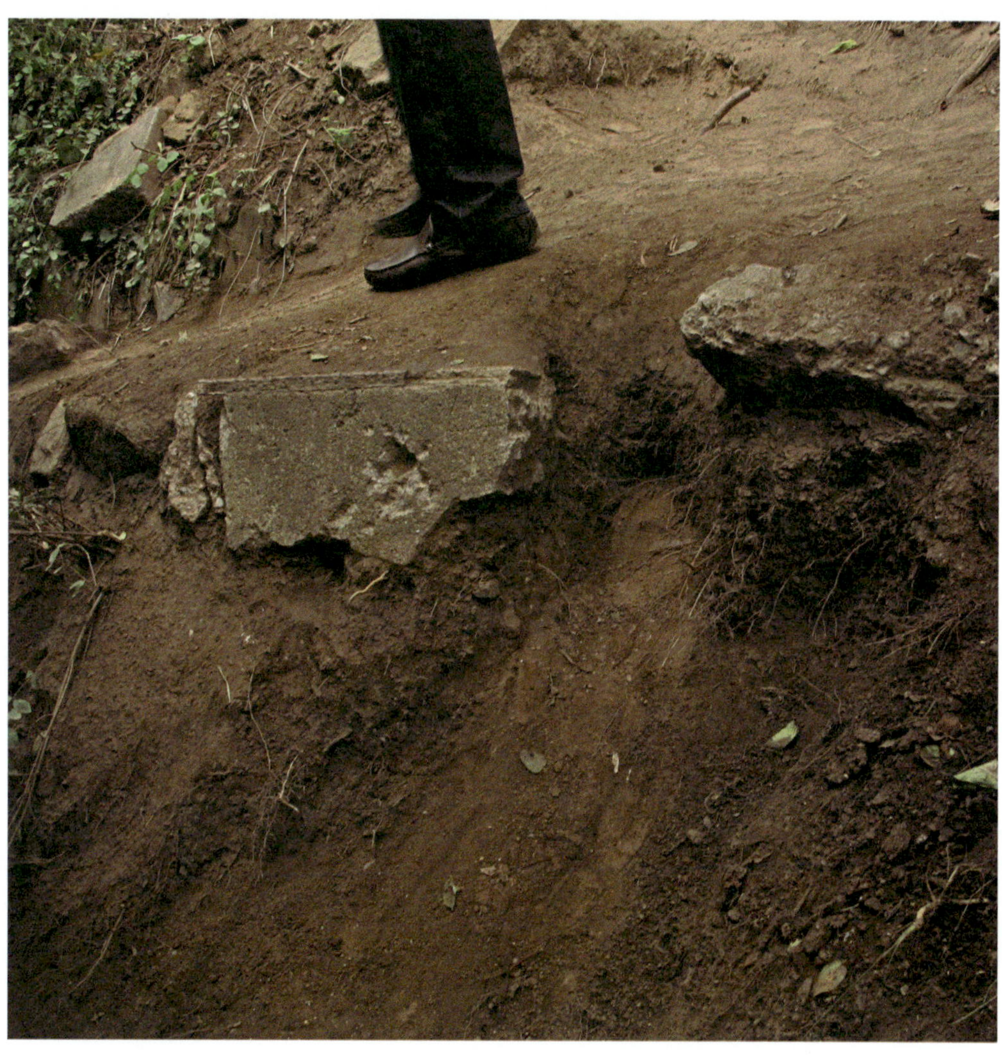

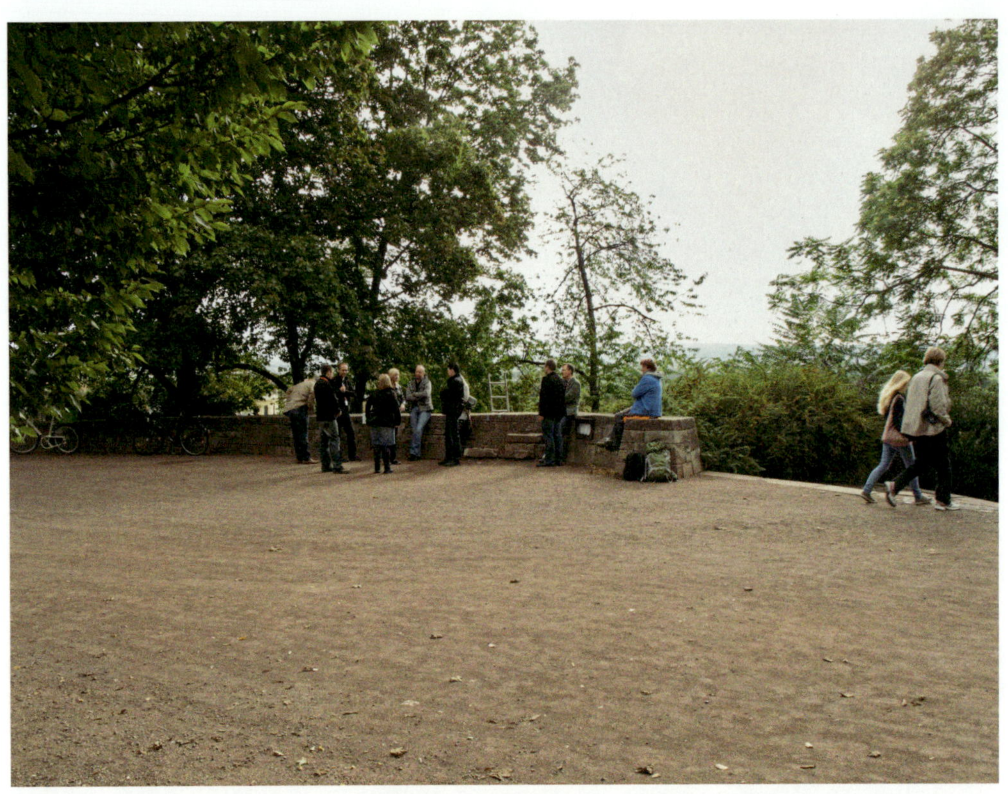

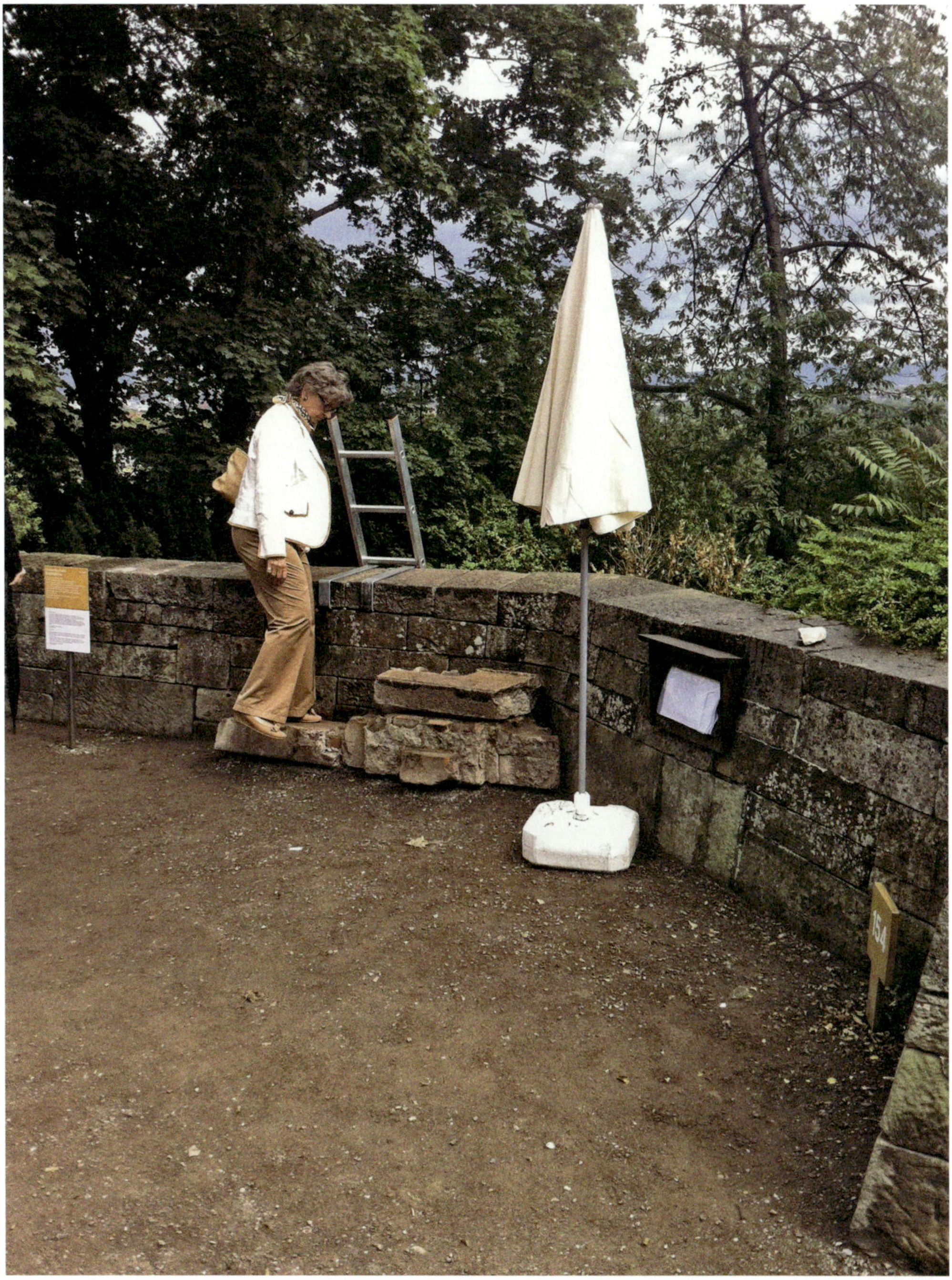

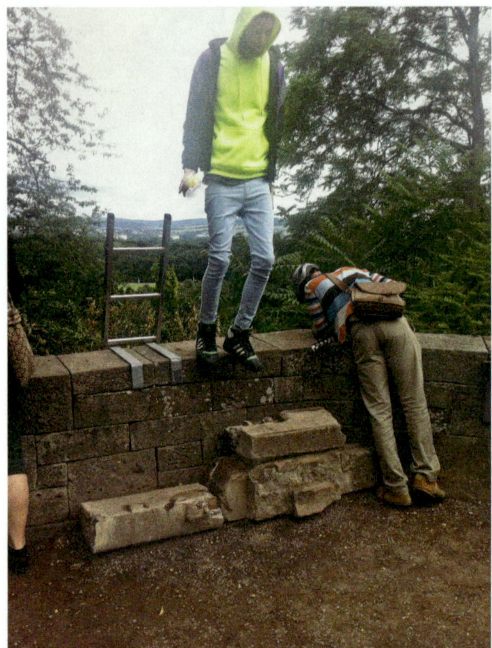
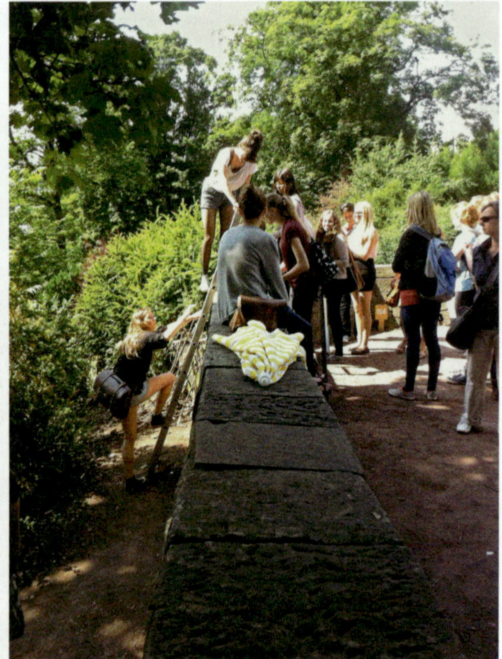

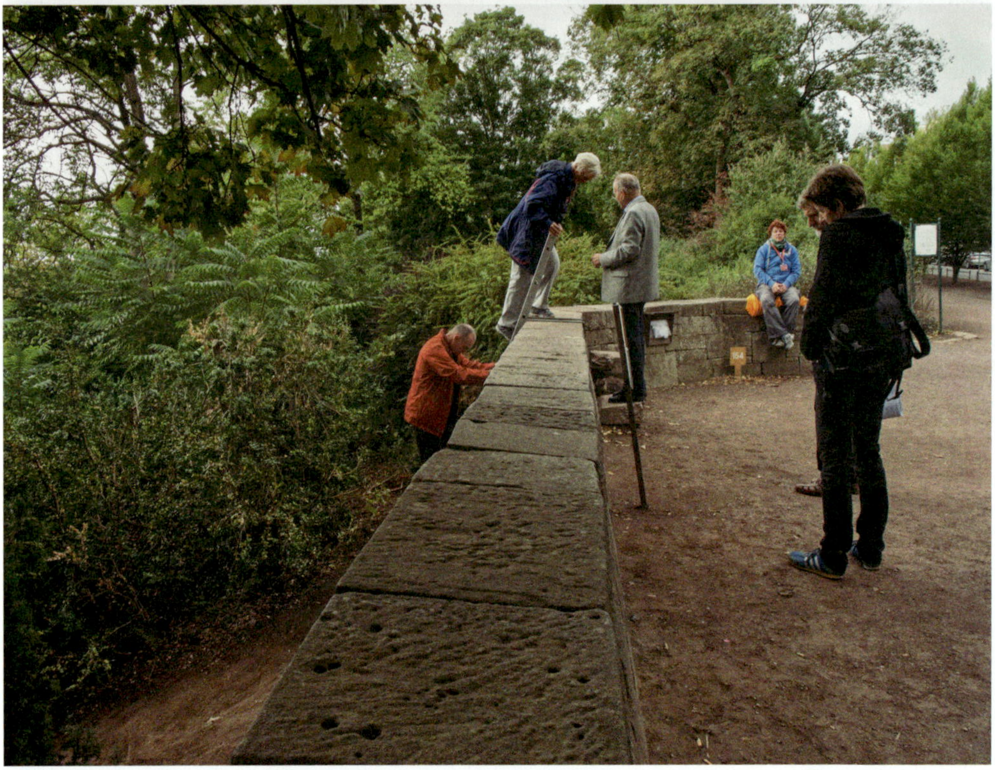

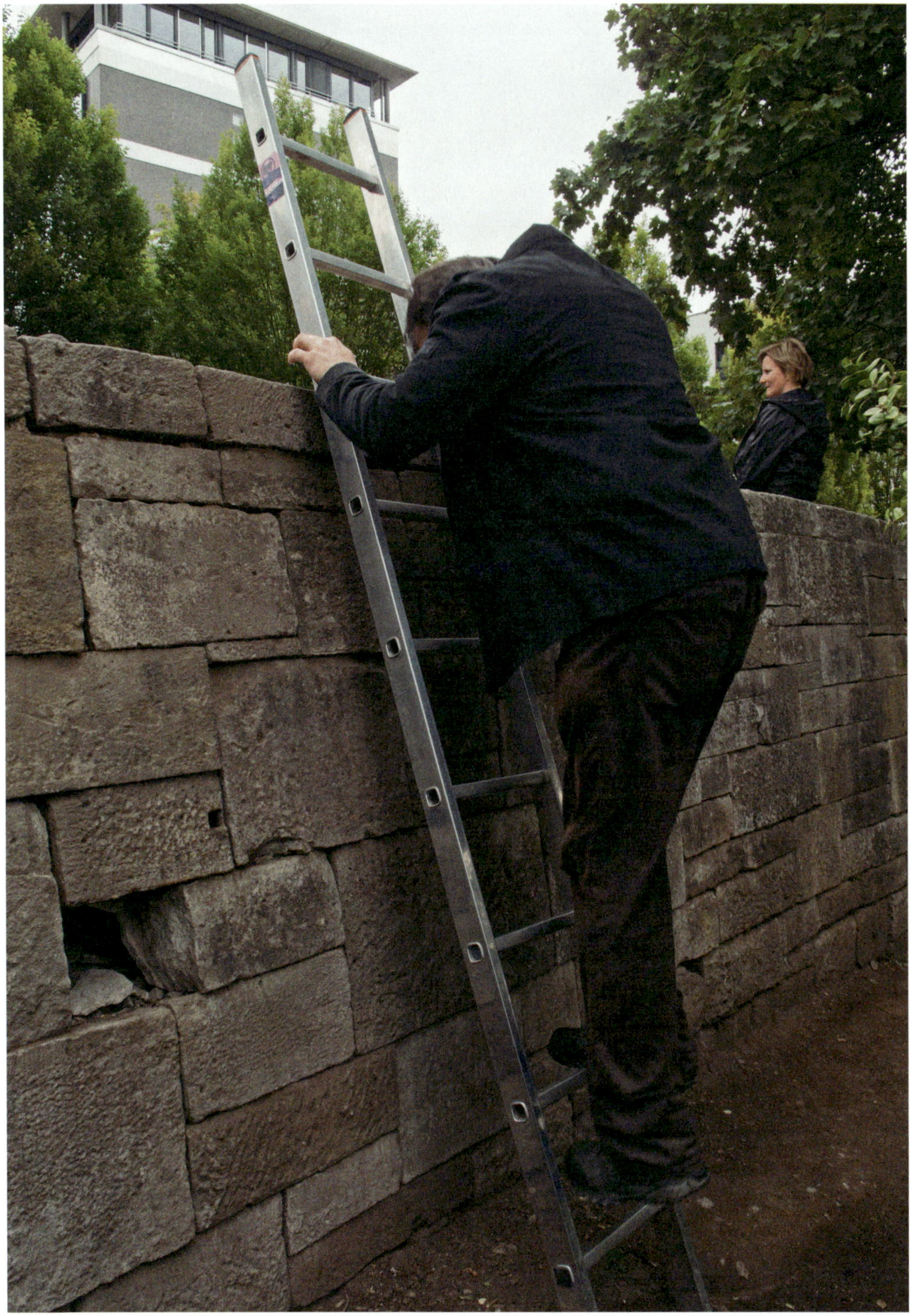

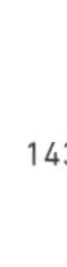

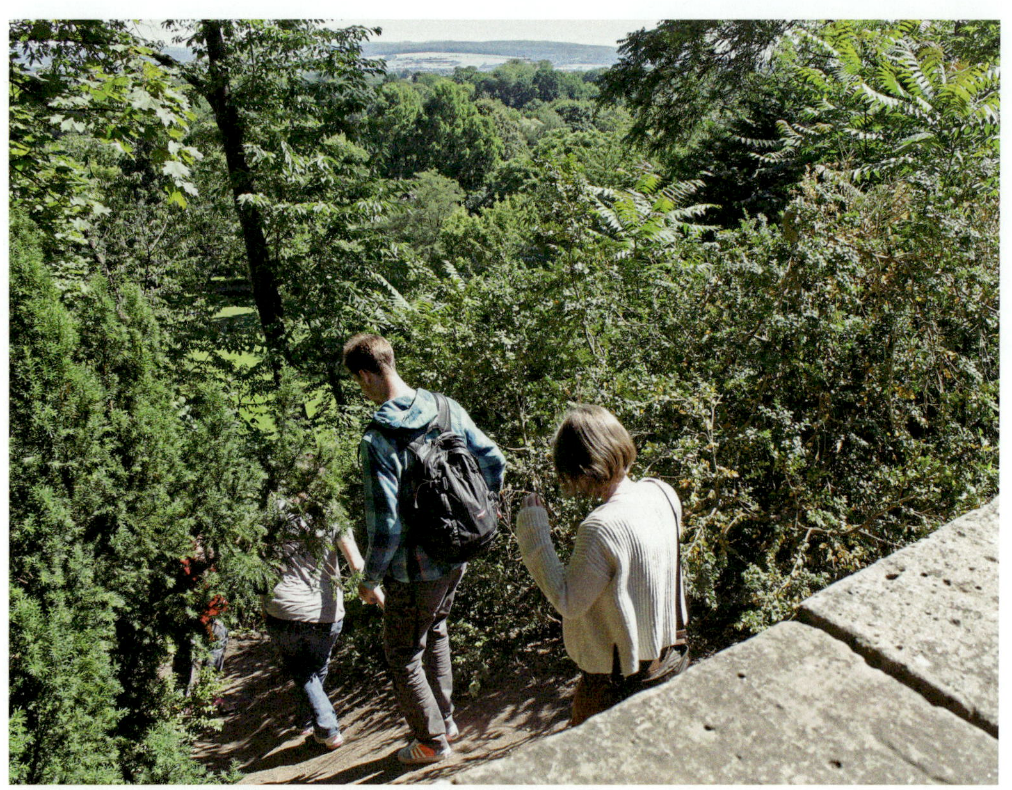

144

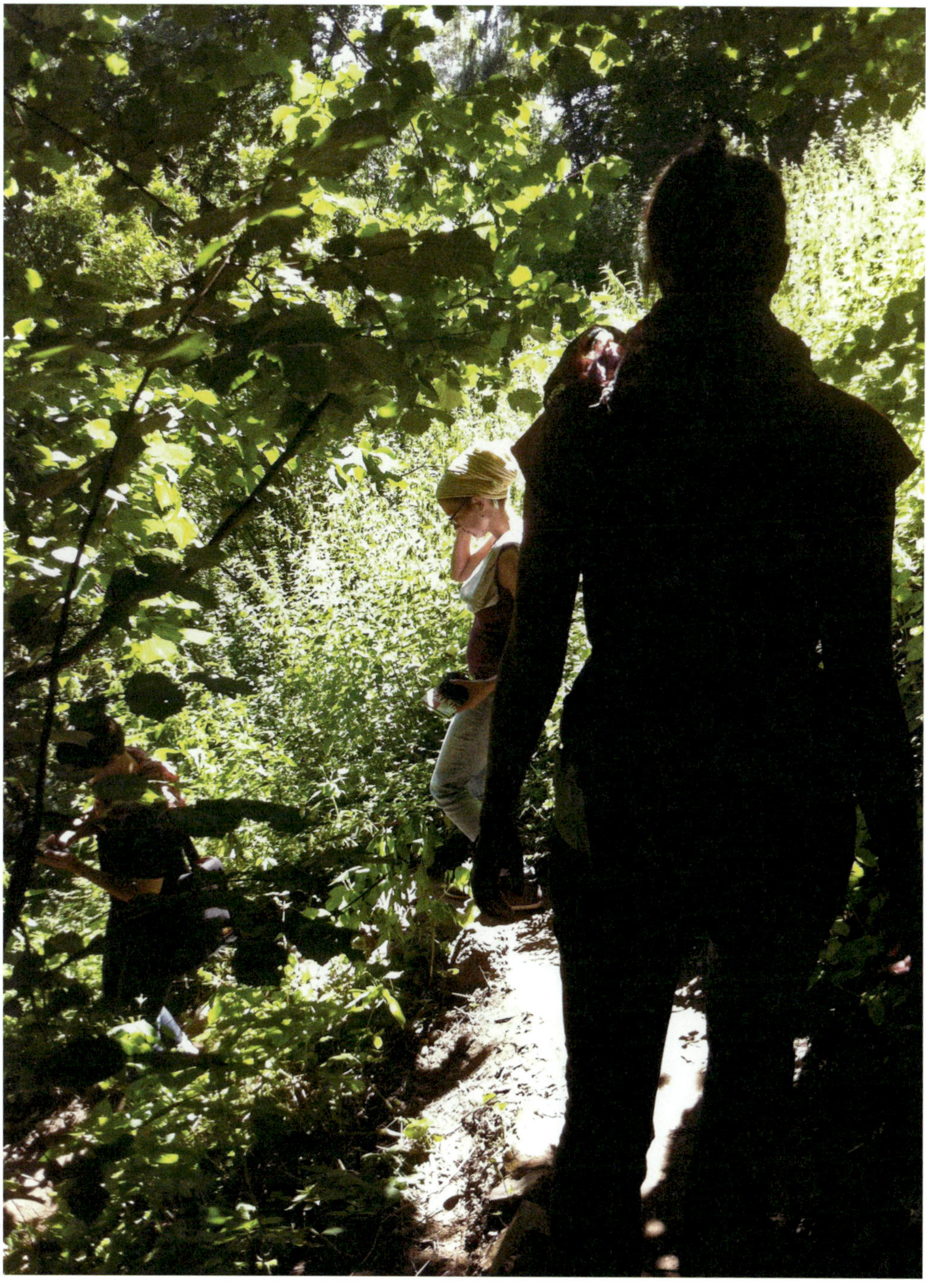

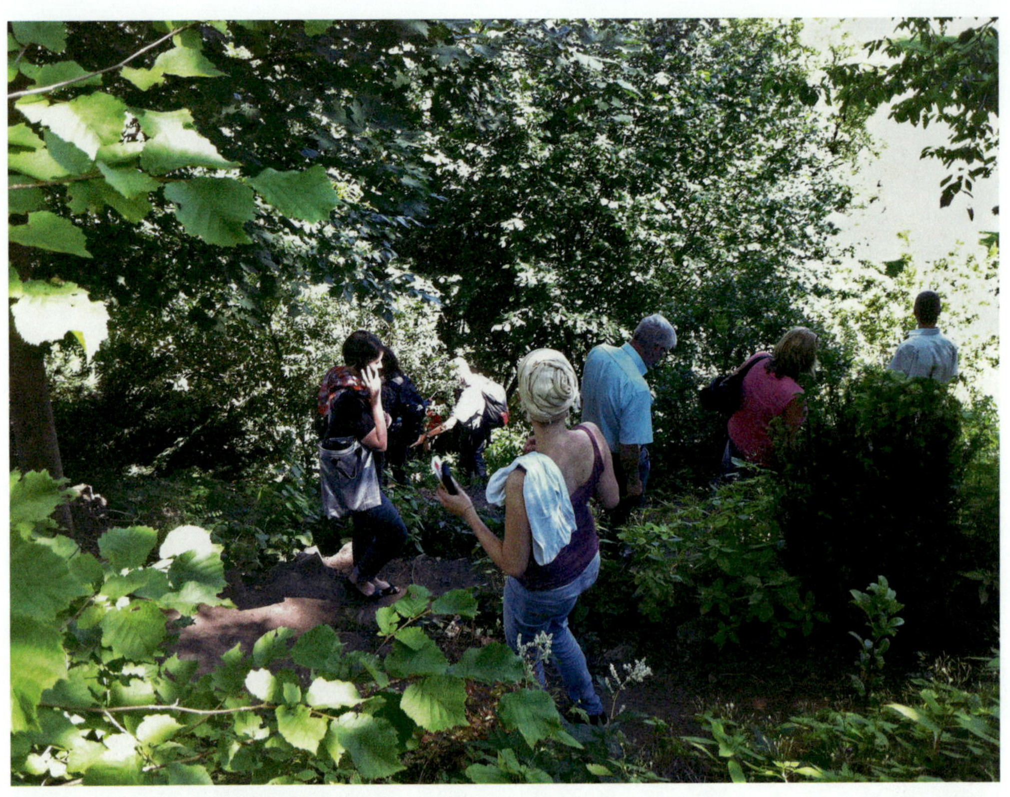

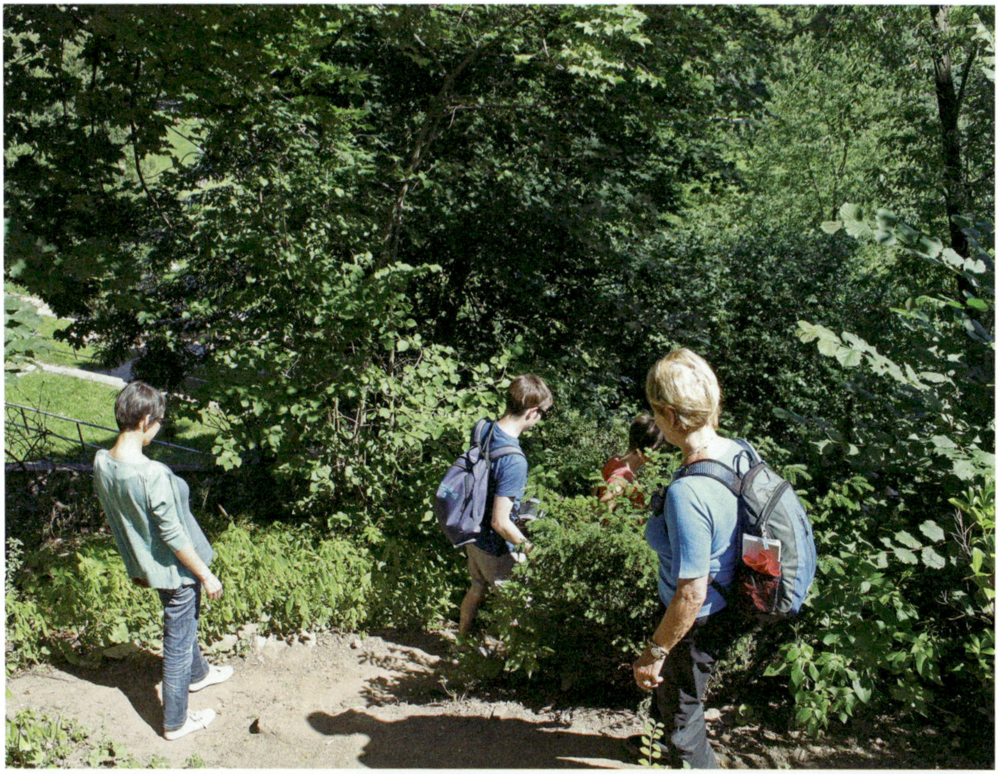

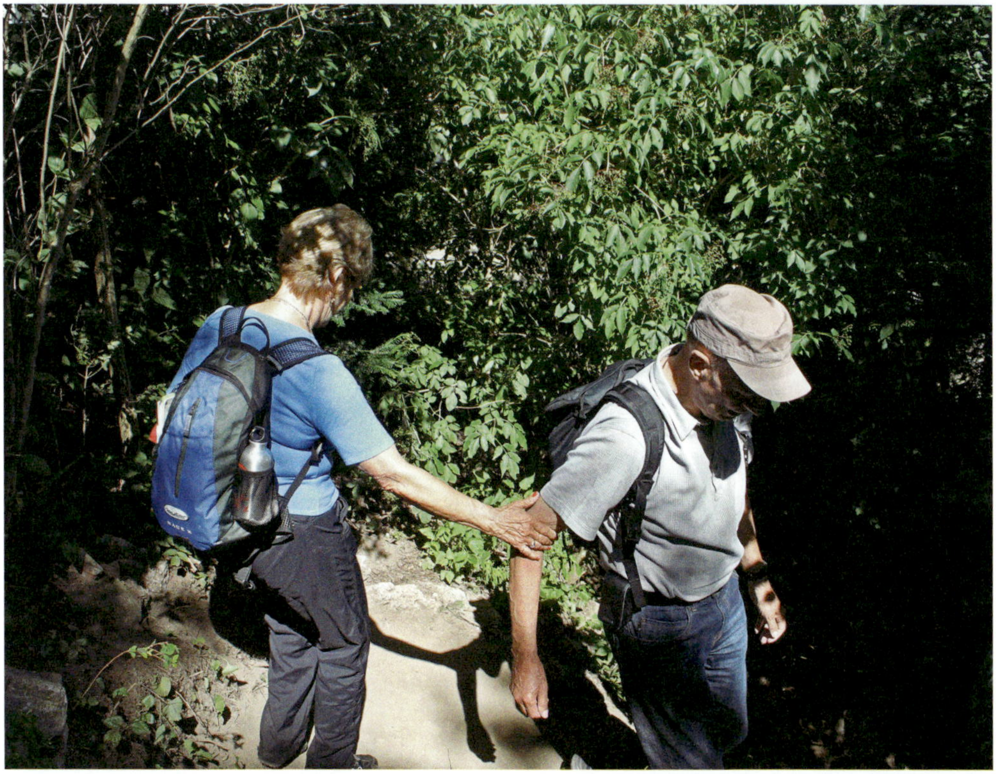

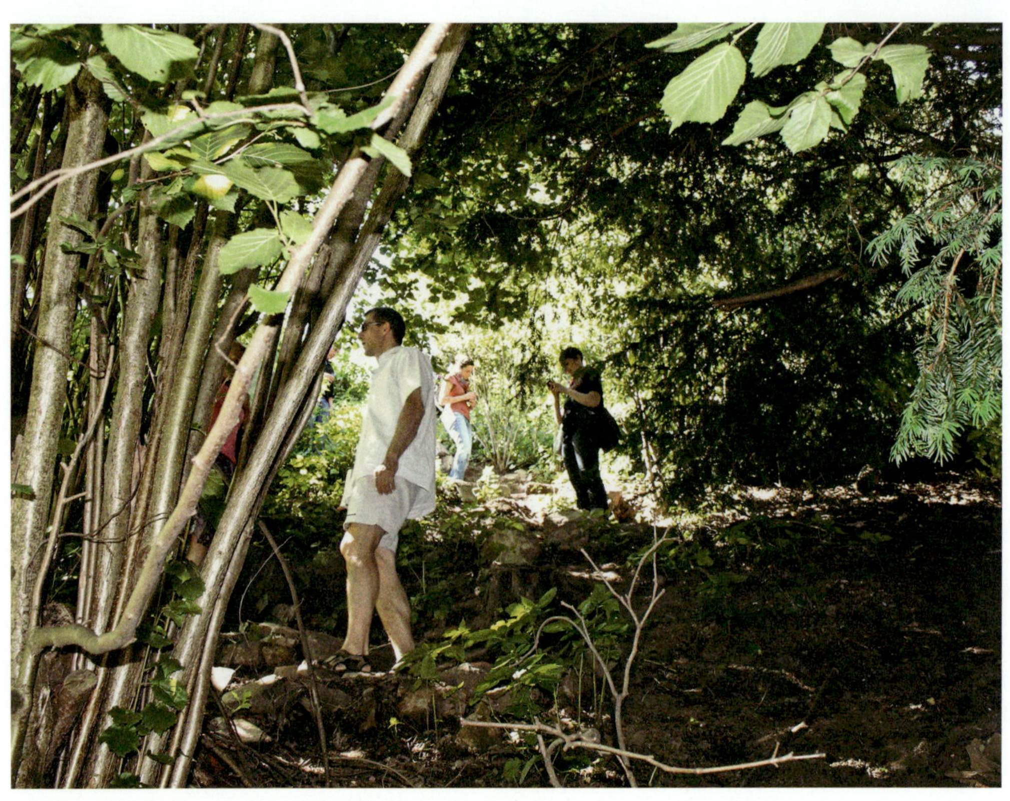

148

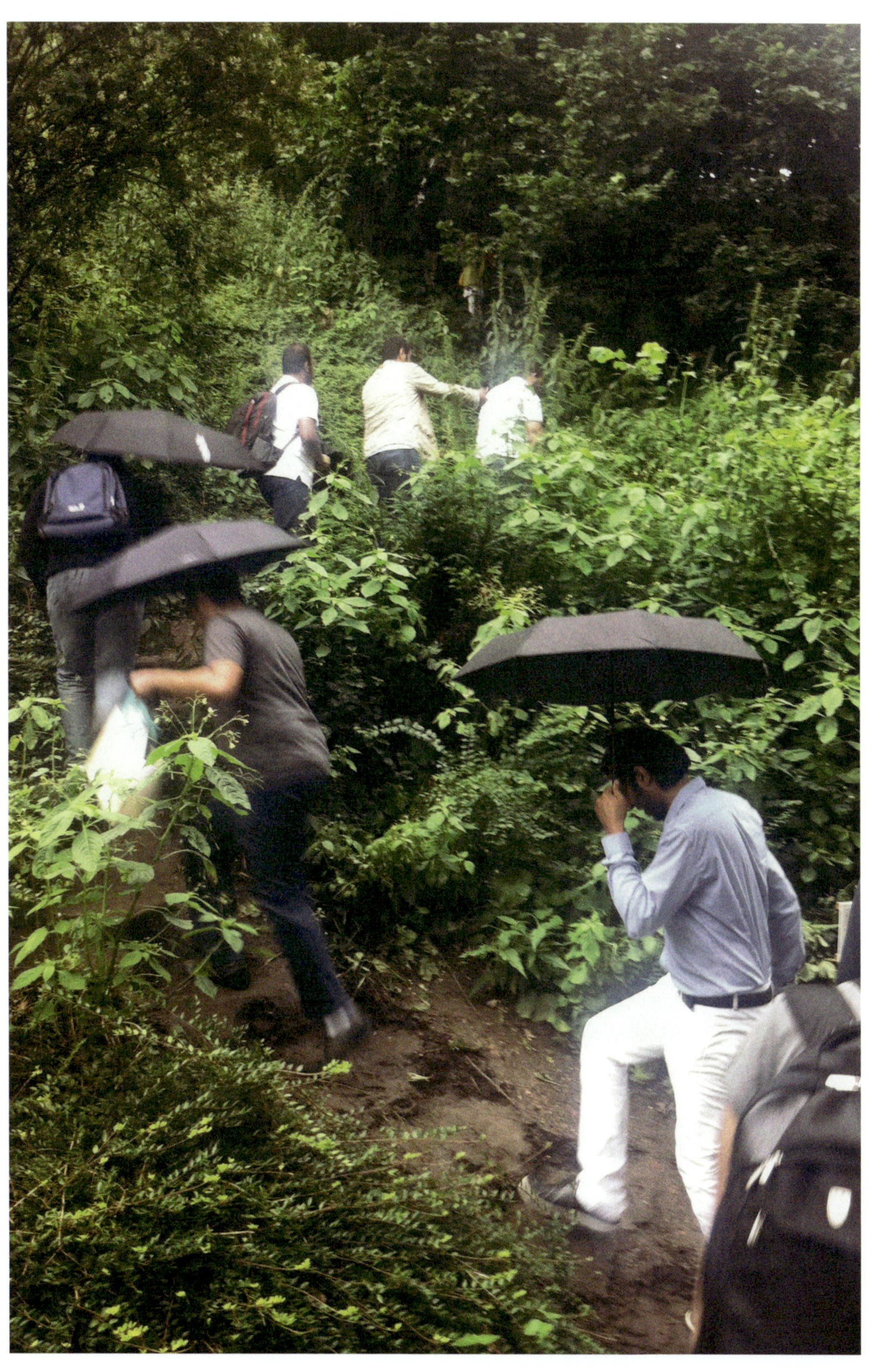

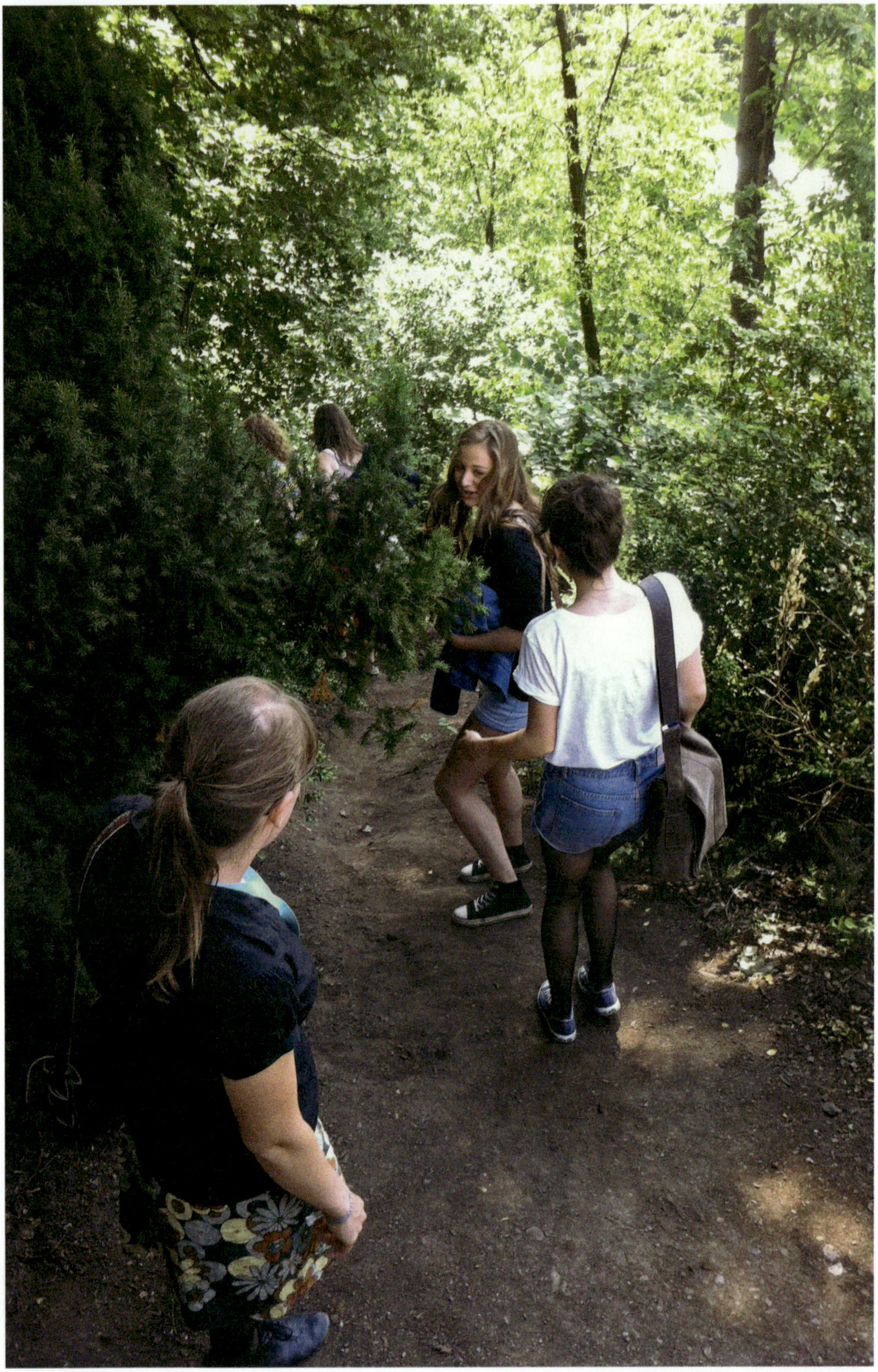

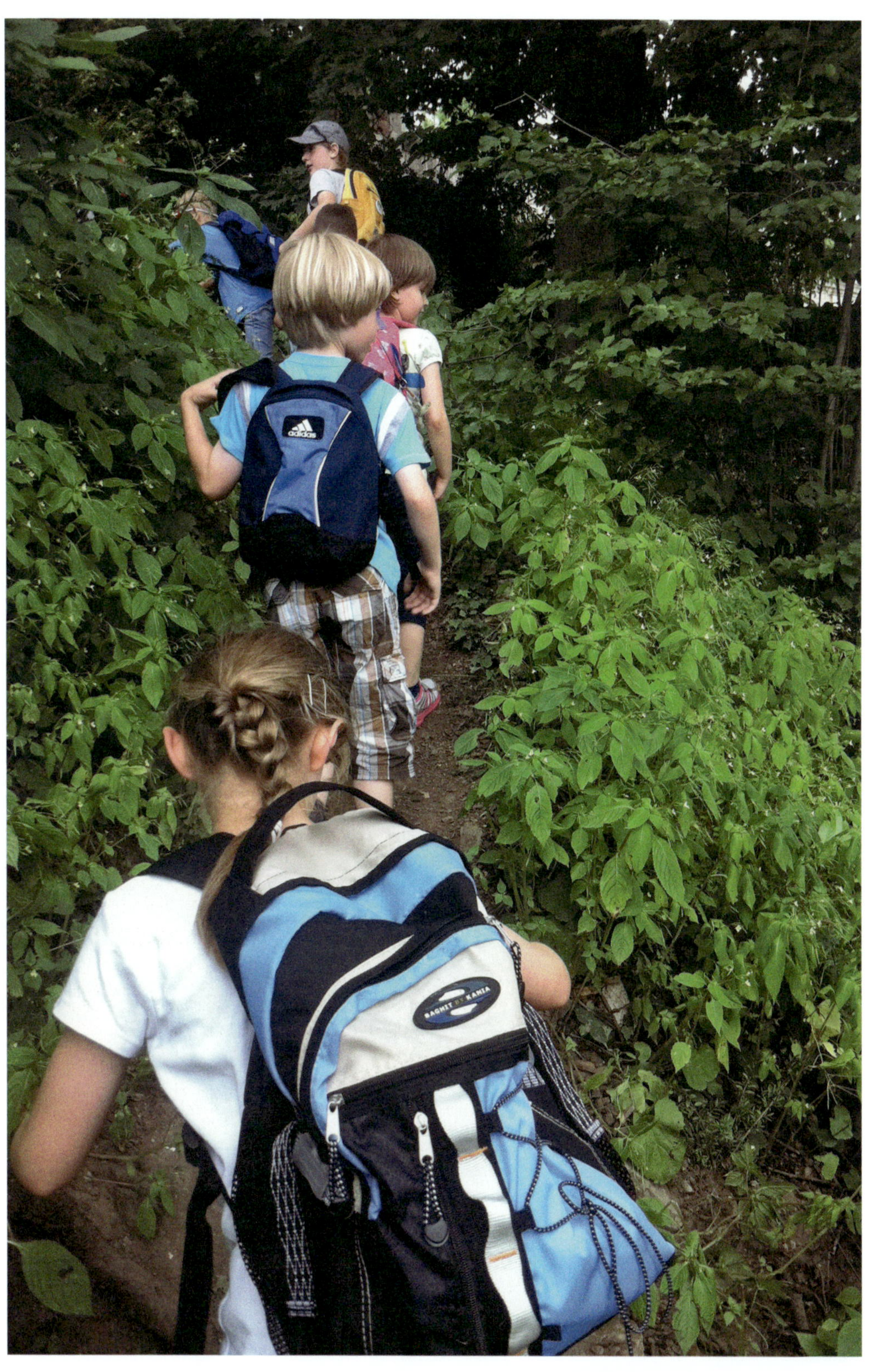

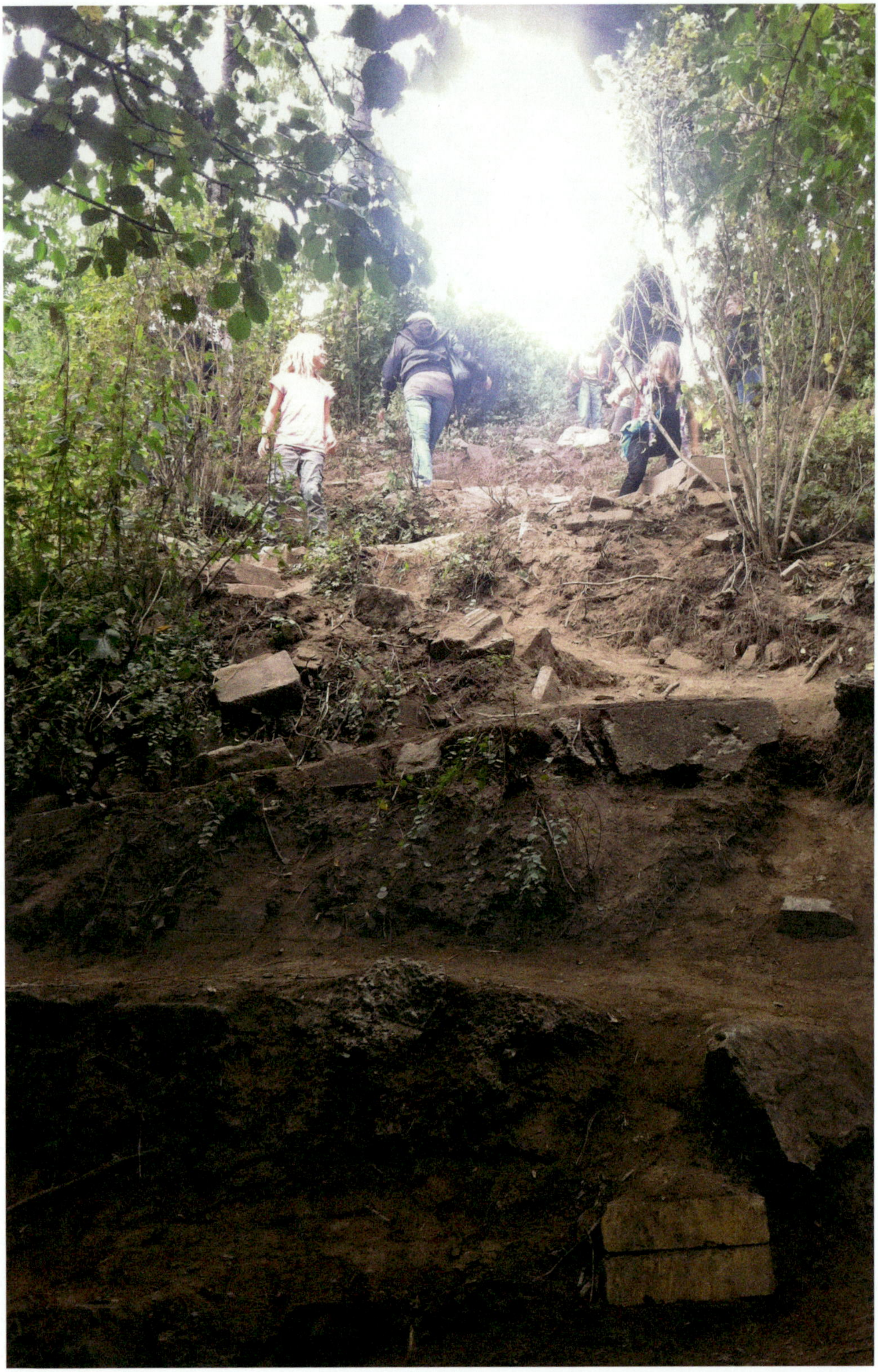

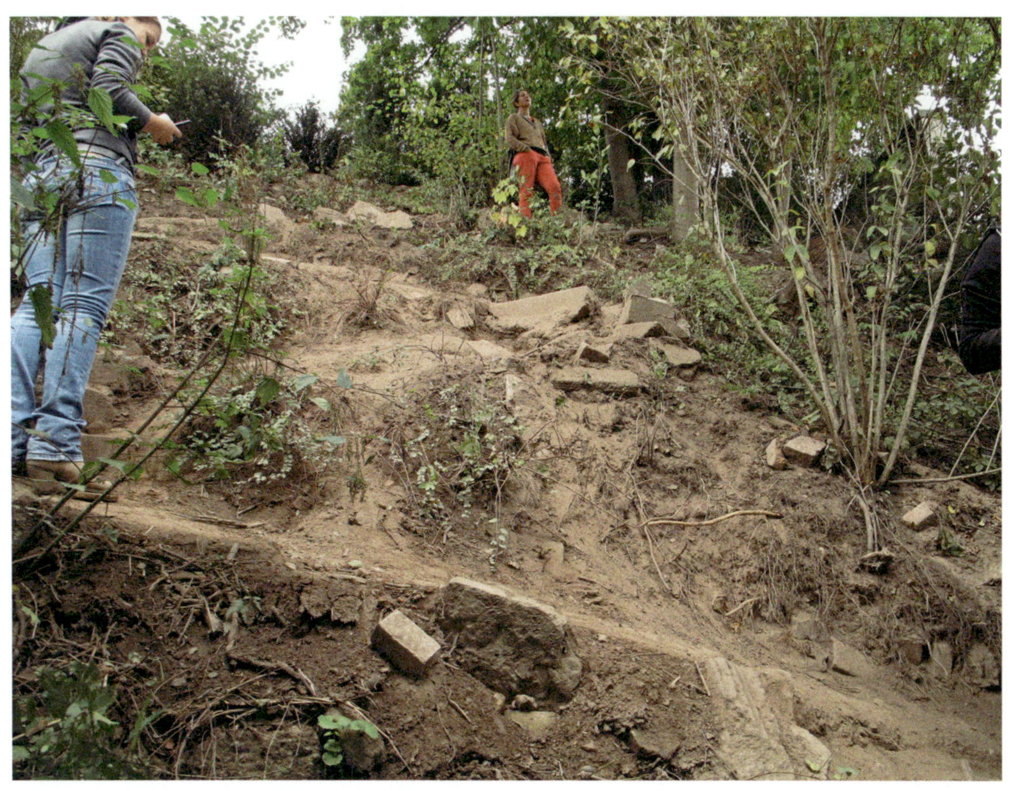

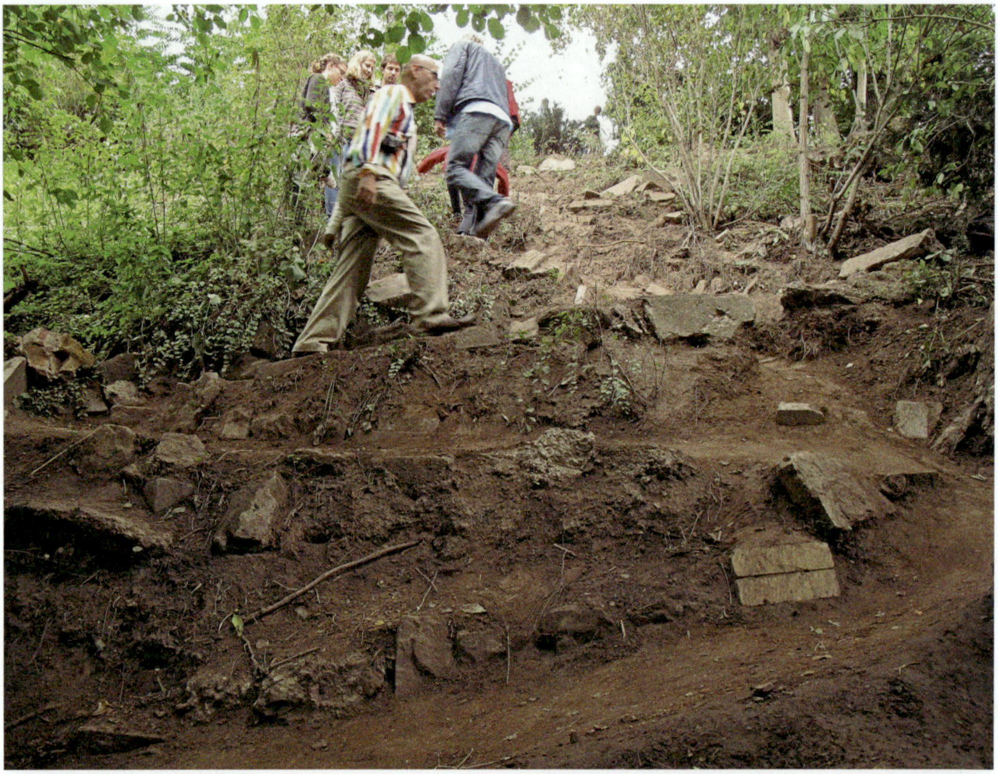

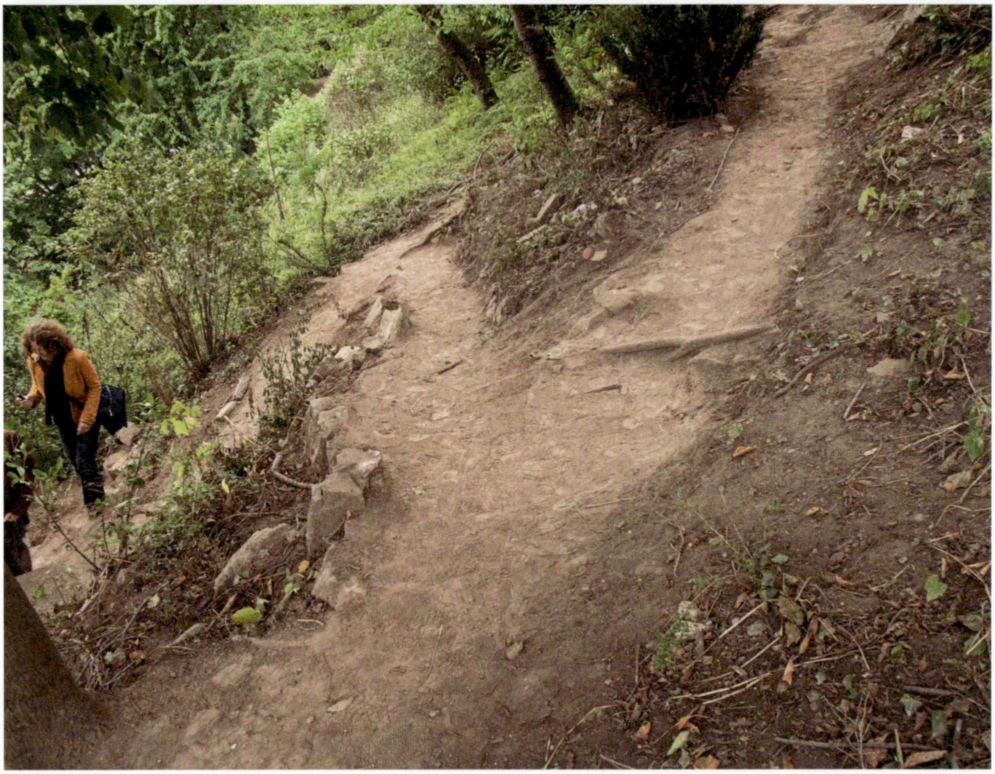

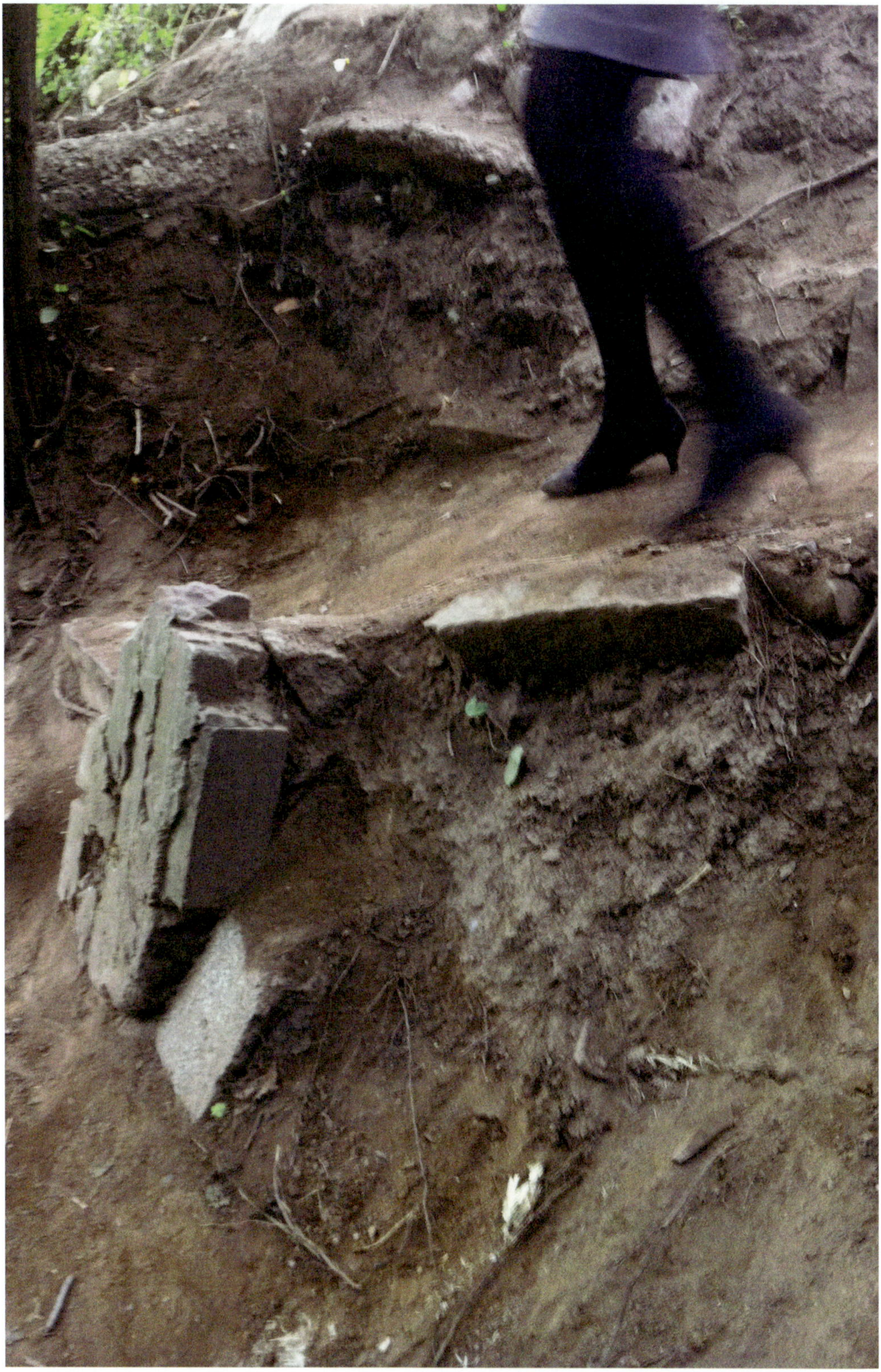

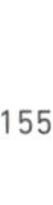

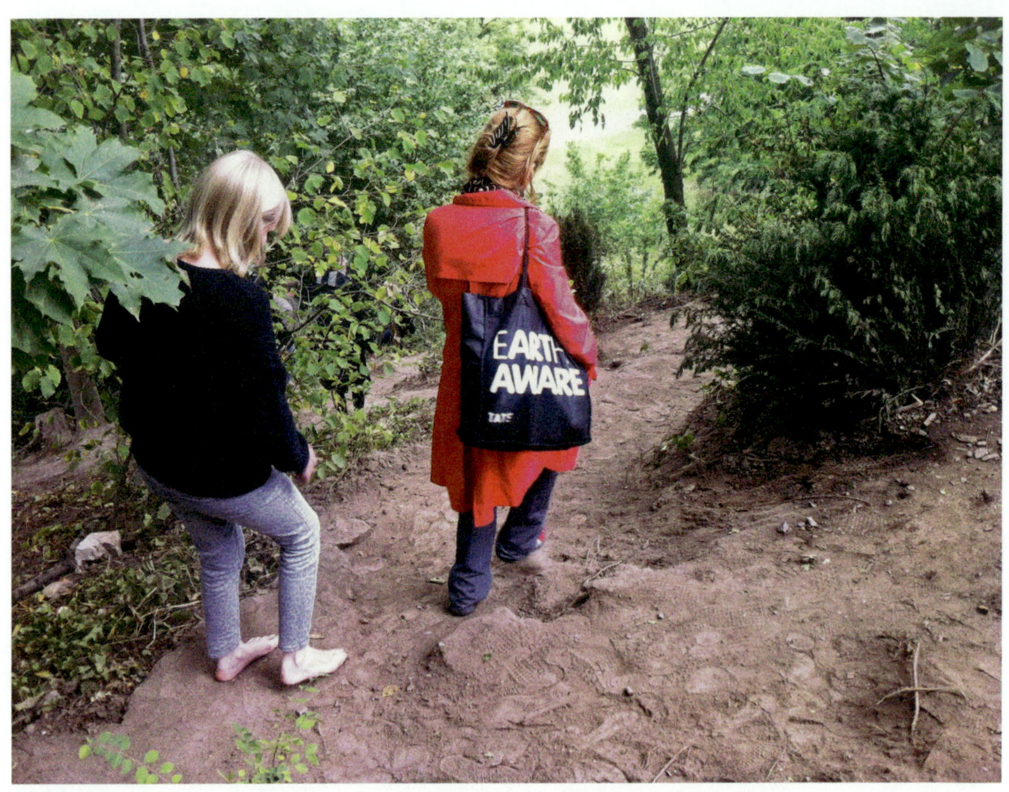

EARTH
AWARE
TATE

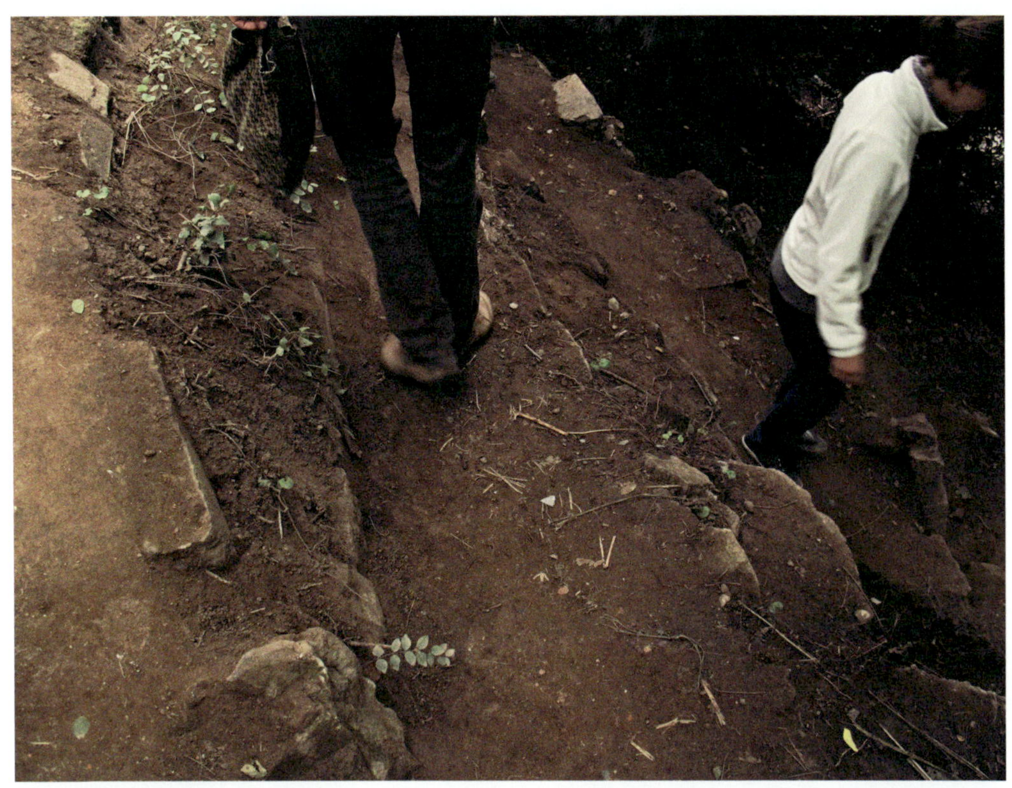

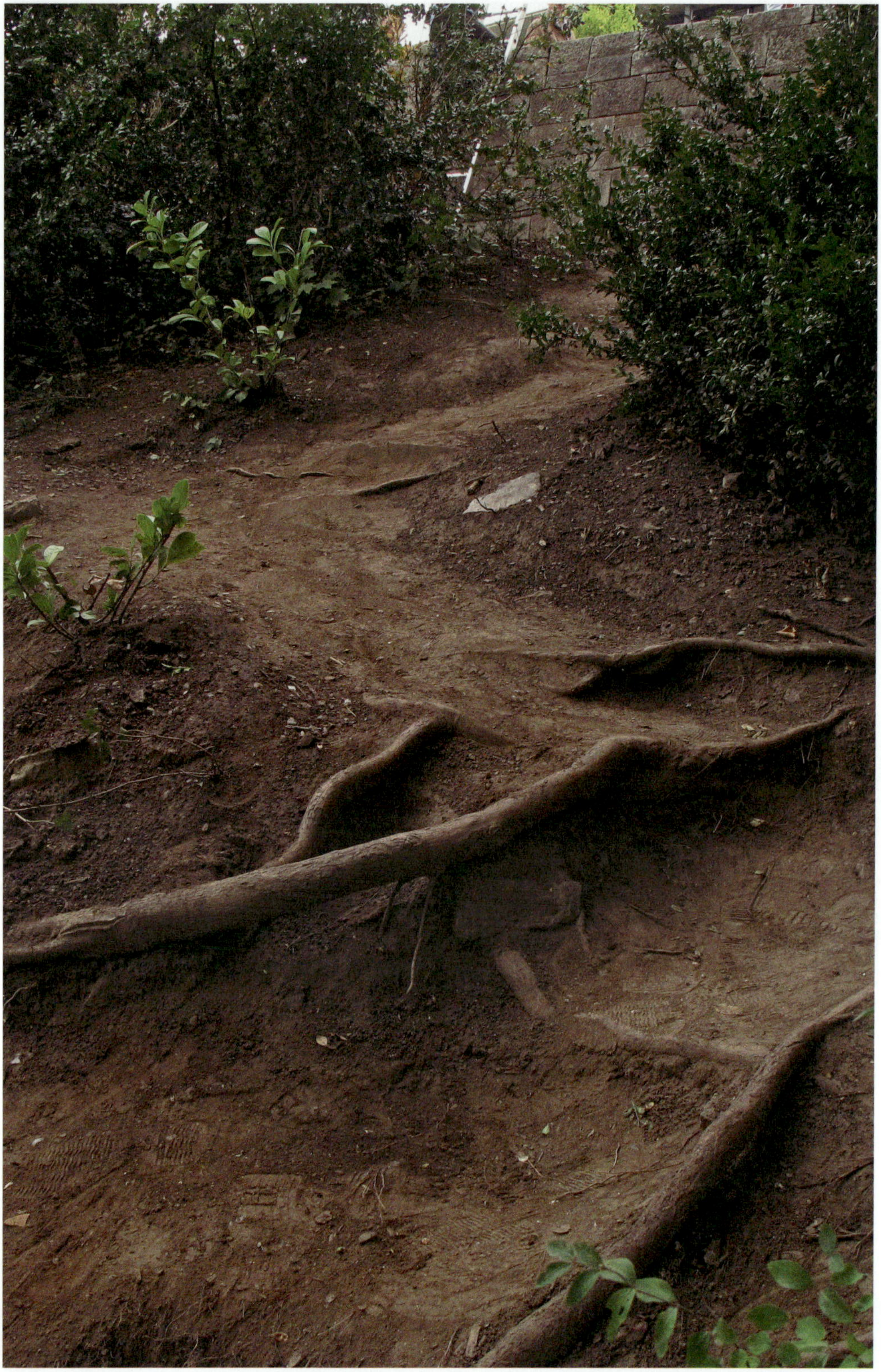

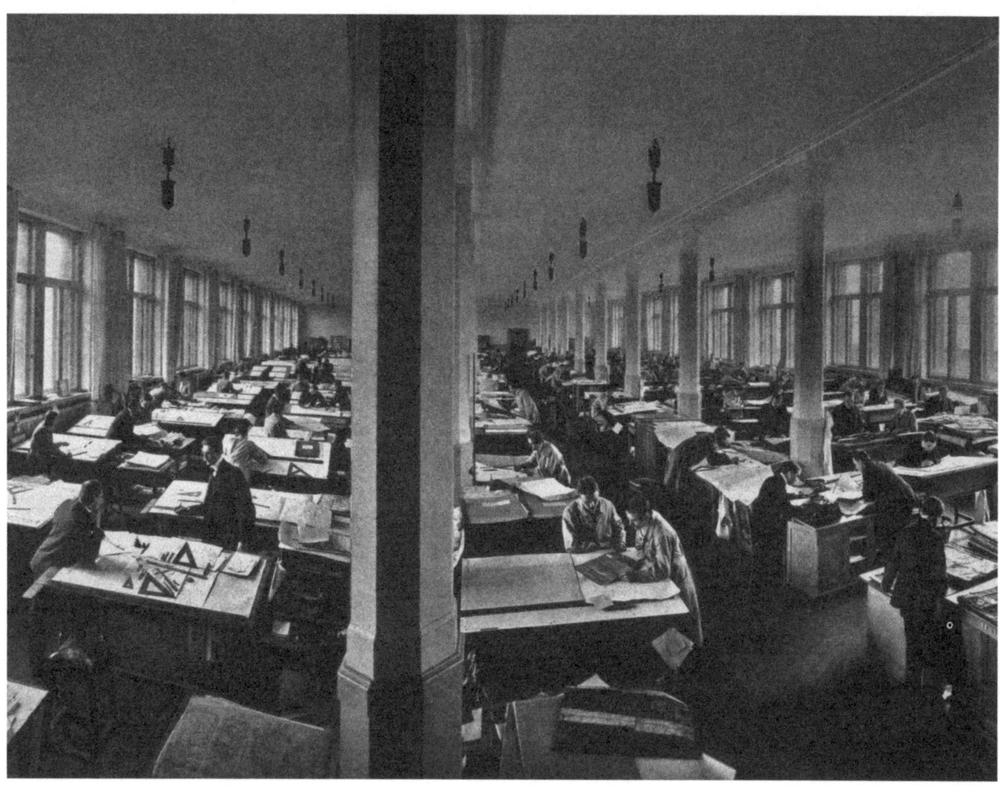

IMAGES FROM THE HENSCHEL PLANT KASSEL (DATE UNKNOWN).
Administration building - drawing office for locomotives
Next pages: Metall cutting factory, workshop for armature production, file forging factory.
[SOURCE: HENSCHEL-MUSEUM, KASSEL. REPRODUCTION: POLA SIEVERDING]

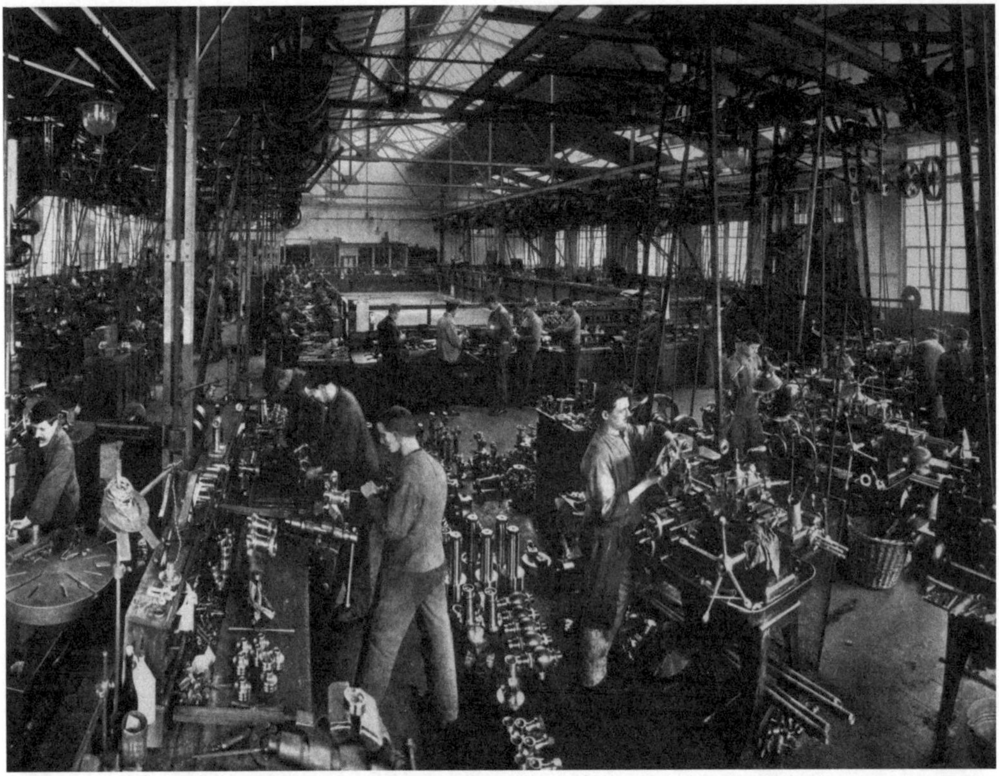

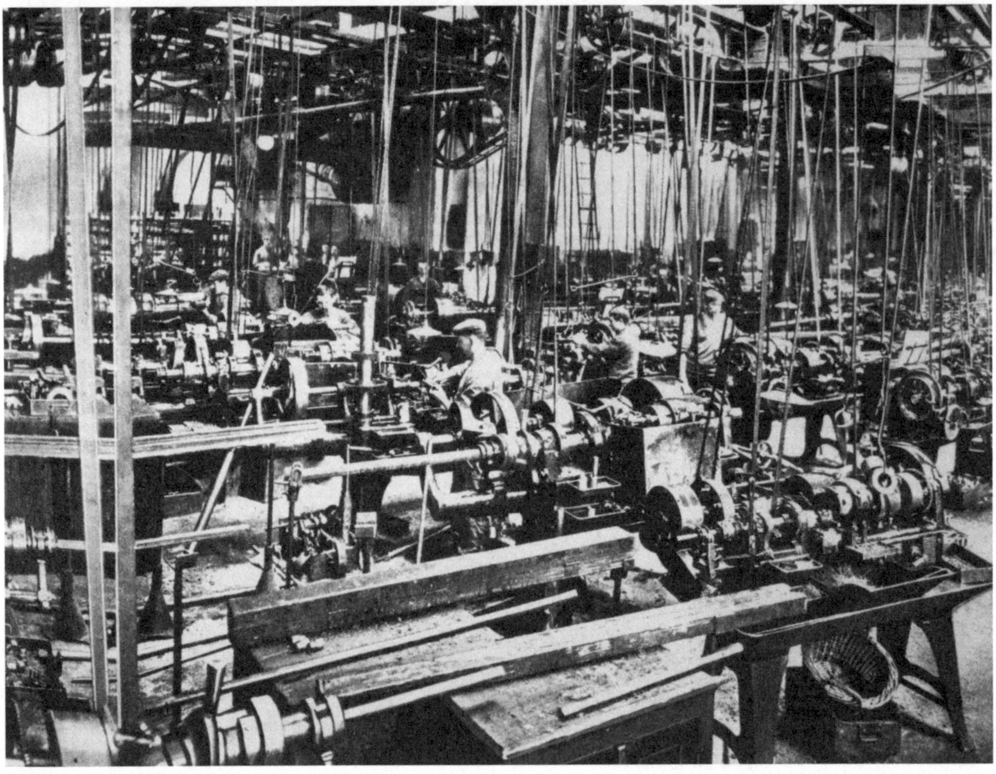

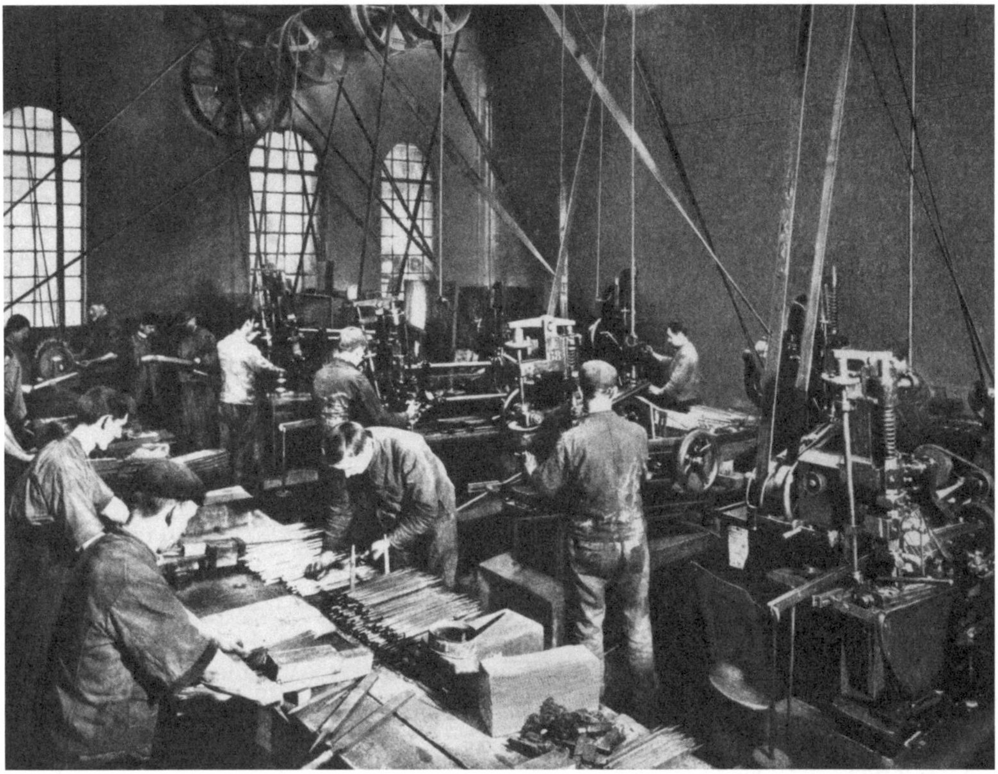

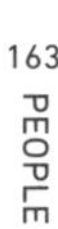

One day while we're busy laying the trail, an older gentleman peeps over the wall and says "If you find something like gold, it belongs to me!" He laughs. As it turns out, his name is Mr. Düsterdieck and he was part of the team of laborers working here in 1953 when the Auehang was extended using rubble.

NATASCHA SADR HAGHIGHIAN ‣ What material is this slope made of?

MR. DÜSTERDIECK ‹ Debris. They bombed Kassel in 1943, and afterwards the debris was cleared from the streets and unloaded here with tipper wagons.

‣ And how do you know this?

‹ Because I was unemployed at the time, and the unemployment agency hired us to do it. That was public relief work. So we were required to work, otherwise we would end up not getting our unemployment benefits. At the beginning we were somewhat grumbly, but afterwards, honestly, the work turned out to be fun.
We were always three men and one wagon, and any pieces of wire or iron that we saw got dug up pretty fast. Things were collected, and starting at four in the evening, the scrap dealers came and bought the stuff from us. They were actually not supposed to come before four o'clock, but they were usually already standing around by noon—not one, but ten, twenty scrap dealers who bought the metal off us.
Back then, sheet metal was worth more than iron is today. And copper could bring in 6.50 or 7.50 Deutschmarks, which was tons of money for one day's work. Each of us went home in the evening with anywhere from forty to fifty Deutschmarks.

‣ On top of your wages?

‹ Yes.

‣ When was that approximately?

‹ That was maybe two years before the first Documenta.
Initially we just worked with shovels and picks and tossed the rubble manually.
After that, when the distances were longer, we got tipper wagons. Railways
were laid for the wagons, and then we loaded them up, worked a bit more,
and then dumped them out.

‣ Where did the debris come from?

‹ From here in Kassel. It all came from the city.

‣ And it was still lying around from 1943 until 1953?

‹ Yes, and then they considered doing the horticultural show here.

‣ How many people were you all together, more or less?

‹ We were two companies. Our company was from Hamburg and Polier was
from Wolfhammer, and down on the slope was a company from Halershausen,
a nursery for plants, and [laughs] they weren't allowed to sell anything. They
said, "You can sell stuff, and we can't . . .". Which is why they worked as slow
as they did. And we guys were up here grinding away, and why? Because it
was our money!

‣ Could you describe again more specifically all the stuff that was in the
rubble?

‹ All of it?! Sheet metal, iron, copper, brass, and we found a lot of jewelry, too
. . . but there was nobody buying gold back then. Up at the top of the Freiheit,
there was a Jewish meeting place, and we sold it to them. There was money
and cigarettes there, too. And the cigarettes were sold again to someone else,
so things were going back and forth the whole time.

‣ So apart from stone, masonry, and bricks, there was a lot of metal in the rubble.

‹ Lots and lots and lots. Up here on the corner of Neue Galerie, where we
were, we even found a wreath made of pewter. We had to watch out that
they didn't swindle us out of that piece.

‣ How many hours a day did you work there?

‹ From early morning until about 4:30 or 5 PM.

‣ How long did these jobs last?

‹ They went on for weeks. We worked from springtime until autumn. In autumn, after we were pretty much finished, came the laying out of the gardens, planting the bushes and trees.

‣ Then soil was dumped out onto the surface?

‹ No. It was all good soil. The old loam houses here in Kassel were often, indeed, made of loam, and there was also mortar and sand.
There were about a hundred men up here. There were fewer people down below, but there was less acreage, too.
Yes, in the early morning the wagon came up, the beer wagon, with a truckload of beer. It came every day.

‣ Do you know exactly where this is? [Shows the image Renaturalisation of the Auehang, see page 168]

‹ That's here, the Neue Galerie. And we worked all the way up to this location.

‣ Here's another view. You can see the Ehrenmal and Schöne Aussicht. And you can also see the extent of the destruction.

‹ Yes, Schöne Aussicht was called "Beamtenlaufbahn" before that. The people from the city hall worked here a lot in earlier times, taking breaks here. They always took two or three-hour breaks.

JASPER KETTNER ‣‣ I don't quite understand completely—in 1943 Kassel was bombed, and the entire city was wasted. And not until 1953 did you come to carry the rubble out of the city?

‹ Well, the bomb raids were in October of 1943, and in 1944 people began with the clean-up operations. But they didn't have any automobiles, you see. So things progressed slowly. In the city, they had a bulldozer. And we had to clear rubble away with our own hands and lay the tracks so the wagons could be driven in. Down here, there were batteries too. They contain a lot of lead, which is why we managed to recover quite some material from there. We took everything with us: sheet metal . . . today, nobody takes big pieces of sheet metal anymore.

▸▸ Right now we're standing here on this rim where Schöne Aussicht becomes the Auehang. Where was this rim before? To what extent has it been enlarged through the addition of the debris?

◂ It started here and ran straight up. Like the wall here. There wasn't anything here. The wall wasn't built until later.

▸ Did you live far away from here back then?

◂ No, in Büttenhausen. We drove up here with our bicycles. You see, the cable car from Büttenhausen to Friederichplatz ran you about 20 pfennig back then. That was a lot of money.

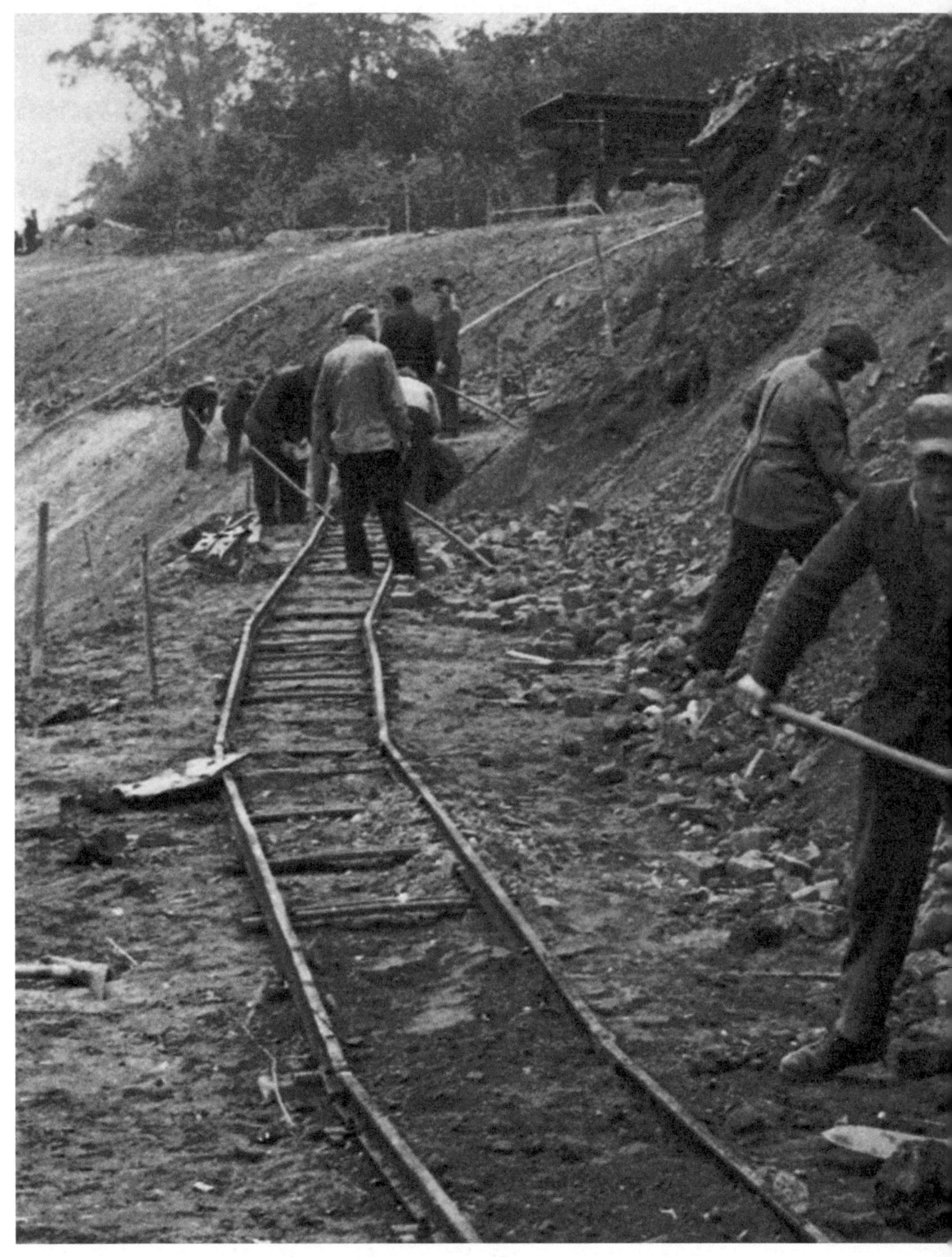

THE RENATURALIZATION OF THE AUEHANG, KASSEL, 1955
Shortly before we lay the trail, Jasper sends me this picture. The caption reads «Renaturalization Work at the Kassel Debris Heap. Construction Work for the German Horticultural Show at the Auehang.»

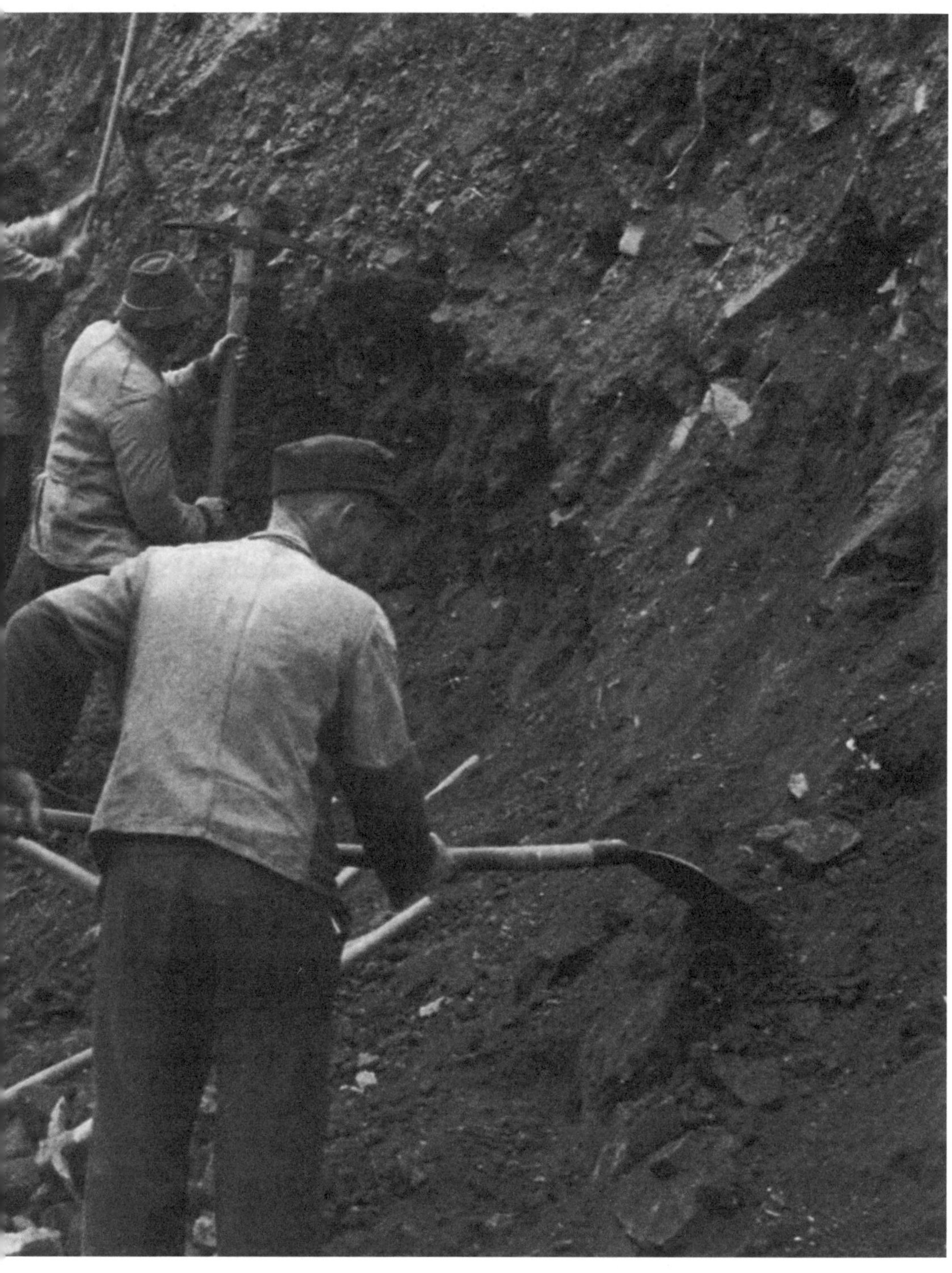

It becomes clear to us that the entire slope is made of debris. Later on we find more images in the city archive and meet Mr. Düsterdieck. Volker Lange brings us rubble from Henschel's Weinberg and Mr. Boßdorf explains to us what kinds of plants are able to grow on debris.

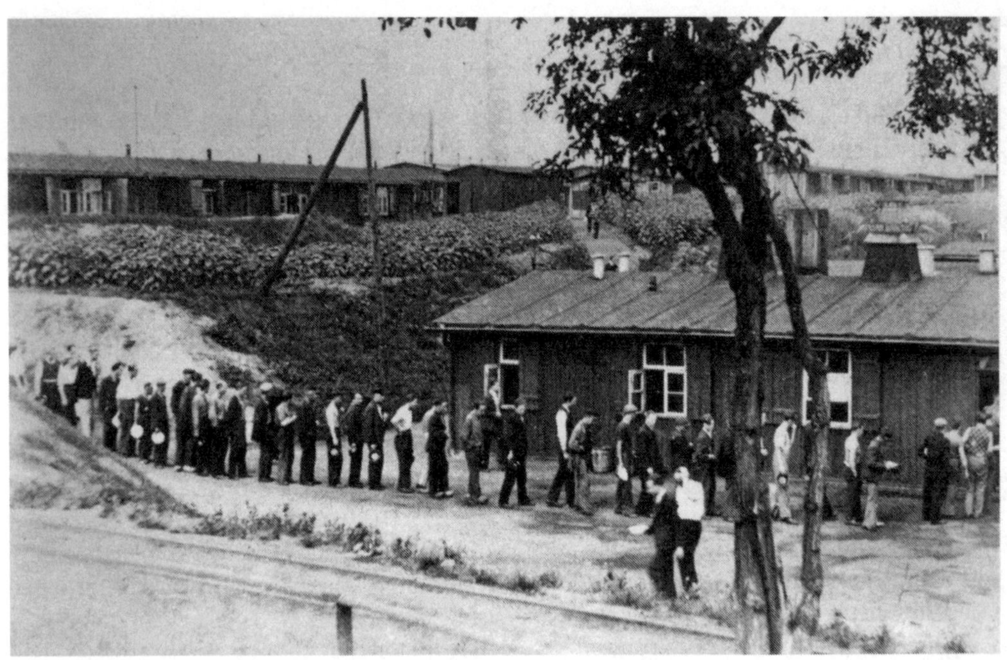

FORCED LABORERS IN FRONT OF THE HENSCHEL CAMP

«I want to see a row ... !» This title was given to this image by Mr. Neuschwander, a former Dutch forced laborer. He secretly took the photograph himself in 1942 at the Henschel Camp in Kassel. The title refers to a command given by the German guards when the foreign forced laborers gathered to wait for their soup.

[PHOTO: PRIVATE. SOURCE: «BREITENAU – ZUR GESCHICHTE EINES NATIONALSOZIALISTISCHEN KONZENTRATIONS- UND ARBEITSERZIEHUNGSLAGERS», GUNNAR RICHTER (EDITOR.), P. 115. REPRODUCTION: POLA SIEVERDING]

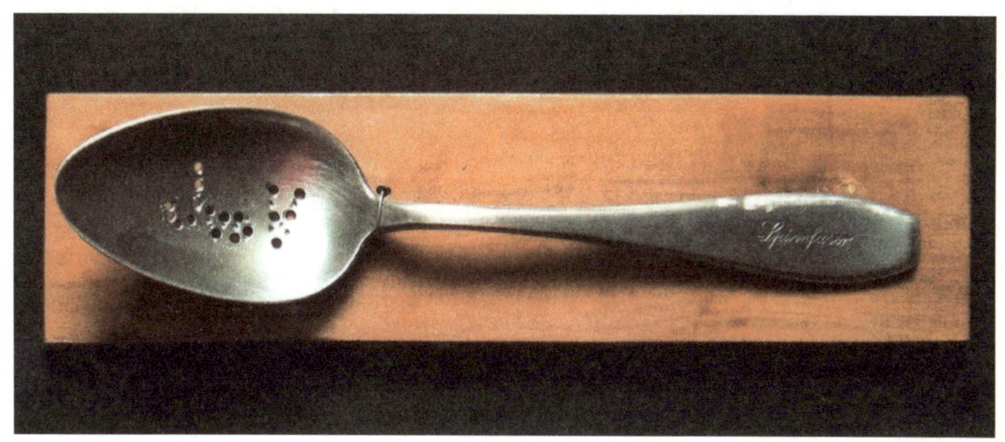

SPOON BELONGING TO JAN VAN DER VLIES

Jan van der Vlies was one of the many Dutch forced laborers who worked and were interned in labor camps in Kassel between 1933 and 1945. He was among those who were transferred from the labor camp to the punishment camp Breitenau for disciplinary reasons. The spoon bears van der Vlies' initials in the form of holes drilled through the metal. This perforation helped both in the recognition of the spoon that belonged to him and in better being able to fish out morsels from the thin soup served in the camp. Today his spoon is exhibited in the Breitenau Memorial.

[SOURCE: «BREITENAU 1933-1945 - BILDER, TEXTE, DOKUMENTE», STEPHAN VON BORSTEL UND DIETFRID KRAUSE-VILMAR. REPRODUCTION: POLA SIEVERDING]

April 2012
Dear Natascha and Pola,

I hope this note finds you both well. We're busy at the Archive, as we always
are when war, misery, and corruption intensify and people can't take it or
fight it anymore and run away. The protests and strikes against the war
mongering in the east and the austerity and border clampdowns in the north
have provoked a goodly number to secede and then they often end up on our
doorsteps, especially when they turn against the craven bankers. Some of
these folks you would know, but there are others new to rebellion and to the
art of not being governed coming from all over now.
In any event, I did have a minute to look into our old records of the deserters
from what's known as World War II or the Second Great European War
(although I don't know why they call it that, since Europe, such as it was, had
been at war with itself and much of the rest of the world for hundreds if not
thousands of years, but that's another matter). The information is sparse but
here's what I can report.

The fragment of a metal spoon that you found in the rubble from the Henschel
estate as you were excavating the trail looks very much like Jan van der
Vlies's spoon. I'm attaching a photo of it. You can see that he's drilled his
initials "JvV" into the spoon, which was a pretty clever way prisoners would
identify their utensils to prevent others from stealing them, and also to make
it a little easier to find something solid to eat in the horrible thin soup they
served at all the work camps, and especially at Breitenau where Jan's spoon
was found.

Jan van der Vlies was a Dutch worker who was captured by the National
Socialists and first sent to Kassel to work as a slave. When exactly he arrived
to the city and what precise work assignments he was given, I don't know.

(If this information is important to you, I know someone I could ask who might know.) It's estimated that there were more than 25,000 foreign workers in Kassel. It's a little confusing because the authorities distinguished among "forced," "foreign," and "guest" workers, but as far as we can tell, they were all unfree and in effect prisoners of war, regardless of whether they were captured as soldiers or captured to be workers. These prisoners of war were used by the city, by large and small companies, by farmers and by individual households to do everything, including domestic service, baking, growing food, building weapons, tanks and roads, sewing uniforms, fixing windows, and maintaining all the prisons and camps in which they were forced to live, of which there were more than 200. Basically, the whole war society and war machine was dependent on the labor of all these captives.

Obviously (and this you already know) the work was brutally hard, and especially in the Henschel armament factories workers were forced to produce weapons under the dual threat of death. First from their National Socialist captors who threatened to kill them if they didn't work and were, in any event, almost starving them to death (remember what happened with the Italians in 1945 at the end of the war?) and then secondly from their liberators, since the Allies were constantly bombing Kassel and all the places where weapons were being made. Even if the conditions had not been quite so deathly, still there would have been a lot of sabotage, open and infrapolitical refusal to work, insubordination, and running away. As it happened, they had a difficult time managing the whole operation and even though they segregated the workers/prisoners by nationality and 'race' to prevent organizing and unity among them (classic prison divide-and-conquer technique), they could not prevent significant resistance from occurring.

We know about the resistance from the overall large number of German soldier deserters who, often prior to taking off, would turn a blind eye to pilfering or hidden weapons or even help civilians escape from custody, or at least look the other way. More directly relevant to your Henschel rubble were the punishment camps set up by Henschel & Son, especially the notorious Möncheberg camp with its isolation cells and escalating punishment levels. And, of course, the fact that 655 men were sent from Kassel to the Arbeitserziehungslager at Breitenau that opened in 1940 and that was attached to the already existing Arbeitshaus from the century before. Breitenau was where the Kassel Gestapo had sent the politicals—the socialists and the communists— in the early 1930s when they had already filled their jails. It was clearly where the most troublesome were sent as a warning to others, including to upstanding German citizens. (People still remembered what happened to Pappenheim.)

And, they transported from B [reitenau] to the big extermination camps and everybody also knew that. Of the 655 workers sent from Kassel to Breitenau only 404 records remain and these show that the vast majority were sent from Henschel. (There appears also to have been quite a bit of organizing or at least individual resistance among the bakers, which is interesting because they were also very active during the Paris Commune.)

As I said, I don't know whether Jan was working for Henschel or not but we can presume that he was part of the contingent of 200 Dutch workers sent to Breitenau, some of whom were later handed over to the police because they weren't responding appropriately to the prison's 'correctional' work regime, which also involved starvation and beatings. The Dutch workers were particularly active as resisters and organizers in the prisoner of war work camps and I heard that the city of Kassel kept special files on them and targeted them for surveillance and persecution. For this reason, we're not sure what happened to Jan, although we hold his memory dear. I have a somewhat blurred photo of some Henschel prisoners lining up to eat, holding their bowls and spoons. In the photo, two men have left the line and are walking out of the frame, towards the viewer. One of the men has his head covered, making it difficult to see his face. I like to think that's Jan starting his escape, dropping his spoon along the way to somewhere else, somewhere safer, somewhere more peaceful.

Who your spoon belonged to and what happened to him, unfortunately I cannot say. Perhaps as committed travelers follow the forks and winding routes on your trail, they will take their questions walking with them and find in that way of walking some of the traces, stories, memories, stray letters, sounds and dreams that constitute the trail's archaeology of knowledge. As always, the Hawthorn Archive embraces you and as always I send you my love.

Avery

PEOPLE

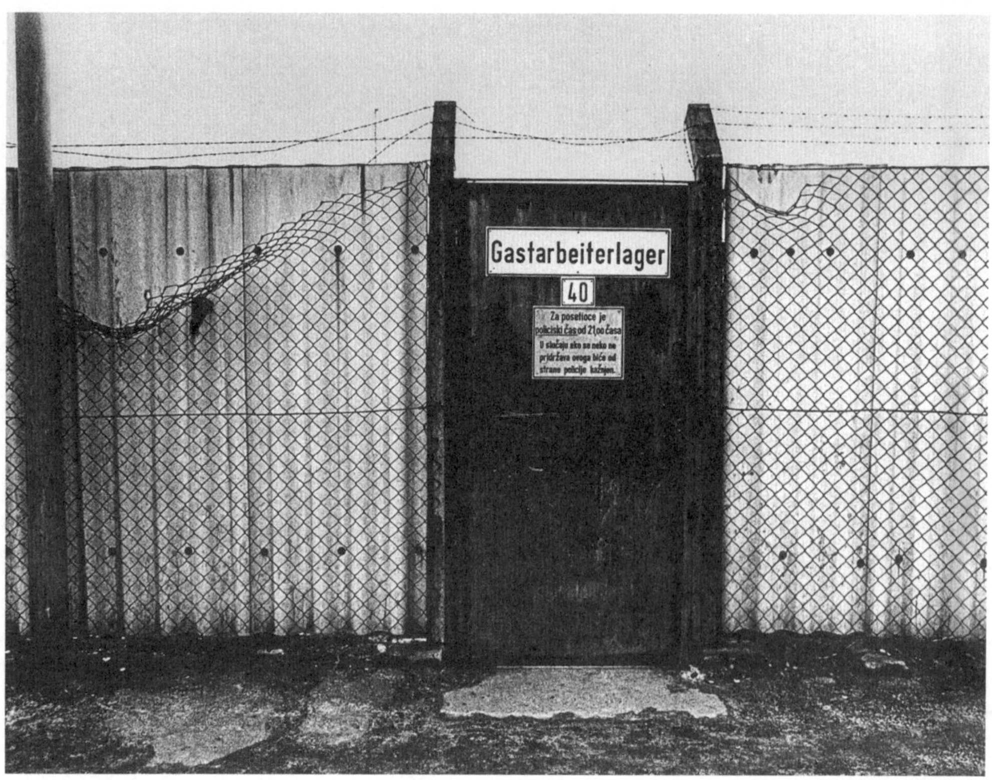

GUEST WORKER CAMP, 1974

Inscription on the door in Serbo-Croat: "Visiting hours end at 21:00 and will be enforced. Those found in violation of this rule are subject to police punishment."

[PHOTO: MANFRED VOLLMER. SOURCE: «FREMDE HEIMAT» AYTAC ERYILMAZ AND MATHILDE JAMIN (EDITORS), RHURLANDMUSEUM ESSEN, 1989. REPRODUCTION: POLA SIEVERDING]

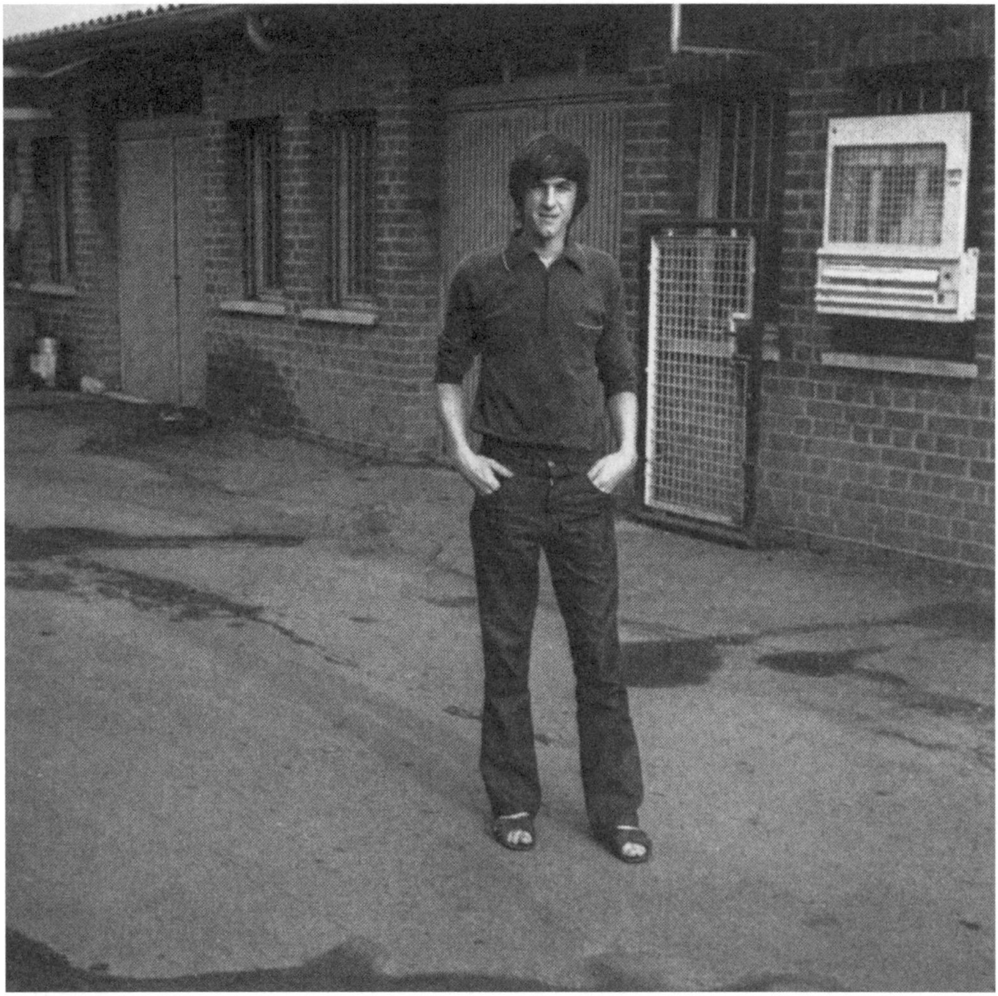

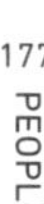

Osman Beganović in front of Henschel's collective worker accomodation at Schenkebier Stanne 2, private photo, 1971

Ayse Güleç is engaged in several projects related to the autonomous organization of migrants. She is director of the educational division of the Schlachthof, a self-determined initiative in Kassel that grew out of a squatting project in the 70s. Ayse assists us in the recording of onomatopoeic animal sounds, read in different languages spoken in Kassel. Over tea, our conversations revolve around the many chapters in the migrational history of Kassel.

HUGUENOTS AND INTEGRATION

NATASCHA SADR HAGHIGHIAN ‣ Migration has written itself into Kassel since long ago in highly diverse ways, inscribed into the city's history and society, even into the cityscape. Back when we laid the trail on the Auehang, we stumbled upon an early chapter of Kassel's migrational history: the Terassengarten, which became a war memorial in the twentieth century, was built in the eighteenth century by Paul du Ry, a Huguenot soldier and engineer who fled from France to Kassel. I was struck by the fact that Landgrave Karl granted asylum on a grand scale to Huguenots at the time, and that he even commissioned Paul du Ry to build an entire urban district for these new inhabitants—the Oberneustadt, or the Huguenottenquartier above Schöne Aussicht. In Kassel the Huguenots were guaranteed religious freedom and the use of their own language, even economic support. Why were they accommodated with such open-heartedness?

AYSE GÜLEÇ ‹ It must have been because during the Thirty Years' War many princedoms were bled dry. There was a shortage of employable men. Many of them died in the war and the land was financially exhausted. In this sense, the Huguenots, who were expelled for their religious affiliation, were welcomed here. Their trades, expertise, and craftsmanship were needed, so there was a demand of sorts, and a usefulness, maybe even an ideology of usability. And we can still see this today in our migrational history. Currently, Germany lacks well-educated, skilled workers, and as a consequence a new law has been passed: Germany now recognizes qualifications belonging to non-EU nationals, migrants in Germany with degrees obtained outside the EU. This wasn't always possible.

To this day, the history of the Huguenots and Landgrave Karl is a very important referential arc when we talk about Kassel and its current situation as a migrational society, and a site of equitable coexistence where people from one hundred and fifty different countries live. With this observation, we want to articulate that a tradition exists, which upholds openness toward other people regardless of their cultural and religious origin. But differences live on, as you mentioned—they were permitted to practice their own religion and speak their own language. The dominant trend in the seventies, eighties and nineties maintained that children of migrant generations ought not to forget their mother tongue. Now, after some time has passed, we are seeing a doctrine which insists that whoever lives here, must speak German. This marks a fundamental change. There are, of course, advocates of bilingualism, but many migrating people have been coming to the realization that the German language is very, very important for living, working, and existing here.

▸ ... and that integration actually means deciding to take on the other identity. The preservation of heterogenous identity is frowned upon; instead you have to become German to be accepted here. That's what I perceive as the undertone of the current concept of integration.

◂ Exactly, and the concept is pared down to language proficiency and not, for instance, to the question of whether one possesses the same rights or not.

FORCED LABORERS AND GASTARBEITER

▸ In the nineteenth century the population of Kassel doubled, and this was linked to industrialization and the intensification of production, which was already happening as early as the nineteenth cetury. But one of the great chapters of this story, as demonstrated by this link, can be read in the production carried out during the Second World War by forced laborers. Ten thousand Kasselers were working in arms manufacture at Henschel, but the demand for war machinery was nonetheless impossible to meet. An additional workforce of twenty thousand was brought in. There were three different categories of worker: forced laborers, foreign workers, and already the first Gastarbeiter [guest workers], who came from friendly countries like Italy. Unlike the Huguenots' role as skilled craftsmen, these workers were doing work they were retrained to do. They were people who had practiced quite different professions before they were displaced to Germany to manufacture tanks in the factories of Henschel and Wegmann.

▸ Can you say something about how these people were housed and what the situation in Kassel was like?

◂ These companies had barrack-like spaces throughout the city. Strangely enough, they were called labor camps, these places where foreign workers and forced laborers were housed. It's horrifying, when you look at the historical chronology, that these camps were utilized later on as housing for other groups of people—the first Gastarbeiter who were recruited after the war, for example. And what's really striking is the shortness of the periods of time separating these different uses. The first recruited Gastarbeiter were housed in these camps only ten years after the forced laborers, and they too worked in factories belonging to Henschel and Wegmann. And this continuity is very, very horrifying. I saw an image in a documentary about the first generation of guest workers in Germany. This image really grabbed my attention, and I can still see it clearly: young, twenty-year-old Italian, Turkish, and Tunisian men who had just arrived at the beginning of the sixties standing in front of a workhouse of sorts—which was once a labor camp—getting their picture taken, and you can even still see the sign that reads "Arbeitslager."

▸ In fact it was already 1955 when the first so-called 'Gastarbeiterverträge' [guest worker treaties] were signed. Italy was the first country, followed by Greece, Turkey, Yugoslavia and Tunisia. And, speaking of chronology, it's perhaps also of interest that in 1955, when the first guest worker treaties were signed, both the first documenta and the first German Horticultural Show took place in Kassel, and the Wirtschaftswunder was starting to really take off. Are there any indications or clues pointing to the existence of a discussion about the almost seamless continuity between forced labor and guest labor in Kassel? Has this caught anyone's eye?

◂ I don't believe so. It has attracted attention in migration research, but I presume that it didn't occur to those who were involved in it at the time.

▸ It's also interesting to imagine the scale of it. Every day forced laborers in groups of two thousand were marched under guard from the labor camp Möncheberg to the factory complexes, half-starved, in torn, ragged clothes,

and in the evening they were marched back. You have to imagine this
happening in a city as small as Kassel, and Möncheberg was just one of
many camps spread out across the entire city. And the forced laborers didn't
only work in arms manufacture.

‹ There were component suppliers too, other factories that the industry was
dependent on.

› Not to mention bakeries and farms that maybe had only one or two foreign
workers, but nevertheless, the whole city had recourse to them. It's of course
attractive to have an additional cheap workforce, which one might not even
be able to afford.

‹ It's really an interesting question whether these people, who lived te
nyears later in these camps, noticed this continuity or not—that forced
laborers once dwelled here. I wonder if they sensed anything, whether or
not something seemed odd to them, whether the euphoria they initially
felt hindered them from seeing the links. The first Gastarbeiter were like
pioneers who didn't know what they were getting into, who cheerfully and
courageously traveled to a new place, not knowing where they would end
up. We're talking about curious, brave, confident people. Surely some of
them must have thought it strange being housed in such big camps. They
must have wondered what might have been there before, but I think these
questions were outweighed by the euphoria that came with a new beginning,
a euphoria that was shared by the city that had recruited them.

› The atmosphere of departure.

‹ The atmosphere of departure and the negation of what happened in those
places . . . people don't talk about this, which is why I think the images
from that time more strongly document the past, revealing the historical
continuitiy.

› It's interesting that quite a lot of images exist of the aftermath of the
bombardment of Kassel, really down to the small details, but there are very
few photographs of the camps. Photographing or making contact with the
forced laborers was forbidden. Propaganda framed the prisoners as wild
rapists, of whom one should steer clear. This was explained by pointing
out how long it had been since these men had been with a woman, as there
weren't any women in the camps.

‹ It was the same thing with the Gastarbeiter.

› Yes, it was a perpetuation of the image of the wild foreigner who couldn't
control his sexual appetites.
I'm always noticing how interesting this temporal analogy to debris is. Kassel
was still 'snowed under' with debris up until the early fifties because the
cleanup lasted so long. And then, in preparation for the German Horticultural
Show, the rubble was dumped over the Auehang, blanketed with earth, and
then flowers—a sea of flowers. Psychologically speaking, this is quite a
strong sign that society is allowing the past to rest, that it is starting afresh.

‹ When you listen to first-hand witnesses, you also notice, however, that
they simply didn't ask the question "what's this place I've ended up in?"
They worked and tried to earn money, and they had fun in their motley
men's groups. For example, people from all over Turkey were coming together,
people who otherwise wouldn't have gotten to know each other.
By the way, the camps also underwent another temporary use. German
minorities who were banished from Czechoslovakia and Poland after the war
were also housed there.

› Expulsion is another issue that is directly linked to migration, leading back
to the cycle of warfare. A city like Kassel produces weapons. These weapons
are deployed to defend Germany's political or economic interests, or, in the
event that they are exported, the interests of other countries. This results in
the expulsion of people, either because they are looking for work, suffering
from political persecution, or fleeing the ravages of war.
At this very moment, all these forms of expulsion are taking place all over
the world. And for one reason or another, some of these people end up in
Kassel, which brings us back to the asylum law.

‹ We were speaking about the Huguenots and how the princedoms were bled
dry. Such a situation reinforces the logic of "war nourishes war." And this
logic applies to postwar Kassel too. The city was destroyed so severely because
the arms industry was located here, which means that Kassel's claim to fame,
namely its economic strength, butressed by the war industry, became the
reason for its destruction. Still, after the war, production was continued, and
today Kassel is still the cutting-edge location for tank production. Starting
in the seventies, after the oil crisis, the first refugees came. In other words,
there was a machinery that made it necessary for people to flee, like the
Kurds in Turkey, for example. Turkey bought tanks from Germany and deployed

them against Kurds; Kurds came to Germany and applied for asylum. The same holds true for many other regions where tanks from Kassel have been deployed. There's a direct link.

RECRUITMENT AND AUSLÄNDERGESETZ [ALIENS ACT]

‣ To add to this, the history of the camp continues in the history of asylum laws. Detention camps exist that regulate to what extent one can leave the facility and what one is allowed to do or not do. In this case, it's the inverse: you can't work.
And then there's the shortage of skilled workers, which was the very reason for granting the Huguenots asylum and welcoming them with open arms: we need engineers to come and build our city. This characterizes the city to this day. The Du Ry family actually designed and built all the landmark buildings in Kassel. In contrast, today we are seeing a rather opaque policy regarding if and when a newcomer, migrant worker, or asylum seeker can have his qualifications recognized in Germany.

‹ So far, migrants have had to go through a depreciation of their professional qualifications, meaning their education or experience was useless and found no recognition here. In the nineties, Germany attempted to recruit foreign workers according to the Green Card model. But nobody wanted to come to Germany. Earlier on, the media had propagated an image—the boat is full, nobody else will be allowed in—and then an invitation was extended once again, but this time only to highly qualified workers, whereupon they realized that nobody at all wanted to come, because Germany was offering such bad conditions. Skilled workers were therefore still sought after for positions that couldn't be filled by German nationals. This led to the German federal government's issuance of a new law as part of the Ausländergesetz instituting the recognition of degrees obtained in foreign countries. This law has been in effect since April 4, 2012. We're assuming that 300,000 persons from non-EU countries will be able to have their associate degrees and university degrees certified and recognized in Germany. This doesn't mean they'll receive a certificate from a German school. They'll simply gain recognition for the education they obtained somewhere else.

‣ That's merely a correction after the fact. It's still based on the principle of rotation while it ignores the question of how people could potentially be welcomed here. The principle that takes effect is the following: now we need

this workforce immediately. They should come and bring their know-how.
But concerning what this means in terms of social and human standards,
there is still a loophole in people's heads: they don't belong here and actually
they shouldn't stay very long at all. As soon as these people are no longer
required, we ask that they leave—because they shouldn't take jobs away
from Germans.

‹ The Ausländergesetz itself is an instrument designed to protect the primacy
of German nationals from those who would come from abroad. It means
nothing more. In other words, the Ausländergesetz enables a differentiation—
who belongs and who doesn't—and other laws are added in order to make
the already existing laws more applicable. The ideology of usability has
always had something to do with economic strength, and it deems work a
very important element.

› It seems schizophrenic to recruit people on such a large scale and simultaneously say "you don't belong, and you have no right to demand anything."

‹ The core issue is that any attempt at nation building, any attempt to answer
the question of what national identity is, always leads to an attempt
at homogenizing everything. Will multilingualism be fostered or should
everyone speak the same language? And how will the rights of nationals be
protected from foreigners, and when? Because sometimes it's loosened. And
one can see the ideology of usability within that, strategies of functionality
as well . . .

› . . . both in synch with the market: demand, production, and the exploitation of resources.

KEMAL ALTUN AND HALIT YOZGAT

‹ Asylum seekers come into play here in a different manner. We just talked
about how Kassel kept producing weapons after the war. In the seventies
asylum seekers started coming to Kassel. This was surely an undesirable
development—the Anwerbestopp [ban on asylum] came already in 1973.
The asylum seekers were fleeing military coups in different countries
where—again—tanks from Kassel were being deployed, after which various
options were explored for regulating or totally pulling the plug on the
asylum application process. Germany had a very unique asylum law, a big

ornament of democracy for postwar Germany. It was tightened more and more, just to be repealed in 1993. Since then, approximately 3.9 percent of all applicants are in fact granted asylum. This means that it's unbelievably difficult to receive asylum here as a victim of political persecution, even as a victim of torture. A well-known example is Kemal Altun, after whom a square in Kassel has been named. It's the square in front of Schlachthof, where I work, and I was part of the initiative to name this square. Kemal Altun came from the Kurdish part of Turkey and applied for asylum in Germany. During his court hearing, he came to the realization that he would be deported, and in the middle of this situation, he chose suicide and jumped from the window.

In Kassel there's another initiative aiming to name a square after Halit Yozgat. Halit Yozgat was murdered here in Kassel, the ninth victim of the Neo-Nazi group from Zwickau called the NSU. He had an internet cafe on Holländische Strasse and was shot there in April 2006. His parents wanted Holländische Strasse to be named after him. For mainstream society, the renaming was quite arduous, not only formally but also emotionally, and now a compromise has been made. A square at the Hauptfriedhof [main cemetery] will be named after Halit Yozgat. I'm citing these events because it's important to see that these historical loops, recurrences, and continuities claim victims.

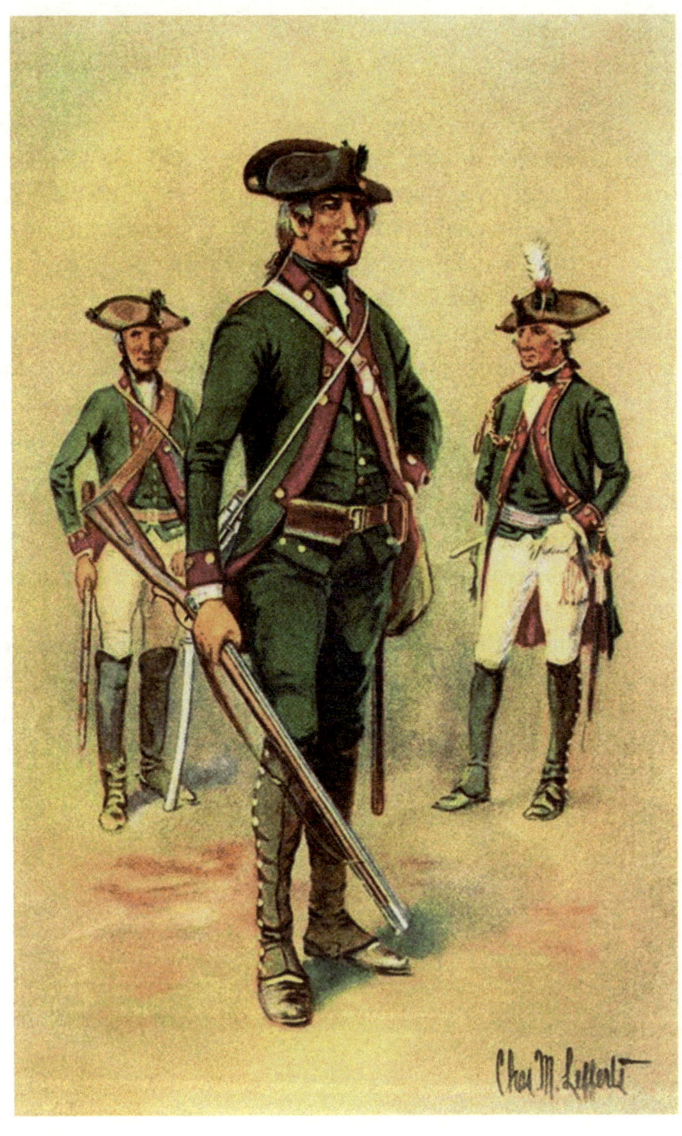

MILITARY POLICE OFFICERS OF THE INFANTRY, LANDGRAFSCHAFT HESSEN-KASSEL, 1776-1783

At exactly the same time Georg Christian Carl Henschel settled in Kassel to cast bells and cannons, Landgrave Friedrich von Hessen-Kassel signed a contract. For the American Revolutionary War, he leased 19,000 soldiers to Great Britain. With the income generated by this soldier trade, the Landgrave financed the establishment of a blooming cultural landscape in Kassel, including not only the construction of the Fridericianum in 1779 and Schloss Wilhelmshöhe in 1786, but also the present-day art collection of Museumslandschaft Kassel. The purpose during recruitment was to enlist as many transient out-of-towners as possible. Riches, gold, and land were promised, but many were attracted to the job by the daily provisions alone. Many were volunteers, although abductions and even drafts did occur. Recruiting officers traveled all over Hesse to remind the sons of farmers and simple craftsmen that they were subject to compulsory military service. In *Intrigue and Love*, Friedrich Schiller thematizes this soldier trade at the beginning of the second act.

[ILLUSTRATION: CHARLES M. LEFFERTS. SOURCE: PUBLIC DOMAIN]

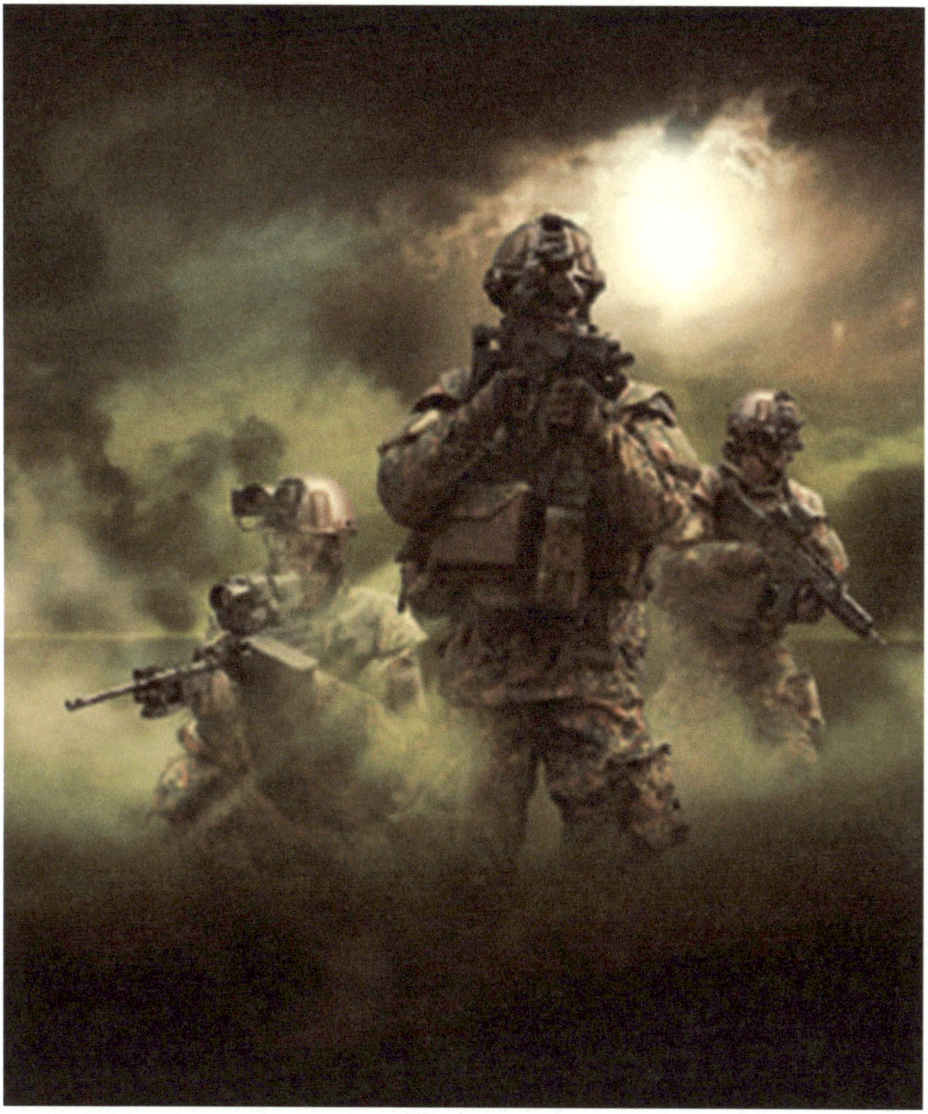

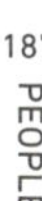

This image is from the Rheinmetall Defense website. It shows the infantryman of the future, able to move more efficiently and better protected.

[ILLUSTRATION: RHEINMETALL DEFENSE]

hätte? – Nicht jetzt noch sich rächte? – Sophie! *(Bedeutend, indem sie die Hand auf Sophiens Achsel fallen läßt.)* Wir Frauenzimmer können nur zwischen *Herrschen* und *Dienen* wählen, aber die höchste Wonne der *Gewalt* ist doch nur ein elender Behelf, wenn uns die *größere* Wonne versagt wird, Sklavinnen eines Manns zu sein, den wir lieben.

S o p h i e. Eine Wahrheit, Mylady, die ich von Ihnen *zuletzt* hören wollte!

L a d y. Und warum, meine Sophie? Sieht man es denn dieser kindischen Führung des *Zepters* nicht an, daß wir nur für das *Gängelband* taugen? Sahst du es denn diesem launischen Flattersinn nicht an – diesen wilden Ergötzungen nicht an, daß sie nur wildere Wünsche in meiner Brust überlärmen sollten?

S o p h i e *(tritt erstaunt zurück)*. Lady!

L a d y *(lebhafter)*. Befriedige diese! Gib mir den Mann, den ich jetzt denke – den ich anbete – sterben, Sophie, oder *besitzen* muß. *(Schmelzend.)* Laß mich aus seinem Mund es vernehmen, daß Tränen der Liebe schöner glänzen in unsern Augen als die Brillanten in unserm Haar, *(feurig)* und ich werfe dem Fürsten sein Herz und sein Fürstentum vor die Füße, fliehe mit diesem Mann, fliehe in die entlegenste Wüste der Welt – –

S o p h i e *(blickt sie erschrocken an)*. Himmel! was machen Sie? Wie wird Ihnen, Lady?

L a d y *(bestürzt)*. Du entfärbst dich? – Hab ich vielleicht etwas zuviel gesagt? – O so laß mich deine Zunge mit meinem Zutrauen binden – höre noch mehr – höre alles –

S o p h i e *(schaut sich ängstlich um)*. Ich fürchte, Mylady – ich fürchte – ich brauch es nicht mehr zu hören.

L a d y. Die Verbindung mit dem Major – Du und die Welt stehen im Wahn, sie sei eine *Hofkabale* – Sophie – erröte nicht – schäme dich meiner nicht – sie ist das Werk – *meiner Liebe*.

S o p h i e. Bei Gott! Was mir ahndete!

L a d y. Sie ließen sich beschwatzen, Sophie – der schwache Fürst – der hofschlaue Walter – der alberne Marschall – Jeder von ihnen wird darauf schwören, daß diese Heurat das unfehlbarste Mittel sei, mich dem Herzog zu retten,

unser Band um so fester zu knüpfen. – Ja! es auf ewig zu
trennen! auf ewig diese schändliche Ketten zu brechen! –
Belogene Lügner! Von einem schwachen Weib überlistet!
– Ihr selbst führt mir jetzt meinen Geliebten zu. Das war
es ja nur, was ich wollte – Hab ich ihn einmal – hab ich
ihn – o dann auf *immer* gute Nacht, abscheuliche Herr-
lichkeit –

ZWEITE SZENE

Ein alter Kammerdiener des Fürsten, der ein Schmuckkäst-
chen trägt. Die Vorigen.

K a m m e r d i e n e r. Seine Durchlaucht der Herzog emp-
fehlen sich Mylady zu Gnaden und schicken Ihnen diese
Brillanten zur Hochzeit. Sie kommen soeben erst aus
Venedig.
L a d y *(hat das Kästchen geöffnet und fährt erschrocken
zurück)*. Mensch! was bezahlt dein Herzog für diese
Steine?
K a m m e r d i e n e r *(mit finsterm Gesicht)*. Sie kosten ihn
keinen Heller.
L a d y. Was? Bist du rasend? *Nichts?* – und *(indem sie
einen Schritt von ihm wegtritt)* du wirfst mir ja einen
Blick zu, als wenn du mich durchbohren wolltest – *Nichts*
kosten ihn diese unermeßlich kostbaren Steine?
K a m m e r d i e n e r. Gestern sind siebentausend Lands-
kinder nach Amerika fort – Die zahlen alles.
L a d y *(setzt den Schmuck plötzlich nieder und geht rasch
durch den Saal, nach einer Pause zum Kammerdiener)*.
Mann, was ist dir? Ich glaube, du weinst?
K a m m e r d i e n e r *(wischt sich die Augen, mit schreck-
licher Stimme, alle Glieder zitternd)*. Edelsteine wie *diese*
da – Ich hab auch ein paar Söhne drunter.
L a d y *(wendet sich bebend weg, seine Hand fassend)*. Doch
keinen Gezwungenen?
K a m m e r d i e n e r *(lacht fürchterlich)*. O Gott – Nein –
lauter Freiwillige. Es traten wohl so etliche vorlaute
Bursch' vor die Front heraus und fragten den Obersten,
wie teuer der Fürst das Joch Menschen verkaufe? – aber

VALET His serene highness begs your ladyship's acceptance of these jewels as a nuptial present. They have just arrived from Venice.
LADY MILFORD (opens the casket and starts back in astonishment).
What did these jewels cost the duke?
VALET Nothing!
LADY MILFORD Nothing! Are you beside yourself? (Retreating a step or two). Old man! you fix on me a look as though you would pierce me through. Did you say these precious jewels cost nothing?
VALET Yesterday seven thousand children of the land left their homes to go to America—they pay for all.
LADY MILFORD (sets the casket suddenly down, and paces up and down the room; after a pause, to the VALET).
What distresses you, old man? you are weeping!
VALET (wiping his eyes, and trembling violently). Yes, for these jewels.
My two sons are among the number.
LADY MILFORD But they went not by compulsion?
VALET (laughing bitterly). Oh! dear no! they were all volunteers! There were certainly some few forward lads who pushed to the front of the ranks and inquired of the colonel at what price the prince sold his subjects per yoke, upon which our gracious ruler ordered the regiments to be marched to the parade, and the malcontents to be shot. We heard the report of the muskets, and saw brains and blood spurting about us, while the whole band shouted— "Hurrah for America!"
LADY MILFORD And I heard nothing of all this! saw nothing!
VALET No, most gracious lady, because you rode off to the bear-hunt with his highness just at the moment the drum was beating for the march. 'Tis a pity your ladyship missed the pleasure of the sight—here, crying children might be seen following their wretched father—there, a mother distracted with grief was rushing forward to throw her tender infant among the bristling bayonets—here, a bride and bridegroom were separated with the sabre's stroke—and there, graybeards were seen to stand in despair, and fling their very crutches after their sons in the New World —and, in the midst of all this, the drums were beating loudly, that the prayers and lamentations might not reach the Almighty ear.

LADY MILFORD (rising in violent emotion). Away with these jewels—their rays pierce my bosom like the flames of hell. Moderate your grief, old man. Your children shall be restored to you. You shall again clasp them to your bosom.
VALET (with warmth). Yes, heaven knows! We shall meet again! As they passed the city gates they turned round and cried aloud: "God bless our wives and children—long life to our gracious sovereign. At the day of judgment we shall all meet again!"
LADY MILFORD (walks up and down the room in great agitation). Horrible! most horrible!—and they would persuade me that I had dried up all the tears in the land. Now, indeed, my eyes are fearfully opened! Go—tell the prince that I will thank him in person! (As the valet is going she drops the purse into his hat). And take this as a recompense for the truth you have revealed to me.
VALET (throws the purse with contempt on the table). Keep it, with your other treasures. [Exit].
LADY MILFORD (looking after him in astonishment). Sophy, follow him, and inquire his name. His sons shall be restored to him. (SOPHIE goes. LADY MILFORD becomes absorbed in thought. Pause. Then to SOPHIE as she returns.) Was there not a report that some town on the frontier had been destroyed by fire, and four hundred families reduced to beggary? (She rings).
SOPHIE What has made your ladyship just think of that? Yes—such was certainly the fact, and most of these poor creatures are either compelled to serve their creditors as bondsmen, or are dragging out their miserable days in the depths of the royal silver mines.
[Enter a SERVANT] What are your ladyship's commands?
LADY MILFORD (giving him the case of jewels). Carry this to my treasurer without delay. Let the jewels be sold and the money distributed among the four hundred families who were ruined by the fire.
SOPHIE Consider, my lady, the risk you run of displeasing his highness.
LADY MILFORD (with dignity). Should I encircle my brows with the curses of his subjects? (Makes a sign to the SERVANT, who goes away with the jewel case). Wouldst thou have me dragged to the earth by the dreadful weight of the tears of misery? Nay! SOPHIE, it is better far to wear false jewels on the brow, and to have the consciousness of a good deed within the breast!
SOPHIE But diamonds of such value! Why not rather give some that are less precious? Truly, my lady, it is an unpardonable act.
LADY MILFORD Foolish girl! For this deed more brilliants and pearls will flow for me in one moment than kings ever wore in their richest diadems! Ay, and infinitely more beautiful!

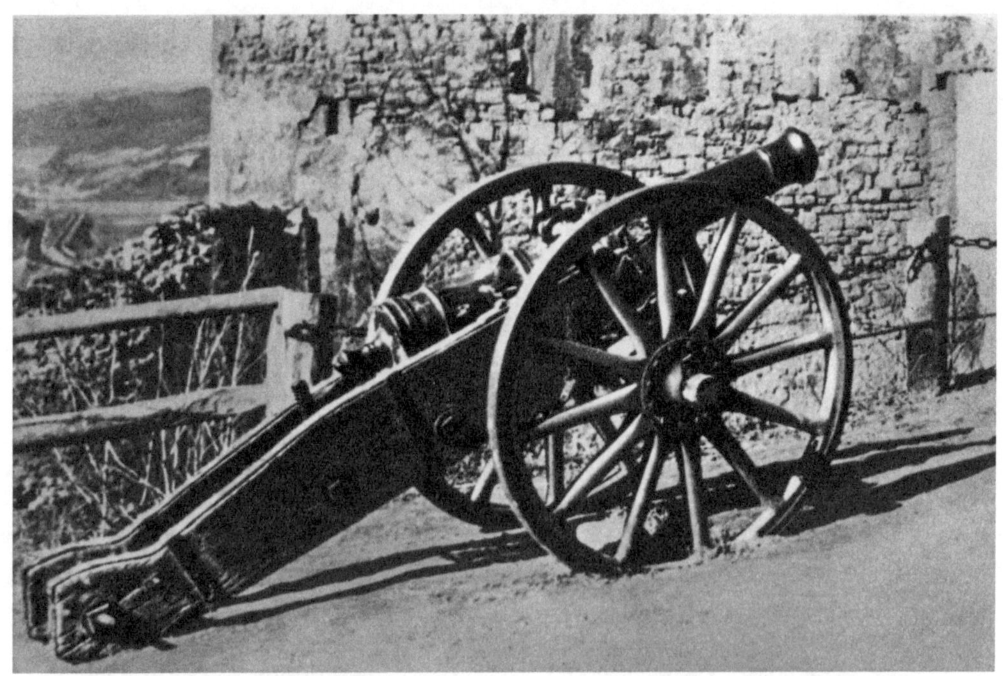

HENSCHEL CANNON ON THE RUDELSBURG (CAST AT THE HENSCHELEI IN KASSEL, 1803)
Georg Christian Carl Henschel came from Gießen to Kassel in 1777, in order to cast bells and cannons, first for Napoleon's brother Jérôme. In 1810 he founded the Henschelei.

[SOURCE: HENSCHEL-MUSEUM, KASSEL. REPRODUCTION: POLA SIEVERDING]

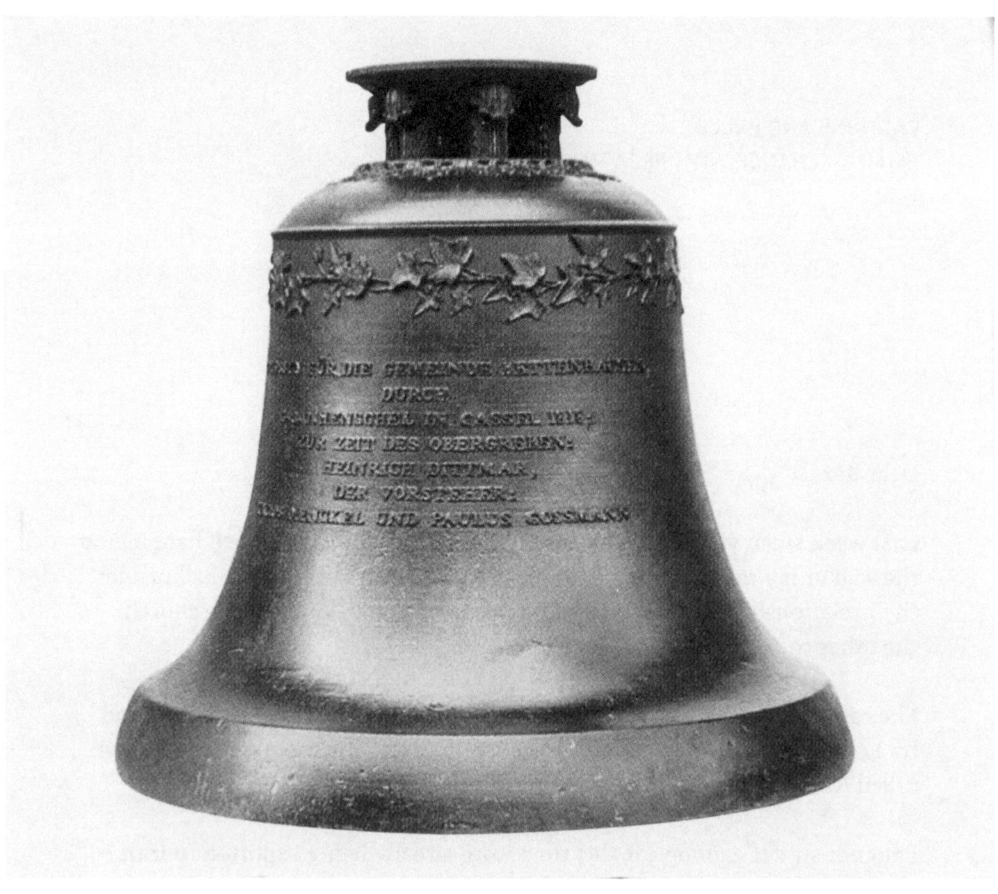

BELL OF BETTENHAUSEN, KASSEL, 1818

This Bell was cast at the Henschelei in Kassel in 1818.

[SOURCE: HENSCHEL-MUSEUM, KASSEL. REPRODUCTION: POLA SIEVERDING]

Dear Reza,

Last week when you looked at the picture of the cannon and bell hanging on the wall of my room, you said: how interesting that both have a ball inside; their relationship is also worth taking note of, one belongs to the church, the other to the army.

The cannon and the bell you saw in those photographs were manufactured by a company named Henschel in the eighteenth century in a German town called Kassel. I will send these photographs to you once again.

I am not sure if cannons at this time were already being exported to Iran, but surely later on, perhaps already in the 1930s when German engineers were constructing the Iranian railroad. It was at this time when Henschel sent sixteen locomotive trains to Iran. I've found a photograph of one of these trains. But this is another story . . .

I would like to know what you meant exactly when you said that the cannon and the bell bear an interesting relationship. What stories do bells carry in Iran? What is the history of the bell in Iran?

Sincerely,
Natascha

Dear Natascha,

The picture of the bell and the cannons on your wall drew me back to the time of my childhood in Tehran, where I grew up in the Christian quarter of the city. Then, I was used to the sound of church bells ringing. Then, cannons would announce the arrival of the Iranian new year. Yet, to tell you the truth, at this point in my life I had never actually seen church bells, nor cannons.

The war between Iran and Iraq had just started and most of my friends and acquaintances were in the process of emigrating from Iran. There was an Armenian girl who lived in my neighborhood. She was the one who showed me our quarter's church bells for the first time. Finding the source of the sound was a big discovery. From that moment on, I would remember her each time I looked up at the church bell towers in our neighborhood.

Around the time when the first air strikes began on Tehran, the church bells in our neighborhood transformed into alarms, signaling danger. Afterwards, they were to remain silent. No one knew what to do in such a situation. My mother wanted to take refuge in the church up the street from us; she believed that certainly the jet pilot would see the church towers and thus not drop his bombs there. She had simple proof: Iraq buys its planes from Europe and so these planes won't bomb churches. A doubtful argument that certainly could not prevent an Iraqi pilot with his modern fighter jet from bombing our neighborhood. Many years later, when I saw the collapse of the World Trade Center, I remembered these words, spoken on that first night when Tehran was being bombed.

I had to wait until my military service to see a real cannon for the first time. It was also during these days that I discovered strange cannons on Iranian television. Iranian television after the revolution would broadcast on New Year's Eve silent comedies and early films from the history of cinema. As if the history of cinema would begin again each year from zero. A huge cannonball chasing down Charlie Chaplin. Harold Llyod with a monster, a cannon tube hanging from its neck, spinning around each other in the midst of the Mexican Revolution. At the necessary moment, the monster would bend down and shoot the cannon.

A cannon, flat and ready, lay on the railroad tracks, facing in the direction of Buster Keaton's train; at any moment it seemed ready to blow the train to bits.

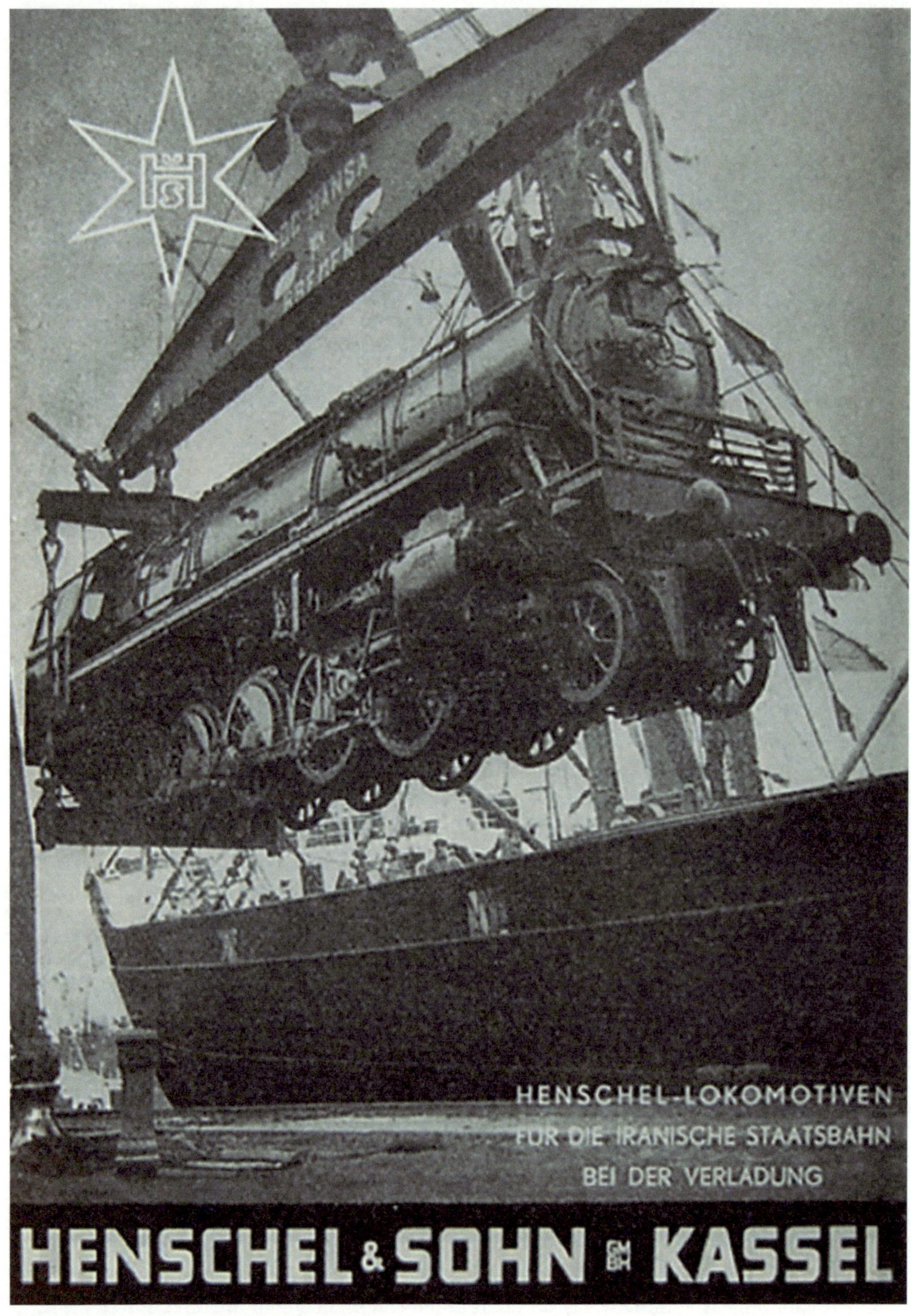

HENSCHEL LOCOMOTIVE FOR THE IRANIAN NATIONAL RAILWAYS; HENSCHEL & SON GMBH, KASSEL

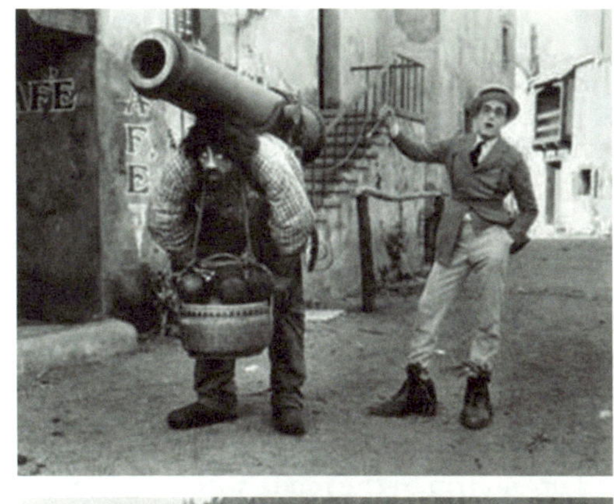
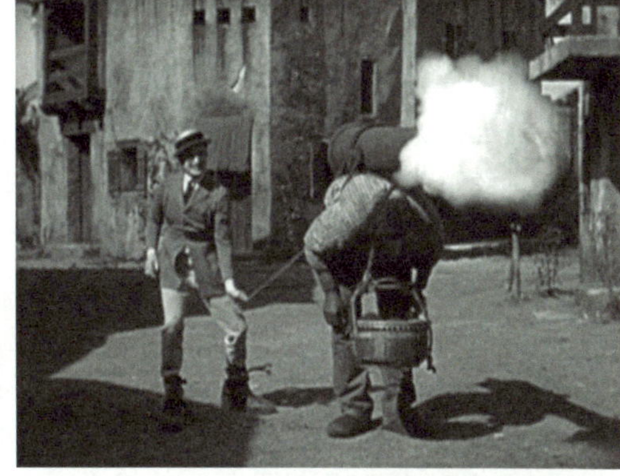
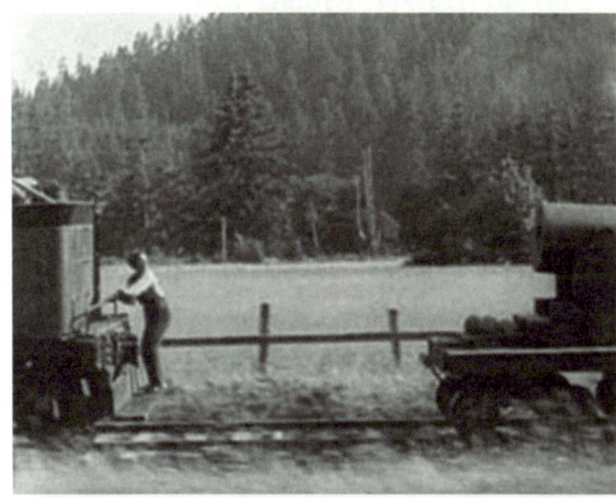
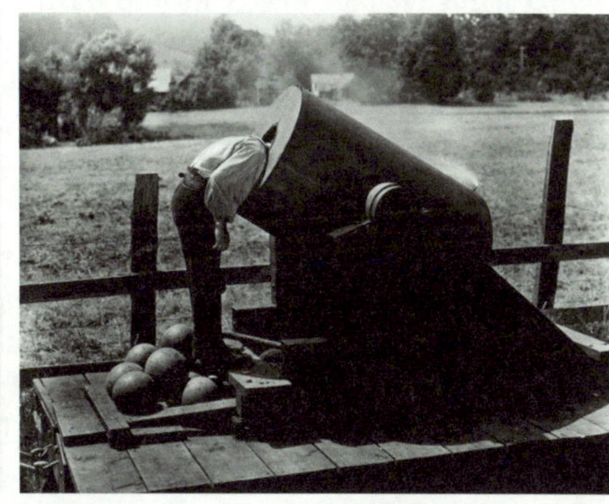
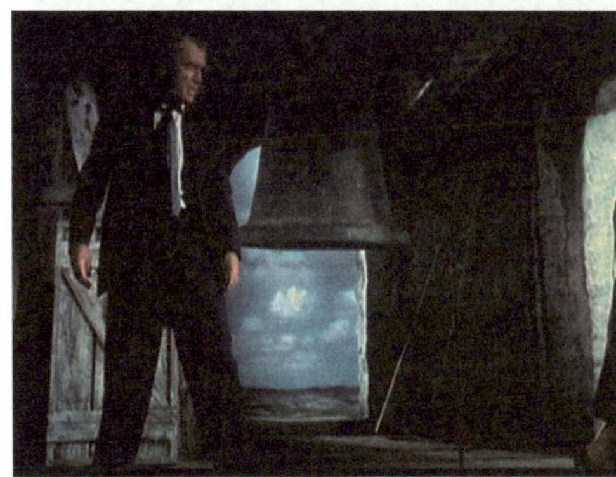
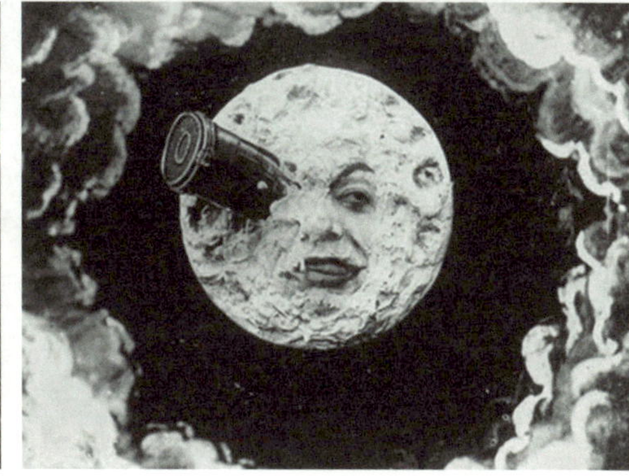

Images attached to Reza Haeri's email

The most interesting idea of all was in George Méliès' film *A Trip to the Moon*.
There they used a cannon to travel to the moon. I still find myself engaged
with these silent films.

Many years later, I encountered an image amongst the many photographs
from the Qajar period showing a condemned man awaiting his execution.
They had tied this man to the mouth of a cannon. It was as if this image
came straight out of one of those silent films. Yet this time there was no
Charlie Chaplin, Buster Keaton wasn't tied up, no trip to the moon was
planned. Here was a man who was most likely being executed for apostacy.
Much of the news and many of the images one sees on television remind me
of Llyod's, Keaton's or Chaplin's films. Although this time there is nothing to
laugh about.

Moreover, I imagine a scene where a woman suddenly falls from atop a bell
tower while a terrified man looks on. Now his fear of heights has gone and
he is no longer dizzy. The bell behind him tolls. Or, take the moment of
Quasimodo's execution by the ropes of Notre Dame's bells, when Esméralda
emerges from the square to save him. Those are the same bells that after the
French Revolution are melted down to make bullets. And finally, I think of
those tourists at the Kremlin in Moscow who take photographs of the Czar's
cannons and bells.

My dear Natascha, I'm not sure what relation any of these images may have
with each other, despite the histories, stories and accounts that lie behind
them individually. They are to one another the cannons and bells of dreams;
from within each, one can hear the resonating sound of the other.

In amity,

Reza

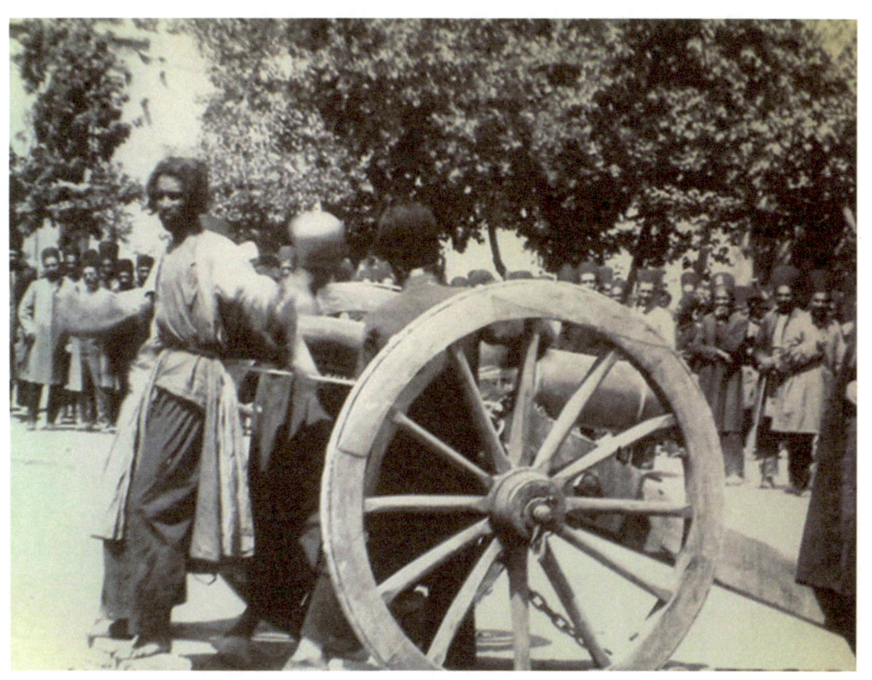

Language

When does a civil vehicle
become a military vehicle?
Which languages are spoken in Kassel?
Language schools, integration courses,
Gastarbeiter, Huguenots in Kassel,
and grammar according to Clausewitz.

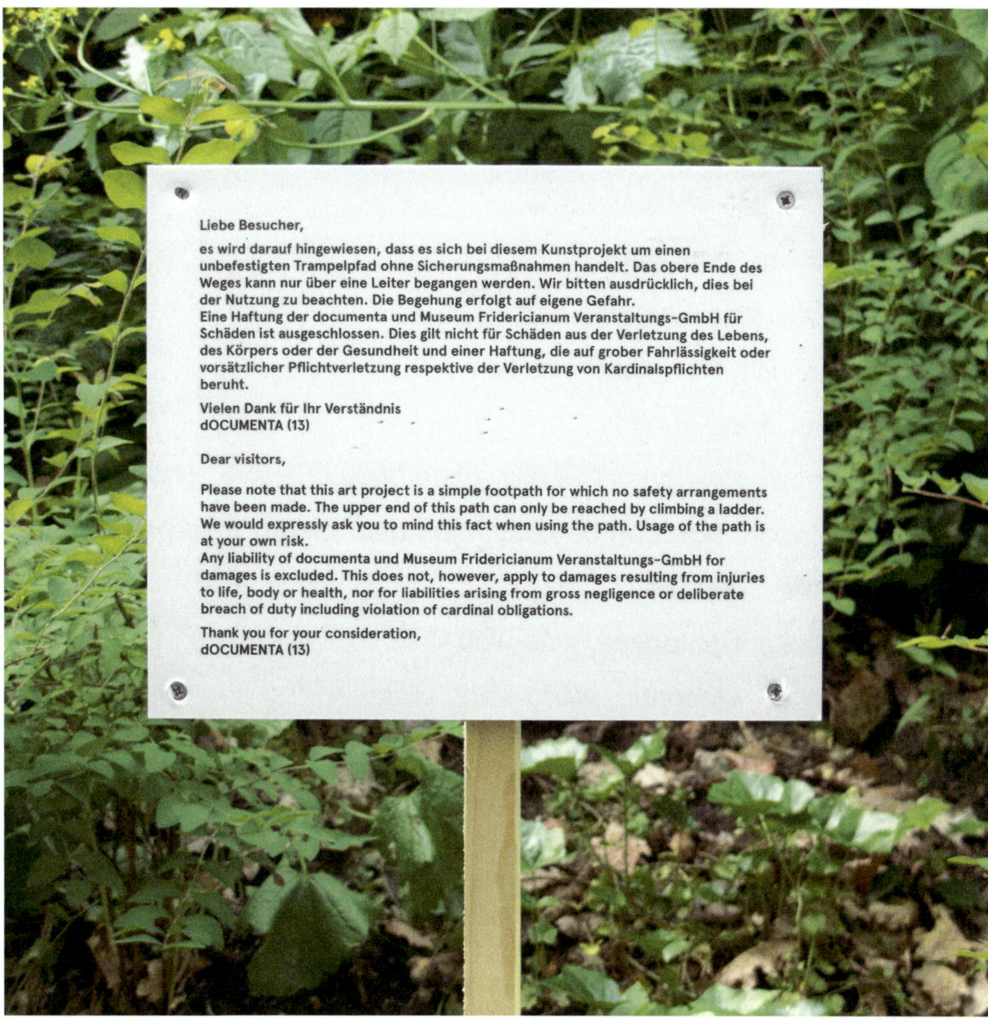

Liebe Besucher,

es wird darauf hingewiesen, dass es sich bei diesem Kunstprojekt um einen
unbefestigten Trampelpfad ohne Sicherungsmaßnahmen handelt. Das obere Ende des
Weges kann nur über eine Leiter begangen werden. Wir bitten ausdrücklich, dies bei
der Nutzung zu beachten. Die Begehung erfolgt auf eigene Gefahr.
Eine Haftung der documenta und Museum Fridericianum Veranstaltungs-GmbH für
Schäden ist ausgeschlossen. Dies gilt nicht für Schäden aus der Verletzung des Lebens,
des Körpers oder der Gesundheit und einer Haftung, die auf grober Fahrlässigkeit oder
vorsätzlicher Pflichtverletzung respektive der Verletzung von Kardinalspflichten
beruht.

Vielen Dank für Ihr Verständnis
dOCUMENTA (13)

Dear visitors,

Please note that this art project is a simple footpath for which no safety arrangements
have been made. The upper end of this path can only be reached by climbing a ladder.
We would expressly ask you to mind this fact when using the path. Usage of the path is
at your own risk.
Any liability of documenta und Museum Fridericianum Veranstaltungs-GmbH for
damages is excluded. This does not, however, apply to damages resulting from injuries
to life, body or health, nor for liabilities arising from gross negligence or deliberate
breach of duty including violation of cardinal obligations.

Thank you for your consideration,
dOCUMENTA (13)

Dog barking   [edit]

- In Albanian, *ham ham*
- In Arabic, *haw haw, hab hab*
- In Armenian, "Հաւ Հաւ," hav hav
- In Batak, *kung-kung*
- In Bengali: *gheu gheu* ঘেউ ঘেউ, *bheu bheu* ভেউ ভেউ, *bhou bhou* ভউ
- In Bulgarian, *bow bow* бау бау, *djaff djaff* джаф джаф
- In Catalan, *bup bup*
- In Chinese, Cantonese, *wōu-wōu* 旺旺
- In Chinese, Mandarin, *wāng wāng* 汪汪[zho 14]
- In Czech, *haf haf*
- In Danish, *vuf vuf, vov vov, bjæf bjæf*
- In Dutch, *waf waf, woef woef*
- In English, *woof, arf, bow wow, ruff*
- In Estonian, *auh auh*
- In Finnish *hau hau, vuh vuh*
- In French, *ouah ouah, ouaf ouaf, wouf wouf*
- In German, *wau wau, waff waff, wuff wuff*
- In Greek, *ghav ghav* γαβ γαβ, *woof*
- In Hebrew, *hav hav* הַב־הַב,[heb 4] *haw haw* הָאוּ־הָאוּ[heb 4]
- In Hindi, *bho bho* भो भो
- In Hungarian *vau vau*
- In Icelandic, *voff voff*
- In Indonesian, *guk guk*
- In Italian, *bau bau*
- In Japanese, ワンワン (wan wan)

Cross-linguistic onomatopoeias – Wikipedia, the free encyclopedia

Rooster crowing   [edit]

- In Albanian, *kikiriku*
- In Arabic, *kuku-kookoo, kuku-reekoo, esku kookoo*
- In Armenian, *tsoo-ghoo-roo-ghoo,* coo-coo-ree-coo
- In Bengali, *Kuk-ku-ruk-kooo*
- In Bulgarian, *cucurigu* кукуригу
- In Catalan, *quic quiriquic*
- In Chinese, Mandarin, *ō ō ō* 噢噢噢 / *wō wō wō* 喔喔喔
- In Czech, *kykirikí*
- In Danish, *kykkeliky*
- In Dutch, *kukeleku*
- In English, *cock a doodle doo*
- In Estonian *kikerikii, kukeleegu*
- In Euskara, *kukurruku*
- In Finnish, *kukkokiekuu, kukko* (cock), *kiekuu* (crowing)
- In French, *cocorico*
- In Georgian, *qiqliqo* ყიყლიყო
- In German, *kikeriki*
- In Greek, *ciciricu* κικιρίκου
- In Hebrew, *quuquuriqu* קוקוריקו[heb 4]
- In Hindi, *ku-kudu-koo*
- In Hungarian *kukurikú*
- In Icelandic, "gaggalagó"
- In Indonesian, *kukuruyuk*
- In Irish, *cuc-adiú-dil-ú*

205

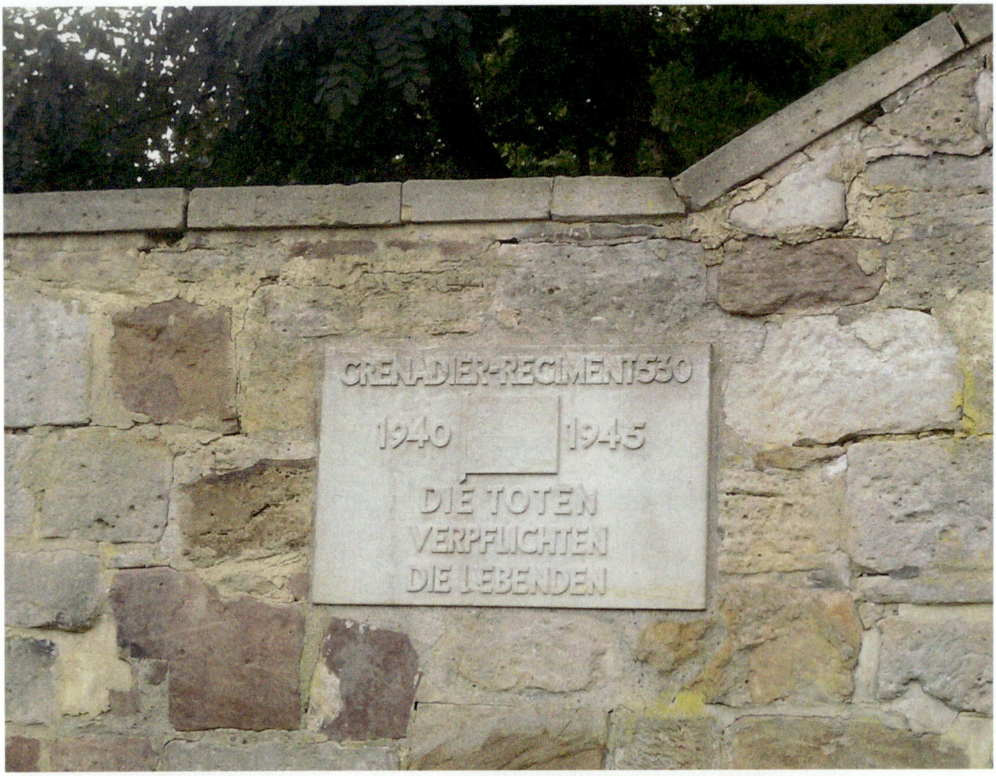

GRENADIER-REGIMENT 530
1940   1945
DIE TOTEN
VERPFLICHTEN
DIE LEBENDEN

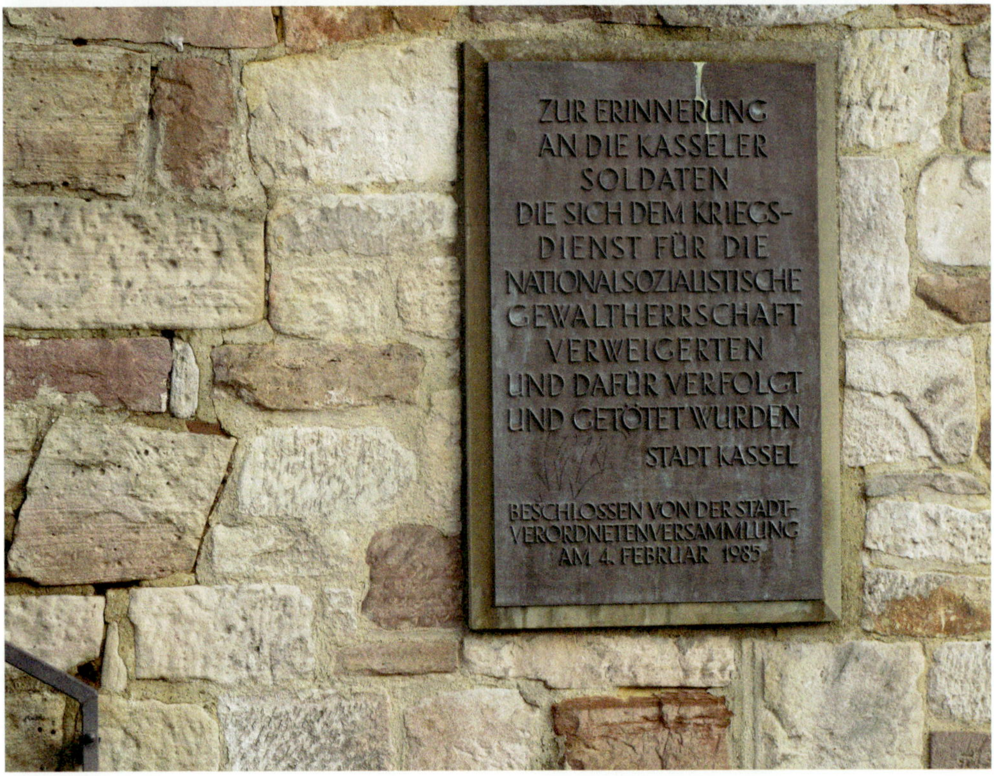

ZUR ERINNERUNG
AN DIE KASSELER
SOLDATEN
DIE SICH DEM KRIEGS-
DIENST FÜR DIE
NATIONALSOZIALISTISCHE
GEWALTHERRSCHAFT
VERWEIGERTEN
UND DAFÜR VERFOLGT
UND GETÖTET WURDEN
STADT KASSEL

BESCHLOSSEN VON DER STADT-
VERORDNETENVERSAMMLUNG
AM 4. FEBRUAR 1985

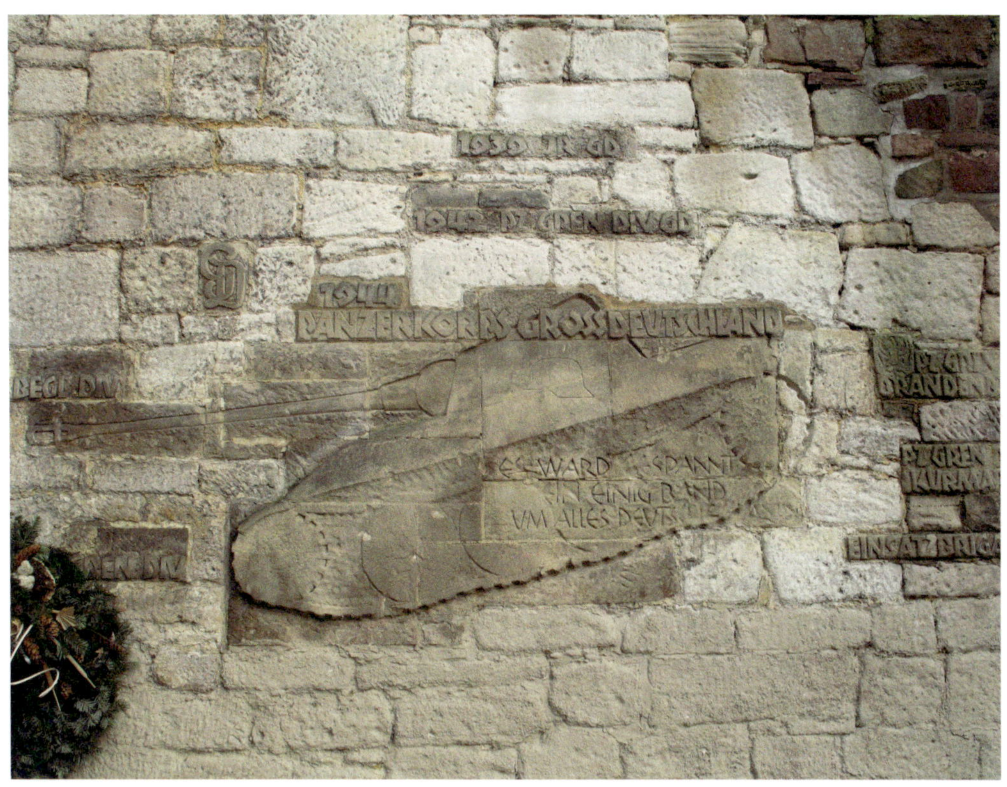

1939 IR GD
1942 IZ GREN DIV GD
1944
PANZERKORPS GROSSDEUTSCHLAND
BEGL DIV
DIV
ES WARD GESPANNT
IN EINIG BAND
UM ALLES DEUTSCH
PZ GREN DIV
BRANDEN
PZ GREN
KURMA
EINSATZ BRIGA

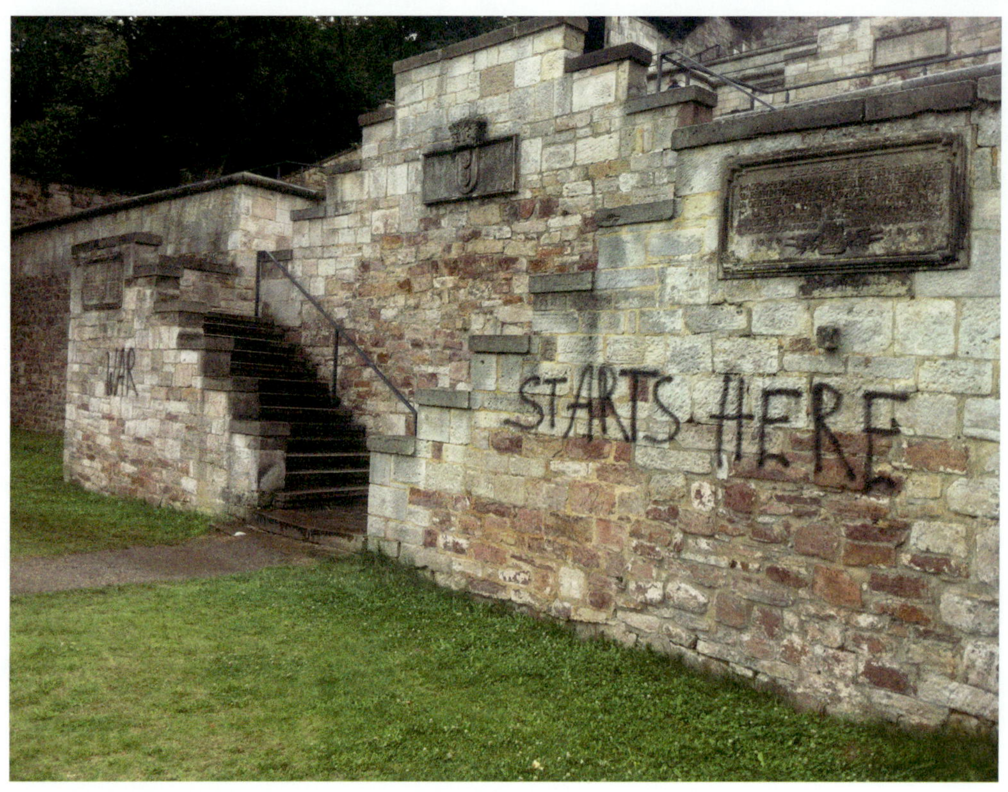

WAR
STARTS HERE

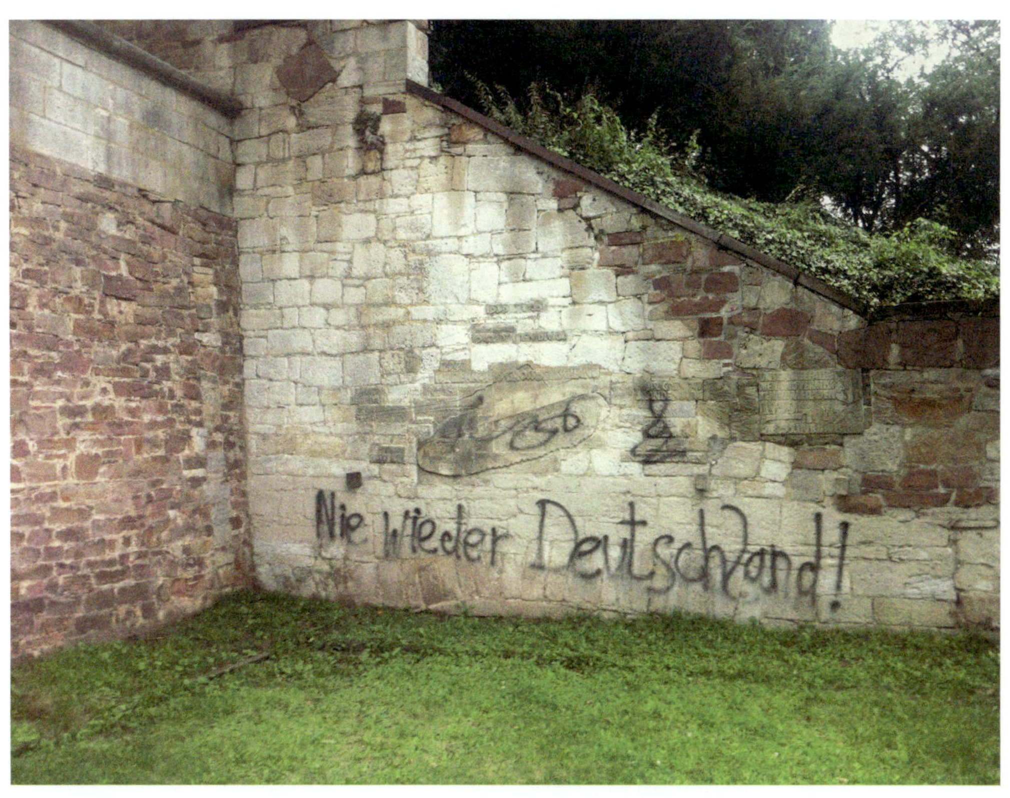

209

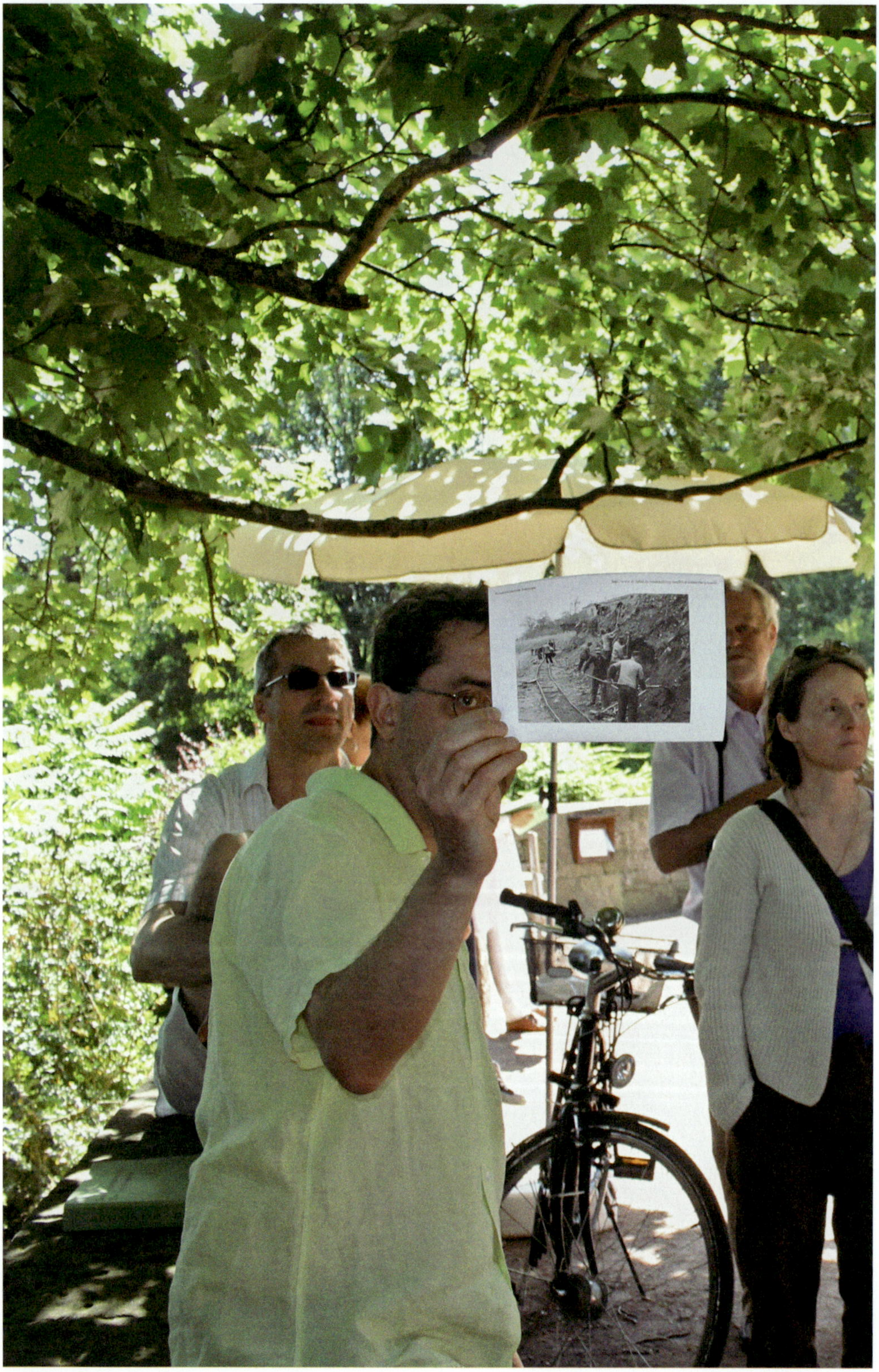

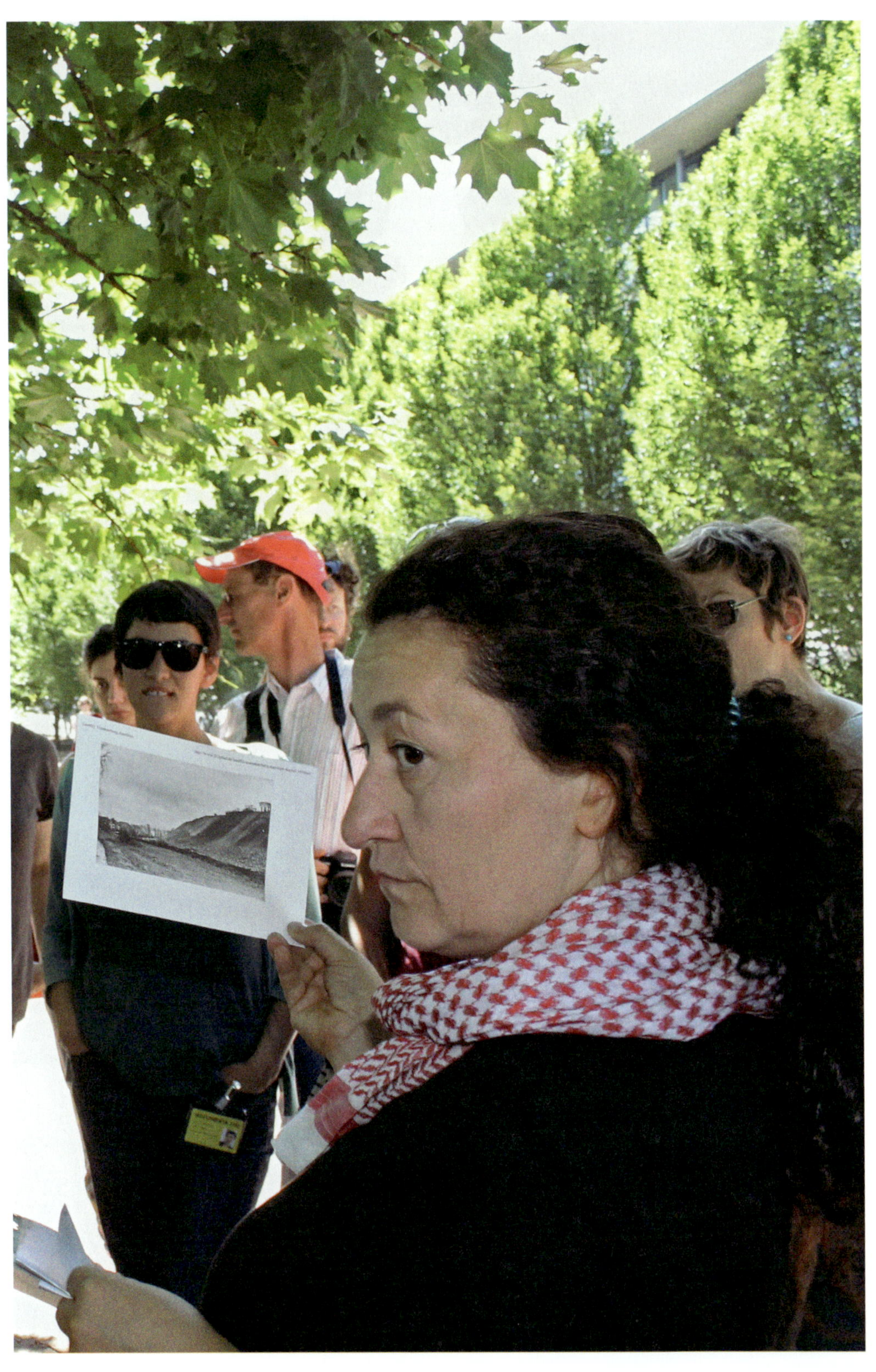

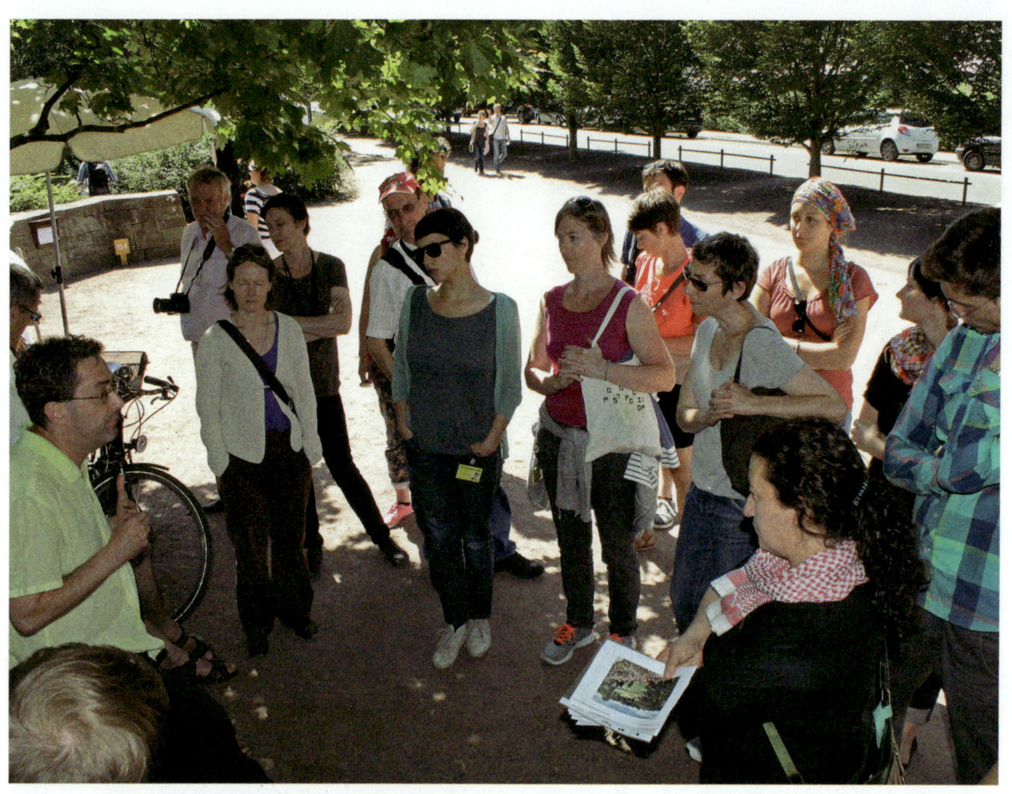

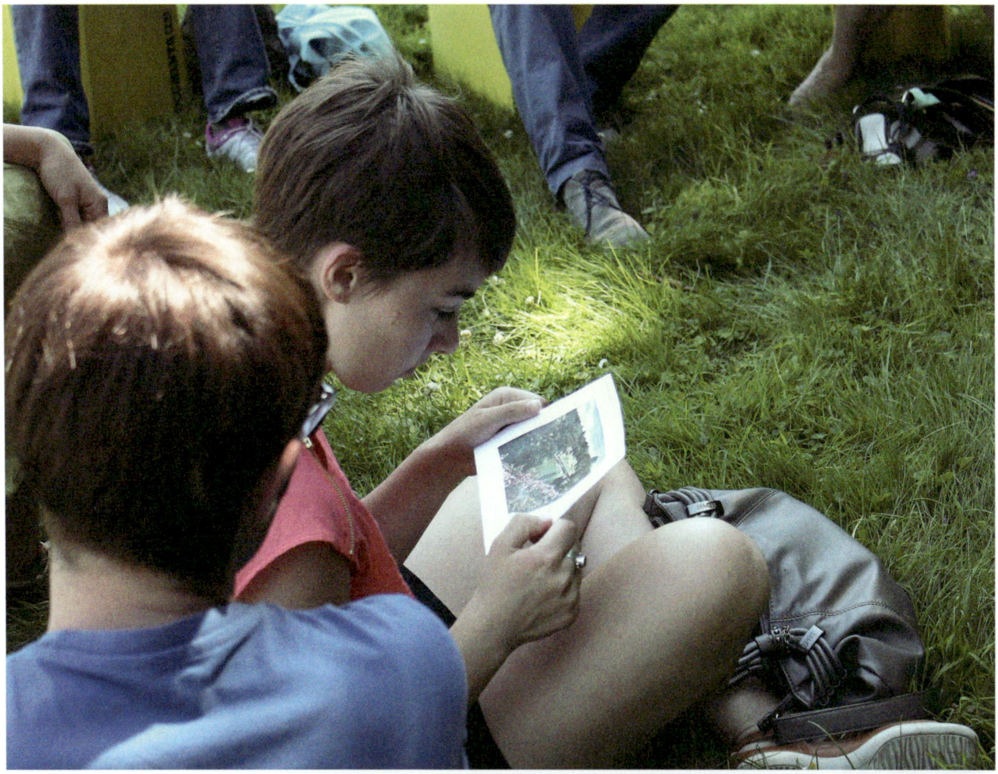

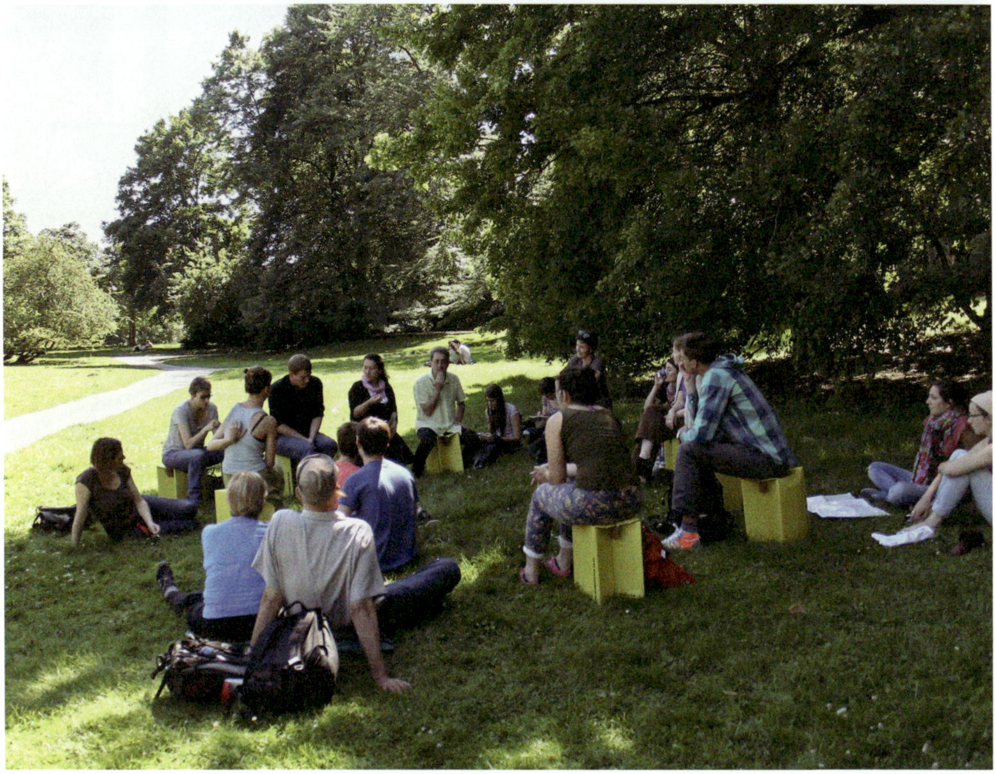

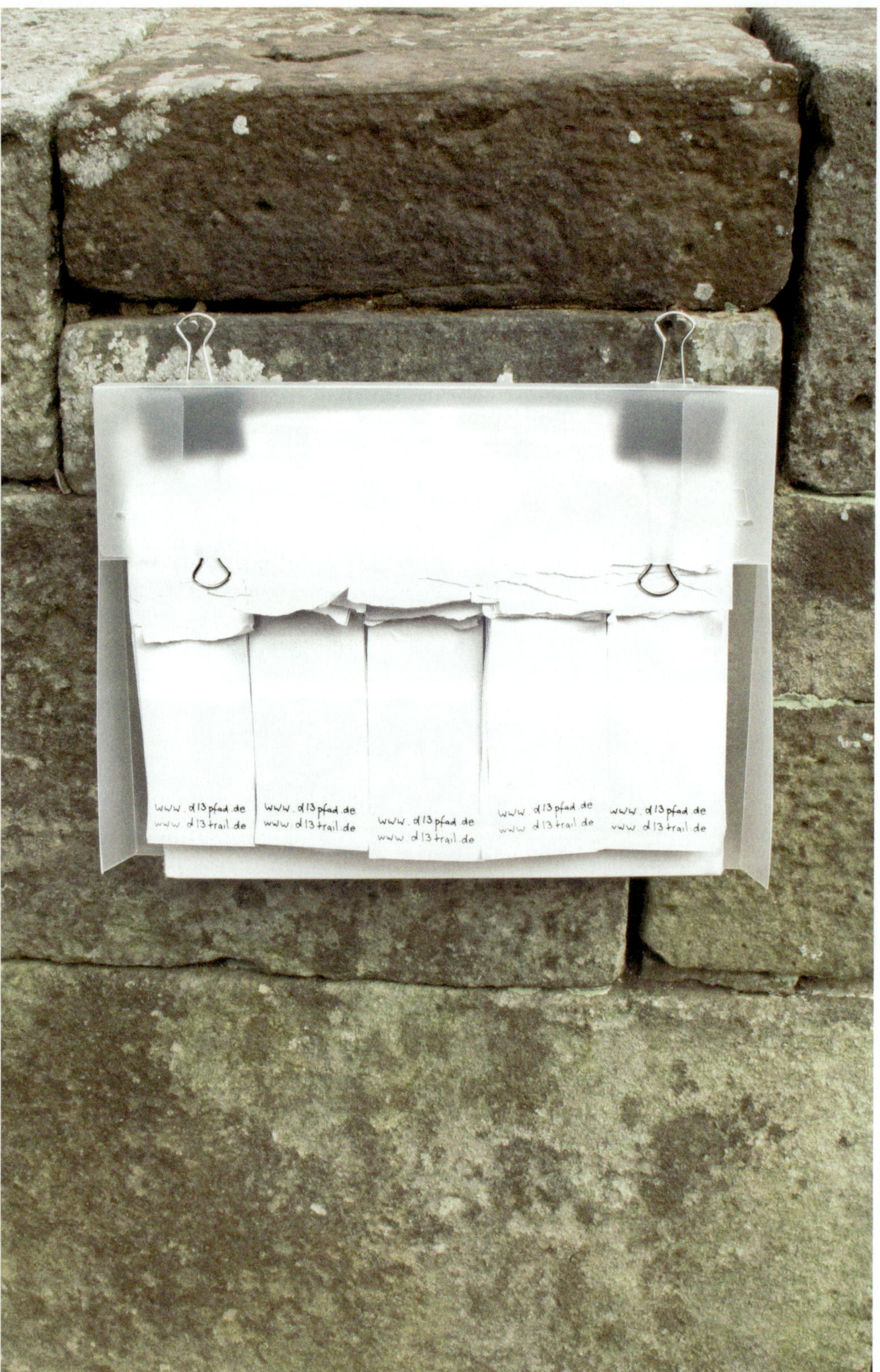
www.d13pfad.de
www.d13trail.de
www.d13pfad.de
www.d13trail.de
www.d13pfad.de
www.d13trail.de
www.d13pfad.de
www.d13trail.de
www.d13pfad.de
www.d13trail.de

Dear Tom,

Since we last talked, the trail has unfolded in many ways, and the research around the rubble and the questions arising from it have become more tangible.

Following your advice, we tried to stay specific in our questions and look at war and destruction and its aftermath—the cleaning up, the sweeping, the burying, not so much in general but more on the basis of a concrete situation.

If you remember, we had talked about the inevitable logic of war and its possible alternatives, about how war makes a mess that requires cleaning up, that the procedure of cleaning up can be a process of healing but also, that it has been delegated to a large extent to NGOs, almost like an appendix to the crisis management of the war machine itself. You differentiated between two incompatible vocabularies to describe the activity of the humanitarian gesture, where one makes the war manageable, or even more plausible, and the other "takes the side of the living" and creates the conditions for living, i.e. making it possible for people to lead their own lives by treating them just like people who have lives to lead, or people who could have lives to lead if they were able to lead them.

Our discussion continued with reflections on the logic of war and its alternatives in terms of considering it a language, where words, gestures, acts and things are exchanged or imposed. You quoted Clausewitz, who stated in *On War* that the language of diplomacy, of politics, and of war is actually the same, only the grammar changes. Clausewitz's argument is that states are permanently rivals and their competition for power and regional hegemony is generally conducted diplomatically and politically. Occasionally this becomes impossible or unsustainable and they resort to another grammar, but it's just a continuation of the same conversation by other means.

Means and grammar are the same thing. And once they've made their point, or once their point has been effectively received by the other party, they don't need to use that grammar of war anymore and can go back to writing, conversing, parleying, and so on.

You pointed out that quite often different grammars are used side by side, that there is a fuzzyness along the edges of the different grammars—diplomatic pressure, sanctions, the exchange of notes, assassination, computer worms— when does war actually start? One usually has peace talks while one is still fighting, as in two different kinds of conversations that are happening simultaneously use different grammars.
You said that this can create some confusion over when a war starts or ends and what the alternatives could be. You suggested there would be a better chance of finding answers when looking at particular wars, looking at the particular situation of one war.

On my return to the rubble of our Kassel trail I tried to be as particular as possible, working with what is there on the trail: the bricks, the plants, the animals, the talk of the transformations the place has gone through, the sto- ries of people involved, the movement of things, plants, people, destruction, death, reconstruction, roses, and art shows.
We tracked the rubble and it led us to the weapons manufacturers, who brought on the devastating bombardments the allied forces carried out over Kassel. The tradition of weapons manufacturing in Kassel goes back to the eighteenth century. During World War II, production was at its maximum capacity, employing 30,000 workers, 20,000 of whom were forced labor. Not only arms as such were produced; civilian production like trains and trucks also became part of military inventories. It seems the grammar of everything changes during wartime, including the grammar of things.

But what grammar does rubble belong to?

After the war, the city was in ruins. For years the rubble was piled up every- where, the rubble which used to be people's houses, garages, shops and work- shops, but also the big factories of Henschel, Fieseler and Wegmann. 85% of the city was destroyed. There was so much rubble that they didn't know what to do with it.

Then in the fifties, at the dawn of the Wirtschaftswunder (German "economic miracle) and in preparation for the BUGA, the national horticultural show, the rubble was eventually cleared away and poured down the slope between Schöne Aussicht and Auepark. It was covered with a thin layer of soil, then with plants that could grow on rubble known as the pioneer species, and then with flowers and more flowers.

I wonder whether by referring to Clausewitz's conception of war one tacitly accepts the language of hegemony—mediating expansionist, dominating, and subordinating policies. Attempts at changing the grammar in this language (for example, from military aggression to diplomacy) and not questioning the language makes me wonder about the rubble again. A city produces weapons, is bombarded and destroyed, plants roses on the rubble and continues to produce weapons. Doesn't this resemble the changes of grammar that Clausewitz proposes—threat, war, diplomacy, threat—without ever questioning the language?

In "Translation, or: can things get any worse?" you describe translation: "a radical translation (as) an active relation between and within languages, not the attempt to overcome language altogether, is the event for which the name politics ought to be reserved." Clausewitz seems to be saying that politics translates solely within one language, but doesn't a radical translation necessitate acknowledging other languages as well? The language of (universal) rights comes to mind as one example.

I would appreciate your comments or thoughts on this.

PS: Pola found this image, *Allegory of Grammar*, from 1659, after Antoine Furetière's *Nouvelle Allegorique, ou histoire des derniers troubles arrivez au royaume d'Eloquence.* Furetière was a French scholar working on a universal dictionary of the French language. What struck me most about this allegory is how implicit the entanglement of language and military strategics is. I am reminded of Allen S. Weiss' research on the culturalization of military planning found in Baroque garden architecture. Like many of these gardens, the terrace garden on the Auehang was also built by a military man. His name was Paul du Ry. The term Bellevue/Schöne Aussicht not only implies a nice view over a landscape but also refers to the vista that facilitates military strategics.

Walter Benjamin says that allegories are, in the realm of thoughts, what ruins are in the realm of things.

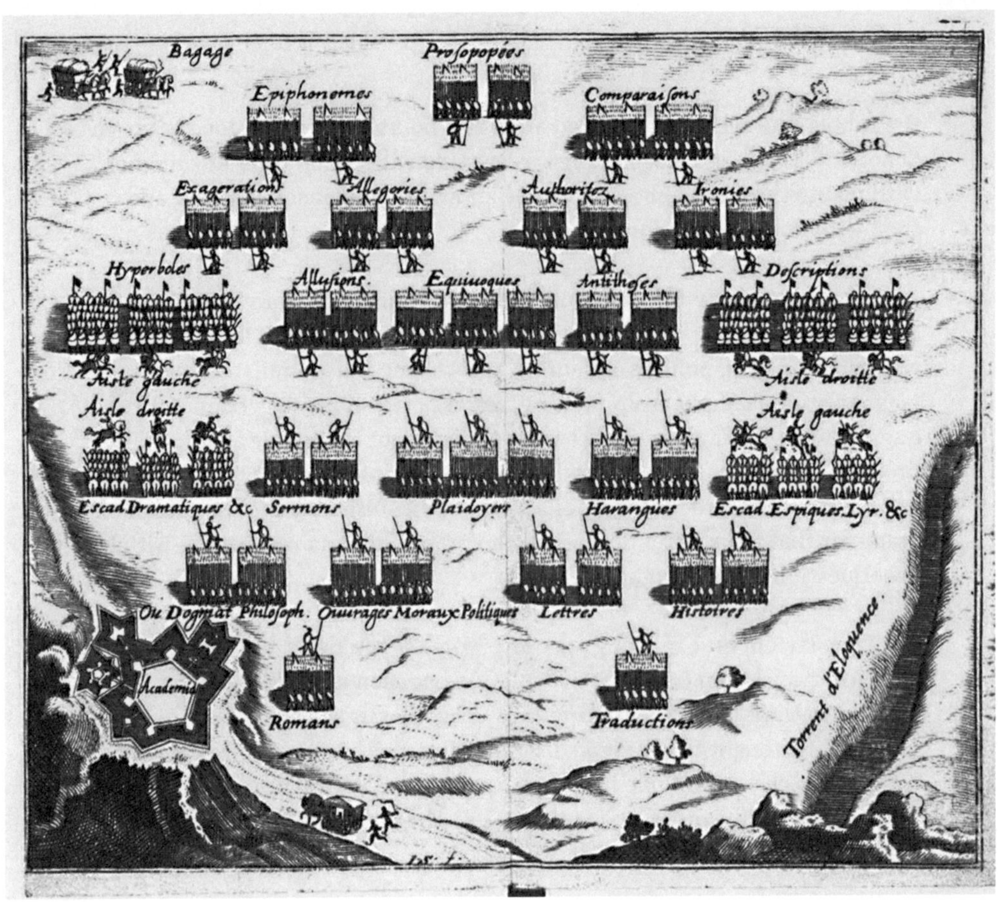

ALLEGORY OF GRAMMAR AND STYLE

Antoine Furetière, "Nouvelle Allegorique, ou histoire des derniers troubles arrivez au royaume d'Eloquence", 1659

B. War is an Instrument of Policy

HAVING made the requisite examination on both sides of that state of antagonism in which the nature of war stands with relation to other interests of men individually and of the bond of society, in order not to neglect any of the opposing elements,an antagonism which is founded in our own nature, and which, therefore, no philosophy can unravel,we shall now look for that unity into which, in practical life, these antagonistic elements combine themselves by partly neutralising each other. We should have brought forward this unity at the very commencement, if it had not been necessary to bring out this contradiction very plainly, and also to look at the different elements separately. Now, this unity is *the conception that war is only a part of political intercourse, therefore by no means an independent thing in itself.*

We know, certainly, that war is only called forth through the political intercourse of Governments and nations; but in general it is supposed that such intercourse is broken off by war, and that a totally different state of things ensues, subject to no laws but its own.

We maintain, on the contrary: that war is nothing but a continuation of political intercourse, with a mixture of other means. We say, mixed with other means, in order thereby to maintain at the same time that this political intercourse does not cease by the war itself, is not changed into something quite different, but that, in its essence, it continues to exist, whatever may be the form of the means which it uses, and that the chief lines on which the events of the war progress, and to which they are attached, are only the general features of policy which run all through the war until peace takes place. And how can we conceive it to be otherwise? Does the cessation of diplomatic notes stop the political relations between different nations and Governments? Is not war merely another kind of writing and language for political thoughts? It has certainly a grammar of its own, but its logic is not peculiar to itself.

Accordingly, war can never be separated from political intercourse, and if, in the consideration of the matter, this is done in any way, all the threads of the different relations are, to a certain extent, broken, and we have before us a senseless thing without an object.

This kind of idea would be indispensable even if war was perfect war, the perfectly unbridled element of hostility, for all the circumstances on which it rests, and which determine its leading features, viz., our own power, the enemy's power, allies on both sides, the characteristics of the people and their Governments respectively, etc., as enumerated in the first chapter of the first book,are they not of a political nature, and are they not so intimately connected with the whole political intercourse that it is impossible to separate them?But this view is doubly indispensable if we reflect that real war is no such consistent effort tending to an extreme, as it should be according to the abstract idea, but a half and half thing, a contradiction in itself; that, as such, it cannot follow its own laws, but must be looked upon as a part of another whole,and this whole is policy.

Policy in making use of war avoids all those rigorous conclusions which proceed from its nature; it troubles itself little about final possibilities, confining its attention to immediate probabilities. If much uncertainty in the whole action ensues therefrom, if it thereby becomes a sort of game, the policy of each cabinet places its confidence in the belief that in this game it will surpass its neighbour in skill and sharpsightedness.

ON WAR, BOOK 8, CHAPTER 6B, CARL VON CLAUSEWITZ (1780-1831)

"Is not war merely another kind of writing and language for political thoughts? It has certainly a grammar of its own, but its logic is not peculiar to itself."

herzlich willkommen in einer parkanlage der mhk•
sie besuchen ein vom land hessen unterhaltenes kulturdenkmal

HESSEN

Vielen Dank, dass Sie zur Erhaltung dieses historischen Gartendenkmals und Landschaftsschutzgebiets sowie zu Ihrer eigenen Sicherheit die folgenden Regeln beachten:

Die Wege sind ausschließlich Fußgängern, Krankenfahrstühlen und Betriebsfahrzeugen der Museumslandschaft Hessen Kassel vorbehalten.

Die übrigen Flächen dürfen nicht betreten werden. Ausgenommen sind speziell ausgewiesene Flächen.

Es ist nicht gestattet, Bäume und Sträucher zu erklettern. Auch das Erklimmen der historischen Parkarchitekturen, Mauern, Mauerreste etc. ist verboten.

Rad-, Kraftradfahren sowie Reiten und die Benutzung von Sportgeräten sind ausdrücklich untersagt.

Hunde sind an der kurzen Leine zu führen, für die Entsorgung des Hundekots ist der Halter verantwortlich.

Lärm jeglicher Art ist zu vermeiden.

Offenes Feuer und Grillen ist untersagt.

Abfall muss vom Verursacher entsorgt werden.

Das Betreten der Anlage geschieht auf eigene Gefahr. Verletzungs- und Lebensgefahr besteht bei Dunkelheit, Gewitter, Sturm und winterlichem Wetter.

Bitte leisten Sie den Anweisungen des Aufsichtspersonals Folge.

Zerstörung, Verunreinigung und Zuwiderhandlungen werden nach den Straf- und Ordnungswidrigkeitsgesetzen verfolgt und entsprechende Schadensersatzansprüche geltend gemacht. Die Ortssatzung bzw. Polizeiverordnung ist in dieser Anlage zu beachten.

Eltern haften für ihre Kinder.

Wir wünschen Ihnen einen angenehmen Aufenthalt!

Thank-you for respecting the following rules for the preservation of this historical garden heritage site and landscape preservation area as well as for your own safety:

The paths are reserved exclusively for pedestrians, motorised wheel chairs and authorised vehicles of the Museumslandschaft Hessen Kassel.

Entry to other areas is prohibited with the exception of specially marked areas.

Climbing trees and shrubs is prohibited. Scaling historical park architecture, walls, and wall ruins etc. is also prohibited.

Cycling, motorcycling, horseback-riding and the use of athletic equipment is expressly prohibited.

Dogs are to be kept on a short leash, the owner is responsible for the disposing of dog excrement.

Noise of any kind is to be avoided.

Open fire and barbecue ist prohibited.

Refuse must be disposed of by the party responsible for it.

Entry to the grounds occurs at one's own risk. A risk of injury or death exists during dark hours, thunder and wind storms as well as winter weather.

Please comply with the instructions of supervisory personnel.

Destruction, pollution and misconduct will be prosecuted pursuant to the penal and administrative offence code and the corresponding claims to compensation will be asserted. Local statutes resp. police regulations are to be complied with on these grounds.

Parents are liable for their children.

We wish you a pleasant stay!

mhk•

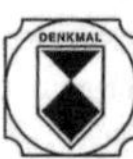
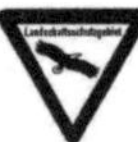

Museumslandschaft Hessen Kassel
Verwaltung Schloss Wilhelmshöhe, 34131 Kassel
Telefon +49 (0)561/ 3 16 80 – 0

PARK RULES FOR THE KARLSAUE, ISSUED BY THE STAATLICHE GARTENANLAGEN OF THE MUSEUMSLANDSCHAFT HESSEN-KASSEL

The situation with the trail on the Auehang constitutes a legal exception that was reviewed and discussed by different lawyers. This is due to the fact that a trail is not an official walkway and, as such, falls completely out of the park's system of rules. The park administration can only take responsibility for official walkways, as Mr. Boßdorf, director of the Karlsaue, explained to me. It therefore cannot be liable for visitors to the trail. For this reason, only a limited amount of the park rules apply to the trail. The exceptional legal conditions under which visitors enter the trail are displayed at the trail's entrances on Schöne Aussicht and in the Karlsaue (see page 203).

Türkisch
Russisch
Polnisch
Englisch
Französisch
Italienisch
Spanisch
Griechisch
Holländisch
Bulgarisch
Rumänisch
Ungarisch
Tschechisch
Slowakisch
Slowenisch
Kroatisch/Serbisch
Albanisch
Kurdisch
Arabisch
Farsi / Dari
Paschtu
Twi
Swahili (Suaheli)
Afrikaans
Amharisch
Tigrinisch
Somali

Ukrainisch
Turkmenisch
Armenisch
Georgisch
Mongolisch
Chinesisch
Vietnamesisch
Japanisch
Koreanisch
Khmer
Burmesisch
Thai
Tamil
Singhalesisch
Hindi
Urdu
Pandjabi
Bengali
Nepali
Marathi
Malayalam
Indonesisch
Tagalog
Cebuano
Tschetschenisch
Aserbaidschanisch
Roma

Michael Boßdorf is the director of the Staatlichen Gartenanlagen of the Museumslandschaft Hessen-Kassel. He assisted us during our construction of the trail in autumn 2011. One day he sent me this list that he had compiled together with his wife. It is a list of languages spoken in Kassel.

Air

Air temperature, air raids, aerial photographs
(which are sometimes called target maps),
and even more aerial photographs.

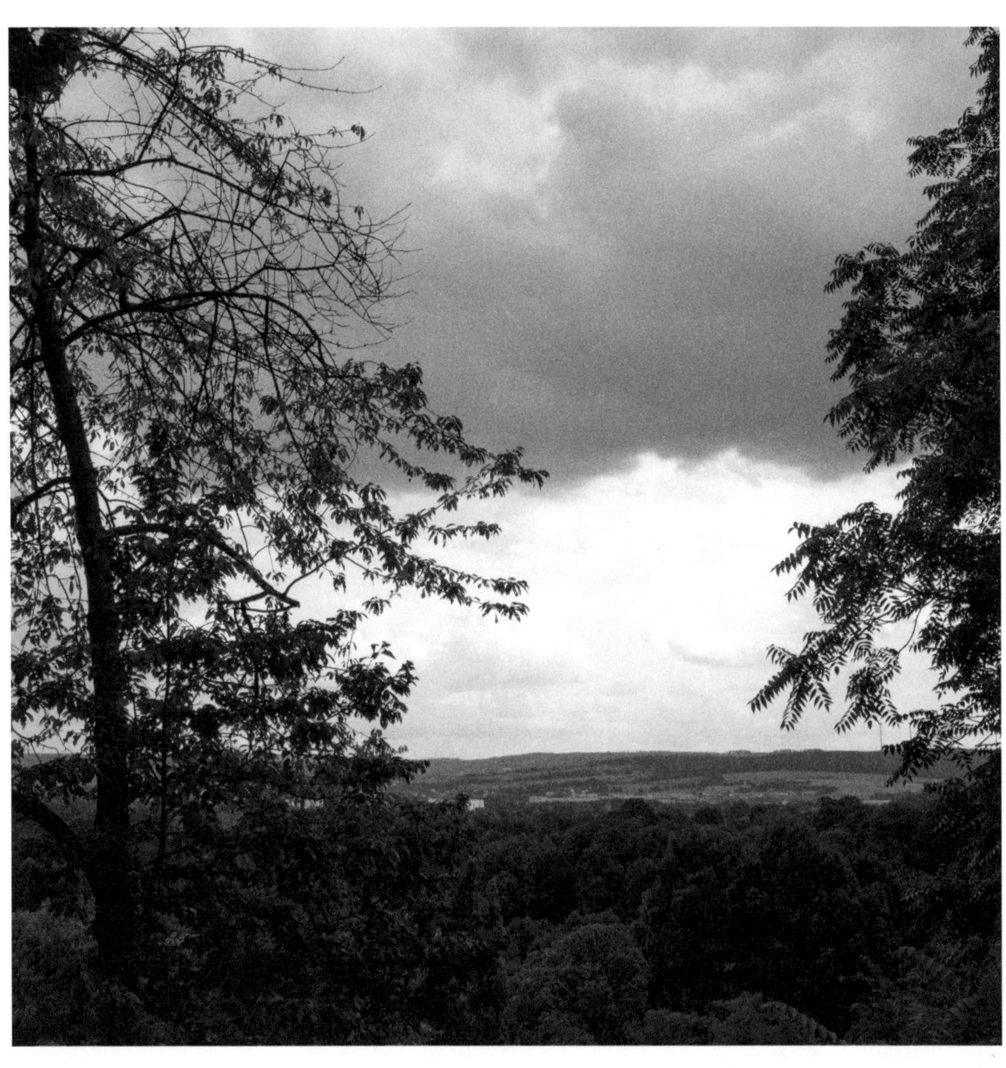

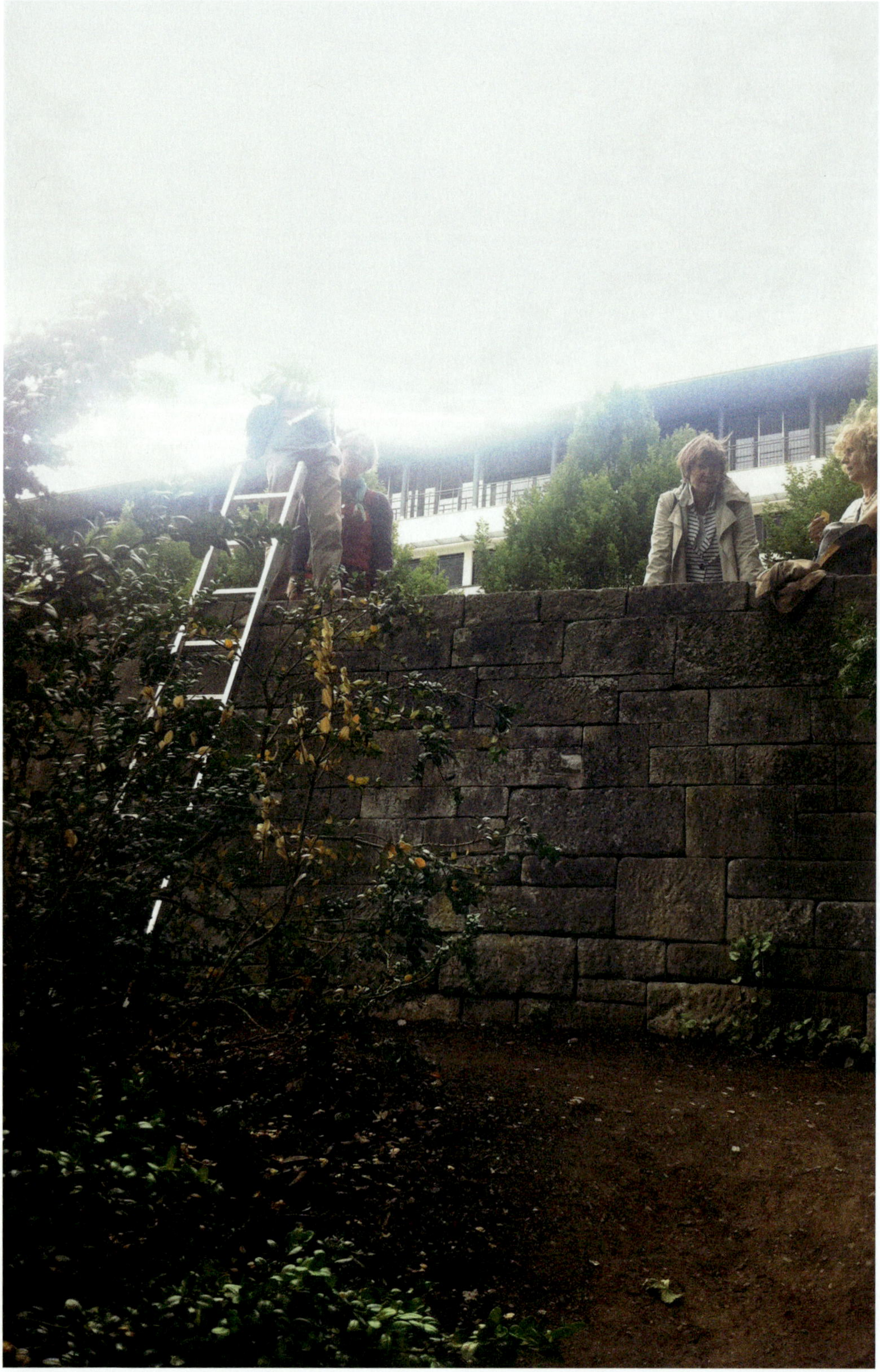

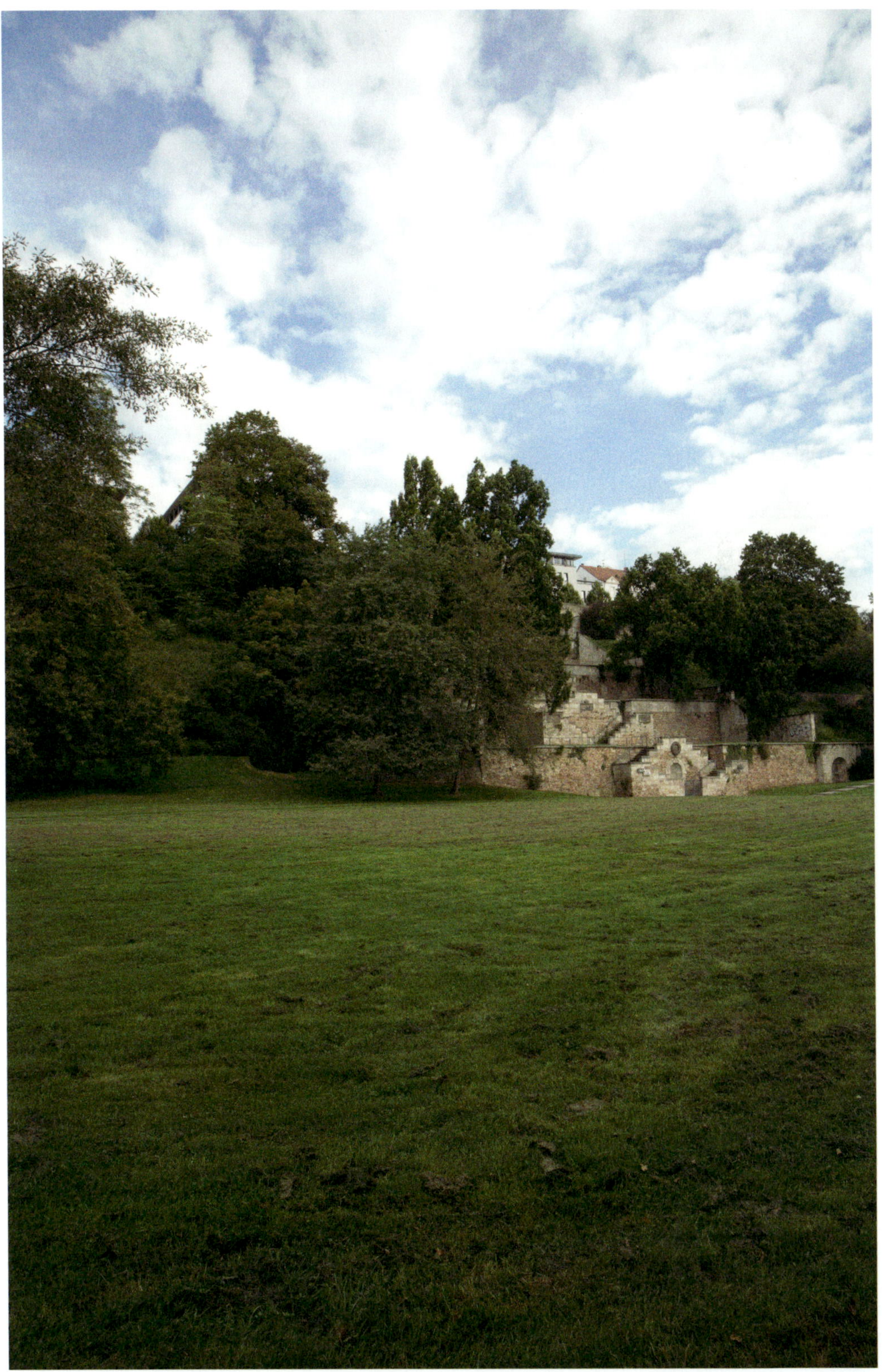

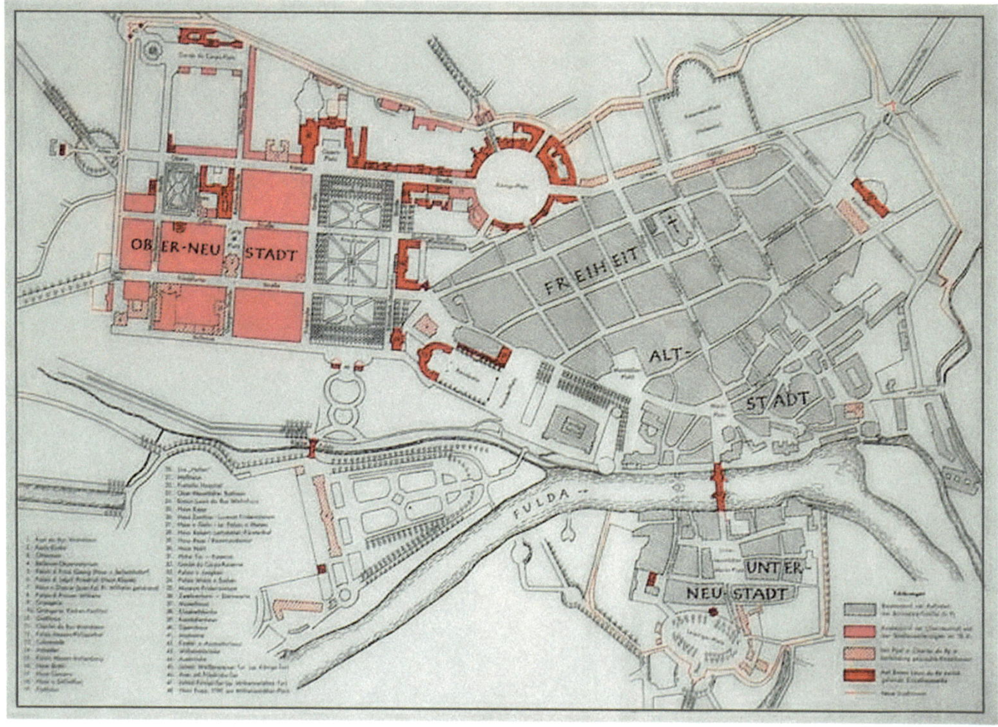

MAP OF THE OBERNEUSTADT QUARTER IN KASSEL

The map shows the Oberneustadt quarter, which was built on top of the former city fortifications, with Strasse Bellevue (today Schöne Aussicht) bordering the Karlsaue. It was built in the eighteenth century for the Huguenots who had fled from France and were granted not only asylum by Landgrave Karl, but also economic support, freedom of religion, and the right to speak their own language. The male population of the Landgraviate of Hessen-Kassel was exhausted by the Thirty Years' War and was in desperate need of craftsmen and master builders. The Huguenots were very welcome, and one of them was the captain of the engineers and master builder Paul du Ry, who built the Prinz-Georg-Palais and Prinzessgarten (today the Ehrenmal, or war memorial for the fallen soldiers of World War I and World War II). Both his son and grandson held the office of the court's highest master builder and built, among other things, the Fridericianum and Schloß Wilhelmshöhe.

[SOURCE: PUBLIC DOMAIN]

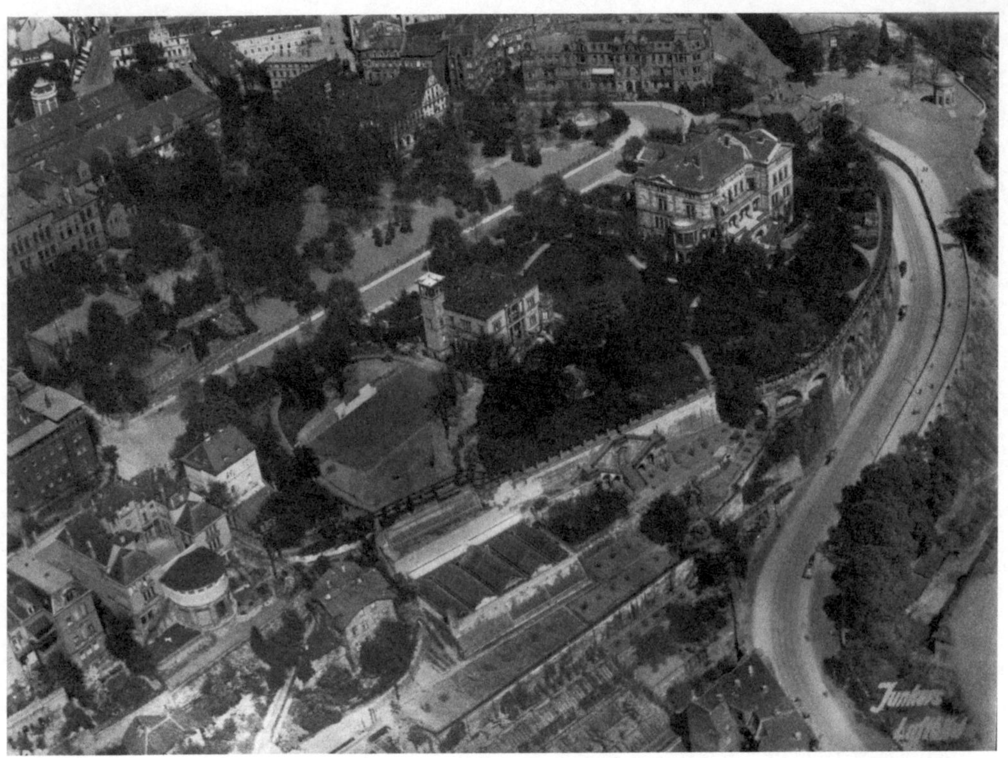

HENSCHEL VILLAS ON THE WEINBERG (CA. 1920s)

[SOURCE: HENSCHEL-MUSEUM, KASSEL. REPRODUCTION: POLA SIEVERDING]

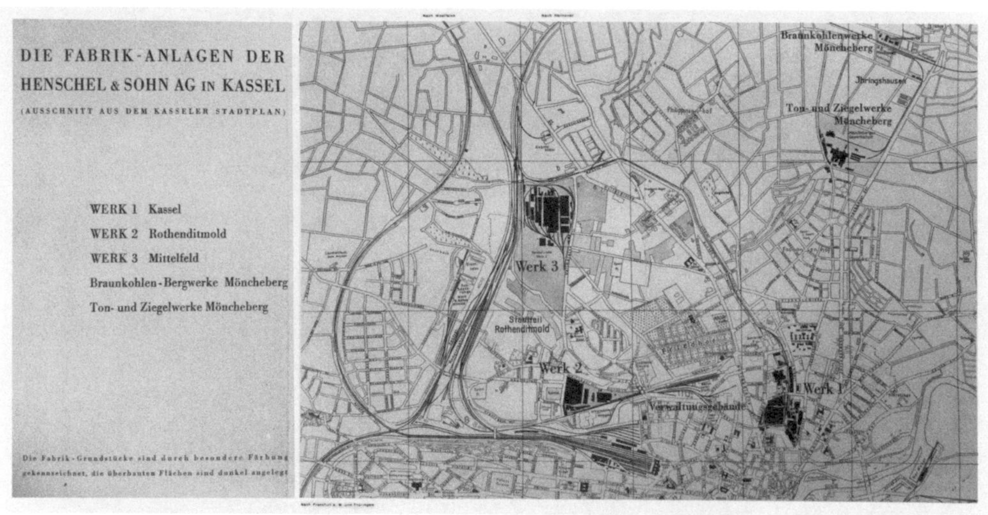

FACTORY COMPLEX OF HENSCHEL & SON AG IN KASSEL

This section of a city map of Kassel, most likely from before 1942, shows the three Henschel plants (Kassel, Rothenditmold, and Mittelfeld) as well as Henschel's clay and brick plants, which were transformed in 1942 into one of the larger forced labor camps. The complex also contained a punishment camp of the Kassel Gestapo.

[SOURCE: HENSCHEL-MUSEUM, KASSEL. REPRODUCTION: POLA SIEVERDING]

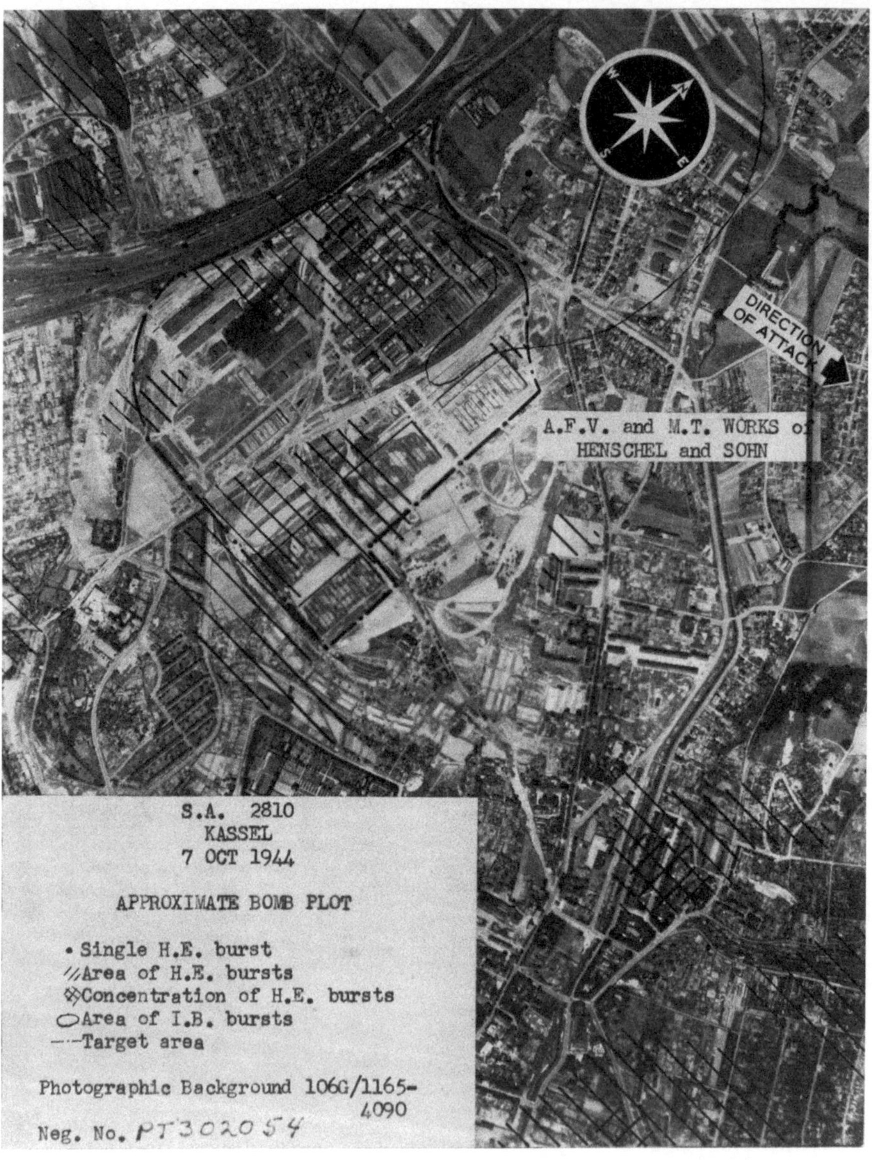

RAID DATA SHEETS

TARGET MAPS AND DATA SHEETS FROM THE R.A.F. AND USAAF FOR THE EVALUATION OF AIR RAIDS ON KASSEL, 1942-45

The data sheets show how many aircraft participated in each attack, how many tons of ammunition were dropped, and which targets were selected. The respective number of Royal Air Force (R.A.F.) and United States Army Air Forces (USAAF) aircraft remaining after the attack is also documented. The target maps contain markings identifying each target and show exact evaluations of the bomb raids on different parts of Kassel. Bomb impacts are circled, targets are shaded. One of the maps marks the labor camp at the Henschel aircraft motor factory at Baunatal (since 1957, the Volkswagen Kassel plant), the horizontal projections of which haven't changed to this day.

[SOURCE: WERNER DETTMAR, KASSEL / THE NATIONAL ARCHIVES, LONDON. REPRODUCTION: POLA SIEVERDING]

"RAID DATA SHEETS."

(EX. 'HARRIS' BLUE BOOKS : DAMAGE DIAGRAMS.)
FOR
KASSEL.

BOMBER COMMAND   8TH USAAF.

RAID DATE	AIRCRAFT ATTACKING	TONS CLAIMED	OBJECTIVE	RAID DATE	AIRCRAFT ATTACKING	TONS CLAIMED	OBJECTIVE
1942				1943			
27/28-8	256	563	TOWN AREA	28-7	54	129	FIESELER BETTENHAUSEN
1943				30-7	94	222	" "
3/4-10	501	1616	" "	30-7	37	87	FIESELER WALDAU.
22/23-10	486	1824	" "	30-7	3	7	TOWN AREA.
26/27-11	1	5	" "	1944			
1944				19-4	106	246	KASSEL/WALDAU.
18/19-3 To 15/16-10	119	145	" "	19-4	51	121	"/BETTENHAUSEN.
1945				19-4	52	114	"/ALTENBAUNA.
6/7-1 To 2/3-3	170	193	" "	22-9	602	1667	HENSCHEL A.F.V & M.T. FACTORY.
8/9-3	268	1142	" "	27-9	248	705	" " "
16/17-3 To 20/21-3	36	29	" "	28-9	138	385	HENSCHEL TANK FACTORY.
				28-9	104	315	HENSCHEL A.F.V & M.T. FACTORY.
				2-10	106	258	BETTENHAUSEN ORDNANCE DEPOT.
				2-10	551	1370	HENSCHEL A.F.V & M.T. FACTORY.
				7-10	67	188	ALTENBAUNA AERO-ENGINE FACTORY.

NUMBER OF AIRCRAFT MISSING FROM R.A.F ATTACKS – 101	NUMBER OF AIRCRAFT MISSING FROM 8 U.S.A.A.F. ATTACKS – see page 2 J.

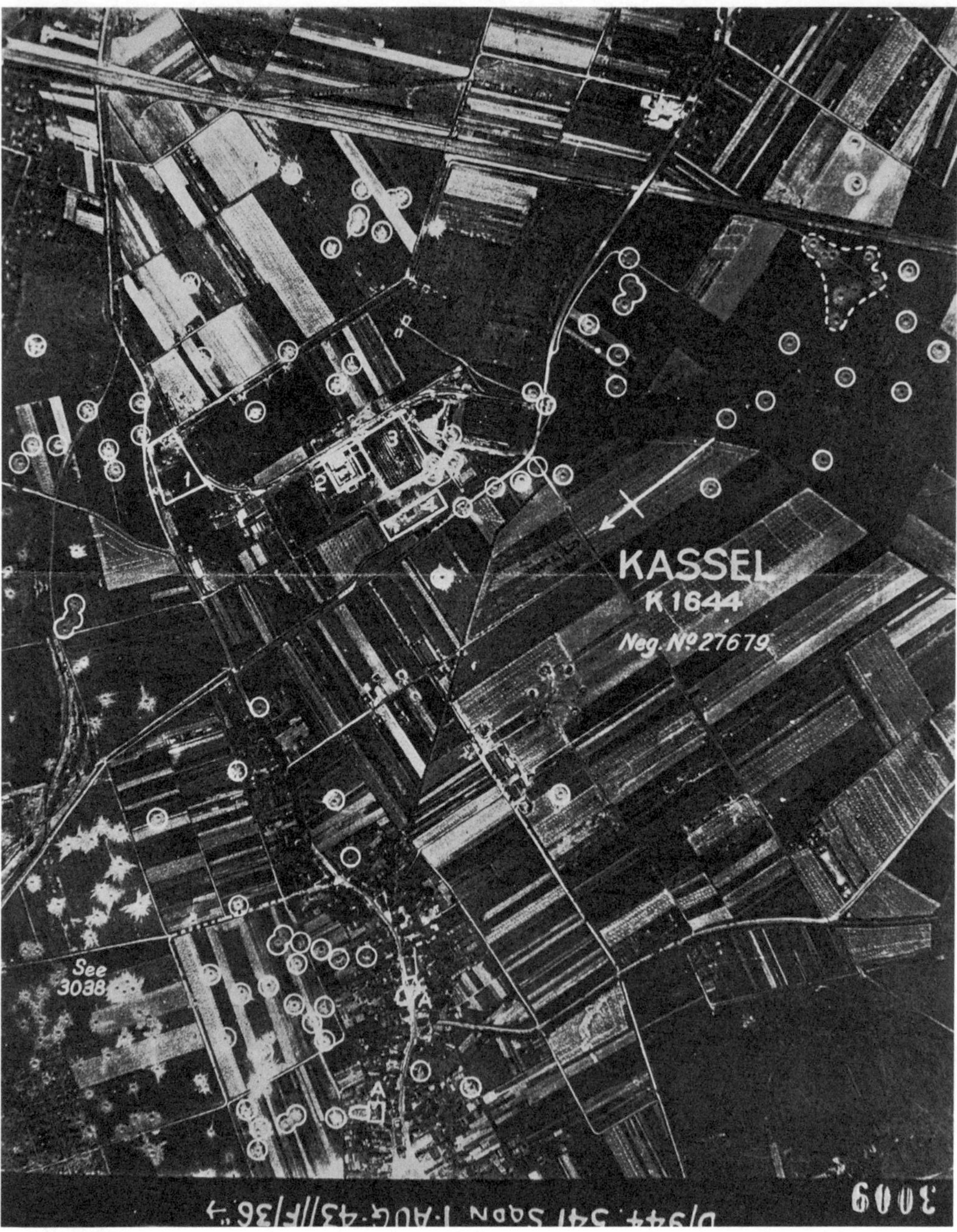
KASSEL
K 1644
Neg. No 27679
1
2
3
See
3038
3009
D/944 541 SqDN 1·AUG·43//F/36"

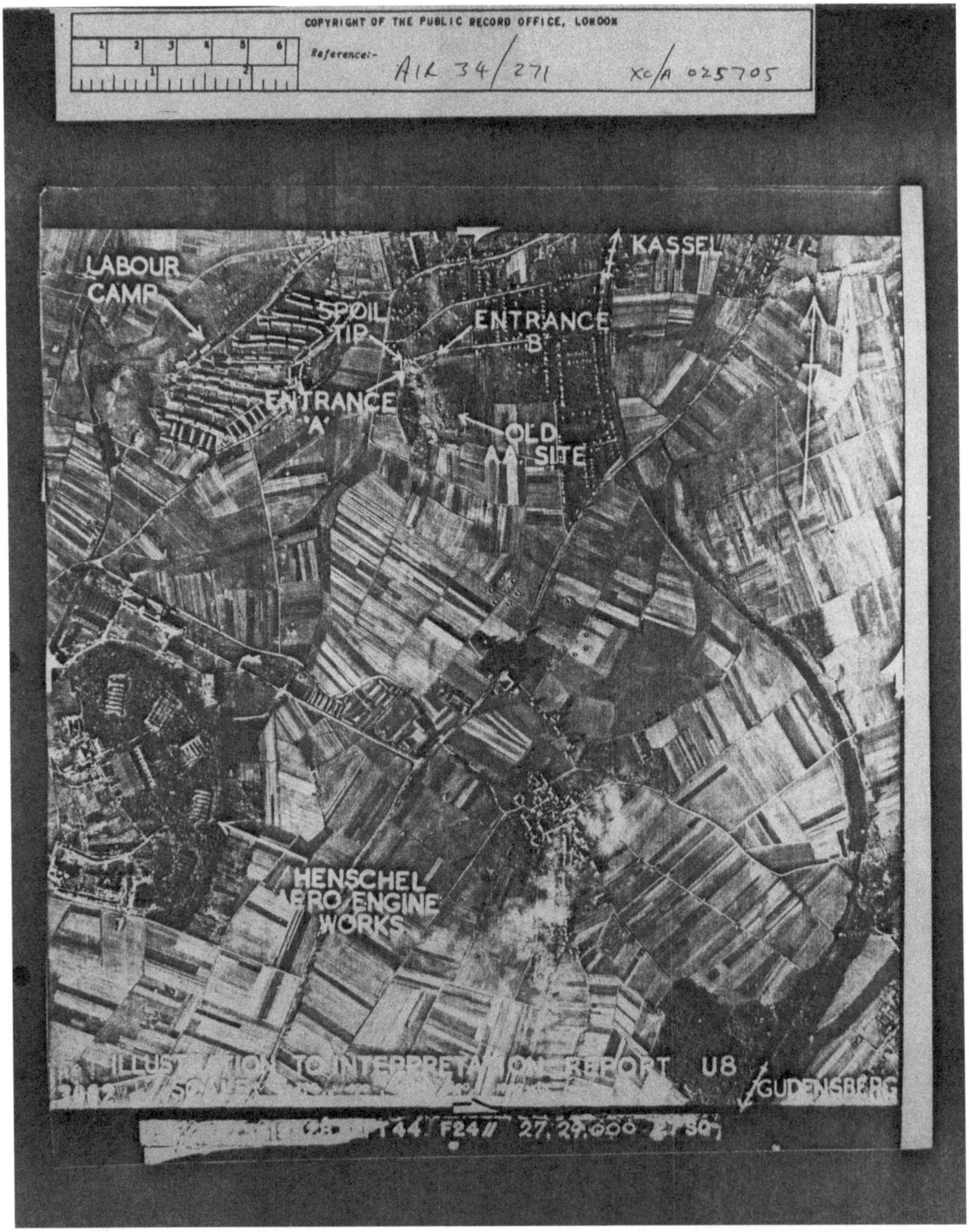

LABOUR CAMP
KASSEL
SPOIL TIP
ENTRANCE B
ENTRANCE A
OLD A.A. SITE
HENSCHEL AERO ENGINE WORKS
ILLUSTRATION TO INTERPRETATION REPORT U8
GUDENSBERG

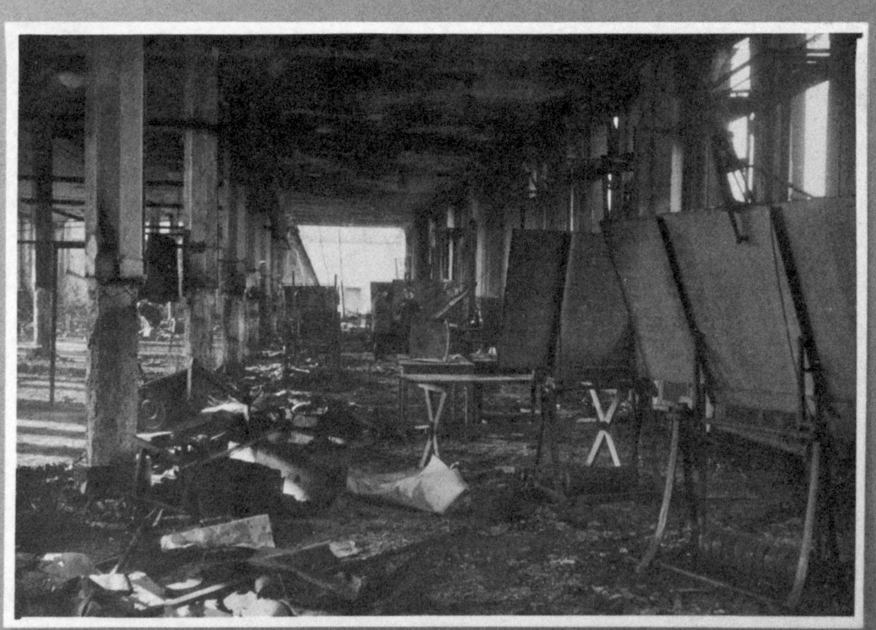

28.2.45   V. 355/ IV 36

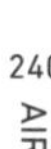

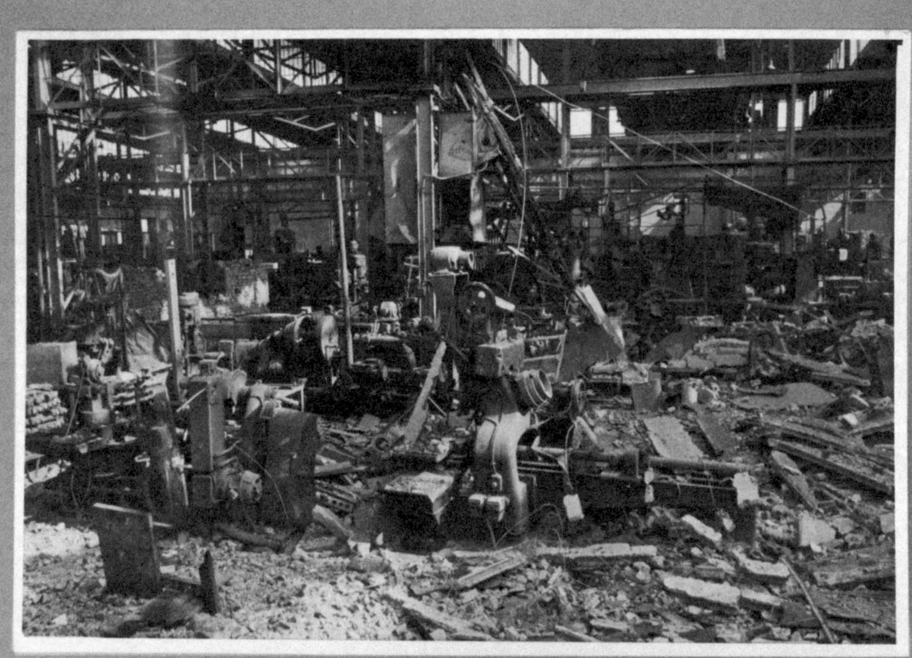

2. 16. 44.   H 1   M 41   V. 373/ I / 1

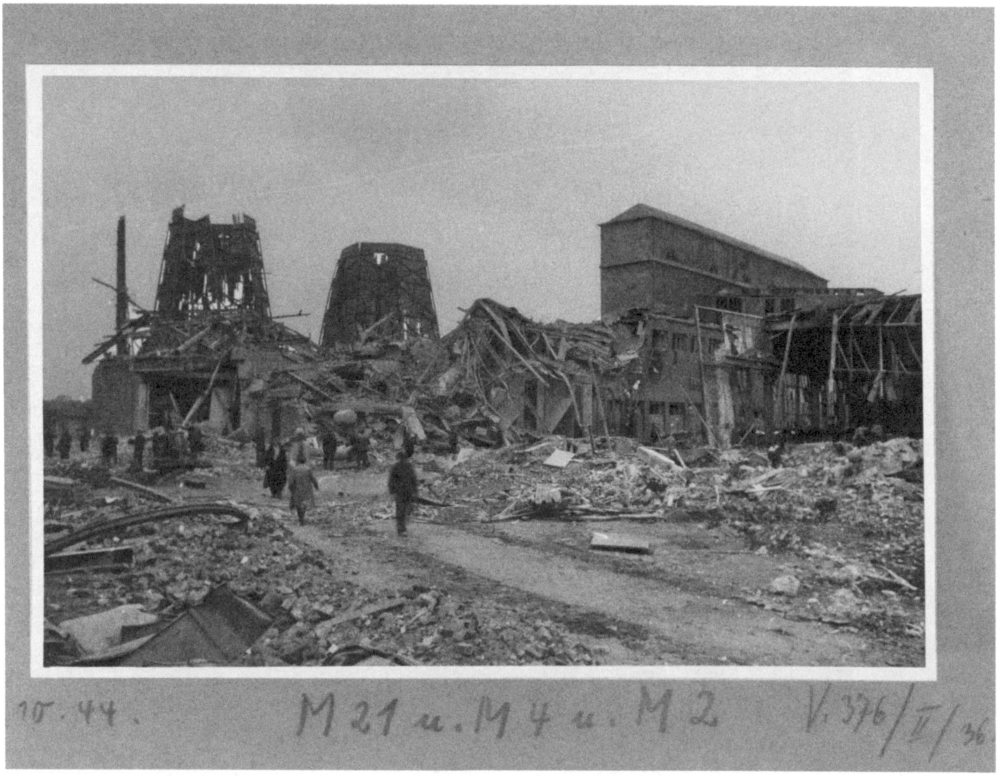

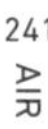

AIR-RAIDS ON THE HENSCHEL WERKE, 1944-1945. - AIR-RAID DAMAGE SUSTAINED BY THE HENSCHEL WERKE

We find these pictures in the Henschel company archive, located at the former Werk Rothenditmold. They show the documentation of bomb damage to the Henschel-plants between September 1944 and March 1945.

[SOURCE: HENSCHEL-MUSEUM, KASSEL. REPRODUCTION: POLA SIEVERDING]

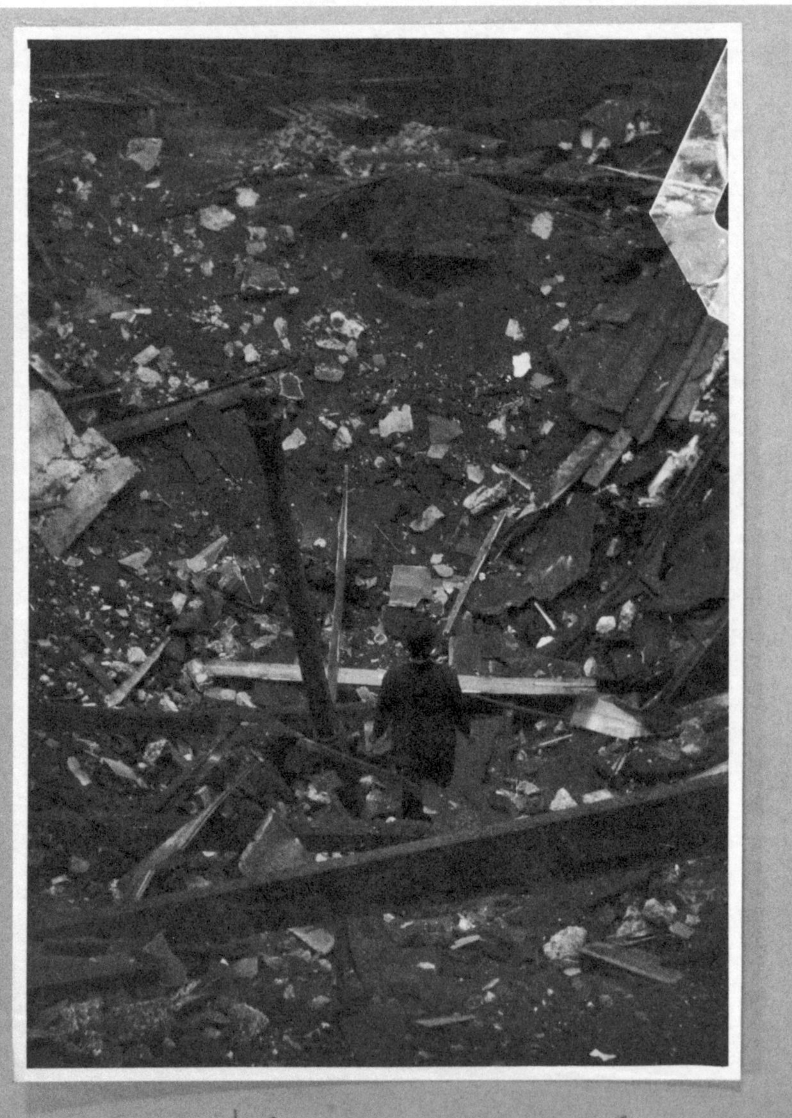

23.9.44.   K 8/9   V. 371/Ⅲ/32

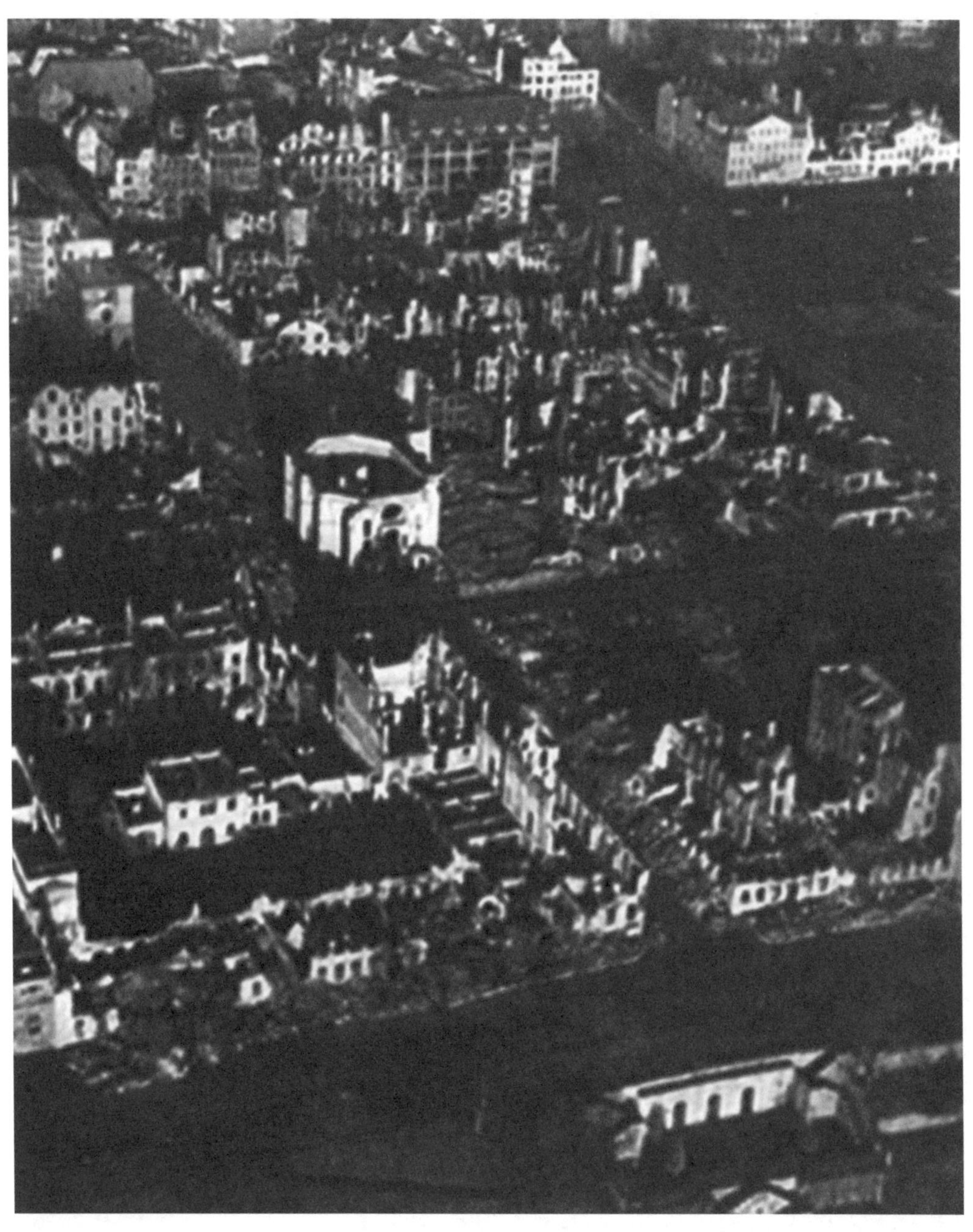

AERIAL PHOTO OF THE DESTRUCTION IN KASSEL OBERNEUSTADT AFTER AIR RAIDS, CA. 1945

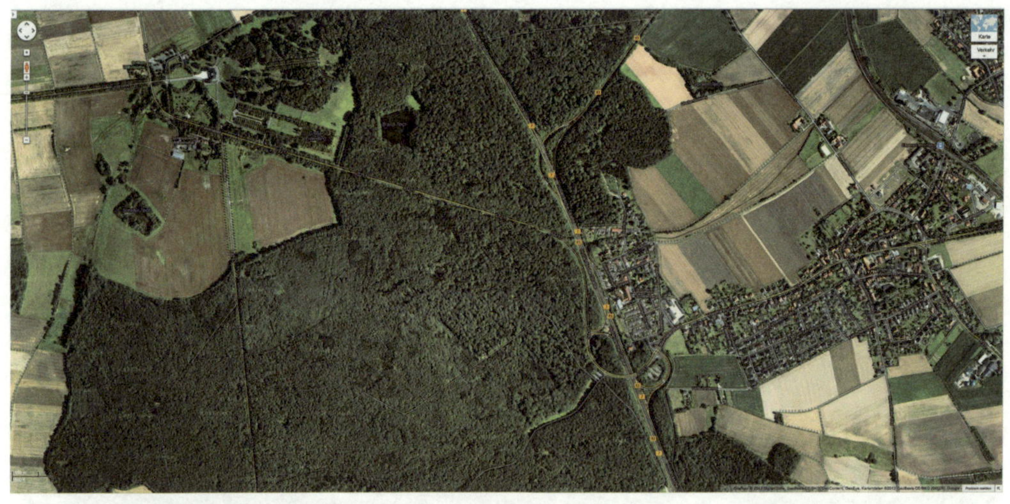

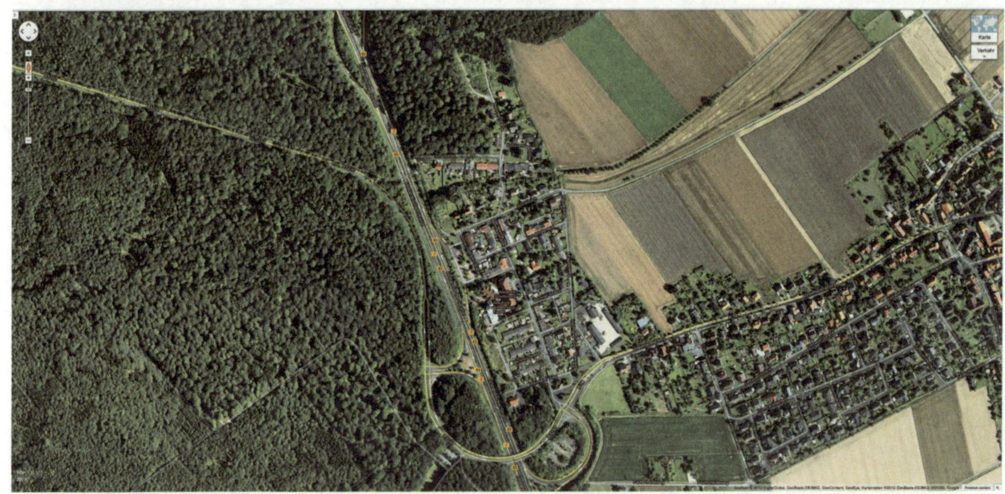

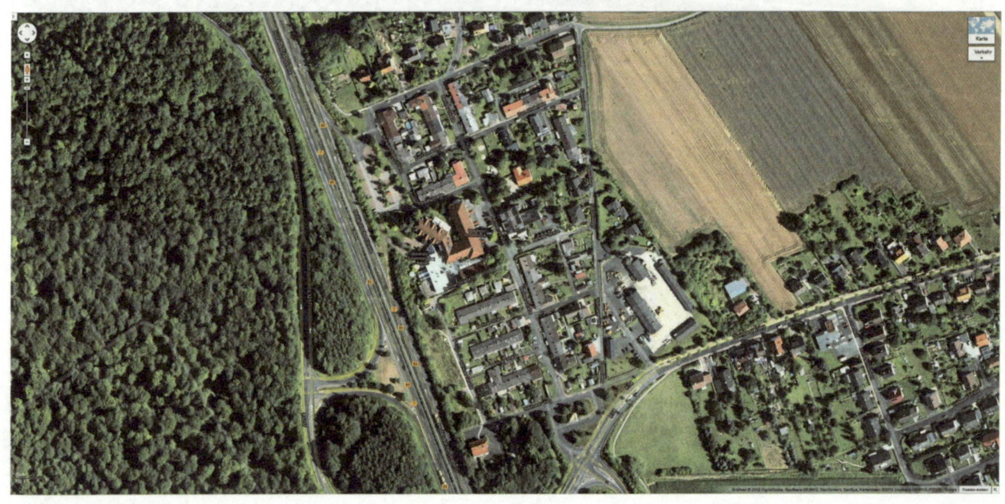

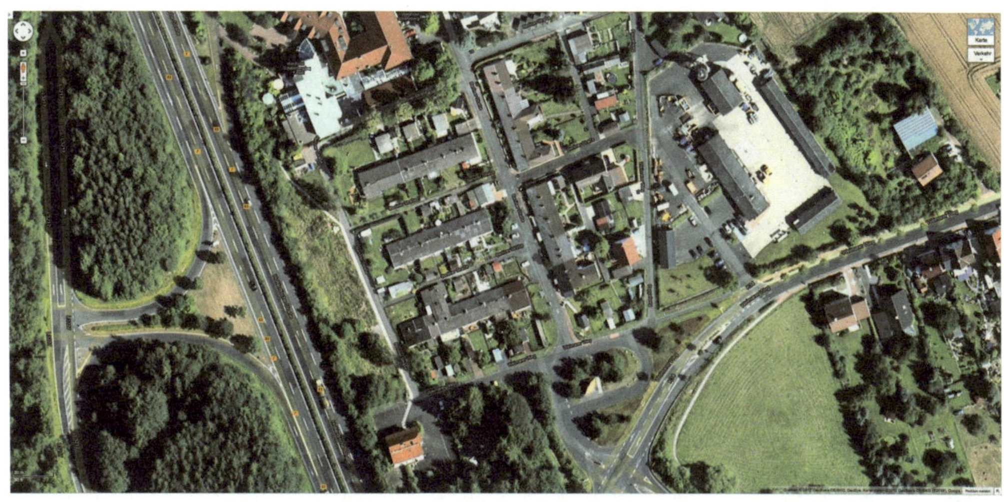

AERIAL PHOTOGRAPH OF THE FORMER SCHÄFERBERG LABOR CAMP, 2012

SCHÄFERBERG, AERIAL PHOTOS, 2012

This aerial photo shows the former labor camp belonging to Henschel at Schäferberg, Kassel, where forced laborers were housed during World War II. After being utilized after the war as housing for German minorities expelled from Eastern Europe, they functioned as housing for the first generation of guest workers, who arrived in Kassel in 1955. The horizontal projection of the Schäferberg camp retains its original form to this day, as do those of many of the other camps. Klaus Mosch-Wicke researched this camp in particular, developing the publication *"SCHÄFERBERG: Ein Henschel-Lager für ausländische Zwangsarbeiter"* (SCHÄFERBERG: A Henschel camp for foreign forced laborers). The following description can be found on page 69f: "The way to Kassel . . . For the workers from the Schäferberg camp, the day started with a long walk to their working premises. According to first hand accounts of Frau I., they boarded the 5:30 train at Mönchehof station, as long as railway operations were not crippled by air raids. Even this meant setting off on kilometer-long marches from the camp to Mönchehof and from Kassel Main Station to Mittelfeld. Every day, however, a certain number of the forced laborers probably had to walk all the way from Schäferberg to Kassel, a hike of about six kilometers. In the event that trains were not running, everyone had to cover the distance on foot. One way lasted at least one and a half hours, and the walk back to camp was an uphill climb. The forced laborers left the camp in the morning at 5 :00 pm and their return never happened until 7:00 pm, at the earliest—14 hours later. To measure the added strain that such a long march imposed, one must visualize these foreigners as they were—starving, usually wearing on their feet only rags, wooden clogs, or, in rare cases, shoes. Under these conditions, the march must have been nothing less than torture, especially in winter. Various eye witnesses recall the 'miserable caravan' that trudged along Holländische Straße through Obervellmar."

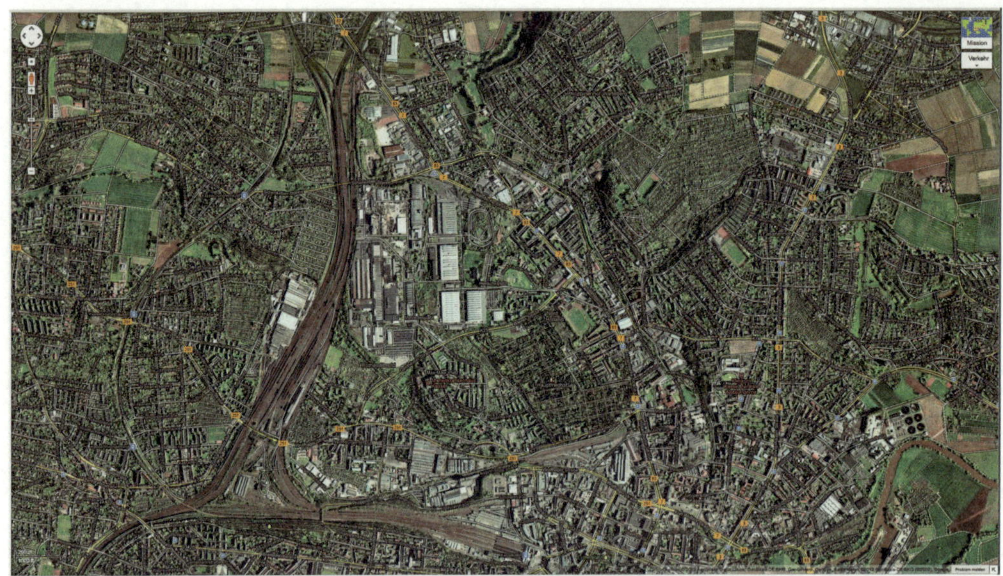

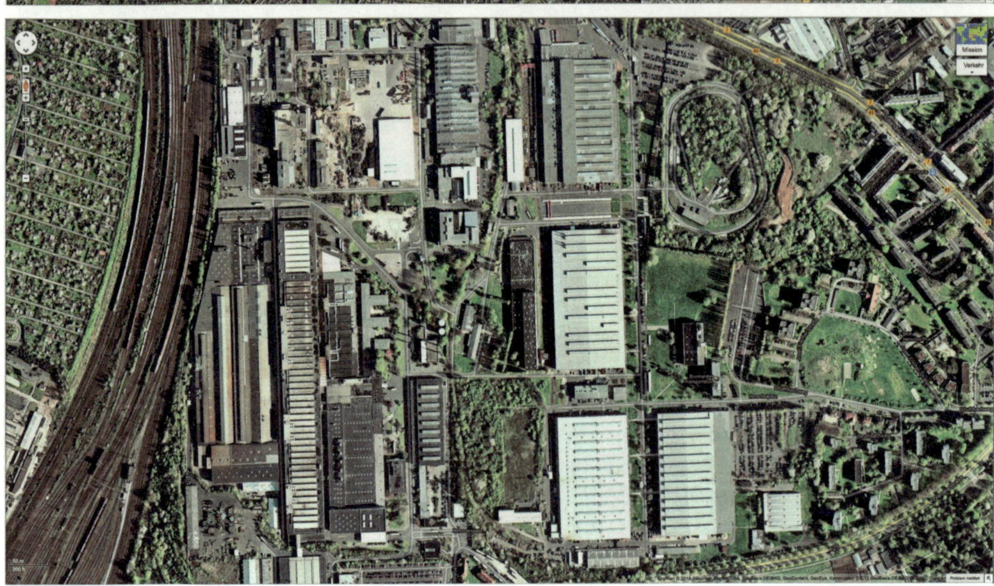

AERIAL PHOTO OF ARMAMENT PRODUCTION SITE, KASSEL, 2012

If one compares current aerial photographs of Kassel with the map of the Henschel-plants from 1945, one can see that the Henschel armament production sites remain. The manufacturing sites as well as the test grounds for track vehicles and wheeled vehicles, which were laid out before 1945, are visible. Today this is the location where the companies Rheinmetall Defense and Krauss-Maffei Wegmann produce the infantry fighting vehicle Puma and parts of the Leopard 2 battle tank.

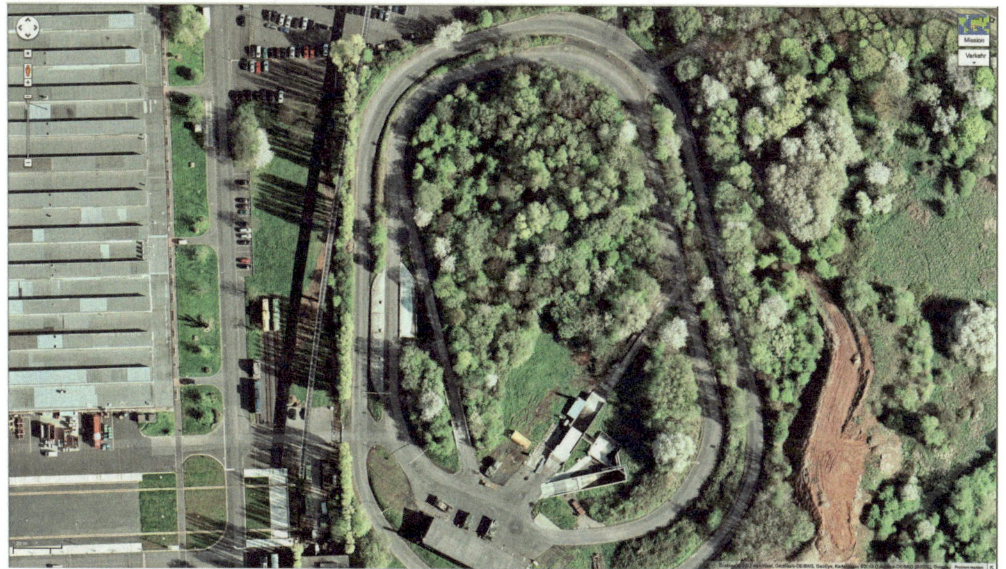

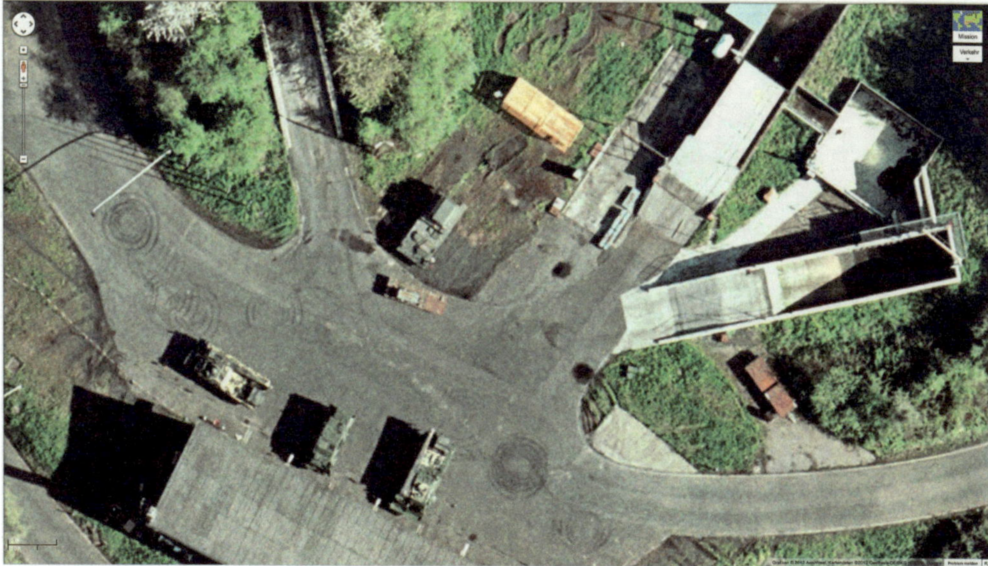

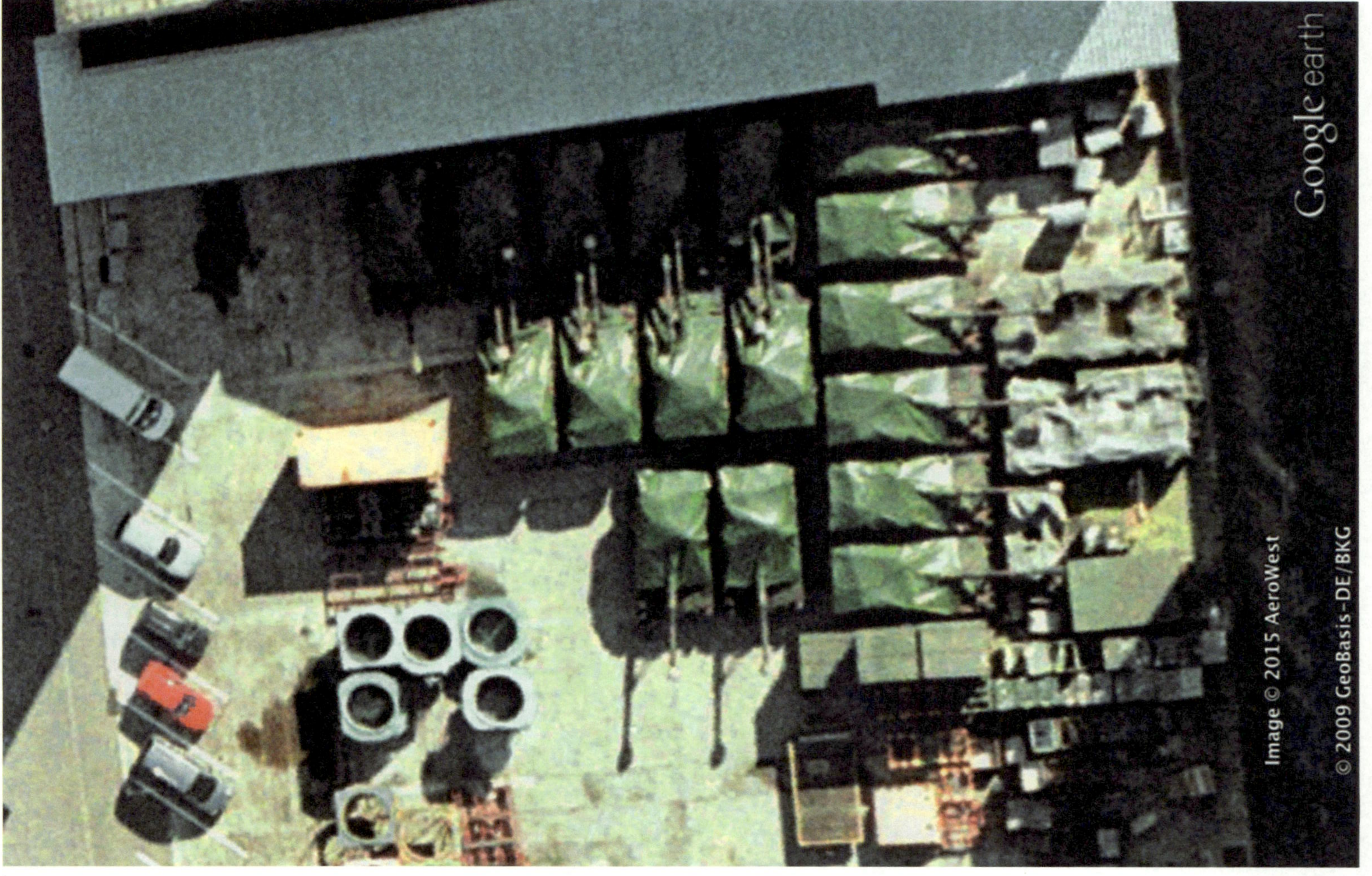

Image © 2015 AeroWest
© 2009 GeoBasis-DE/BKG
Google earth

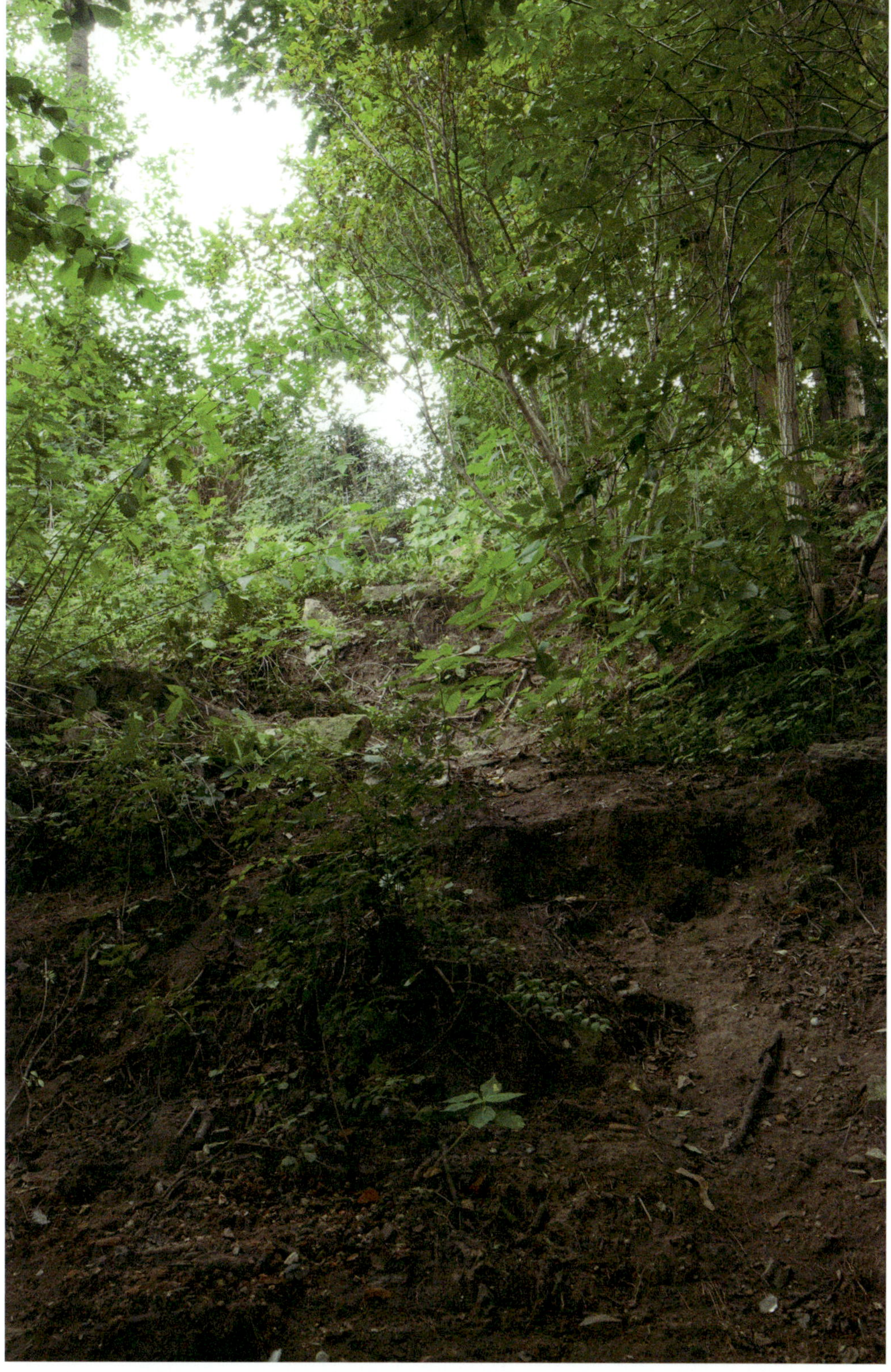

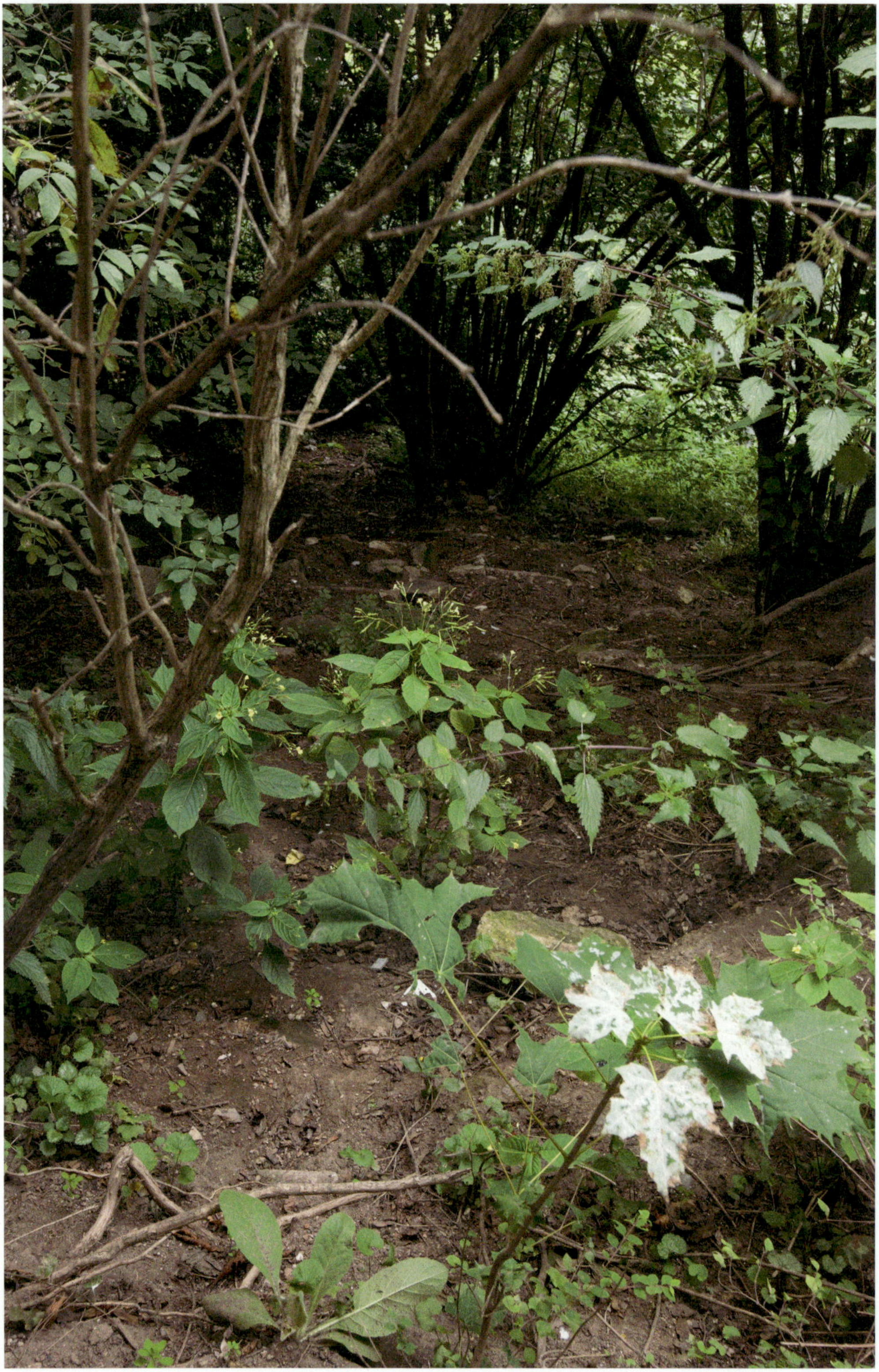

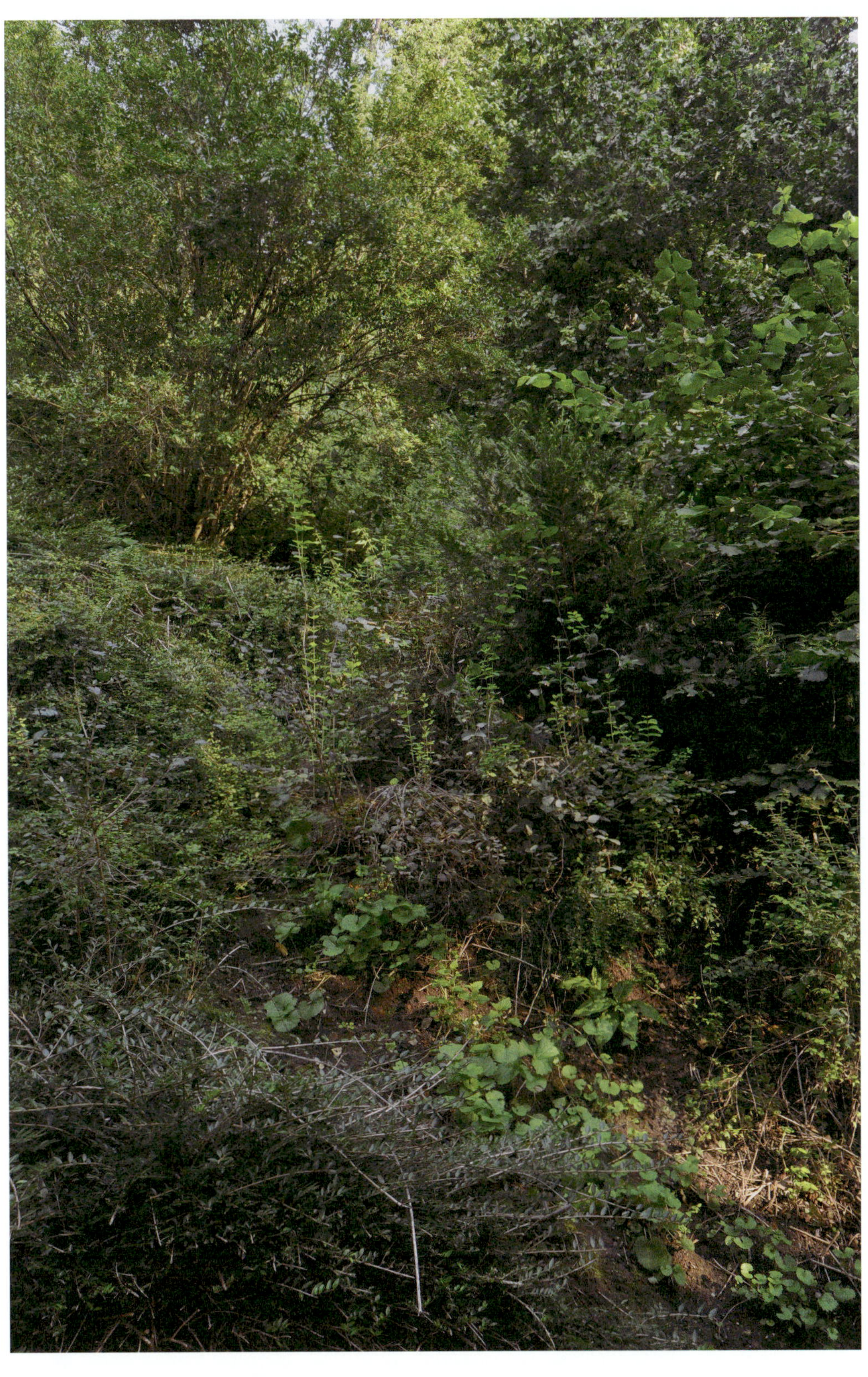

COLOPHON

EDITED BY Natascha Sadr Haghighian, Pola Sieverding, Jasper Kettner
DESIGN Ça ira!

CONVERSATIONS WITH Michael Boßdorf, Herr Düsterdieck, Anselm Franke, Avery Gordon, Ayse Güleç, Reza Haeri, Tom Keenan, Volker Lange, Helmut Weich, Allen S. Weiss

TRANSLATION William Wheeler, Ashkan Sepahvand, Natascha Sadr Haghighian, Daniel Hendrickson
TRANSCRIPTION Ute Waldhausen
COPY EDITING Ashkan Sepahvand, Natascha Sadr Haghighian, Pola Sieverding, William Wheeler, Soheyla Sadr
REPRODUCTION Pola Sieverding
IMAGE TREATMENT max-color
IMAGE CREDITS Natascha Sadr Haghighian: pages 5, 6, 8-9, 10, 11, 12, 14, 33, 34-35, 36, 37, 38-39, 40 bottom, 41, 42, 43, 45 top, 46, 75, 76, 77, 82, 84, 85, 139, 140, 142 bottom, 143, 153, 154, 157, 158, 204, 205; Jasper Kettner: pages 7, 13, 40 top, 44, 45 bottom, 78, 79, 141, 142 top, 145, 146, 149, 150, 151, 152, 155, 156, 206, 207; Nils Klinger: pages 80-81, 83; Pola Sieverding: pages 86, 108-109, 110, 203; Tom Keenan: pages 107, 204 top; Rosa Maria Rühling: pages 144, 147, 148, 208, 209, 210, 211; Kati Liebert: pages 227, 228, 229, 230, 251, 252, 253
COVER DRAWING Ashkan Sepahvand
WEBSITE www.d13pfad.de

PHYSICAL TRAIL
CONCEPTION AND IDEA Natascha Sadr Haghighian
CURATORIAL ASSISTANT AND ADVISOR Jasper Kettner
TRAIL CONSTRUCTION DREAM TEAM Angela Anderson, Ashkan Sepahvand, Ute Waldhausen, Alexander Geißler, Lea Brede, Klaus Wichmann
PROGRAMMING Erik Wiegand
SOUND RECORDING Natascha Sadr Haghighian, Ute Waldhausen
SOUND EDITING Ute Waldhausen
dOCUMENTA (13) took place from 9 June until 16 September 2012

KINDLY SUPPORTED BY
Kulturverwaltung des Berliner Senats
documenta archiv
Haus der Kulturen der Welt, Berlin

PRINTED BY Oktoberdruck, Berlin
BOOKBINDER Reinhart & Wasser, Berlin
FONTS Tabac G4 (Tomáš Brousil, Suitcase Type Foundry) Din Next (Linotype)
PAPERS Munken Pure, PROFIbulk naturmatt Bilderdruck

PUBLISHED BY Spector Books, Leipzig, 2015 - www.spectorbooks.com
ISBN 978-3-95905-013-5

THANKS TO

Ayse Gueleç, Ute Waldhausen, Ashkan Sepahvand, all Kassel residents who lent their voices to the trail, Michael Boßdorf, Christine Litz, Carolyn Christov-Bakargiev, Chus Martinez, Lucky 5, Carroll/Fletcher, Erik Wiegand, Avery Gordon, Anselm Franke, Thomas Keenan, Volker Lange, Reza Haeri, Helmut Weich, Herr Düsterdieck, Angela Anderson, Ulrike Uhlig, Erik Stein, Sabine Wiegand, Sven Becker (Bexen), Gerd Mörsch, Stadtarchiv Kassel, Henschel-Museum, our barkeeper from Würgeengel, J's Bar, Bad Muskau

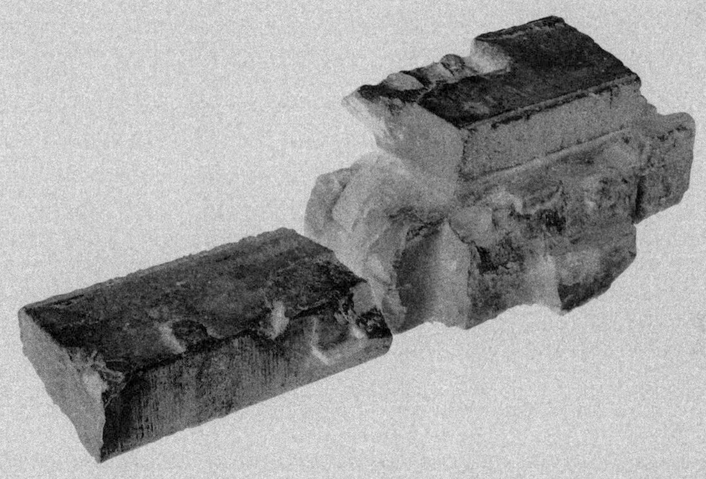